D0893294

Burying Uncertainty

Burying Uncertainty

Risk and the Case against
Geological Disposal of
Nuclear Waste

K. S. Shrader-Frechette

UNIVERSITY OF CALIFORNIA PRESS

Berkeley / Los Angeles / London

University of California Press
Berkeley and Los Angeles, California

University of California Press
London, England

Copyright © 1993 by The Regents of the University of California

Library of Congress Cataloging-in-Publication Data
Shrader-Frechette, K. S., 1944–
    Burying uncertainty: risk and the case against geological
disposal of nuclear waste / K. S. Shrader-Frechette.
        p.   cm.
    Includes bibliographical references and indexes.
    ISBN 0–520–08244–3.—ISBN 0–520–08301–6 (paper)
    1. Radioactive waste disposal in the ground—Environmental
aspects.   2. Radioactive waste disposal—Risk assessment.
    I. Title.
    TD898.2.S48   1993
    621.48'38—dc20   92–35083
                                                              CIP

Printed in the United States of America

1 2 3 4 5 6 7 8 9

The paper used in this publication meets the minimum requirements
of American National Standard for Information Sciences—Perma-
nence of Paper for Printed Library Materials, ANSI Z39.48–1984 ∞

To Kang

Contents

Acknowledgments

Much of the work in this volume originated as a result of research (1984–1987) supported by the National Science Foundation, Ethics and Values Studies, under grant ISP-82-09517, "Ethical and Value Issues in Siting Radioactive Waste Facilities," and work (1991) supported by the U.S. Department of Energy and the state of Nevada under grant 685873, 9.3.7, 4-C, "Expert Judgment in Assessing Radwaste Risks." Any opinions expressed in this book, however, are mine and do not necessarily reflect the views of either the National Science Foundation, the U.S. Department of Energy, or the state of Nevada.

For reading and criticizing earlier versions of this book, I am grateful to many persons, but especially to Bill Freudenburg, Steve Frishman, Reed Hansen, Carl Johnson, Charlie Malone, Naomi Oreskes, Gene Rosa, Joe Strolin, and Richard Watson. Whatever errors remain, of course, are my responsibility. Dan Wigley has done excellent work as my research assistant, and I look forward to reading his books some day. Thanks also to Jeannine de Bolt and Marty Wortman for superb work in word processing. Finally, I am grateful to the University of South Florida for giving me a distinguished professorship that has enabled me to spend a significant amount of time in research for this volume.

My greatest debt is to my husband, Maurice, the brightest and most loving critic of my work, and to our children, Eric and Danielle. They make everything worthwhile.

Preface

More than three hundred years ago, John Milton wrote that "books are not absolutely dead things," but "contain a potency of life in them to be as active as that soul was whose progeny they are." I hope that this book has such potency, the potential to help change things. I hope that it helps us all—citizens of the world, guardians of the future, and stewards of the planet—to reexamine our current policy of permanent geological disposal of high-level radioactive waste. My thesis is that, because the scientific uncertainties are so great and the ethical burdens so severe, we ought to delay our decision about permanent geological disposal in order to determine whether the future will be able to give us better scientific and ethical guarantees of containment. As Thomas Jefferson put it, in a letter to George Washington: "Delay is preferable to error."

Because I am committed to the belief that philosophy ought to encompass more than autopsies on dead theories, I attempt to show that we ought to use philosophy of science, epistemology, and ethics to help shape contemporary science, public policy, and democratic thought regarding radioactive waste. If we do not, the penalty will be poorer science, weaker public policy, and less effective democracy.

Despite our societal failure to deal adequately with the problem of nuclear waste, there are a number of excellent discussions of the difficulties surrounding high-level radioactive waste. Among the many superb volumes are the Blowers, Lowry, and Solomon analysis, *The*

International Politics of Nuclear Waste (1991); the Carter study, *Nuclear Imperatives and Public Trust* (1987); the Dunlap, Kraft, and Rosa collection, *The Public and Nuclear Waste* (1993); the Freudenburg and Rosa anthology, *Public Reactions to Nuclear Power* (1984); the Kasperson collection, *Equity Issues in Radioactive Waste Management* (1983); the Lenssen essay, "Nuclear Waste" (1992); the Monitored Retrievable Storage Review Commission's study, *Nuclear Waste* (1989); and the many studies of the U.S. National Academy of Sciences/National Research Council, including *Social and Economic Aspects of Radioactive Waste Disposal* (1984), *Rethinking High-Level Radioactive Waste Disposal* (1990), and *Ground Water at Yucca Mountain* (1992).

Given the many excellent analyses in whose debt I remain, why is yet another book on nuclear waste needed? One reason is that virtually all the earlier works deal either with the technical aspects or with the political difficulties associated with radioactive waste disposal. The technical volumes usually do not address adequately the *epistemological* and *methodological* problems associated with quantitative risk assessment and repository siting. Except for several of the equity issues, the political books usually do not assess, in any detailed way, the great variety of *ethical* presuppositions built into alternative scenarios for dealing with high-level radioactive waste. This volume is a first, and very modest, step toward a more comprehensive analysis of the waste problem.

Another reason for the book is that there is no study that examines existing, state-of-the-art scientific, ethical, and political justifications for siting a current high-level radwaste repository. This work focuses, in part, on the proposed Yucca Mountain (Nevada) facility, designed to be the world's first permanent repository for high-level, commercial radioactive waste. My argument is, in part, that there are serious doubts about the scientific and ethical problems latent in the very best risk studies of the allegedly best sites for high-level repository sites (such as Yucca Mountain); therefore, there ought to be serious doubts that we are ready for permanent geological disposal, if indeed we shall ever be. Delay is preferable to error.

1

The Riddle
of Nuclear Waste

Italians have not been able to protect Renaissance art treasures for even as long as *one* thousand years.[1] Egyptians have not been able to protect the tombs of the Pharaohs for even as long as *four* thousand years, and some of the graves were looted within centuries. Yet, we in this generation have an obligation to protect our nuclear wastes for more than *ten* thousand years—a period longer than recorded history.

It is ironic that we have been civilized for only about 10,000 years, yet we face the task of protecting high-level radwastes, a dangerous and "massive source of potentially valuable energy," in perpetuity.[2] We face the task of storing radionuclides such as plutonium, which has a half-life of 24,000 years, but remains dangerous for more than 250,000 years. We have been separated from the apes for only about 5 million years, yet we face the task of safeguarding iodine-129, which has a half-life of 16 million years but remains dangerous for more than 160 million years.[3] We in the United States have been a nation for only about 200 years, yet we face the task of storing technetium-99 having a half-life of 200,000 years. Given the short span of our experience in handling these materials, how can we deal adequately with long-lived radioactive waste?

Although he may not have intended to do so, J. R. R. Tolkien, in *The Lord of the Rings*, suggested an answer to the riddle of nuclear waste. The ring gave mastery over every living creature. But because it was created by an evil power, it inevitably corrupted anyone who at-

1

tempted to use it. How should the hobbits, who held the ring, deal with it? Erestor articulated the dilemma: "There are but two courses, as Glorfindel already has declared: to hide the Ring forever; or to unmake it. But both are beyond our power. Who will read this riddle for us?"[4] The purpose of this book is to "read the riddle" of nuclear waste, to provide another alternative to the two current options of either permanently disposing of the waste or rendering it harmless. The argument is that permanent geological disposal of high-level radioactive waste is, at least at present, both scientifically uncertain and ethically questionable. Yet despite a variety of attempts, there is no proven way of reducing it to something that is not extremely lethal.[5] What ought to be done? We shall argue that the best option, drawn from a number of undesirable alternatives, is to place our high-level radwastes in negotiated (with the host community), monitored, retrievable, storage facilities (NMRS), at least for the foreseeable future—the next century—and that we should continue testing proposed sites for permanent, deep, geological disposal.[6] The rationale for our NMRS solution is both scientific and ethical. We need to reduce uncertainties about present and future radionuclide contamination. We need to protect members of present and future generations. We need to leave open the option of discovering and using technical processes that would render the waste less harmful.

The Status Quo: Promoting Permanent Disposal

The proposal to abandon the policy of permanent geological disposal of high-level radioactive waste, at least for the foreseeable future, is contrary both to most government positions and to most scientific opinions on the issue. As early as 1955, researchers representing the U.S. National Academy of Sciences (NAS) recommended permanent isolation of high-level radioactive wastes in mined geological repositories, a position the NAS spokespersons hold today.[7] This basic approach to disposal of high-level radioactive wastes is still being pursued in virtually every nation in the world. As Don U. Deere, chair of the U.S. Nuclear Waste Technical Review Board of the NAS, confirmed in 1990: "There is currently a world-wide scientific consensus that a deep geologic repository is the best option for disposal of high-level waste. The Board believes that there are no insurmountable technical reasons why an acceptable deep geologic repository cannot be developed."[8]

The most fundamental reason that virtually all governments and nuclear-risk experts have pursued a policy of developing repositories for permanent geological disposal of high-level radioactive materials is that they wish to maximize waste isolation. Another argument in favor of permanent geological disposal is that it minimizes both costs and hazards, especially transport risks to and from a storage facility. Still another reason for permanent disposal is that we, members of the present generation, should solve the high-level radioactive waste problem, not merely store the radionuclides and leave the burden to members of future generations.[9] The underlying assumption of this rationale for disposal is that only a *permanent* geological repository addresses important ethical obligations to future persons.

The technical disadvantages of permanent geological disposal of high-level radioactive wastes include the lack of experience with long-term isolation and the difficulty of knowing geological features and processes at the great depths and over the long time periods required. Some persons also oppose permanent geological disposal because they claim that it is impossible to assure isolation of the wastes underground. Other arguments against permanent disposal focus on technical uncertainties, on political difficulties associated with siting the facilities, on ethical problems related to imposing such a risk on members of future generations, and on the importance of the retrievability of the waste so as to leave open the options for future storage or disposal.[10]

The Mistakes of the Past

The main rationale for permanent disposal is the need to safeguard high-level wastes, to isolate them in perpetuity. Because some persons do not believe that radwastes can be isolated in perpetuity, however, they are critical of policies dictating permanent geological disposal. One of their reasons for doubting the feasibility of permanent disposal is that no one has ever accomplished it. They claim that, despite advances in knowledge and technology, inductive evidence argues against the possibility of permanent geological isolation of high-level wastes. There are no plausible inductive arguments for the success of permanent geological disposal of high-level radwaste, given data on nuclear waste storage for less than *one* century, and no data for the minimum storage period of *thousands* of centuries. What data we do have are not comforting. As we shall explain later, regulatory, safety, political, and financial questions have repeatedly forced the U.S. Department of Energy (DOE) to delay planning and opening facilities for nuclear waste. And, in the past, hundreds of people have died in radwaste accidents.

The worst such accident occurred when thousands of acres—twenty-two square miles—in what was then Soviet Kasli were rendered uninhabitable by high-level nuclear waste that went critical more than three decades ago.[11] At the current premier U.S. facility in Hanford, Washington, over 500,000 gallons of high-level radwaste have leaked into the soil, then into the Columbia River, and then into the Pacific Ocean.[12] Indeed, members of the U.S. Congress and the U.S. General Accounting Office (GAO) have admitted that DOE facilities have caused extensive soil and water contamination at Fernald (Ohio), Hanford (Washington), Idaho Falls (Idaho), Lawrence Livermore (California), Oak Ridge (Tennessee), Rocky Flats (Colorado), and Savannah River (South Carolina). Congress said recently that 1,061 DOE sites require a massive cleanup that may cost from $130 to $300 billion. Poor management and storage of radioactive materials and waste has occurred at all these facilities, in part, because DOE managers have repeatedly violated the agency's own environmental regulations as well as U.S. laws regarding hazardous wastes. Likewise DOE administrators have withheld funds and information from persons interested in DOE-facility safety, penalized whistleblowers who attempted to correct problems, and failed to spend the money necessary either to avoid or to clean up extensive radioactive contamination. As a result, members of Congress have charged that the DOE has lost credibility.[13]

At the nuclear waste facility containing more plutonium than any other commercial site in the world, a low-level radwaste installation in Maxey Flats, Kentucky, government and industry scientists were wrong by six orders of magnitude when they predicted how fast the stored plutonium would migrate. Because the facility was for low-level radwaste—largely from the commercial fuel cycle of reactors throughout the United States—workers buried the radioactive materials in allegedly impermeable shale. They used no canisters for containment. Officials of the nuclear engineering company that operated the site, however, were confident about the adequacy of the facility. They said that the possibility of offsite migration of the waste was "essentially nonexistent."[14] They reassured citizens that it would take twenty-four thousand years for the plutonium to travel one-half inch onsite. It went two miles offsite, however, less than ten years after the facility opened.[15] Although the geology, the storage methods, and the types of waste stored at Maxey Flats are different from those at the proposed facility in Yucca Mountain, Nevada, several of the assessment methods at the two sites are similar. Hence, mistakes at sites like Maxey Flats may have something to teach us about proposed repositories such as Yucca Mountain.

Current plans for future U.S. storage of high-level radioactive waste call for deep geological emplacement of steel canisters in host rock. Federal regulations require the steel canisters to resist corrosion for as little as three hundred years. Nevertheless, the DOE admits that the waste will remain dangerous for longer than ten thousand years. Government experts from the DOE also agree that, at best, they can merely limit the radioactivity that reaches the environment; they claim that "there is no doubt that the repository will leak over the course of the next 10,000 years."[16] It is likely that such leaks might occur through groundwater transport. On the basis of past leaks at nuclear-waste facilities, U.S. government researchers have extrapolated and have said that future leaks should occur at a rate of two to three per year. Using government-estimated exposure levels (580 person rem) at each radwaste site, each existing facility could cause approximately 12 cancers and 116 genetic deaths per century, if future leaks occur at the same rate as past ones.[17] These numbers appear relatively small until one realizes that, for ten thousand years, the cancer deaths alone could be in the hundreds of thousands per storage site. Admittedly, there are new waste technologies that might reduce these government figures. Any new technology, however, is unavoidably dependent upon fragile and short-lived human institutions and human capabilities. Faulty technology, after all, did not cause the Three Mile Island or Chernobyl accidents. It was human error. Likewise human error could well be the insoluble problem with managing high-level rad-waste.

Perhaps, however, the difficulties encountered with nuclear waste in the past have been due mainly to poor management practices, to inexperience, to outdated technology, or to individual cases of corruption.[18] Also, perhaps the leaks and contamination have occurred at existing U.S. waste facilities because none of them was designed to be permanent. As monitored facilities, these sites obviously did not maximize waste isolation. Nevertheless, the conflict between isolation and monitoring raises a fundamental dilemma: waste cannot be both easily monitored and completely isolated from the biosphere. These are incompatible goals, just as maximizing both safety and short-term economic efficiency (in storing radwaste) are incompatible goals. Because nuclear waste cannot be easily monitored and completely isolated at the same time, one could argue that, on the one hand, if scientists and engineers had maximized radwaste isolation and foregone monitoring, then installations like Hanford might have been more secure. On the other hand, one could argue that if scientists and engineers had maximized monitoring and minimized radwaste isolation, then leaks at facilities like Hanford might have been discovered more quickly. As a consequence, goes the argument, serious leaks and contamination might not have occurred.

To determine how much confidence we might be able to place in new scientific advances and recent disposal technology for permanent isolation of high-level radwaste, we must examine the best available techniques for assessing and managing the nuclear waste. Later in this book we shall examine the methods being used at the site proposed as the first permanent high-level radwaste repository in the U.S., at Yucca Mountain, Nevada. This examination should provide us with some idea of whether Yucca Mountain will be a more reliable location for storing nuclear waste than such facilities as Fernald, Hanford, Idaho Falls, Lawrence Livermore, Maxey Flats, Oak Ridge, Rocky Flats, and Savannah River.

Summary and Overview

To evaluate the feasibility of permanent disposal of high-level radioactive waste, we need to provide a context for discussion of this issue.[19] In chapter 2, we shall summarize the cultural, historical, legal, political, and scientific framework within which governments and industries began to generate nuclear waste. The chapter also will discuss why the wastes are so hazardous and why, to date, they have not been permanently stored. Chapter 3 explains some of the methodological factors responsible for the contamination at existing radwaste sites and for the flaws in assessments of proposed nuclear waste facilities. Given these factors, the chapter argues that scientific optimism about the models and predictions for successfully disposing of radioactive waste is misplaced. It is misplaced, in large part, because scientists, engineers, and managers have not been sufficiently sensitive to two potential sources of difficulties with probabilistic or quantitative risk assessment: methodological value judgments and questionable scientific inferences. One of the greatest abuses of quantitative risk assessment (QRA) has been to cloak the value judgments of QRA behind a veneer of technical precision.[20] In this volume we shall strip away several layers of technical methods so as to reveal the methodological value judgments and faulty inferences that often cause assessment difficulties. Scientists and engineers frequently have made methodological value judgments, for example, that certain hydrogeological models were capable of predicting future migration of radionuclides, despite the long time frame of the proposed repositories. Often they have also made the invalid inference, for instance, that because they knew of no way that radioisotopes could migrate at a particular site, therefore the wastes would not do so. Indeed, many scientists and engineers in general appear to have forgotten how the methods of probabilistic risk assessment often rely on subjective value judgments. Chapter 3 explains how these value judgments occur in science. It also shows, in many cases, that these subjective value judgments have caused scientists and engineers both to underestimate the risk posed by radwaste and to overestimate their ability to contain it.

Many scientists and engineers would argue, however, that the failure to assess nuclear risks accurately and to manage them safely in the past is no indicator of our future shortcomings in this area. Hence, to determine whether or not we can adequately assess and manage the prospective hazards associated with high-level radioactive waste, our analyses must be based on the best available risk studies of nuclear waste disposal and management. In chapter 4, we shall evaluate the success of current efforts to assess the risk associated with the nation's first proposed permanent high-level repository for commercial radwaste. The site is at Yucca Mountain, Nevada. The thesis of chapter 4 is that given the best available assessment methodology and the best available disposal technology, many scientists and engineers continue to underestimate the risks of permanent geological disposal. Indeed, a U.S. National Academy of Sciences (NAS) representative noted recently that the "methodology the Department (DOE) has selected [for evaluating the Yucca Mountain site] represents 'state of the art' and is adequate."[21] Yet in virtually all cases of *estimating* the magnitude of the risks of geological disposal, including the case of the proposed premier U.S. facility at Yucca Mountain, scientists and engineers have erred through an overconfidence bias. We shall argue that they have underestimated the risks by virtue of methodological value judgments (see chapter 3) about factors such as long-term extrapolations, model simplifications, sampling assumptions, questionable interpolations, and human error.

Chapter 5 argues that many risk assessors not only underestimate the disposal risk, but also that they subjectively evaluate it. In virtually all cases of *evaluating* the acceptability of the risks of geological disposal of high-level radioactive waste, including the case of the proposed Yucca Mountain facility, DOE assessors have employed subjective scientific, ethical, and political value judgments that are questionable. These subjective value judgments include assumptions about the adequacy of single-site studies, about the acceptability of certain risks and risk reductions, about the improbability of worst-case scenarios, about the relevance of "average risk" calculations, and about the justifiability of limited-liability protection, the lack of informed consent to risk, and utilitarian risk distributions. Making some subjective judgments is, of course, unavoidable even in science. The point of chapter 5 is that often scientists are unaware of their subjective judgments, and often they make judgments that are wrong.

Continuing to analyze state-of-the-art risk-assessment methodology and radwaste-disposal technology, chapter 6 argues that current scientific methods and practices in this area do not merely fall victim to questionable and subjective value judgments about risk. More importantly, they often employ logical, methodological, and ethical inferences that are problematic. Chapter 6 shows that in virtually all assessments of the risks of geological disposal of radioactive waste, including the case of the proposed premier U.S. facility in Yucca Mountain, DOE assessors have used questionable inferences. These include the appeal to ignorance, begging the question, affirming the consequent, the appeal to authority, as well as the expertise inference, the de minimis inference, the consent inference, the inference of specious accuracy, and the inference of the multiple maximand.

Chapter 7 assesses a number of policy conclusions based on the presence of unexamined (and often questionable) value judgments and inferences in current state-of-the-art risk assessments of proposed high-level radioactive waste repositories. The chapter begins with the recognition that all scientific and technological problems, especially

those requiring long-term predictions, involve methodological uncertainties and value judgments. (Of course, the value judgments
that occur in science are not typically moral or ethical. They are normative, however, in that they are based on methodological rules or
goals.) Scientists and engineers who designed the Waste Isolation Pilot
Project (WIPP) underground repository for military nuclear waste, for
example, made the methodological value judgment that the facility
needed to be built to withstand no more than a 5.5 earthquake (on
the Richter scale). Even before the WIPP repository was open, however, a 4.8 quake occurred. The 2 January 1992 earthquake was cen-
tered only 60 kilometers from the facility.[22] Even though such value
judgments occur throughout science, the chapter argues that there are
several unique characteristics of the problem of permanent geological
disposal of nuclear waste that render uncertainties and value judgments associated with it more troubling than in other areas of science.
As a result, geological disposal may not be, at present, the scientifically
best option, at least for high-level and certain long-lived wastes, such
as many transuranics. The chapter argues that there are at least three
reasons that the ordinary problems of empirical imprecision and scientific value judgments are more serious in the area of permanent geological disposal: the longevity of the wastes, the magnitude of possible
accident consequences, and the potential for human error or social
amplification of the risks of radwaste disposal. Chapter 7 also argues
that it is impossible, at present, to defend permanent disposal of high-
level nuclear wastes anywhere without relying on three invalid inferences: the appeal to ignorance, affirming the consequent, and begging
the question. Because these flaws constitute insurmountable obstacles,
at present, to a rational and scientific defense of permanent geological
disposal, the chapter argues that they are insurmountable obstacles, at
least for the foreseeable future, to sanctioning the policy of geological
disposal of high-level radioactive wastes.

Continuing to draw policy conclusions on the basis of the uncertainties surrounding permanent geological disposal of high-level
wastes, chapter 8 analyzes several key ethical problems associated with
disposal. These include: inadequate liability coverage; failure to provide free informed consent to members of future generations; and
sanctioning utilitarian (rather than egalitarian) distributions of the
risks. Chapter 8 argues that permanent geological disposal cannot be
justified until ethical problems—about such matters as due process,
consent, and equal treatment—have been either resolved or greatly re-

duced. Because these problems are, in principle, solvable, they do not constitute insurmountable obstacles to geological disposal. The chapter argues, however, that reducing these three obstacles, at present, would likely be prohibitively costly.

If permanent geological disposal of high-level radioactive waste, at least at present, poses massive scientific and ethical problems, then what is to be done? Chapter 9 argues that generating less waste in the future, together with above-ground storage (for the next century) of those high-level wastes that we do create, is the most desirable logical, ethical, and scientific alternative, at present. Because the main focus of this volume is to evaluate the current policy of permanent geological disposal, the discussion of temporary above-ground storage is not comprehensive. Rather, the purpose of chapter 9 is to sketch briefly an important alternative to current radwaste policy. Above-ground storage avoids question-begging appeals to future geological conditions that are unknown, and it places a greater ethical burden of radwaste risk on the present persons who have generated it, rather than on future persons who are likely to be its victims. Moreover, by keeping the waste accessible, at least for the short term (100 years), above-ground storage leaves open our scientific options for better radwaste management in the future. Nevertheless, one of our long-term policy choices might include permanent geological disposal. For the foreseeable future, however, this volume concludes that permanent geological disposal is both scientifically and ethically questionable. The containment of radioactive wastes, according to one U.S. Senator, is the single greatest responsibility ever consciously undertaken by the human race.[23] If his assertion is correct, then such a responsibility may require considerably more scientific precision and ethical sensitivity than we have exhibited thus far.

2

Understanding the
Origins of the Problem

Radioactive wastes have been called the Achilles Heel of the nuclear industry because after nearly half a century of nuclear technology there is still controversy surrounding how to deal with them. Perhaps because they are worried about human error and about scientists' claims to store waste safely in perpetuity, citizens and members of environmental groups have been in turmoil over the issue of nuclear-waste storage. Almost everywhere, they have proclaimed NIMBY: "Not In My Backyard." From Taiwan and Argentina to Japan and Siberia, citizens have protested plans to build nuclear-waste facilities.[1] In the United States, several groups have charged in lawsuits that radiation-exposure standards for proposed sites are too lax and violate the Safe Drinking Water Act. Over the last few years, Congress has been besieged with dozens of bills proposing to delay, abandon, or change the repository program established under the 1982 U.S. Nuclear Waste Policy Act.[2]

In spite of the current controversy surrounding atomic energy, 26 nations have commercial nuclear plants. All of them produce irradiated (spent) fuel and other toxic wastes. In 1992 there were 418 commercial nuclear reactors in the world, 112 of them in the United States, and 154 of them in Europe.[3] The U.S. government predicted in 1973, however, that there would be 1,000 fission plants generating power in the United States by the year 2000.[4] Cost overruns, public opposition, and concerns about safety have made it unlikely that this prediction will ever be fulfilled. Part of the reason is that accidents like

11

those at Chernobyl and Three Mile Island have done much to inflame public opposition to commercial nuclear fission. U.S. Department of Energy (DOE) representatives admit that Chernobyl could cause up to 28,000 fatal cancers in the former Soviet Union, Scandinavia, and Europe over the next 50 years, and other scientists and policymakers claim that the number of fatal cancers caused by Chernobyl will be as high as 475,000.[5] Also, U.S. Nuclear Regulatory Commission (NRC) data indicate that the United States has a fifty-fifty chance of having another accident the size of Three Mile Island or larger.[6] Given such data, it is no surprise that no new commercial reactors have been ordered in the United States since 1974.[7]

In fact, the commercial nuclear fission programs in all developed nations either have been cut back or have come to a standstill, except in France, where the utility employs fast breeder, rather than fission, reactors. Moreover, the apparent reasons for the success of the French nuclear program—the fact that it is centralized and government owned—are unique and not necessarily transferable to other nations. The French utility is protected from market forces, protected from environmentalists' criticisms, and protected from public participation in decision making. Even with these benefits, the French utility now has a debt of $30 billion, due to its commitment to nuclear power. In 1982 this debt had accumulated to $152 billion, although part of it was forgiven by the government. At least part of the reason for the expensiveness of French nuclear electricity is the fact that there are numerous safety problems and maintenance takes longer and longer, leading to considerable downtime for the reactors.[8]

In the United States during the 1980s, radioactive waste doubled, the costs of nuclear-generated electricity quadrupled, and mishaps exceeded 34,000 in number.[9] Despite the fact that most developed nations have begun to reject commercial nuclear fission, however, radioactive waste remains an international problem. All radwastes can be deadly and, as a consequence, they need to be isolated from the accessible environment. The scientific and technical consensus—as already mentioned in the previous chapter—is that we ought to achieve isolation by permanent geological disposal of all high-level nuclear wastes. To evaluate the disposal option, however, we need to understand the technical, historical, and legal issues surrounding the origins of radioactive waste. Because the main concern of this volume is high-level radioactive wastes such as spent reactor fuels, we shall focus mainly on them.

Radioactive Waste:
Technical Background

Commercial and military reactors are the main producers of the radioactive waste that results from the fissioning or splitting of uranium or plutonium atoms, a process that creates new radioactive elements or radionuclides. Most fission reactors split apart uranium-235; the breeder reactors used in France convert non-fissionable uranium-238 into plutonium-239 after irradiation by neutrons. Some of the radionuclides created by neutron absorption and fissioning have higher atomic numbers than uranium, and they are called "transuranic elements." Other radionuclides are lighter than uranium, and they are called "fission products." Each of the more than eighty such products created in the fission reactor is capable of releasing ionizing radiation. Radiation is the energy transferred as particles or waves move through space or from one body to another. Radiation is "ionizing" when it is able to remove orbital electrons from other atoms or molecules and hence able to change their structure and molecular charge. The fact that ionizing radiation can change the structure of atoms or molecules is what accounts for its ability to cause carcinogenic, mutagenic, and teratogenic damage—to induce, respectively, cancer, genetic defects, and birth defects.[10]

Whenever objects or persons absorb energy and change structure as a result of ionizing radiation, they become radioactive, that is, they emit radiation in the form of alpha particles, beta particles, or gamma rays. Alpha particles are positively charged helium atoms; they contain two protons and two neutrons. Because alpha radiation is the most densely ionizing, it is potentially the most dangerous of the three forms of radiation, even though it is the least penetrating. If an alpha-emitter like plutonium, a transuranic, enters the body, it can cause significant cellular damage or even death. Beta particles have the same charge and mass as electrons. Streams of beta particles (beta radiation), such as those from strontium-90 and cesium-137, can cause skin burns. Usually accompanying alpha and beta emissions, gamma rays are high-energy, short-wave-length radiation. Like x-rays, gamma rays are a type of electromagnetic radiation. Because gamma rays (like x-rays) are so highly penetrating, several feet of concrete or rock are required for adequate shielding. Iodine-131 is an example of a gamma emitter. Even though they are naturally present, at low levels, throughout our environment, all three types of ionizing radiation are harmful if they are inhaled, ingested, or somehow incorporated into the body. Gamma rays and x-rays are especially dangerous because they can damage or destroy living tissue, even from a distance of several feet or more. Despite their risk, however, we employ x-rays because of their benefits, for example, in medical diagnosis. Because x-rays and gamma radiation lose very little energy as they travel through the air, they can act at great distances. Alpha emitters, however, must be in touch with live tissue to cause harm. Nevertheless, because they can lodge in the body, they can deposit a very large quantity of energy in a given volume of tissue.

The most common measure of the intensity of radioactivity is the curie (Ci), named after Marie Curie who, with her husband Pierre, discovered radium in 1898. (A curie is the quantity of a radioactive isotope which decays at the rate of 3.7×10^{10} disintegrations per second. Originally it was the amount of radioactivity given off by one gram of radium.) One nuclear reactor may contain over 10,000 megacuries of radioactivity. (A megacurie is 1 million curies.) In general, the greater the intensity of the radioactivity, the greater the potential damage that it can inflict. Short-term effects of chronic exposure to radiation are radiation sickness—nausea, vomiting, dizziness, headache, and so on. Long-term effects of chronic exposure to radiation are cancer, reproductive failure, birth defects, genetic effects, and death. One reason why the effects of exposure to radiation are so serious is that there is *no threshold* for increased risk as a result of exposure to even small amounts of radiation; also effects of radiation are *cumulative*: successive exposures increase one's risk of harm.[11] In 1989 members of a U.S. National Research Council Committee argued that an acute dose of radiation is three times more likely to cause cancerous tumors and four times more likely to induce leukemia than was thought in 1980. Hence, despite the known effects of radiation, current standards may be too lenient. Identifying dangerous radiation effects is also difficult because many of them are latent. For example, at the Oak Ridge National Laboratories, where many persons received high doses of radiation, it took twenty-six years for the cancer rate to exhibit a statistically significant increase. Much radiation damage also remains undetected because few persons do epidemiological studies to measure its effects on humans.[12]

Radioactive Waste:
Historical Background

Standard accounts of nuclear history are often misleading regarding the source and the magnitude of our difficulties with radioactive waste. Some persons have claimed that we face the problem
of nuclear waste both (1) because of military activities and important
hospital uses of nuclear medicine and (2) because a number of utilities
were eager to provide inexpensive electricity for a great number of
people. Both these myths are untrue. High-level radwaste is, for the
most part, neither medical nor military, nor is it generated as a result
of inexpensive electricity. Such waste consists of spent fuel rods from
reactors and residues from fuel reprocessing. Less than 1 percent of
high-level waste is from medical activities.[13] Moreover, at least in the
United States, approximately half of the high-level waste now needing
storage is from commercial nuclear fission, not military activities.[14]
Also, the commercial half of the waste, primarily spent fuel, is expected to rise dramatically by 1995, to 11 times the metric tons now
needing to be stored, whereas the military waste will increase very
slowly and remain close to current levels. For example, U.S. spent
fuel, currently about 7,000 metric tons, will rise to more than 70,000
metric tons by 1995. The upshot is that by 1995 most high-level and
low-level radwaste, especially in Europe, will be from commercial reactors, not from military activities, and certainly not from medical
processes.[15]

The problem of radioactive waste, moreover, exists neither because
industry was eager to generate electricity nor because fission was an
economical means of doing so. At the beginning of the atomic era, industry was reluctant, both on economic and on safety grounds, to use
fission to generate electricity. Worried about safety, all major U.S. corporations with nuclear interests refused to produce electricity by
means of fission unless some indemnity legislation was passed to protect them in the event of a catastrophic accident.[16] The top lobby-
ist for the nuclear industry, the president of the Atomic Industrial
Forum, has confirmed what numerous government committee reports
show. Commercial nuclear fission began, and was pursued, only because government leaders wanted to justify continuing military expenditures in nuclear-related areas and to obtain weapons-grade plutonium.[17] Moreover, at least in the United States, fission-generated

electricity began only because the government provided more than $100 billion in subsidies (for research, development, waste storage, and insurance) to the nuclear industry. Congress also gave the utilities a liability limit (in the Price-Anderson Act) which protects licensees from most of the public losses and claims in the event of a catastrophic nuclear accident. The current U.S. liability limit is approximately $7.2 billion, less than 5 percent of the cost required to clean up Chernobyl, which was not a worst-case accident. Similar liability limits for commercial nuclear fission exist in other countries, such as Canada, where there is a $75 million government and industry liability limit for nuclear accidents. Since the costs of such accidents can run into the hundreds of billions of dollars, the constitutionality of these liability limits has been challenged in every nation in which they exist.[18]

In 1976, twenty years after commercial fission reactors began operating, the *Wall Street Journal* proclaimed them an economic disaster. Nuclear electricity has proved so costly that year 2000 projections for nuclear power plants are now approximately one-eighth of what they were in the midseventies.[19] The few U.S. nuclear manufacturers still in business have remained so by selling reactors to other nations, often developing countries. Yet many of the commercial reactors going to these countries may not be in their best interests, as later chapters of this volume will suggest. Indeed, commercial nuclear fission may be the current version of infant formula. In the infant formula controversy of the last two decades, U.S. and multinational corporations made great profits by exporting infant formula to developing nations. They were able to do so only by coercive sales tactics and by misleading foreign consumers about the merits of their products. Some diplomats also have charged that developing nations have been misled about the merits of commercial nuclear fission. Other officials have claimed that developing countries are seeking fission-generated electricity as a subterfuge for obtaining nuclear weapons capability, through the plutonium byproduct.[20] India exploded its first nuclear bomb, for example, by using plutonium produced by a reactor exported by Canada. Whether or not military subterfuge is the reason for the commercial survival of nuclear fission, the few countries still developing atomic energy do not have uncontroversial grounds for subscribing to the myth of the safe, economical atom. As Chernobyl and other accidents show, nuclear fission is obviously an expensive and very dangerous way to boil water and to run a turbine.

Every year, each 1000-MWe reactor discharges about 25.4 metric tons of high-level waste as spent fuel.[21] For three hundred commercial reactors, worldwide, the annual high-level radwaste is 7,620 metric tons. Only 10 micrograms of plutonium are almost certain to induce cancer, and those several grams of plutonium, dispersed in a ventilation system, are enough to cause thousands of deaths.[22] Moreover, as even industry experts admit, each of the 7,620 metric tons of high-level waste produced annually has the potential to cause hundreds of millions of cancers for at least the first three hundred years of storage, and then tens of millions of cancers for the next million years,[23] in the (perhaps) unlikely event of its dispersal. These cancers could be prevented, of course, with isolation of the wastes for a million years. That is why most plans for high-level radwaste storage call for defense in depth, for sealing the waste in a ceramic material and for burying it deep underground in stainless steel or copper canisters. Nevertheless, U.S. EPA (Environmental Protection Agency) reports have warned that we cannot count on institutional safeguards for the waste beyond a hundred years.[24] Despite the fact that long-term safeguards for radioactive waste, especially high-level waste, are not likely to be guaranteed beyond a century, scientists, engineers, and industrialists have been generating nuclear waste ever since the end of the nineteenth century. In 1895, Roentgen discovered the x-ray, and in 1896, Becquerel and the Curies discovered natural radioactivity. Ever since that time, scientists and medical doctors experimenting with radionuclides or x-rays, for example, have been generating nuclear waste. Large volumes of radioactive waste were not created, however, until the atomic bomb program of World War II. The United States and the former Soviet Union both built uranium enrichment plants during the war. Both countries therefore started to develop light-water, nuclear fission reactors (that use enriched uranium fuel) because this was the technology used in their military efforts. Canada, France, and Great Britain, however, began work on reactors moderated by graphite or heavy water. Using unenriched uranium, these reactors cost more to build than the enriched uranium reactors of the United States, but they are safer by virtue of being better able to withstand a loss of cooling.[25]

The effort to collect the plutonium needed for atomic bombs during World War II was part of a U.S. defense effort known as the Manhattan Project. In 1942, the Manhattan Engineer District Project was formed, and in December of the same year Enrico Fermi directed a team that produced the world's first nuclear chain reaction. By January 1943, the U.S. federal government researchers were overseeing the building of the first atomic bombs at Oak Ridge, Tennessee, and Hanford, Washington. On 16 July 1945, the world's first atomic bomb, using plutonium, was exploded in New Mexico. On 6 August 1945, the United States dropped the first nuclear warhead, employing uranium-235, on Hiroshima. Sixty-five thousand persons perished in the blast. Days later, another atomic bomb was dropped on Nagasaki.

Although the discussion in this volume focuses on the current policy of geological disposal of high-level radioactive waste, much of which is from commercial reactors, it is important to note that many of the problems associated with decision making regarding radwaste stem from the military origins of the first nuclear technology. The Manhattan Project, with its military focus, has left a legacy of secrecy, centralization, and technocracy which has dominated nuclear-related decision making for at least three decades in the United States This three-part legacy led to haste, to temporary solutions, to a lack of public participation in regulating nuclear energy, to institutional self-protection, and to public policy that was neither properly debated nor scrutinized through scientific peer review. For example, in 1986, in response to public demand, the U.S. Department of Energy released 19,000 pages of formerly classified documents on the operations at the Hanford facility (used to develop the atomic bomb and to store radioactive waste) during the 1940s and 1950s. The documents reveal that U.S. military researchers had conducted radiological experiments on local people, without either their knowledge or their permission. In 1945 alone, the Hanford facility, devoted to wartime production of plutonium, routinely released through its reactor exhaust stacks 340,000 curies of radioactive iodine. (Current standards permit less than 1 curie of iodine to be released each year at the facility, and even in 1945, this deliberate release far exceeded U.S. government environmental standards.) Numerous other accidents and deliberate releases occurred at Hanford, many of which were designed for the purpose of developing a monitoring methodology for intelligence efforts regarding the Soviet military program. Such experiments were made possible only because of the secrecy that shrouded the nuclear industry in all countries in its early years.[26]

From 1940 through 1945, the United States spent $2 billion to develop the first atomic bombs used during World War II. Thereafter, the government took twenty years and more than $100 billion in subsidies to develop the first commercial nuclear reactors used to generate electricity. Scientists were optimistic about the "Atoms for Peace" program; it provided a nonmilitary rationale for continuing the development of nuclear technology and for obtaining weapons-grade plutonium that could be used for military purposes.[27] Nobel-winning scientists, such as Henry Kendall, now claim that the present U.S. government subsidies for commercial reactors are running on the order of $20 billion per year; if these subsidies were removed from nuclear electricity, Kendall and others claim that the costs of fission-generated electricity would double.[28]

Between 1948 and 1953, the United States built and tested a submarine reactor at Idaho Falls under the leadership of Admiral H. G. Rickover. The submarine *Nautilus* went to sea in 1955, powered by a nuclear reactor using enriched uranium fuel. All of the Polaris missile-carrying submarines of the United States use nuclear reactors.[29] In 1951, the Experimental Breeder Reactor at Arco, Idaho produced the first commercial nuclear electric power. In 1956, the first full-scale nuclear fission power plant began to operate at Calder Hall in northwestern England. Only after the passage of the 1957 Price-Anderson Act, limiting nuclear liability in the event of an accident, did the U.S. industry agree to begin using atomic energy for commercial generation of electricity. The first U.S. commercial nuclear plant (in Shippingport, Pennsylvania) was ready to begin operation in 1957; it was a light-water reactor. Also in 1957, the United Nations established the International Atomic Energy Agency to promote the peaceful uses of nuclear power. In 1958, the former Soviet Union opened its first commercial reactor near Chelyabinsk. By 1970, nuclear plants had opened in Canada, France, Great Britain, India, Italy, Japan, the Netherlands, Spain, Switzerland, the United States, and the former Soviet Union.[30] Even before the U.S. accident at Three Mile Island in 1979, however, commercial nuclear fission was already in economic trouble, as the preceding remarks indicate. As this brief history of nuclear technology also reveals, reactors came into use as part of military efforts to create an atomic bomb. Despite widespread sponsorship and use of this technology, no country evaluated nuclear fission, prior to its commercial employment, in order to determine whether or not it was a desirable means of generating electricity. Instead, driven by military applications, nations promoted commercial use of nuclear technology as a way to support weapons development.

The Current Status of High-Level Radioactive Waste

As a result of the use of nuclear technology for almost a century, many countries of the world have created radioactive wastes.

The bulk of these wastes, as was already mentioned, comes from civilian, rather than military, uses. Hence, even if we were successful in stopping military generation of radioactive wastes, we would still face the problem of radwastes created by commercial reactors. Scientists and engineers are currently employing a variety of techniques to manage and store these wastes. In countries that reprocess the nuclear materials, the high-level waste is in liquid form or vitrified. Otherwise, it is stored, usually in pools of water at the reactor site, until it is cool enough for geological emplacement. Emplacement often occurs from twenty to fifty years after the waste is created.[31] Reprocessing high-level radioactive waste is desirable, at least in the sense that it reduces its volume and makes plutonium available for use as fuel in breeder reactors. Reprocessing does not, however, reduce the radioactivity of the waste. It creates greater volumes of intermediate-level and low-level radioactive wastes. Reprocessing is not desirable in the sense that it makes use of the waste for weapons—in other words, proliferation—much easier. Currently, the United States, Canada, and Sweden are the only major nuclear nations that do not have their spent fuel, their high-level radwaste, reprocessed. Other Western countries, including Japan, contract for reprocessing services with Britain and France, although Japan is building its own reprocessing plant. The former Soviet Union manages spent fuel from its country and from Eastern Europe.[32]

As was already mentioned in chapter 1, most governments and nuclear-industry representatives prefer permanent, deep geological disposal of high-level wastes and spent reactor fuel. Currently, there are sites under investigation for permanent disposal in Argentina, Finland, France, Germany, South Africa, Sweden, Switzerland, and the United States. Although preferred sites exist in Argentina, Germany, South Africa, and the United States, no permanent repository has yet been chosen anywhere in the world. Geological disposal is also the selected method of managing intermediate wastes, although so far, only the WIPP site in New Mexico has been built for possible permanent disposal of military transuranic wastes; there are other sites under consideration in several countries.[33]

Short-lived intermediate-level wastes and low-level wastes likewise are placed in shallow land-burial trenches in France and in the United States, or in sub-seabed repositories in Sweden. Some low-level radioactive wastes are also incinerated or emitted into the air, rivers, or seas, as from reprocessing plants in Britain and France. Currently, the greatest source of radioactive pollution of the world's seas and oceans is the Windscale reprocessing facility in Sellafield, United Kingdom. Until 1970, the United States dumped intermediate-level and low-level wastes into the oceans, and until 1983, the British dumped them (on behalf of their own country and on behalf of Belgium, Switzerland, and the Netherlands) into the oceans. Most radioactive wastes, however, currently remain in storage, presumably waiting until governments come up with a final disposal site or management plan.[34]

Radioactive Waste: Legal and Regulatory Background

Nuclear wastes, and especially high-level wastes, are subject to a number of laws and regulations throughout the world. Many of these restrictions have been developed in cooperation with the International Atomic Energy Agency (IAEA). Although the IAEA was founded in 1957, only recently has the agency developed several guidelines to govern the management of nuclear waste. These are: (1) for effluents containing radionuclides in amounts below authorized radiological protection limits (based on the recommendations of the International Commission for Radiological Protection, the ICRP), one can follow the strategy of "dilute and disperse" to the environment — "the solution to pollution is dilution"; (2) for waste containing only short-lived radionuclides, one can follow the strategy of "delay and decay"; (3) for waste containing significant amounts of long-lived radionuclides, one can follow the strategy of "concentrate and confine." Only in late 1988, however, did the IAEA establish its first formal radioactive waste policy body, the International Radioactive Waste Management Advisory Committee.[35]

In 1957, the same year that the IAEA began, two other organizations were also created, both of which have played a role in oversight of nuclear waste. The Organization for European Economic Cooperation and Development (OECD) created a European Nuclear Energy Agency (ENEA) that became the NEA in 1972 when Japan acceded to the OECD. In 1975 the NEA established a radioactive waste management committee that facilitates sharing of member information and sponsors research on land and sea disposal of nuclear wastes. The other group that came into being in 1957 is the European Economic Community's (EEC) Nuclear Agency, Euratom, whose members own commercial nuclear materials in the EEC as well as design and operate several nuclear facilities.[36]

Through United Nations agreements, member states have also accomplished some regulation of nuclear energy and radioactive waste. At the U.N. Convention on the High Seas held in Geneva in 1958, for example, each nation agreed to take measures "to prevent pollution of the seas from the dumping of nuclear waste, taking into account any standards and regulations which may be formulated by the competent international organization."[37] Sea-dumping of radioactive wastes by some member states, however, continued until 1983. This and other examples suggest that despite the international guidelines and information exchanges regarding radioactive waste accomplished through the IAEA and related agencies, it was not until the Chernobyl accident in 1986 that countries actually began to accept transnational regulation of nuclear technology. Even so, policy and execution regarding radioactive waste remains largely a matter of national law.

Because of the great differences, country to country, in laws and regulations concerning nuclear energy, and because the United States has the single largest commercial nuclear program in the world, we shall discuss only U.S. laws and regulations regarding nuclear energy and high-level radioactive waste. Much U.S. regulation in this area began in 1946 with the Atomic Energy Act and the establishment of the Atomic Energy Commission. The Atomic Energy Act of 1954 emphasizes both domestic and international uses of the atom, and it also provides for control of "source material" (uranium and thorium) and "by-product material" (radioactive substances).

In 1957, under threat from all major companies with nuclear expertise to "withdraw from the nuclear field" unless indemnity legislation was passed to protect the industry, Congress passed the Price-Anderson Act, an amendment to the 1954 Atomic Energy Act. This amendment provides that the law will "hold harmless the [nuclear] licensee and other persons indemnified" from public liability claims (arising from nuclear accidents) in excess of $560 million. (As was already mentioned earlier in this chapter, the limit was raised to approximately $6 billion in 1988. Even so, the liability limit currently is less than 5 percent of the cost required to clean up Chernobyl.) The liability ceiling provided by the Price-Anderson Act was passed with the proviso that the limitation would be effective for only ten years. The Joint Committee on Atomic Energy assured Congress that the limitation was needed only for a decade, that the problems of nuclear safety would be solved by 1967, and that the fear of public liability would no longer block economical private nuclear insurance. The problems with reactor safety have not been resolved, however, and the Price-Anderson Act, with minor amendments, has been extended in 1967, 1977, 1987, and 1988.[38]

Until 1975, the Atomic Energy Commission (AEC) was responsible in the United States for both promoting and regulating nuclear energy. Numerous lawsuits charged that the AEC had covered up problems at nuclear facilities and that it had not done a credible job of insuring safety.[39] Indeed, the agency suppressed studies that raised questions about the safety of commercial nuclear energy, and it abolished the National Academy of Sciences' committees on radioactive waste; M. King Hubbert, chair of the National Academy of Sciences' Division of Earth Sciences, noted: "There has never been an agency any more ruthless than the AEC . . . they were a law unto themselves."[40] Because of numerous problems of bias and credibility, the AEC was abolished through the U.S. Energy Reorganization Act, although many of its employees simply moved to successor agencies. The 1975 act created the Energy Research and Development Agency (ERDA) to promote nuclear energy and the Nuclear Regulatory Commission (NRC) to assess safety. Two years later, the Energy Organization Act of 1977 replaced the ERDA with the Department of Energy (DOE).

Throughout all these changes in U.S. agencies regulating nuclear plants, the Environmental Protection Agency (EPA) has been responsible for monitoring pollution from radioactive waste facilities. Created in 1970, the EPA has responsibility for air and water standards, limits on pollutants, and control of radioactivity. The EPA also provides for public participation regarding its functions through meetings, hearings, and advisory group reviews. The relationship among the three agencies (the NRC, DOE, and EPA) that most directly affect the handling, storage, and disposal of radioactive waste is complex. More than any other U.S. agency, the EPA provides radiation-protection standards. The NRC licenses and regulates waste disposal and management under EPA standards. The DOE does research and development, advises and helps with waste programs, and has been charged with operating defense and high-level commercial-waste repositories.

In addition to the restrictions set by the current DOE, NRC, and EPA, several laws also control regulations and policy regarding nuclear energy and radioactive wastes. The National Environmental Policy Act of 1969 (NEPA), for example, has as its purpose to prevent or eliminate damage to the environment and biosphere, including humans. The act also created the Council on Environmental Quality (CEQ), a group that reports to the president. NEPA's most important provision requires that every federal action that may significantly affect the environment must be accompanied by an environmental impact statement (EIS). The EIS describes alternative actions, social and economic effects, public comments on the actions, agency responses to these comments, and includes reports of relevant hearings.

In 1982, Congress passed the Nuclear Waste Policy Act (NWPA), perhaps the single most important piece of legislation affecting high-level radioactive waste disposal. The act mandated permanent disposal of radwaste, a policy that had for years been the conventional wisdom (see chapter 1). Containing timetables for the DOE to accomplish permanent, underground disposal of high-level waste, the NWPA governs commercially generated materials, but allows for disposal of defense wastes, given presidential approval. The act also set up a nuclear waste fund to pay for disposal through a fee imposed on the waste generators and therefore on consumers. The fee is one-tenth of a cent per kilowatt hour, or about a sixtieth of the cost of electricity paid by the consumer. The NWPA also requires an Office of Civilian Radioactive Waste Management, with its director reporting to the secretary of energy. Perhaps most important, the act provides guidelines for site selection of possible high-level radioactive waste repositories.[41]

Under the guidelines of the 1982 NWPA, the DOE selected a number of sites as potentially acceptable for the first permanent high-level radwaste repository in the United States. They were in Washington, Utah, Texas, Mississippi, Louisiana, Nevada, the Great Lakes area, and the Appalachian range. In 1987, the choice of sites was narrowed to Hanford (Washington), Yucca Mountain (Nevada), and Deaf Smith (Texas). After much political compromise, Congress passed the Nuclear Waste Policy Amendments Act of 1987; one of its main provisions was to mandate study of only one site, Yucca Mountain. Other special features in the act are the requirements to create a Nuclear Waste Review Board in the National Academy of Sciences; to ship spent fuel in NRC-approved packages, with state and local authorities notified of shipments; and to provide an analysis, between the years 2007 and 2010, of the need for a second repository.[42] Only if the Nevada site is found unacceptable will other possible locations be considered. Currently scientists and engineers are studying the hydrogeology, seismicity, volcanism, and climate of the Nevada location.

However, on 5 January 1990, the Nevada attorney general filed a court petition seeking a "notice of disapproval" of the Yucca Mountain site under the NWPA. The petition failed, and Nevada has appealed it to the U.S. Supreme Court.[43] The U.S. Supreme Court, however, denied further review. It said that discussion of constitutional issues (related to Nevada's support of an absolute right to veto the selection of the Yucca Mountain site) was premature. In other words, Nevada's alleged right to veto the site can be discussed only after the site is formally selected for a repository, after all licensing and permitting procedures are completed.[44] Because 80 percent of Nevadans oppose the facility, the DOE plans for Yucca Mountain remain in question.[45] Some persons have even argued that the DOE may have to abandon its current plans and consider other options, such as subseabed disposal or above-ground storage.[46]

In addition to the DOE, the NRC also controls disposal of high-level radioactive waste through regulations that ultimately are published in the *Code of Federal Regulations*, 10 CFR 60. Some of the most important provisions of the code are that a high-level radwaste facility should:

- pose no unreasonable risk to public health and safety;
- employ multiple barriers to prevent waste migration;
- meet performance objectives for its components and system;
- meet site characterization requirements such as geological stability, slow groundwater movement, lack of propensity to flood, and remoteness from populations;
- provide retrievability of the wastes for up to fifty years;
- employ waste packages that are dry, inert, and that take account of all possible effects;
- have waste packages that remain secure for at least three hundred years;
- be built in an area where groundwater travel time from the repository to public water sources is at least one thousand years;
- allow less annual release of radionuclides than a thousandth of a percent of the amount of radioactivity that is present one thousand years after the repository is closed;
- be studied such that predictions about safety are made with conservative assumptions and by calculations that take account of uncertainties.[47]

Some of the problems with 10 CFR 60 are that the code employs qualitative language, such as "unreasonable risk," and that it mandates somewhat incompatible goals, such as retrievability (for fifty years) of the waste and permanent disposal.

Conclusion

How ought one determine whether permanent geological disposal of high-level radioactive waste, as prescribed through 10 CFR 60, is a reasonable policy alternative? One important measure is whether current studies of state-of-the-art waste technology provide reasonable assurance that the NRC and DOE requirements, such as those just listed, can be met. In addition to looking at the quality of the site studies, another source of information about reasonable future waste policies is past government performance in the area of radioactive waste management. At least some of this information is not reassuring. For example, a recent report on the environmental contamination and containment record of the U.S. Department of Defense (DOD) and the DOE argued that these departments were "amongst the worst violators of the hazardous waste laws." The report concluded with the statement that the DOD and DOE attitude varied between "reluctant compliance and active disregard for the law." At the Fernald uranium-fuel processing plant in Ohio, for example, the DOE facility each year illegally dumped 109 million gallons of highly radioactive wastes into storm sewers. Current estimates for cleaning up the U.S. (DOE and DOD) nuclear weapons plants are more than $300 billion.[48]

Later in this volume, we shall examine in more detail the previous record of U.S. government agencies in managing radioactive wastes. We shall also evaluate the quality of the best site studies done in connection with high-level radioactive waste disposal, the assessments currently being performed at the proposed premier site at Yucca Mountain. Both of these investigations should provide some insight into the feasibility of permanent geological disposal of high-level nuclear waste. Before beginning these two analyses, however, it is important to know exactly how reliable any scientific studies of risk can be. The purpose of the next chapter is to show that unavoidable methodological value judgments sometimes undercut the practice of science and risk assessment and therefore jeopardize many conclusions about radioactive waste disposal.

3

Reliance on Value Judgments
in Repository Risk Assessment

In a recent book, I. S. Roxburgh, a proponent of geological disposal of high-level radioactive waste, optimistically outlined
the characteristics of evaporites, crystalline rocks, and argillaceous
rocks as repositories. Next he spent several chapters enthusiastically
discussing sub-seabed disposal, groundwater movement, and physico-
chemical processes that retard radionuclide movement. After a lengthy
and detailed scientific argument for permanent geological disposal,
Roxburgh admitted that the three main methods of repository risk
assessment (expert judgments, fault trees, and simulations) are "to a
large extent reliant upon qualitative judgements."[1] How could one
admit both that assessment of repository risks is largely a *qualitative*
enterprise, even though risk assessment yields *quantitative* conclusions? How could reliable quantitative results be based on reasoning
that is "to a large extent reliant" on qualitative judgments?

The purpose of this chapter is to resolve the puzzle over how and
why quantitative risk assessment (QRA) of radwaste repositories is in
part qualitative, even though the site studies are allegedly quantitative
and reliable. We shall argue that the solution to this puzzle is that the
site studies are not as quantitative and reliable as has often been alleged. In this and subsequent chapters, we shall show that both the
site studies and the risk assessments—indeed all of the sciences—unavoidably involve qualitative, value-laden judgments about method,
some of which are reasonable and some of which are not. And if they
do involve such judgments, then in order to evaluate a given practice

of science or risk assessment we must be able to evaluate the quality of the methodological value judgments imbedded in it. Hence, although even the best quantitative assessments rely on some qualitative judgments, we need to evaluate both the extent of these judgments and the evidence supporting them, in order to determine whether they are defensible. In this chapter, we shall outline some of the ways in which science in general and QRA in particular are value laden. That accomplished, in subsequent chapters we shall survey both the types and the defensibility of value judgments used in state-of-the-art assessments of proposed high-level repositories, notably in the current Yucca Mountain studies.

Science and Methodological Value Judgments

Sometimes QRAs are less valuable, objective, and scientific than they should be. As examples of scientific explanation and prediction, QRAs can go wrong in two main ways, with respect to the *data* employed in their premises or with respect to their *methods*. A central focus of our analysis is QRA methods used at proposed repository sites like Yucca Mountain and how we may improve them. We can improve them in the same way that we strengthen scientific methods: by a persistent critique of specific (QRA) arguments and by using tried canons of logic to assess the reliability of specific (QRA) conclusions.[2]

Our methodological analysis of the arguments used in QRA focuses on two of the important ways in which the move from premises (about scientific data) to conclusions (about risk evaluation) can go wrong. Either the *inferences* used to justify the move from premises to conclusion may be suspect, or the *methodological value judgments*—in terms of which we interpret the inferences, data, premises, and scientific theories—may be questionable. *Inferences* are processes of reasoning that we use in deriving conclusions from premises, and they may be valid or invalid. If we are given the premise, "A entails B," for example, we use an invalid inference if we draw the conclusion, "B entails A." Or, for instance, if we are given the premises, "A entails B," and "B entails C," then we use a valid inference—transitivity—if we draw the conclusion, "A entails C."

Methodological value judgments are interpretations of inferences, data, premises, or theories—interpretations that rely on our commitment to particular methodological values. For scientists, methodological values include simplicity, predictive power, external consistency, accuracy, and so on. Whenever we employ or apply inferences, data, or premises in the arguments of science or QRA, we must interpret them. Typically these interpretations take the form of methodological value judgments. For example, someone committed to the methodological value of predictive power might make the methodological value judgment that if models of some phenomenon had not been tested with actual field data, then they alone were an insufficient basis for drawing conclusions. Because of this methodological value judgment, such a person might discount the predictive value of computer models. Similarly, for instance, someone committed to the methodological value of external consistency—rather than predictive power— might make a quite different methodological value judgment. Such a person might judge that untested models of some phenomenon, provided that they were consistent with available data, were a sufficient basis for drawing conclusions about the phenomenon. In chapters 4 and 5, we shall discuss some of the methodological value judgments that occur frequently in QRAs of proposed respository sites. In chapter 6, we shall investigate some of the questionable inferences used in QRA.

Because some methodological value judgments are more plausible, logical, or defensible than others, and because QRA conclusions are often highly sensitive to methodological value judgments, it makes sense to assess them. Moreover, even though many methodological value judgments are defensible and reliable, nevertheless they all are somewhat subjective. They are somewhat subjective because they are *interpretations* of inferences, data, premises, or theories. They are also somewhat subjective because scientists may disagree about the relative importance of different methodological values in terms of which we make methodological value judgments. We term methodological value judgments "value judgments" because they are partially subjective, because they are a function of methodological values or norms (predictive power and so on), and because they are often more controversial than judgments about empirical data.

When a scientific explanation/prediction or QRA relies on problematic inferences or value judgments, often those inferences or value judgments are suspect because they are based on erroneous or questionable *assumptions,* rather than on confirmed data or valid logic. Assumptions are propositions that are suppositions, that are taken for granted. Often they are taken for granted because it is impossible or impractical to confirm them. For example, one assumption underlying the Yucca Mountain work is that safe, geological storage of high-level radwaste is possible in perpetuity. Although there is evidence for this proposition, it cannot be confirmed because of the long time period. Hence it is taken for granted; it is an assumption. Because methodological value judgments can be substantiated, but never fully confirmed, they are assumptions (about methodological values). Not all assumptions, however, are methodological value judgments; they might be judgments about things other than values. Generally, the more plausible methodological value judgments are based on more plausible assumptions. Likewise, all invalid or unsound inferences typically rely on some incorrect assumption or supposition, whereas valid or sound inferences usually rely on correct assumptions or suppositions about the relationship between given premises and a conclusion.

Later, when we analyze some of the problematic methodological value judgments (chapters 4 and 5) and inferences (chapter 6) in repository QRAs, we shall discuss the most problematic assumptions on which these value judgments and inferences rest. In some instances, we shall show that the QRA arguments fail to meet the conditions for an adequate scientific explanation. In the strictest sense, the logical and empirical conditions of adequacy for a scientific explanation are (1) that each conclusion is a logical consequence of certain premises; (2) that the premises contain general laws that are required for deducing each conclusion; (3) that the premises have specific, empirical content capable of being tested; and (4) that the premises state propositions that are true.[3] Typically, arguments that employ questionable methodological value judgments or invalid inferences, such as begging the question, violate one or more of these four conditions. We do not believe, however, that the QRAs of proposed repositories always should be faulted for failing to meet one or more of these four strict conditions for a deductively adequate scientific explanation. Indeed, much of science fails to meet one or another of these conditions at some time. Nor do we believe that QRA should be faulted for including methodological value judgments. Most areas of science rely on such judgments. Rather, an important point of our subsequent chapters is (1) that many QRAs are questionable because their arguments fail to provide even good inductive, probabilistic, or retroductive grounds for their conclusions, and (2) that many QRAs contain methodological value judgments that are highly questionable; such judgments do not provide good reasons for the conclusions of many QRAs.

Quantitative Risk Assessment
and Value Judgments

Many of the flaws that threaten the objectivity of risk assessments at radwaste sites occur in part because all science and all quantitative risk assessment (QRA) are laden with unavoidable methodological value judgments, at least some of which are questionable. Many of these value judgments concern how to estimate and evaluate particular risks. They deal with factors such as model reliability, sampling, extrapolations, human error, credible worst cases, and so on. Although not all methodological value judgments are avoidable in QRA, and although one can never be absolutely certain whether a particular methodological value judgment is correct, nevertheless the reliability of any particular such judgment often can be assessed on the basis of the evidence for and against it. For example, it is possible to assess the methodological value judgment—that a particular hydrogeological model is reliable—by evaluating the evidence for and against it based on analogous cases, past events, short-term predictions, and so on. A substantial part of this evidence will be an evaluation of the range of uncertainty associated with the model.[4] The methodological value judgments—which inject some degree of subjectivity into all science—occur at all three stages of risk assessment:

- risk identification,
- risk estimation, and
- risk evaluation.

Such value judgments likewise appear in the risk management occurring after assessment. Indeed, as a prominent group of risk assessors recently concluded: "While it is common to separate the technical steps of exposure and dose-response assessment from risk management, an important conclusion of this study is that risk-management decisions are part of nearly every risk assessment step." The group of risk assessors then illustrated, in a lengthy table, "for each risk assessment step, the types of risk management decisions typically made in response to selected uncertainties." In other words, they showed that methodological value judgments arise even at the allegedly purely technical stages of risk assessment, because even technical experts must make management decisions about how to deal with technical uncertainties.[5]

Such value judgments are particularly troublesome because they are often not recognized as value judgments. In fact, proponents of the "standard account" of QRA believe that it is more neutral and value free than it is. They typically maintain that risk assessment is a largely nonqualitative, *scientific discipline* to be perfected along hypothetical-deductive lines[6] and that if they merely discover the correct algorithms they will have the power to predict and assess risks in a wholly neutral way, much as Einstein and Bohm hoped for deterministic, predictive power for quantum mechanics. Proponents of the standard account of risk assessment also believe that it is possible to separate the allegedly purely technical steps of risk assessment from risk evaluation and risk management.

Critics of the standard account argue, however, that QRA—and especially its third stage, risk evaluation—is not merely a *scientific investigation* but also a *political procedure* to be negotiated among scientists, engineers, policymakers, and the public.[7] They argue that because of the many unavoidable methodological value judgments involved in the process, risk assessment is neither always nor wholly objective.[8] Just as physicists do, assessors must make value judgments about which data to collect, about how to simplify myriad facts into a workable model, about how to extrapolate because of unknowns, about how to choose statistical tests to be used, and about how to select sample size. They must make value judgments in determining criteria for NOEL—no-observed-effect level,[9] in deciding where the burden of proof goes, which power function to use, what size test to run, and which exposure-response model to employ.[10] Although such judgments are also methodological assumptions, it is important to recognize that they are judgments about methodological *values*, values such as reliability, simplicity, predictive power, completeness, explanatory adequacy, and so on. Because such assumptions are *value judgments*, they can be wrong. They represent partially subjective aspects of allegedly objective risk estimates and evaluations.

Because risk assessors must continually make methodological value judgments at every stage of their analysis, proponents of the standard account of QRA err when they claim to be able to separate some allegedly purely technical aspect of risk assessment. They also err when they claim that risk assessment can be isolated from risk management. Because every part of assessment involves methodological value judgments, and because even scientific conclusions have implications for risk-management recommendations, risk assessment is not completely separable from risk management.[11]

One of the main goals of this volume is to reveal the way that risk assessments of proposed high-level radioactive waste repositories are laden with methodological value judgments. Although no scientific enterprises are completely free of subjectivity, at least with respect to methodological value judgments, and although not all value judgments are problematic, obviously the best science and risk assessment are the least subjective. Certainly the best science is free of the logically invalid inferences that we shall discuss later in this volume. Once we are aware of the unavoidable methodological value judgments inherent in all risk assessment, we shall be forced to assess which judgments are subjective in a damaging sense. We shall also be forced to recognize more clearly the role of public and democratic decision making in shaping our evaluations of acceptable risk, especially uncertain risks. The more questionable are the subjective methodological assessments of scientists and risk assessors, the more ought members of the public to decide how much uncertainty about risk they are willing to bear. The public must decide how safe is safe enough, how safe is fair enough, how safe is voluntary enough, and how safe is equitable enough. In other words, to the degree that risk assessors' judgments involve both ethics and uncertainty, risk analyses ought to be open to challenge from the very public likely to be affected by such assessments. Our account of the methodological value judgments inherent in risk assessment of repositories is thus one part of a much larger argument that risk evaluation and radwaste policies are not the sole prerogative of scientists, engineers, or policymakers. Such policies are not their sole prerogative because risk decisions are not wholly objective accounts of science and because risk decisions often affect everyone. They are laced with values, and on questions of value facing citizens in a democracy—particularly value questions affecting human welfare— the public has the right to play a role in policy determination.

One of the most important threats to epistemologically naive accounts of complete objectivity in risk analysis is the postulate or value judgment that one ought to define risk only as a compound measure of the probability and magnitude of adverse effect. This measure is often expressed in terms of average annual probability of fatality. Using this definition alone, risk analysts often presuppose that one is justified in identifying/interpreting "real risk"[12] in terms of fatalities and in ignoring other factors, such as risk-induced stress,[13] injuries, financial losses, sociopolitical effects, and threats to due process rights or to rights of future generations. Proponents of the standard account

of QRA often ignore such aspects of risk because of their narrow, evaluative definition of risk, and because the social and ethical aspects of
risk are among the most difficult to handle. Thus, even at the risk-
identification stage, value judgments (about what types of risks to
consider) are unavoidable. Moreover, because of incomplete data and
long years of testing, assessors are forced to interpret and to extrapolate from the information that they do have and hence to make
methodological, pragmatic, and epistemic value judgments about how
to identify risks.

Value Judgments in Estimating Risks

In estimating the magnitude of risks, assessors may
rely on methodological value judgments that, although not always erroneous, are sometimes question-begging and/or misleading. Every
time one makes the methodological value judgment that a certain interpolation of missing data is acceptable, or that one ought to extrapolate from laboratory to field data, one is making a methodological
value judgment about a factual situation, as all scientists do. To the
degree that values are involved, the factual judgment could be incorrect. Obviously, however, value judgments about factual situations are
never wholly avoidable because data are rarely complete. Hence, assessors are forced to use value judgments to "fill in the gaps." These
judgments focus on methodological values such as simplicity, heuristic
power, completeness, explanatory adequacy, and so on.

At the second stage of risk assessment, risk estimation, one must
make many value judgments about the validity of extrapolation from
high to low doses, from animals to humans, and from one group of
humans to another. The problems associated with such extrapolation
are well known in science, as when health physicists try to estimate a
dose-response curve for low-level radiation exposure given data points
only for higher-level exposures. Environmentalists, industry representatives, and members of health-physics associations have each extrapolated, respectively, to a dose-response curve for radiation that is typically (1) logarithmic or supralinear, (2) quadratic, linear-quadratic,
or linear with a large threshold, and (3) linear with no threshold.
Subscribing to different value judgments about the low-dose end of
the curve, they have claimed, respectively, that low-level radiation is

very dangerous, not very dangerous, and moderately dangerous. To get some idea of the differences in the estimates produced by using different value judgments to support alternative models for radiation dose-response curves, consider the excess incidence of cancer cases predicted, other than leukemia and multiple myeloma. For a 10-rad exposure, the quadratic model predicts 560 excess cancers per million persons exposed, whereas the linear-quadratic predicts 4,732 excess cases, and the linear model predicts 10,630 excess cancers. Thus there is a 20-fold difference between the quadratic and the linear models! And there is an 86-fold difference between the predictions of the quadratic and the supralinear models. However, the National Academy of Sciences' Committee on Biological Effects of Ionizing Radiation claims that there is no reason to prefer one model over the other at low doses. Their position suggests that one methodological value judgment about which curve to use is not always more objective than another.[14]

Estimating the population at risk and the dose received is just as problematic because risk estimators must assume that their theories provide a reasonable measure of exposure; that the exposure is related in some clear way to the administered dose; that the absorbed dose is a specific function of the administered dose; that phenotypic variation in populations does not inordinately affect the dose received; that the critical organ dose is related precisely to the absorbed dose; and that the effect is a particular function of the critical organ dose. Because actual measurements of particular doses, for example, of radiation, cannot be made in all situations, a mathematical model of assumed exposure must be used, and assessors must make a methodological value judgment as to its suitability. Sometimes these judgments differ radically; toxicologists, for example, typically view the notion of a safe threshold dose as controversial, whereas engineers, who sometimes equate dispersal with dilution, tend to assume some threshold below which a substance is no longer harmful. Neither group, however, typically addresses synergistic consequences,[15] even though seemingly unimportant pathways of exposure can assume great significance owing, for example, to biomagnification or food-chain effects.

Moreover, it is rare that a substance is uniformly distributed across pathways and time. Numerous studies have shown that the target dose, pathway, and persistence of a toxic or hazardous substance, for example, are difficult to predict. Predictive difficulties plagued epidemiologists tracing the distribution of radiation after the Chernobyl nuclear accident on 25 April 1986. Maps showing the areas of greatest radionuclide deposition look like Rorschach drawings; the distribution did not follow a predictable pattern based on prevailing wind direction and the rotation of the earth. Instead, numerous factors, such as rainfall patterns and the height of the radioactive plume, affected the highly irregular spread of radiation following the accident.[16] Also, even if pathways of various toxins could be determined exactly, phenotypic variations among populations are such that one person could be two hundred times more sensitive to a chemical or to radiation than another, even when both received equal doses.[17] Given such situations, the assessor often is forced to make a number of highly interpretative, value-laden judgments about how to estimate a given level of risk.

Value Judgments in Evaluating Risks

Risk assessors also make methodological value judgments whenever they evaluate the acceptability of risks and compare one risk to another regarding acceptability. For example, whenever one claims that so long as the risk to the public from high-level radioactive waste is no greater than that arising from uranium ore the risk is acceptable, then one is making a value judgment about risk. We shall say more later about this particular value judgment. At this point it is important to note, however, that precisely because such judgments involve values, they could be erroneous with respect to scientific, ethical, political, or social norms. They represent a second area in which QRA can go wrong.

Highly evaluative judgments characterize the third stage of hazard assessment, risk evaluation, because analysts typically use economic and psychometric methods to determine whether a risk is acceptable to society. In doing so, assessors are forced to make a number of subjective judgments, such as whether monetary-term parameters can adequately represent the real cost or benefit of a thing; whether the *magnitude* of risks, costs, and benefits is more important than their *distribution*;[18] whether past societal risk levels reveal desirable risk levels for the present; whether past hazards ought to have been accepted; whether the preferences people express via instruments such as surveys provide reliable indicators as to acceptable risks; and so on.

All the assumptions, extrapolations, and erroneous inferences that may arise during the three stages of hazard assessment arise in large part because nearly all situations of risk identification, estimation, or evaluation—like many situations in science—are empirically underdetermined. There are often less data than needed to describe such situations clearly and completely. Because they are empirically underdetermined, risk assessors are forced to make some methodological value judgments so as to interpret the data available to them. At root, these assumptions and inferences often reduce to the problem of getting a grip on causality. This is difficult since causes are not seen; they are inferred on the basis of their effects. Cancers, for example, do not wear tags saying they were caused by their subject's smoking, or by use of oral contraceptives, or by diet drinks, or by breathing the emissions of the chemical plant next door. Moreover, we know statistically how much of one agent causes cancer in *general*, but we can never determine whether a substance caused a *particular* cancer. We can only make a methodological value judgment to support inferences about what caused a certain cancer.

Risk victims everywhere are typically able to show a statistically significant increase in certain types of injuries/deaths, a *correlation* between increased dose and increased response, but no *cause* of particular cancers, for example. Without proof of causality, they can claim no benefits. In the absence of proof and complete data, they are forced, like risk assessors everywhere, to rely on methodological value judgments, on inference, extrapolation, and simplification.[19]

Conclusion

In summary, methodological value judgments in quantitative risk assessment (QRA)—as in all science—typically fall into a number of categories. They are, for example, value judgments about the acceptability of

- a given definition of risk
- a given description of what factors are at risk
- a given simplification of the situation
- a given way of selecting and deleting data
- a given aggregation of the data
- a given sample size

- a given statistical test
- a given model for exposure
- a given dose-response model
- a given extrapolation from the data
- a given price/value for risk avoidance.

Each of these and other methodological value judgments enables us to respond to a situation that is uncertain or empirically underdetermined. Yet because our response involves a value judgment, it could be wrong. It could lead to error in the risk assessment. Because methodological value judgments are both unavoidable and potentially erroneous, we must learn to deal with them. We need to take account, explicitly, of all the relevant methodological value judgments on which our scientific conclusions depend. We need to determine whether the evidence tends to substantiate these value judgments or to call them into question. By using more reliable methodological value judgments in QRA, and by becoming more aware of the value judgments we do make, we shall provide better QRA and better public policy.

In subsequent chapters, we shall provide examples of methodological value judgments occurring in some of the best contemporary repository risk assessments. We shall argue that these subjective judgments often are not as reliable as others we might make. As a consequence, our policies about permanent disposal are not as reliable as we might like. Indeed, if our later arguments are correct, then our value-laden policies may be "an interminable trek toward an ever-receding mirage," the goal of permanent disposal.[20]

4

Subjective Estimates
of Repository Risks

Claude Bernard, the foremost French physiologist of his day, wisely warned that "true science teaches us to doubt."[1] It teaches us, as the previous chapter argued, that all science and risk assessment rely on methodological value judgments about the merit of factors such as experimental designs, theories, standards of proof, observations, explanations, curve-fits, and estimates. However, one measure of the degree to which we should doubt any particular scientific conclusion is the extent to which it relies on hidden, unjustified, or controversial value judgments about methods. If a conclusion is extremely sensitive to some methodological value judgment, then it is important to know how plausible the value judgment is. Otherwise one could place misguided confidence in an unreliable conclusion.

In arguing for permanent geological disposal of high-level radioactive waste, proponents often rely on the scientific conclusion that repository risk estimates are low. Such estimates, of course, depend on methodological value judgments. Department of Energy (DOE) researchers, for example, have admitted that their estimates regarding geohydrology, geochemistry, and waste-container lifetimes are "nonconservative" and "realistic" regarding the proposed Yucca Mountain waste facility.[2] The DOE scientists justify their "nonconservative" methodological value judgments by claiming that limited data force them to "rely heavily on professional judgment attended by expressions of the level of subjective confidences in findings."[3] Whether we call them "professional judgments" or "methodological value judgments," nonconservative risk estimates present a problem for all risk assessments. Proponents of permanent repositories for nuclear waste, however, are likely to believe that such value judgments do not threaten the objectivity of their claims about the safety and feasibility of disposal. Recognizing the presence of the judgments, they may believe that they have only an insignificant effect on their conclusions. Opponents of geological disposal, however, are likely to believe that estimates of repository risks are highly sensitive to questionable methodological value judgments and that such judgments could play havoc with allegedly low estimates for the risks of disposal. Who is correct, the proponents or the opponents? How justified are the methodological value judgments associated with risk estimates for high-level radwaste disposal?

One of the best ways to determine both the defensibility of disposal-related value judgments—and the degree to which risk conclusions are sensitive to them—would be to examine some state-of-the-art assessments of proposed repositories. In the United States, there is only one site, Yucca Mountain, Nevada, that is currently being considered for a high-level repository. Because the Yucca Mountain studies represent some of the latest, most expensive, and best available risk assessments, they provide a number of clues about the status of methodological value judgments used in risk estimation, the second stage of QRA. Indeed, as we noted in chapter 1, the U.S. National Academy of Sciences has confirmed that the Yucca Mountain assessments are "state-of-the-art."[4] In this chapter, we shall analyze eight of the methodological value judgments that are central to Yucca Mountain risk *estimates*. (In the next chapter we shall analyze value judgments associated with risk *evaluations,* the third stage of QRA.) Most of these value judgments are paradigmatic instances of the types of subjective assessments that underlie all assurances of repository feasibility and safety. Moreover, we shall argue that at least some of these methodological value judgments threaten the validity of claims about the suitability of Yucca Mountain for high-level radioactive waste. We also shall argue that similar difficulties are likely to plague any optimistic risk estimates associated with permanent geological disposal of nuclear wastes.

Repository Risk Estimates Rely on Questionable Value Judgments

Probabilistic risk-assessment conclusions about Yucca Mountain, although typically optimistic about site suitability, are also highly sensitive to a number of assumptions or methodological value judgments. For example, most site assessors have concluded that, as U.S. regulations require (see chapter 2), no radionuclides are likely to reach the water table at Yucca Mountain in less than 1,000 years. Other assessors, particularly those from the state of Nevada, have concluded that groundwater travel time from the disturbed environment to the accessible environment could be as short as 978 years and that, as a result, Yucca Mountain would not meet government standards for a repository.[5] Conclusions about groundwater travel time, however, are highly sensitive to a number of assumptions about the rate of fracture flow and infiltration, that is.[6] Many of the conclusions about radionuclide migration are also highly sensitive to a number of value judgments about the reliability of the simulations used, the validity of a variety of extrapolations and interpolations, the lack of need for more site-specific data, and so on. If different value judgments and assumptions were used then, quite different conclusions about radionuclide migration and repository containment could very likely be drawn. As one group of assessors put it, for example: "The use of a low net infiltration rate for this problem made it not unexpected that there was no predicted radionuclide release to the water table. Other rates would probably result in considerably different transport results."[7]

Similarly, in a review of the Yucca Mountain Site Characterization Plan, evaluators criticized the fact that much of the report comprises theoretical designs based on large assumptions. As a result, claimed the reviewers, the likely success of the designs proposed within the report is highly questionable from a technical point of view. Further, the evaluators charged that the problematic designs are based on technical errors and on oversimplifications. They concluded that many of the concepts within the Yucca Mountain plan have not been developed to the degree necessary to insure scientific integrity.[8] The purpose of this chapter is to examine several examples of the ways in which the Yucca Mountain risk assessments—despite the areas in which they are technically successful—may have gone wrong, either through logically questionable inferences or problematic methodological value judgments, and to learn what, if anything, these difficulties tell us about the general question of permanent geological disposal.

The forthcoming analysis of problematic methodological value judgments (chapters 4 and 5) and questionable inferences (chapter 6), will uncover a number of specific difficulties which, although they are neither mutually exclusive nor exhaustive, are typical of quantitative risk assessments (QRAs) of proposed repositories. Value judgments about model reliability, for example, often intersect with other value judgments about the plausibility of certain simplifications in the treatment of site phenomena. Similarly, there are a number of methodological value judgments that are not even mentioned in this analysis. Specific transportation-related judgments, for instance, are not included, both because assessors and decision makers appear to be aware of many of the shortcomings in this area and because a number of contracts have already been offered for studies to assess transportation impacts associated with Yucca Mountain. Our point in assessing these methodological value judgments is neither that our survey is exhaustive nor that methodological value judgments ought to be avoided. As we mentioned earlier, such value judgments are unavoidable in both science and risk assessment. Hence, the problem is not the methodological value judgments as such, but (1) the frequent absence of any ideas about the limits of error or uncertainty associated with them and (2) the tendency of assessors to be overconfident about the effects of their methodological value judgments.

Value Judgments about Long-term Risks

One of the most basic methodological value judgments used in estimating the risk of radionuclide migration (at Yucca Mountain and at other proposed permanent sites) concerns extrapolations on the basis of short-term studies. Indeed, geologists who are asked to make predictions typically are forced to make methodological value judgments when they extrapolate either to the *past* or to the *future* on the basis of what they observe in the *present*. Often geologists use internal features, stratigraphy, and morphologic expressions of rocks, for example, or general principles describing dynamic geological processes operating through time, when they make inferences and methodological value judgments about past geologic events.[9] Frequently geologists, for instance, use the absence of certain phenomena in the past and present as evidence for denying the likelihood that a specific geologic process will occur in the future. Yet such an inference is questionable because one ought not simply assume from the absence of something that it was never there and that it will never be there. As Watson points out, "it is a *non sequitur* to argue from the absence of something [like given rock] in the past to the conclusion that it will not be present in the future."[10] There must also be other evidence, for example, for a process of rock removal, in order for the inference to be reasonable. Likewise, there must be "other evidence" when geologists extrapolate to the past or to the future on the basis of present data. Geologists know that, in general, the less we know about the processes and evidence supporting such inferences/extrapolations/methodological value judgments, the greater is the likelihood that we are wrong. Moreover, the smaller the empirical base used for such extrapolation, all things being equal, the greater the chance that it is not, or will not be, representative of past and future events and processes.

One problematic methodological value judgment made in many Yucca Mountain studies is that short-term tests (for several years or less) provide adequate information for very precise predictions of long-term behavior, for example, isolation of the waste for ten thousand years and container integrity for one thousand years.[11] This methodological value judgment—about the validity of a long-term inductive conclusion based on short-term data—is highly controversial, in part because the extended time horizon for any high-level repository is several times longer than recorded human history.[12] As MIT geologist, K. V. Hodges, a peer reviewer for the Yucca Mountain Early Site Suitability Evaluation (ESSE), put it, the Congressional mandate for siting a high-level repository is for *predictive* information ten thousand years into the future. Geology, however, as he points out, is an *explanatory* and not a predictive science.[13] Or, as Dartmouth geologist N. Oreskes noted: "The extrapolation of short-term to long-term studies at Yucca Mountain flies in the face of 300 years of geological practice. The question is, how did they get away with *that*?"[14] "Predictive geology," according to Hodges, "is predicated on the assumption of a sort of inverse uniformitarianism: the past geologic record is the key to future geologic activity."[15] Yet at least since the recent revolution in plate tectonics, uniformitarianism—in any precise, predictive sense—has been largely abandoned by geologists. As Hodges continues,

earthquake prediction is one of the most visible examples of predictive geology. . . . but it remains a hit-or-miss proposition. Perhaps predictive geology will improve in the future. . . . but DOE, the Congress, and the American people need to confront the fact that the earth science community does not have the tools necessary to generate models that will permit the prediction of future tectonic activity *with a high degree of accuracy*. . . . tectonic predictions, when stripped of statistical sound and fury, are not much better than educated guesses.[16]

Moreover, says Hodges, it is likewise "patently absurd" that we attempt to predict the probability of volcanic disruptions over ten thousand years. In asking for such predictions, claims Hodges, we are "asking the impossible."[17]

Indeed, the entire (fourteen-person) DOE peer reviewer group for the Yucca Mountain Early Site Suitability Evaluation confirmed Hodges' conclusions about the impossibility of reliable ten-thousand-year predictions for any waste repository site. They said:

Many aspects of site suitability are not well suited for quantitative risk assessment. In particular are predictions involving future geological activity, future value of mineral deposits and mineral occurrence models. Any projections of the rates of tectonic activity and volcanism, as well as natural resource occurrence and value, will be fraught with substantial uncertainties that cannot be quantified using standard statistical methods.[18]

If the Yucca Mountain peer reviewers are correct, then obviously making precise long-term geological predictions on the basis of short-term data is questionable.

Although long-term prediction is a problem in any area of science, the Yucca Mountain predictions are particularly problematic as compared to those in other areas of science not only because they deal with thousands of years but also because U.S. government regulations require the predictions to be very precise (see later sections of this chapter for discussion of this point). They specify allowable levels of radionuclide releases over thousands of years. Thus, it is the precision of the long-term predictions that make them more problematic at Yucca Mountain than in other applications of science. Moreover, in cases such as Yucca Mountain, precise long-term predictions about safety are especially questionable because the potential dose commitments of radioactive isotopes (such as C-14, Pu-239, and I-129)—all with possibly serious health effects—extend from hundreds of thousands to millions of years.[19] In other words, long-term precise predictions are more problematic in cases where their being wrong could lead to a human or environmental disaster. Such a disaster is especially worrisome because the Environmental Protection Agency has explicitly warned that it is "impossible" to predict anything regarding the success of radioactive waste management beyond one hundred years.

The agency has noted that institutional controls are particularly problematic beyond a period of one hundred years.[20] Indeed, when the State of Nevada did a review of the Yucca Mountain Site Characterization Plan in 1989, focusing on the hydrogeological pathways for possible radionuclide escape, one of its seven major "concerns" was using short-term studies as the basis for long-term site predictions.[21]

One of the main worries about making the value judgment that a long-term repository risk is acceptable—given only short-term, incomplete data—is that some unforeseen catastrophic event could occur centuries from now that would compromise the integrity of the long-term facility. Yet the waste would be retrievable by U.S. regulations (see chapter 2) for only fifty years after the repository is opened. Because catastrophes have occurred in the past, there are grounds for similar worries about disruption of the waste-disposal facility. The U.S. landscape has a number of craters created by meteor hits, for instance, some of which (in Iowa and Arizona) are quite famous. Yet the annual probability of a meteor strike is quite low, just as the probability of repository flooding is likely small.[22] When one is considering long-term predictions for something like the Yucca Mountain repository, however, even meteor hits, volcanism, or seismic activity, all of which have a low annual probability, assume major proportions. In the case of volcanism or seismic activity, for example, it is not necessary to assume that the disruptive event would unearth the waste canisters. Rather, even a small seismic dislocation of some geological features might be sufficient to change the location and flow of groundwater that could flood the repository and leach the waste. Moreover, even if the per-year probability of dangerous seismic or volcanic activity is quite low, for example, 10^{-6}, this figure means that during the lifetime of the repository such an event would be virtually certain. An annual probability of 10^{-6} converts to a 10^{-3} likelihood over a thousand years. This is a quite high probability, and it is especially disconcerting when one considers the possible catastrophic consequences.

Obviously, it is questionable whether one can make an inductive prediction that guarantees the radwaste "permanent isolation from the biosphere"—as several risk assessors claimed—on the basis of inductive data obtained during only one or several decades.[23] Moreover, most of the Yucca Mountain experiments have been done and data have been obtained over periods of far less than a decade. Investigations of 304 days duration and 9 years duration, for instance, have both been called "long-term" studies.[24] However, data from 6-, 11-, and 18-month experiments, rather than multiple years, is more typical of Yucca Mountain investigations.[25] Tests on migration of spent fuel and groundwater transport of radionuclides, for example, are typically only months in duration, for example, 2, 6, and 12 months.[26] Even for tests as long as 3.5 years or 3 years duration, respectively, tests used to determine the degree and extent of spent-fuel migration or the integrity of the waste canisters,[27] researchers have been forced to extrapolate and make the methodological value judgment that behavior over 3.5 years will be representative of that over 10,000 or more years.

In the case of waste canisters, experiments of three years' duration are particularly problematic, because the future temperatures in the repository are expected to be as great as 200 degrees Celsius in the immediate vicinity of the waste,[28] causing changes in the surrounding rock.[29] Moreover, in some experiments, all of the canisters made of the nuclear waste-package reference material have failed and showed stress-corrosion cracking when they were exposed to a one-year test in groundwater and tuff at the expected temperature of 200 degrees Celsius.[30] Nevertheless, the DOE expects the canisters—presumably improved somehow—to last from three hundred to one thousand years. All of these problems suggest that long-term experiments are essential. The shorter the time of the experiment, all things being equal, the more questionable the inductive value judgment that the data support precise predictions about repository behavior thousands of years in the future.

Loan companies find it difficult to predict mortgage rates for more than thirty or forty years given nearly a century of information. Yet DOE risk assessors have predicted confidently that "meteorological conditions . . . for over 40 years" provide a firm basis for concluding "that any radiological emissions would be effectively dispersed before they reach highly populated areas" near a proposed permanent repository.[31] How could one know about dispersion ten thousand years hence? And how could one predict population centers so far into the future? Of course, once a repository were built, the location of such a facility might influence the site and growth of future cities. Nevertheless, Las Vegas, as it exists today, would have been unlikely fifty years ago, before the Hoover Dam, and the fastest growing cities a decade ago were not substantial even one hundred years ago.[32] Yet risk assessors, with far less inductive information, are attempting to predict precise phenomena associated with permanent repository behavior and its consequences for periods of time that are many orders of magnitude longer. Many of the radioactive isotopes that would be stored at sites like Yucca Mountain—such as I-129, Np-237, Cs-135, U-238, Zr-93—have half lives that are in the millions of years.[33] During such long time periods of radiotoxicity, changes in climate, groundwater, precipitation, and volcanic activity could occur.

Yucca Mountain risk assessors, for example, need to predict precise phenomena associated with future climate, weather, mineralogy, and water composition, even though climate and weather are the most variable and rapid natural processes influencing the repository, and even though mineral reactions are currently occurring there.[34] Even DOE researchers admit that "the climatic changes that are possible during the next 10,000 years of Yucca Mountain may cause changes in the hydraulic gradient. . . . The extent of these changes is uncertain."[35] Major variations in the climate of Nevada have occurred during the last forty-five thousand years, and the U.S. Geological Survey claims that future climatic changes probably will occur within the time the waste materials are hazardous.[36] Precipitation patterns are likewise fluctuating, and assessors must be able to predict them in perpetuity. The precipitation data for Yucca Mountain, however, covers only approximately the last thirty years,[37] yet ten-thousand-year precipitation predictions are crucial to the safety of Yucca Mountain because percolating water could infiltrate and transport radioactive leachate, once the containers have been breached. Hence, to assume that the thirty-year precipitation data are adequate—for precisely predicting the risks associated with a permanent repository—represents a methodological value judgment that is somewhat questionable, especially in light of the fact that both precipitation and its variability appear to have increased at the Nevada site.[38]

Ultimately, value judgments that short-term data provide an adequate basis for inferring extremely precise long-term behavior rely on an inductive inference, on the assumption that the future will be like the past. This is the basic assumption of all historical geology. The DOE has made exactly this methodological value judgment every time it has concluded, for example: "Yucca Mountain . . . would meet the U.S. Environmental Protection Agency standards . . . if present hydrologic, geologic, and geochemical conditions (as presently understood) persist for the next 10,000 years."[39] How could one guarantee, however, that such conditions will persist? Likewise, how could the DOE justify its methodological value judgments that the future will be like the past? The DOE has concluded, for example, regarding the Yucca Mountain site, that "extreme weather phenomena are neither frequent enough nor severe enough to be expected to significantly affect the safety of repository operation." The DOE has also claimed that "no severe meteorological conditions have been recorded or are expected to occur in the region that would contribute to radionuclide releases." Even more surprisingly, the DOE has affirmed that "on the basis of the geologic record, no dissolution [of subsurface rock] is expected during the first 10,000 years after repository closure, or thereafter."[40] How could one affirm that there will *never* be rock dissolution at Yucca Mountain? Or that neither "extreme weather" nor "severe meteorological conditions" will occur at the site? Do the DOE assessors have enough data to make these predictions? When the time periods at issue are so great, inductive value judgments such as these are extremely questionable. Long-term judgments about the suitability of Yucca Mountain for a waste repository are especially questionable because of the existence of lakes in the Great Basin of Nevada during the Wisconsin period—2 million years ago—and because moderate variations in climate are sufficient to cause large changes in the hydrological budget of some of the closed basin systems in Nevada.[41] An evaluation of the Quaternary history of the Yucca Mountain area reveals that, like other areas proposed for radwaste sites, it has undergone geomorphic change in the last million years, and it may undergo catastrophic landslides in the future.[42] Other assessors have calculated the probability of a volcanic disruption hazard given the natural historic seismicity of the Yucca Mountain region as 10^{-6} per year.[43]

Methodological value judgments about precise long-term predictability at Yucca Mountain are also questionable in light of the fact that some assessors argue that the water table at Yucca Mountain could rise 130 meters if precipitation increased by 100 percent.[44] This is a significant and possible increase, since *average* precipitation levels, for a decade, often vary by two orders of magnitude.[45] At Yucca Mountain, for example, water tables stood at 926 meters (approximately 2,938 feet) only 14,000 years ago. High water tables were northeast of the Nevada Test Site (NTS) until only 7,000 years ago, and on the NTS 700,000 years ago.[46] Nonetheless, some assessors claim that the water table at Yucca Mountain was never more than 200 feet above its present position[47] and that radwaste will be emplaced more than 650 feet below the surface and more than 600 feet above the water table.[48] The water table is currently between 728 and 775 feet above sea level.[49] Even if there were a significant climate change and a doubling of rainfall, a recent (1992) panel of the National Academy of Sciences argued that the water table at Yucca Mountain would rise, at most, by 400 feet; although this is a significant rise, the panel concluded that the proposed repository would not be at risk of groundwater infiltration.[50] Such conclusions appear reassuring until one realizes that the same NAS panel warned that its modeling results involve very "large uncertainty," that there are few data to constrain the complex hydrologic system at Yucca Mountain, and that its predictions "depend heavily on expert judgment" because of the "unprecedented" exactitude required for 10,000-year predictions.[51] Because high-level radwaste requires essentially "permanent isolation from the biosphere,"[52] some geologists have said that any planned repository must be built under the assumption that groundwater will eventually come in contact with the high-level waste.[53] The DOE, however, has continued to assume that because the water table has been constant for several decades, therefore, it is likely to remain so in the future.

Making the methodological value judgment that short-term hydrogeological tests provide accurate predictions for long-term behavior has been one of the reasons for the erroneous underestimation of the potential for offsite radwaste migration at the low-level radioactive facility at Maxey Flats, Kentucky. As we pointed out in chapter 1, although the Maxey Flats site is disanalogous in many ways to the proposed Yucca Mountain site, several problematic risk-assessment methods appear to be similar at the two locations. The geologist (from the New Jersey Geological Survey) who did the original studies at the Kentucky site drilled and studied the wells for only ten days. As a result, he concluded that they were dry and that hydraulic conductivity was very low at the site.[54] On the basis of his analyses, the Kentucky facility was opened the year he did his studies. Years later, other geologists and risk assessors observed the wells for a year and concluded that because some of them were filled with water, therefore hydraulic conductivity was quite high.[55] Just as the longer-term studies gave the more accurate results—and a less optimistic picture of the Maxey Flats radioactive waste site—so also there is reason to question the methodological value judgment that short-term studies at proposed high-level sites, like Yucca Mountain, provide accurate data for precise long-term predictions. Moreover, as we have already argued, given the longevity of the proposed Nevada site, the problems related to methodological value judgments about long-term predictions at other sites, and the difficulties with accurate geological predictions, there is reason to believe that this value judgment is problematic. It poses a serious difficulty for any proposal to site a permanent geological repository either at Yucca Mountain or anywhere else on the supposition that precise long-term predictions about hydrogeology are reliable.

Value Judgments about Model Reliability

A more basic methodological value judgment is not only that one can predict long-term geological behavior on the basis of short-term data but that one can model a geologically heterogeneous site, like Yucca Mountain, with "highly nonlinear" flow characteristics,[56] and that such models provide adequate and precise knowledge upon which to base future predictions about radwaste migration. Such judgments about the adequacy of modeling are questionable, both because the models cannot be validated in the field over the long term and because, if empirical data were available, one would not need to employ models in the first place. Admittedly one can often determine that a given model is probably wrong, as does Watson when he criticizes the chronostratigraphic model on the grounds that it is false to Earth history and that it gives rise to pseudo-problems of correlation and inclusion.[57] Typically, however, one does not have the data to confirm a long-term geological model. Assessors are forced to use models to evaluate all proposed repository sites simply because they have inadequate data and theories to use in characterizing the area over the long term.[58] They do not know how the hydrology, geology, waste packages, and so on will perform over centuries, and so they use models of the situation—Monte Carlo simulations, for example.[59]

One frequent rationale for substituting modeling and simulations for actual empirical testing is that modeling and simulations have been used before in assessing the probability of nuclear accidents.[60] Probabilities related to nuclear accidents, however, are notoriously inaccurate. For example, all of the accident-frequency values obtained from operating experience in U.S. nuclear reactors fall outside the 90-percent confidence band of calculated expert probabilities in the best nuclear risk assessment ever performed (WASH 1400).[61] Different assessors' probability estimates associated with various reactor events typically vary by four orders of magnitude.[62] Hence, the use of nuclear accident simulations does not necessarily provide a justification for the value judgment that repository modeling is reliable. Indeed, speaking for the state, the Nevada attorney general criticized the DOE and its assessors for doing modeling of the Yucca Mountain site, modeling that depends on major untested assumptions, without validating the models in the field; spokespersons for the state of Nevada also warned that the uncertainty in the models (for possible radionuclide transport) was one of their seven major "concerns" about the reliability of Yucca Mountain studies.[63] Many risk assessors, however, typically assume that models alone are sufficient to demonstrate the acceptability of a particular repository site. They repeatedly affirm that such models, together with computer codes, "demonstrate the safety of a final storage site for nuclear wastes."[64]

Much of the problem with model uncertainty in the risk assessments of repository sites arises from the fact that all the laws and theories used to explain site characteristics and possible radwaste migration are based on highly idealized notions. Many assessors at Yucca Mountain, for example, use highly idealized continuum models (such as porous-media models)—that assume the underlying rock is solid and unfractured—rather than discontinuum models formulated to account for the effects of discrete fractures.[65] They do so because continuum models are simpler and more efficient to use and because they have no superior alternatives.[66] Assessors also employ continuum models on the grounds that matrix flow predominates over fracture flow at Yucca Mountain, a highly questionable assumption.[67] Thus, there are a variety of reasons for believing that the idealized hydrogeological models at Yucca Mountain may not be accurate.[68] Indeed, external reviewers argue forcefully that, in general, the quality control on the Yucca Mountain modeling is poor.[69]

Another example of idealized, therefore value-laden and questionable, methodological judgments used in repository assessments are those that assume Darcy's Law is an accurate way to represent Yucca Mountain site hydrogeology. Virtually all of the risk assessments that discuss transport time of groundwater at radwaste sites rely ultimately on variants of Darcy's Law.[70] It states that groundwater flow velocity is proportional to the hydraulic gradient. This law, however, is an empirical, causal, and mathematical idealization.[71] Describing flow in porous media, Darcy's Law assumes that flow occurs through the entire cross-section of the material, rather than through pores and between solids, as actually happens. The law further assumes that velocity is uniform and the path straight, and it relies on average values of hydraulic variables applicable to volume elements. Moreover, because the corrections in Darcy's Law—needed to make it applicable to a particular site—must be based on laboratory or field results and do not come from the fundamental law itself, it is not obvious that good scientific theory actually supports some of the generalizations in which Darcy's Law is employed. For example, its use at Yucca Mountain is particularly problematic in part because the law is not suitable for conditions of fracture flow.[72]

Of course, hydrogeologists might argue, in most situations, that the idealizations and value judgments central to models based on Darcy's Law are not significant and that they could lead only to minor errors. However, the combined effect of numerous value judgments and small errors might be great, particularly in a situation of fracture flow. After all, siting a high-level radwaste repository requires long-term hydrogeological prediction, very slow groundwater migration time, and adequate information in the present. Such requirements mean that it is impossible to confirm that the Yucca Mountain laboratory and field results used in connection with Darcy's Law are accurate. Hence the problem of idealization remains.[73] In his classic essay on methodology, Milton Friedman claimed that idealizations were a problem in science only to the degree that the predictions resulting from them could not be checked. Because predictions for sites like Yucca Mountain cannot be checked over the long term, it is clear that they remain part of a classical scientific problem.[74]

The methodological value judgments about the adequacy of modeling proposed repository sites are also more questionable than those in many other areas of science because the site specifications to which the models must conform are sometimes very precise and therefore could be quite difficult to meet. For example, in the Yucca Mountain case, assessors are required to guarantee, by virtue of 10 CFR 60.113, "substantially complete containment" within the waste packages for three hundred to one thousand years and a controlled release rate from the engineered barrier system for ten thousand years of 1 part in 10^5 per year for radionuclides present in defined quantities one hundred years after permanent closure.[75] Given such precise requirements for the Yucca Mountain repository, it is questionable whether a simulation, a model, of the site could provide information that is firm enough to meet such specific requirements. The more stringent the site specifications, the more accurate must be the information used to meet the specifications. The methodological value judgment about the accuracy of modeling is questionable because of the long time frame of the prediction, the specificity of the requirements, and the fact that the simulation or model cannot be checked. Despite these three problems, most risk assessors base their Yucca Mountain conclusions on a variety of sophisticated models.[76] Yet only rarely do the assessors openly admit that their models are uncertain by virtue of being based mainly on "conceptual designs."[77] As a result, the methodological value judgments about the adequacy of modeling appear to have at least the potential to cause serious errors in QRA conclusions about Yucca Mountain and other proposed sites.

Value Judgments about Simplification of the Phenomena

Because real hydrogeological systems at proposed repository sites like Yucca Mountain are often quite complex, risk assessors frequently must make a further methodological value judgment that the simplifications of their models do not seriously misrepresent the situation they are attempting to understand and to predict. Indeed, risk assessors admit that simplifications of many hydrogeological phenomena are necessary in order to formulate analytic solutions to problems of hydraulic conductivity, infiltration, and so on.[78] According to the way that we are using the term "simplicity," one model or theory has more simplicity if it postulates fewer principles, laws, properties, or entities than another.[79] To render the real hydrogeological system at Yucca Mountain mathematically and scientifically tractable, for example, risk assessors have had to make certain methodological value judgments about simplifying the situation.[80] These include simplifications such as that all radionuclides have identical transport retardation factors, or that all radionuclide releases are instantaneous.[81]

Other common simplifications in permanent repository risk assessments are that water flow will be one-dimensional;[82] that percolation will be downward only through the unsaturated zone, but horizontal through the saturated zone;[83] that temperature and moisture are constant;[84] or that there is a normal distribution of cumulative releases of radionuclides to the water table.[85] All of these value judgments about simplification have been made in the Yucca Mountain situation, even though they are almost certainly counterfactual, and even though they have been criticized by external reviewers.[86]

Schedule constraints also often force a number of simplifications in risk studies.[87] Such simplifications obviously are not completely accurate representations of the real world but, in the case of Yucca Mountain, assessors make the methodological value judgment that they are accurate enough to describe the phenomena. This methodological value judgment is problematic, of course, to the degree that the simplifications are likely to underemphasize the likelihood of radwaste migration. At least three factors illustrate the underestimating effect of simplifications. Models that do not consider the growth of Ra-226 and other radionuclides in the long-lived decay chain stemming from the uranium and plutonium in the waste underestimate the health hazards of the waste.[88] Likewise, oversimplifying the physical processes in the unsaturated zone and the biological and chemical processes in the entire groundwater system may lead to underestimation of radionuclide transport and health hazards; if one assumes that adsorption of radionuclides reduces their hazard to the public, one may thereby forget that adsorbed radionuclides in the unsaturated zone may act as a very long-term contaminant source to the underlying saturated zone.[89]

A third example of simplification that causes an underestimation of risk has to do with synergism. Assessors, including those at Yucca Mountain, typically assume that many hydrogeological variables—such as percolation flux, hydraulic conductivity, effective matrix porosity, and fracture porosity—are independent; they make this assumption of independence because they do not have data that enable them to correlate the variables.[90] Yet obviously the combined effects of at least some of these factors could enhance the velocity of waste or water transport. Indeed, in the case of Yucca Mountain, outside evaluators have argued that oversimplifications in the description of the relevant hydrogeology compromise the scientific integrity of the site characterization plan.[91]

The methodological value judgment that phenomena and models may be simplified in order to provide an acceptable description and explanation of the site is problematic in part because simplicity is not always a good criterion for theory acceptability in science. It is not always a good criterion because if two empirically underdetermined or vague theories were both equally able to account for certain empirical results, then scientists following a criterion of simplicity could be forced to choose a crude, suspect, single-factor theory simply because it was the simpler of the two. More generally, as Friedman has pointed out, using simplicity to choose from among theories, all of which are consistent with the facts, is bound to lead to counterintuitive conclusions about the most acceptable scientific theory. This is because for any such theory there is a simpler one also consistent with the facts. Hence, because science strives for strong—not safe—hypotheses, using simplicity as a criterion for theory choice in science could lead to accepting theories that are weaker with respect to explanatory power.[92] Moreover, using simplicity as a criterion for theory choice in explaining characteristics of proposed repository sites is more problematic than in other areas of science. Given the inadequacy of the data and the heterogeneity of the Yucca Mountain site, for example, it is not clear that the simplified explanatory premises have a very high probability of being true.

In a highly applied risk-assessment situation, choosing a theory on the basis of simplicity, even though the empirical data are highly underdetermined, could lead to dangerous consequences. In such a case it might be better to admit that there is no adequate theory. For example, if one admitted that the simplified theories used to predict radwaste migration at Yucca Mountain might be inadequate, then this admission might have the virtue of preventing a questionable theory from being used as the basis for public policy that declares Yucca Mountain acceptable. The oversimplified models and theories used at Yucca Mountain bring to mind some of the scientific, health, and policy problems that arose when scientists and risk assessors made similar simplifications at the Maxey Flats low-level radwaste facility. Just as at Yucca Mountain, many of the Maxey Flats' scientists simplified the situation by assuming that there was only vertical movement of water above the water table. Yet, offsite migration at the Kentucky facility occurred in part through horizontal movement above the water table,[93] horizontal movement that was ruled out on the basis of a methodological value judgment.

Likewise, approximately twenty years ago there was a conflict between two groups of geologists evaluating the groundwater-flow theories for the proposed radwaste site in Maxey Flats, Kentucky. The geologists from several universities (Georgia Tech and Auburn, among others) and from several consulting groups and industries (primarily EMCON and Nuclear Engineering Company, NECO) used an extremely simple single-factor flow theory premised completely on the low permeability of the shale on site. They concluded that the radwaste could not migrate offsite for centuries.[94] The geologists from several government agencies (USGS and EPA) rejected the simple flow theory of the academic and industry geologists and claimed that many factors—such as possible fissures, fractures, and hairline cracks between bedding planes—not merely the low permeability of the shale, had to be taken into account.[95] Offering a theory with less simplicity and more explanatory parameters and properties, they claimed that radwaste could well migrate offsite. Because groundwater flow on the Maxey Flats site was so slow and so difficult to monitor directly, both theories were empirically underdetermined and hence equally consistent with the facts. As a result, policymakers chose the theory with more simplicity, the low permeability theory of the industry and academic geologists. Their choice has proved dangerously wrong, because plutonium traveled offsite only several years after the facility was opened.[96] Maxey Flats became known as "the world's worst nuclear dump."[97] The moral of the story is that the greater the empirical underdetermination of theories and models, the more dangerous it is to evaluate them in terms of the criterion of simplicity alone because the more likely it is that many "simple" theories are all consistent with the limited data. In the case of Yucca Mountain, the empirical underdetermination of the site is quite serious. Several of the DOE peer reviewers noted that modeling of flow at the site is "to a large extent based on simplifying assumptions which have not been fully verified by field observations."[98]

Value Judgments about
Reliability of Sampling

One of the methodological value judgments that is most crucial to the simplifications necessary to model any repository site is that sampling—via boreholes, wells, groundwater, or volcanic tuff cores—provides an adequate empirical base for predicting hydrogeological behavior at the location. At Yucca Mountain, risk assessors made a number of value judgments about sampling. The DOE assessors made the methodological value judgments, for example, that hydraulic-conductivity values obtained from the southeastern part of the Yucca Mountain area "are representative of the values along the flow path."[99] In arriving at such judgments about the representativeness of their sampling, they subjected cores of tuff, for instance, to a variety of stresses in order to infer inductively how it might behave as a high-level waste repository. They also took samples of special glass and irradiated it for given periods in order to determine the leach rates of various radioactive elements.[100] Similarly, they subjected samples of spent fuel to tests for thousands of hours to determine the rate of oxidation.[101] In addition, they examined samples from two deep boreholes in order to draw conclusions about the nature of the aquifer.[102]

In all their sampling activities, Yucca Mountain researchers have typically made the value judgment that a given number of boreholes or tuff samples, for example, 2, 7, 20, 29, were sufficient and were representative enough to enable them to draw reliable inductive conclusions about site characteristics such as fracture transmissivity, permeability, and hydraulic conductivity.[103] However, the epistemological difficulty with relying on sampling in order to understand the hydrogeology of a site is that one never knows when the number of samples collected is enough, because one never knows if they are representative or if the samples have captured the heterogeneities of the site. One often cannot adequately describe a site on the basis of several dozen boreholes; to attempt to do so would be like characterizing a large library on the basis of examining several dozen books.[104] It is well known, for example, that the host tuffs at Yucca Mountain are "highly variable."[105] Different tuff samples react differently to the same environmental constraints. Often the samples are not representative of these differences, or it is not known whether they are representative and hence whether geostatistical techniques give accurate estimates of variance. As late as 1988, for instance, assessors mentioned that they had just completed "the only hole drilled to date that penetrates the base of the tuff sequence and enters the underlying Paleozoic dolomite basement."[106]

Different samples used in adsorption studies appear to present a particular problem at Yucca Mountain. For example, when researchers used various samples of groundwater and tuff in order to study potential transport of radionuclides from a repository, they found that the adsorptive properties of the radionuclides on tuff were a function of time, temperature, and particle size, among other characteristics.[107]

They also found that sorption values for various types of tuff differ, for example, by at least four orders of magnitude.[108] Thus, representative adsorption samples are difficult to obtain, and conclusions about adsorption are dependent both on problematic samples and their representativeness, as well as on the models constructed from them.[109] Moreover, assessors are not able to check the representativeness of the samples used in adsorption studies because much of the data and theory underlying sorptive barriers are incomplete, unknown, or undeveloped.[110] In part because methodological value judgments about adsorption appear to have contributed to an underestimation of radionuclide transport at low-level radwaste sites like Maxey Flats and to a false belief that plutonium would not migrate rapidly,[111] there is reason to be cautious about any conclusions based on adsorption sampling.

Sampling methods used in repository risk assessments also often fail to be representative because researchers have sometimes modified the conditions under which they run experiments on samples. For example, in some Yucca Mountain cases, hydrogeologists used crushed-rock samples (not merely columns) to determine adsorptive values.[112] Yet adsorption of radionuclides at Yucca Mountain, once containment has been breached, obviously will not occur in crushed rock but in fractured, intact rock. Moreover, the fractured, intact rock is less likely to adsorb radioactive materials (and retard migration) than is crushed rock.[113] Hence, use of crushed-rock samples probably contributes to an underestimation of the risk of migration.

Despite general methodological problems with sampling and particular difficulties with the representativeness of the Yucca Mountain samples, many of the Yucca Mountain researchers remain confident that the adsorption values and radionuclide transport values "are being confirmed."[114] Obviously, however, by using different samples or different groundwaters or more extensive sampling or less crushed tuff, one could draw quite different conclusions about the adsorptive properties of the radionuclides or the transmissivity of the tuff; thus, one could draw different conclusions about the likelihood of radwaste migration offsite. Simply considering the possibility that plutonium can form pseudo-colloids—which can facilitate transport—could change assessment conclusions about radwaste migration. It is conceivable, therefore, that for different samples under different conditions, for example, plutonium might not be adsorbed or captured as assessors predict.[115] And if sampling fails to provide accurate predictions, then the methodological value judgments (about the types and numbers of sampling that ought to be done) may not provide a firm scientific basis for drawing general conclusions about site suitability.

When researchers sampled infiltration of precipitation at two Yucca Mountain sites, for example, they found hydrological activity at one location but not at the other.[116] Such results suggest that methodological value judgments about interpolating or extrapolating (from existing to missing sample points) could lead to difficulties, even if one employed geostatistics. Indeed, external reviewers have warned that many technical assumptions—methodological value judgments—about the site are not supported by field conditions and may be inappropriate to the Yucca Mountain system.[117] Of course, in hydrogeological situations one obviously must make some types of methodological value judgments, both about the quantity and the representativeness of the sample data. The problem is not the methodological value judgments about sampling as such because they occur in all science and QRA, as we explained in chapter 3. The real problem with such judgments, in the repository case, is the frequent absence of any ideas about the limits of errors associated with such judgments. If one is ignorant about the limits of error, then the idealizations, extrapolations, interpolations, and simplifications could lead to false predictions, just as they did at Maxey Flats and at other nuclear waste facilities. Moreover, in the case of the long time horizons associated with permanent repositories, it is impossible to know the limits of error to any precise degree because of the short-term data, the absence of long-term model confirmation, and the inductive inferences associated with both.

In risk assessments of the Maxey Flats site, sampling problems similar to those at Yucca Mountain caused serious difficulties and apparently contributed to the lack of knowledge about the facility's potential for radwaste migration. When industry geologists drilled wells at Maxey Flats, they found that they were dry, perhaps because their samples did not occur in areas where fractures happened to exist. When USGS geologists did other sampling, using well tests, however, they noted that some of the wells filled rather rapidly.[118] Because of difficulties associated with sampling, its representativeness, and its quantity, different scientists at Maxey Flats obtained contradictory empirical results. For this reason, there are grounds for questioning repository risk data that are based on inadequate sampling. There are also grounds for questioning the methodological value judgment that

Yucca Mountain sampling has already provided a reliable source of information about the site.

Admittedly, virtually all areas of science employ methodological value judgments about sampling. Much science would be impossible without sampling. Our point here is not that sampling is bad. The point, rather, is that in certain situations—characterized by heterogeneous phenomena and inadequate data to support very long-term predictions—the most reliable sampling is done in an extremely conservative, thorough, way. Because some Yucca Mountain sampling involved questionable methodological value judgments, for example, about factors such as using crushed rock, the sampling does not appear to have been done, in all cases, in a conservative way. Hence there are grounds, in cases like Yucca Mountain, for questioning some of the optimistic judgments of site suitability, given that they are based on limited sampling. There are also grounds for questioning the use of sampling as a basis for accurately assessing repository risk because the greater the number of boreholes drilled, for example, the more precisely we can characterize a proposed site. But such precision is bought at a price, since less drilling means less tendency to compromise site integrity, and more drilling (more accuracy) means a greater likelihood of compromising site integrity.[119] Hence, conclusions about site suitability need to reflect accurately the limits imposed by sampling.

Value Judgments
about Laboratory Predictions

In assuming that sampling can provide an accurate description of sites like Yucca Mountain, some risk assessors also make the additional methodological value judgment that laboratory analyses of samples provide an adequate basis for conclusions about field behavior.[120] Rather than doing a sufficient number of experiments in the field, for example, hydrologists and geologists at Yucca Mountain have done laboratory experiments on cores of tuff taken from the field.[121] Using laboratory data about site geochemistry, about behavior of crushed (not solid) tuff, about sorption, and about retardation of radionuclide transport, for example, assessors extrapolate from laboratory results in order to draw conclusions about all these factors on site.[122] One of the things assessors wish to determine in their laboratory studies is whether "fracture healing" (in which fractured rock samples become sealed when water flows through them at elevated temperatures) can prevent leakage of radionuclides.[123] Because the assessors' conclusions about field behavior are *extrapolations* from premises about laboratory behavior rather than deductions from premises about field behavior, they are obviously questionable. Moreover, because of the many disanalogies between laboratory and field behavior at Yucca Mountain, the conclusions are questionable even on inductive grounds.

Obviously, there are many disanalogies between laboratory and field behavior of a core of tuff, any one of which could account for erroneous estimates of future radionuclide transport at sites like Yucca Mountain. Admittedly some assessors have been sensitive to these disanalogies and have emphasized the importance of field studies to check models and samples.[124] Nevertheless, the very use of samples investigated in a laboratory setting requires one to make untested methodological value judgments about the degree of fit between the laboratory conclusions and those of the field. Like value judgments about sampling, judgments about the accuracy of using laboratory data to describe field conditions occur in many areas of science. The problem is not with the methodological value judgment that one can use the laboratory data in this way, but with risk assessments of sites like Yucca Mountain, studies that have failed to test this value judgment as completely as possible by experiments in the field. In other words, the problem is not with laboratory data and associated methodological value judgments, but with applications that appear lacking in scientific conservatism and adequate field confirmation.

Value Judgments about Fractured, Unsaturated Media

Another methodological value judgment central to risk assessment of many proposed high-level repositories like Yucca Mountain is that despite the discontinuous, nonhomogeneous nature of the fractures in the geological substrate, nevertheless it is possible to predict, with reasonable accuracy, the path and rate of potential radioactive migration, once containment of the canisters has been breached.

This value judgment is a potential problem for virtually any repository because there might be fracture flow, and because it is "generally the case" that all rock sites are fractured.[125] Yet most fractures are not uniform, and hence they cannot easily be modeled. Such heterogeneities prevent a "comprehensive flow analysis," as at the Stripa Mine in Sweden.[126] Modeling the fractured substrate is especially problematic for the unsaturated zone at Yucca Mountain, because very little is known about it. Also, the volcanic tuff itself is quite heterogeneous, with eight orders of magnitude of variation sometimes occurring in the saturated hydraulic conductivities.[127] Nevertheless, risk assessors claim to have demonstrated that "methodologies are available for characterizing fracture flow" through saturated fractures.[128] They say that such methods are "suitable" for determining fracture flow, or "adequate" and "valid."[129] An alternative methodological value judgment, one to which representatives of the state of Nevada appear to subscribe, is that given the discontinuities and heterogeneities in the fractures, such characterizations are impossible because the flow is likely to be random and unpredictable. Indeed, recognizing that travel time through fractures is faster than through any rock matrix,[130] representatives of the state of Nevada have warned that the great uncertainty regarding flow through heterogeneous, fractured material is one of their seven major hydrogeological "concerns" about Yucca Mountain.[131]

At Yucca Mountain, risk assessors are attempting to model the site and to predict possible releases of radionuclides through the fractures.[132] Because they have inadequate empirical data,[133] and because behavior of heterogeneous, partially saturated, or saturated sites is not at present mathematically tractable, they use models that assume a more homogeneous hydrogeological situation. The models assume, for example, uniformly spaced or parallel fractures.[134] Often they ignore the fact that drying is more or less rapid along different fractures.[135] Yet all these heterogeneities could be enough to alter substantially the predicted rates of radionuclide migration at Yucca Mountain and at other proposed sites. Such predictions are scientifically suspect, at least in part, because they are not derived from any general scientific laws about fracture flow in a heterogeneous environment. Indeed there are no precisely predictive laws for such an environment. The methodological problem with value judgments about fracture flow is not, however, that they rely on no predictive general laws, since much of science involves no such laws. Rather, the real difficulty here is that U.S. government regulations for repositories require precise predictive power over thousands of years, whereas the science available for QRAs of repository sites is not as precise and predictive as regulations appear to require.

One of the major methodological value judgments about hydrogeologically modeling a heterogeneous site has to do with rate of infiltration. Infiltration of water into a site is largely a function of precipitation which, as we mentioned already, is highly variable. Infiltration, in turn, is highly variable from one spot to another at Yucca Mountain, for example, because of differences in the underlying hydrogeology, especially the presence of fractures. In some Yucca Mountain studies, researchers showed that rainwater on site evaporated and had no influence at depth; yet they cautioned, for example, that five feet of water entered boreholes, via fractures, at one of their sampling spots.[136] This sort of heterogeneity, with no infiltration at depth anywhere except for one place where five feet of water accumulated, is exactly the sort of nonuniformity that could play havoc with methodological value judgments about our ability to predict radwaste migration.

Infiltration is particularly important at sites like Yucca Mountain because although less than 3 percent of precipitation onsite likely infiltrates deeply enough to recharge the saturated zone, nevertheless concentrations of infiltration in time or space, according to some assessors, could supply enough flux to cause fracture flow on site.[137] Assessors have warned that the rock at Yucca Mountain could act as a sink for infiltrating water, and that "significant winter recharge could occur . . . due to snow melt."[138] Climate change to wetter conditions could also cause more infiltration and enhanced fracture flow.[139] Given the possibility of fracturing because of the heat of the waste,[140] and given the possibility of intense rainfall at a particular location, the assessors' claim that fracture flow is "unlikely" or "not credible"[141] is a questionable methodological value judgment. It is questionable, in part, because fracture flow is so sensitive to a relatively small change in the percolation rate. If the percolation rate increases by only one order of magnitude above conservative values, this might be enough to initiate fracture flow. Fracture flow, in turn, could significantly reduce the travel time of water between the repository and the water table.[142]

A few assessors have warned about the reliability of the models for fractured media,[143] cautioning that the hydraulic parameters are "poorly known" and basic issues are "unresolved."[144] Such worries are likely part of the reason why representatives for the state of Nevada, responding to the conceptual design of the Yucca Mountain Site Characterization Plan, claimed that "one of the most disturbing aspects is the lack of attention given to the geohydrologic setting and its performance at the Yucca Mountain site."[145] Likewise, when the fourteen DOE peer reviewers assessed the 1992 *Early Site Suitability Evaluation* for Yucca Mountain, they said that the biggest conceptual issue in the ESSE was whether there was likely to be fracture flow at Yucca Mountain and therefore groundwater travel time from the disturbed zone to the accessible environment in less than one thousand years.[146] The DOE peer reviewers also criticized the ESSE for lacking a detailed discussion of fracture flow and for relying on simplified models for a heterogenous site.[147] Hence even the outside evaluators appear disturbed by the value judgments about precise prediction of flow in fractured media at Yucca Mountain.

Some researchers, however, appear to believe that the site models can be "verified" or are "valid."[148] (We discuss verification problems later, in chapter 6.) One difficulty with methodological value judgments about using models to predict fracture flow, however, is that past judgments about flow through fractures (at other radioactive waste sites) have been overly optimistic about radioactive containment, and they have resulted in serious error. Indeed the methodological value judgment at the Maxey Flats radwaste facility, that no flow through fractures was likely, was one of the key mistakes that led to offsite release of radionuclides, including transuranics, less than a decade after the facility was opened.[149] This methodological value judgment about Maxey Flats is uncomfortably similar to the claim that fracture flow is "unlikely" or "not credible" at Yucca Mountain.[150] On the surface, the Maxey Flats, Kentucky facility appears to have little to teach us about sites like Yucca Mountain. In most respects, the Nevada and Kentucky cases are quite dissimilar. The Nevada site, in an area of low rainfall, is for deep burial of high-level, heavily shielded radwastes, whereas the Kentucky facility, in a region of high rainfall, was for unshielded, shallow land burial of low-level and transuranic wastes. Nevertheless, the two sites have at least two apparent similarities. Both are hydrogeologically heterogeneous sites, and both are plagued by fractures in the underlying rock.

The Kentucky predictions went wrong, in part, because the scientists focused on the alleged impermeability of the shale underlying the site but underestimated the potential for migration through its hairline fractures. Similarly, at least some risk assessors have argued that

Yucca Mountain is full of fractured tuff through which contaminated water could migrate.[151] Another similarity between the two sites is that once the high-level radwaste canisters and the fuel cladding at Yucca Mountain have been breached, allegedly between three hundred and one thousand years after emplacement, then the underlying geology and hydrology will determine the extent of the waste migration because of precipitation, infiltration, and leaching. Ultimately, therefore, both high-level and low-level sites face the same problems of geological containment. Hence, some of what happens regarding low-level radwaste migration, decades after the waste is stored, could provide a preview of part of what happens regarding high-level radwaste migration centuries after it is deposited. Thus, low-level sites, like Maxey Flats, and proposed high-level sites, like Yucca Mountain, may have some pregnant similarities, despite their obvious dissimilarities. These similarities suggest that our mistakes at Maxey Flats may have something to teach us about potential problems at sites like Yucca Mountain.

At Maxey Flats, the radioactive releases occurred within nine years, although they were predicted to occur after centuries or even after thousands of years.[152] Scientists employed by promoters of the facility presented simple, low-permeability models for the underlying shale, and policymakers concluded that the possibility of offsite migration was "essentially nonexistent."[153] The U.S. Geological Survey (USGS) project director, however, later explicitly said that any simple quantitative model for the site was impossible because Maxey Flats is a poorly permeable, fractured, geological system. Any prediction of flow paths was impossible, he said, because of the highly irregular hairline fractures and the fracture intensities.[154] Because prediction of fracture flow at Maxey Flats would require detailed information about the spatial distribution and hydraulic properties of each of many hairline fractures in a variety of successive strata (e.g., Nancy Shale, Henley Shale, Ohio Shale, and so on), the USGS project director concluded that groundwater flow at Maxey Flats could not be predicted.[155] Any model, he said, would presuppose conditions for its accuracy that were not met at Maxey Flats, conditions such as "uniform transmission of water through the rocks."[156] Although his warnings were ignored by state promoters of the site, he concluded that "hydraulic conditions do not meet the requirements for the method of analysis."[157] His argument years earlier about the Maxey Flats site is quite similar to current claims by Yucca Mountain assessment reviewers that the untested

Yucca Mountain models are not appropriate for the complex site hydrogeology.[158] In both cases, a major threat was/is fracture flow, and in both cases, risk assessors were/are using untested models that may not account adequately for fracture flow.

Given the fractured tuff and the heterogeneity of the hydrogeological site, caused in part by incomplete information, by irregular fractures, and by no information about the long-term future, one might well be justified in concluding at Yucca Mountain, just as one concluded at Maxey Flats, that the hydraulic and geological conditions do not meet the requirements for the idealized methods of analysis that presuppose uniformities. Indeed, at any proposed geological repository facing similar heterogeneities, the same charge would hold. If site conditions such as fractured tuff do not meet the conditions for analysis, then it could be quite dangerous to make the methodological value judgment that one can accurately predict radwaste migration in the heterogeneous, fractured media at sites like Yucca Mountain. Just as the DOE peer reviewers warned in their 1992 evaluation, methodological value judgments about fracture flow could represent a serious deficiency in Yucca Mountain QRAs and in repository studies generally.

Value Judgments that Interpolations Are Acceptable

Still another major methodological value judgment in many repository risk assessments, including some of those at Yucca Mountain, is that accurate interpolation of sparse and irregularly spaced data is possible. A number of assessors make this assumption[159] even though the data are not uniform, even though infiltration, for example, occurs at some locations but not at others,[160] and even though low groundwater-flow rates are guaranteed only for unsaturated conditions where infiltration has not compromised the repository site.[161] Heterogeneities in the hydrology and geology onsite indicate that curve-fitting techniques could fail to provide an accurate picture of hydrogeology at sites like Yucca Mountain. This may be why, for example, the state of Nevada listed uncertainties regarding infiltration and groundwater travel time as among its seven major "concerns" regarding site hydrogeology.[162] Of course, the problem here is not with methodological value judgments about interpolation, as such, because all scientists must make judgments about interpolation. The problem is that the use of value judgments about interpolation at Yucca Mountain appears insufficiently careful and conservative given the heterogeneity of the site.

Value Judgments that Human Error Is Not Significant

Another problematic methodological value judgment that is implicit in a number of repository risk assessments, including many of those at Yucca Mountain, is the presupposition that human error is not a significant contributor to risk at the site. In one of the official DOE documents, this value judgment is made quite clear: "Because of the plans to mark the site and to use other passive means to prevent human intrusion into the repository, and because of the intention to ensure that the site will have little value in unique resources, large-scale human activities that would inadvertently affect the repository are not likely to take place at the site. Accordingly, the only scenarios currently considered for this case are those involving occasional random exploratory drilling at the site."[163] Indeed, DOE risk assessors seem almost completely to ignore the effects of human error in thwarting repository containment. The DOE environmental assessment for Yucca Mountain concludes: "No impediments to eventual complete ownership and control [of Yucca Mountain] by the DOE have been identified. Therefore, on the basis of the above evaluation, the evidence does not support a finding that the site is not likely to meet the qualifying condition for post-closure site ownership and control."[164]

As the policy position of the DOE makes clear, the DOE discounts not only large-scale human error and inadvertent activities causing intrusion into Yucca Mountain, but also organized sabotage and terrorism. Indeed, virtually 99 percent of the DOE research on Yucca Mountain, as revealed in its own Program Assessment, is on physical science topics related to the risk. There is almost nothing on possible socioeconomic problems caused by the facility or on human aspects of risk.[165] Indeed, in the 1992 *Early Site Suitability Evaluation* (ESSE) for Yucca Mountain, the DOE researchers bluntly stated that "unmitigatable social and/or economic impacts are not expected to occur" at Yucca Mountain.[166] If our earlier questions about site stability for ten thousand years are plausible, however, then there are equally pressing questions about possible social impacts.

Typical Yucca Mountain risk assessments, apparently following the position of the DOE, also make the same controversial methodological value judgment that human error at the site will be insignificant. For example, assessors assume that risk managers will have to deal only with radioactive "releases that would be expected from the repository under undisturbed conditions," that is, conditions where human accident, error, or sabotage does not disturb the site.[167] After explicitly ignoring human errors, accidents, and other disruptive features, the same assessors conclude that "even for the highest credible flux . . . releases of radioactivity to the accessible environment in 10,000 years after closure are significantly less than the limits imposed in the draft standards (40 CFR 191) for environmental radiation protection."[168] After ignoring such human disruptions of the site, risk assessors typically conclude that Yucca Mountain will meet government environmental requirements; indeed, after ignoring these human factors, they usually put a quite precise figure on the risk involved. For example, they say that the site will cause "less than one health effect every 1,400 years."[169] Such confident and optimistic predictions seem questionable in the face of assessors' tendency to ignore an important class of risk factors, namely, human causes of repository failures.

Because the vast majority of the DOE-funded Yucca Mountain studies deals with purely physical, nonhuman processes, it appears that DOE policymakers and assessors presuppose either that human error is unimportant at Yucca Mountain, or that it is poorly understood and therefore can be ignored in favor of what is better understood (physical-transport mechanisms for radwaste). Both value judgments about Yucca Mountain fly in the face of previous inductive evidence about estimates of human error either at other facilities or at Yucca Mountain. For example, several risk assessors calculated the likelihood of human disruption onsite after the first century. They said that the probability of drilling at Yucca Mountain could be as high as 5×10^{-2} to 2×10^{-3} per year.[170] If the estimates of some scientists about human disruption at Yucca Mountain are so high, it is questionable whether many assessors ought simply to ignore this human factor and then conclude that the risk of disruption at Yucca Mountain is quite low. Given that there is an active gold mine within fifteen miles of Yucca Mountain and several inactive mines within ten miles,[171] it does seem reasonable to believe that future drilling might occur nearby.

Moreover, it is conceivable that future generations might try to use the buried waste, because of its "potentially valuable energy."[172]

The methodological value judgment by the DOE—that one can ignore the human-caused risks at Yucca Mountain—is all the more problematic, both because the U.S. Environmental Protection Agency (EPA) does take account of human error in its assessment of the impacts associated with repositories,[173] and because the EPA claims that "the most important cause of radionuclide release appears to be human intrusion."[174] Also, it is obvious that many precise aspects of human behavior far into the future are not predictable.[175] Moreover, even in a probabilistic sense, it is not clear that good reasons support the value judgment that human error at the Yucca Mountain site will be insignificant. After all, if the EPA claim is correct, and if the human contribution to technological accidents is typically as high as 90 percent (in the case of the airlines and the chemical industry),[176] then human error/intrusion could be a significant repository risk. After all, U.S. Office of Technology Assessment authors conclude that more than 60 percent of accidents involving hazardous materials are the result of human error.[177] Hence, it is not surprising that some reviewers have explicitly criticized the DOE failure to give sufficient attention to human error at Yucca Mountain. They have charged that "the most striking weakness of risk assessments for the proposed Yucca Mountain repository is their failure to address the social amplification of risk."[178]

Human error is one of the major contributors to risk in the cases where government radioactive waste facilities have caused large-scale contamination and threats to welfare. At the Maxey Flats site, for example, the facility was closed only a decade after it was opened in 1962. Offsite migration of radionuclides caused the closure, and the facility received much government attention and adverse publicity. Yet more than fifteen years after its well-documented problems of poor containment, the government has failed to oversee and clean up Maxey Flats effectively. Indeed, social and human factors amplified the risk even after it was brought to public attention. As late as 1987, wells to monitor contamination on site revealed that tritium levels in the Maxey Flats groundwater exceeded the Environmental Protection Agency limit by 6 orders of magnitude.[179] The Maxey Flats situation suggests not only that humans cause a significant amount of the risk from radioactive waste management, but that once their failures are brought to light, both individuals and institutions often amplify, rather than correct, the risk.[180] One important question also raised by the Maxey Flats case is this: why should one believe that humans at Yucca Mountain and at other proposed repositories will not amplify the radwaste risk, given that they have done so at Maxey Flats, at Fernald, at Hanford, at Savannah River, at Oak Ridge, at Rocky Flats, at Idaho Falls, and at Lawrence Livermore? Indeed, many corrections for safety and environmental problems were not made adequately at these and other facilities. The risk was amplified, in large part, because the government did not wish to bear the cost.[181] The DOE has admitted that it caused soil and water contamination at all these places, that it withheld information from the public, that it violated its own regulations, that it failed to tell workers when they were handling plutonium, and that it used retaliation against employees who were whistleblowers.[182]

The U.S. General Accounting Office (GAO) pointed out, for example, that Savannah River, Rocky Flats, Hanford, Idaho Falls, Maxey Flats, and West Valley (New York) all have extensive onsite contamination. Indeed, as we mentioned in chapter 1, the GAO identified 1,061 DOE sites that currently require a massive cleanup; the government estimates that this cleanup will require from $130 to 300 billion.[183] Presumably the existence and continuation of contamination at these major DOE facilities indicate that no hazardous site is free from problems caused by human error.[184] Indeed, the GAO said that contamination at DOE facilities is so extreme that the government knows precisely neither the extent of it nor what is needed to clean it up. Government representatives have also testified that the DOE has lost its credibility[185] and that the complacency at the DOE is similar to that existing at Chernobyl before the accident.[186]

At the nuclear feed materials plant at Fernald, Ohio, for example, the company (under DOE supervision and instruction) repeatedly broke environmental regulations, contaminated the site, and illegally stored radioactive materials. Fernald workers even processed plutonium for twenty-two years without wearing respirators.[187] DOE managers gave the facility repeated permission to break its own regulations and to make regular discharges of uranium into nearby rivers, permission that was given from the very beginning of the operation of the plant.[188] In-house recommendations for correcting safety problems and reducing risks were ignored, even when workers died.[189] At the Fernald facility, DOE authorities made "no attempt" to monitor releases or to "take corrective measures" once problems had occurred.[190]

Indeed, the DOE shipped 2,500 tons of thorium sludge in corroding steel containers to Fernald, to be stored there, even though Fernald had no use for the waste.[191]

At the Maxey Flats facility, the government-supervised company (Nuclear Engineering Company, NECO, later called "U.S. Ecology") illegally dumped radioactive materials offsite and refused to admit investigators to the facility once offsite radioactivity had become a problem.[192] For government administrators even to allow Maxey Flats to dump 950 pounds of special nuclear materials (plutonium, uranium-233, and enriched uranium 235) in an area with average annual rainfall of 48 inches, in shallow soil trenches 25 feet deep,[193] suggests human error, ignorance, mismanagement, or corruption. Moreover, given DOE's previous problems with violating environmental regulations and with secrecy, as illustrated in such problems as the Fernald facility, it is clear that assessors may be wrong to discount the problem of human error at any repository, including Yucca Mountain. Discounting human error at the proposed repository is extremely problematic because external reviewers have already criticized the DOE for lack of coordination at the Yucca Mountain site,[194] for ignoring the social contributors to risk,[195] and for allegedly using Yucca Mountain as a justification for its own self- and predetermined policies.[196]

Representatives from the Hanford nuclear facility and from Yakima Nation, near Hanford, likewise have criticized "DOE's reckless environmental and safety practices at Hanford."[197] Texans have testified before Congressional committees that the DOE's handling of the proposed radwaste site in their state caused them to have "no confidence" in the DOE's technical ability and responsiveness to legitimate public concerns.[198] Residents of Mississippi accused the DOE of not sharing data about their state's possible radwaste site with them,[199] and numerous state geologists have accused the DOE of technical deficiencies caused by its own political agenda.[200] Nevadans have charged the DOE with secrecy in the face of Yucca Mountain studies, with not consulting with them, and with failure to fund Nevada requests for research about the site.[201] Indeed, Nevada had to sue the DOE to get funding for independent technical studies of the Yucca Mountain site.[202] As a result, the GAO concluded that the DOE has not allowed the states and Native American tribes to participate in the high-level waste siting program to the extent intended by the Nuclear Waste Policy Act of 1982.[203] All these problems suggest not only that human error is likely to occur at Yucca Mountain and other proposed geological repositories, contrary to what many government risk assessors claim, but also that such error may arise in part through the bias, mismanagement, and lack of concern of the very government agencies that ought to be protecting the public interest.

One common denominator among many of the problems of human error may be the institutional shortcomings of agencies such as the DOE. To the degree that the difficulties are institutional, the human risk-amplification problem may be even greater than we have suggested so far. Hence, making the methodological value judgment that human error will not be a significant contributor to repository risks—at places like Yucca Mountain—seems highly questionable. The value judgment appears capable of compromising QRA conclusions about repository safety.

Problems with Yucca Mountain versus Problems with Permanent Disposal

Many of the eight methodological value judgments (e.g., about the reliability of conclusions based on sampling) surveyed in this chapter are widely used throughout science and risk assessment. Hence, the difficulty is not with using these value judgments, as such, but with drawing stronger conclusions from them than are warranted by the existing scientific theories and inductive data. At Yucca Mountain, for example, we argued that some of the DOE site-suitability conclusions appeared to be stronger than were warranted by the limited quantity and the questionable representativeness of the evidence. In general, however, there are no basic problems with employing many methodological value judgments (such as those related to sampling, extrapolation, and use of laboratory data) in science and risk assessment. Indeed, in many areas of science, there simply are no viable alternatives to making a variety of such judgments.

However, a number of methodological value judgments used in the Yucca Mountain case do present difficulties. They appear to exemplify "bad science." They suggest that, were certain value judgments— regarding risk estimation, for example—handled differently at Yucca Mountain, the scientific conclusions about the site might be somewhat different. Some of these examples of "bad science" include the value judgments that models not validated and confirmed by field data are accurate; that simplifying assumptions adequately represent the site, even though they have not been checked by actual observations; that laboratory data provide an accurate account of field conditions; that one can precisely predict site hydrology despite fractured, inhomogeneous conditions; and that, despite the site heterogeneities, one can interpolate to obtain specific and representative hydrological and geological data.

Obviously, if "bad science" was responsible for all of the flawed methodological value judgments about risk estimation that we have criticized at Yucca Mountain, then these problems would argue only against repository sites chosen on the basis of flawed studies. "Bad science" would not argue generally against permanent geological disposal of radwaste. But this raises the question whether the problems we have exposed in this chapter represent difficulties that might be avoidable at other proposed repository sites or in other risk studies. Do these problems with value judgments about risk estimation argue only against "bad science" and "bad risk assessment" or also against any permanent radwaste repositories?

At least two of the methodological value judgments criticized in this chapter appear to present obstacles to any permanent geological disposal of radwastes anywhere. These are the value judgments that short-term data can be used to confirm precise conclusions about long-term (ca. 10,000 years) site acceptability, and that human error and risk amplification do not threaten the security of a permanent repository. If the arguments in this chapter have been correct, then both short-term scientific data and the potential for human error militate against any precise, optimistic predictions regarding long-term (10,000 years) repository suitability and safety. Indeed, as we showed early in the chapter, and as the Yucca Mountain peer reviewers for the DOE confirmed, there can be no reliable geological predictions regarding volcanism and seismicity, because geology is essentially an explanatory, rather than a precise predictive science. As we also argued, and as the Yucca Mountain peer reviewers and various social scientists admitted, beyond fifty or one hundred years, precise predictions about human and institutional errors and behavior are not reliable. This being so, short-term geological data and the potential for human intrusion into the repository exacerbate the more general problem of accurate long-term prediction.

Federal regulations (see chapter 2) stipulate that precise thousand-year predictions—regarding either geological factors like seismicity or social factors like repository intrusions aimed at securing natural resources—are required to guarantee the safety of a permanent repository. If such accurate long-term predictions are at present impossible, then a scientifically defensible siting of a permanent repository, at least at present in the United States, likewise appears impossible.

5

Subjective Evaluations
of Repository Risks

Recent risk assessments done by the Ford Foundation-Mitre Corporation and the Union of Concerned Scientists (UCS) used identical data—probabilities and consequence estimates—associated with the risk of commercial nuclear fission reactors. Yet their risk evaluations were contradictory. The Ford Foundation assessment recommended use of nuclear energy, and the UCS study advised against it. How could two studies that agreed on the probabilistic and scientific data reach opposed conclusions? The answer is that the two studies used different methodological rules, different methodological value judgments at the third (risk-evaluation) stage of assessment. The Ford group used the Bayesian expected-utility rule, whereas the UCS analysts used a maximin rule. The moral of the story is that even when they are based on the same data, risk-assessment conclusions can be highly sensitive to methodological assumptions about how to evaluate given risks.[1]

One obvious question raised by the contradictory Ford-Mitre and UCS conclusions is whether similar contradictions would arise if one challenged the methodological rules and subjective judgments used to evaluate risks associated with high-level radwaste repositories. As we did in the last chapter, one way to answer this question would be to examine state-of-the-art risk assessments, some of the best of which are being done for the first proposed U.S. high-level, permanent waste repository in Yucca Mountain, Nevada. In the previous chapter, we questioned many of the methodological value judgments typically used at stage two, *risk estimation*, of the QRAs for proposed repositories. In this chapter, we investigate similar judgments typically employed at stage three, *risk evaluation*, of QRA. We shall argue that Yucca Mountain assessors use at least eight questionable methodological value judgments to evaluate repository risks. Because many of these value judgments are both necessary to, and typical of, justifications for permanent geological disposal, problems with them raise questions about the whole enterprise of permanent burial of high-level radioactive wastes.

Value Judgments that a Given Magnitude of Risk Is Acceptable

One of the most basic judgments typical of repository risk evaluation is that the magnitude of the radiological hazard alone determines risk acceptability and that a particular magnitude of risk is acceptable, regardless of other considerations. Many risk evaluations, at Yucca Mountain and elsewhere, rely on the methodological value judgment that predicting hazardous events having a certain low probability of occurrence is sufficient to provide a guarantee of facility safety. Obviously, however, no particular level of probable safety is ever known to be enough. No premises about some level of safety are alone sufficient to justify a conclusion about site acceptability because site acceptability is a function of normative and evaluative premises. It is not a logical consequence of particular empirical claims. Hence, value judgments about the acceptability of some level of risk cannot be justified on purely empirical grounds. One assessor, studying ground motion at Yucca Mountain, based his "conservative estimates" of risk on the value judgment that predicting ground motion that had a one-in-ten chance of occurring was a sound basis for seismic design of the repository.[2] However, we could just as easily argue that we ought to design for a one-in-a-hundred or a one-in-a-thousand chance of particular ground motion. Other groups of risk assessors concluded that there had been no "significant" fault-related movement on the Yucca Mountain Site in the last 500,000 years,[3] and that moderate earthquakes would likely occur at Yucca Mountain at recurrence intervals of tens of thousands of years.[4] The obvious question this raises, however, is whether 500,000 years of no "significant" fault-related movement or 10,000 years of no moderate earthquakes is enough. Should there have been 5 million years of no such significant movement? Or more or less? Choosing a level of designed safety obviously involves value judgments.

Some risk assessors calculated the probability of a volcanic disruption hazard at Yucca Mountain as 10^{-6} per year,[5] whereas others have estimated this risk as between 10^{-8} and 10^{-9} per year,[6] with the probability of volcanism exceeding 10^{-4} over 10,000 years.[7] Not only do these numbers cover a wide range, but there is no certain way to be sure that the possibility of volcanism is ever gone; volcanism at an individual center may last 500,000 years, contrary to what many Yucca Mountain assessors have assumed. Moreover, Yucca Mountain is relatively free of faults, but the paucity of faults does not guarantee safety from future volcanic disruption.[8] Hence, the obvious question is: why is the methodological value judgment—that the risk of volcanism is acceptably low—reliable? As we argued in the previous chapter, even the DOE peer reviewers, such as K. V. Hodges, have themselves argued that it is "patently absurd" to think that there are reliable predictions for geologic events 10,000 years in the future.

The annual probability of various accidents involving radionuclide releases at Yucca Mountain, according to some risk assessors, is between 10^{-6} and 10^{-9}.[9] Obviously these volcanic and accident risks are small, per year, but the inference that such values are "low enough" represents a highly questionable methodological value judgment (in part) because, over centuries, the probability is much higher. For example, if the probability of volcanic disruption is 10^{-6} per year, then for 10,000 years, that probability would be 10^{-2}, an extraordinarily high risk. The value judgment about the acceptability of such a risk is questionable in part because, although the per-year risks may appear low, the risks to future generations, whose members have no say in contemporary decisions about Yucca Mountain, are higher than those that we would likely accept for ourselves. Indeed, a value judgment that such future risks are acceptable arguably fails to take account of citizens' concerns about issues such as due process, equal protection, compensation, and the rights of future persons. (See later sections of this chapter and chapter 8 for a discussion of equity issues related to problems of radioactive waste.) The apparent failure to take adequate consideration of the rights of future generations, in making the ethical judgment that a given level of risk is acceptable, is particularly apparent in the radiation standards to be used at Yucca Mountain. European scientists are quite critical of the fact that U.S. radiation dose limits do not extend beyond 1,000 years for the individual and 10,000 years for the population. European regulatory protection against radiation extends up to 1 million years—990,000 years longer than U.S. protection.[10] Moreover, European waste containers have longer projected lives—100,000 years, and not the 300 to 1,000 years of the U.S. canisters. This is one reason that the Swedish nuclear program has been so successful, for example, with its emphasis on long-lived engineered barriers.[11] The fact that other countries are making much more conservative plans for managing and containing high-level radwaste suggests that typical U.S. levels of acceptable risk, whether from volcanism or radwaste canisters, may not be adequate. Hence, the value judgment that given levels of risk are scientifically, ethically, socially, and politically acceptable is highly controversial. One reason for the controversy is that such judgments appear to rest on a highly questionable, short-term, utilitarian justification. (Later in the chapter and in chapter 8 we shall discuss utilitarian ethical judgments.)

In assuming that a given number of years of canister reliability—or a given number of future cancers caused annually by Yucca Mountain—is acceptable, assessors presuppose that the magnitude of a risk, alone, is grounds for acceptance. Obviously, however, equity of distribution, compensation, free and informed consent, as well as other social considerations also play a major role in whether a given number of cancers, for example, is acceptable. After the first several hundred years, cancers caused by the Yucca Mountain repository are predicted to be roughly one hundred to one thousand per year, approximately the same number that would occur as a result of naturally occurring uranium-ore bodies.[12] It is not clear, however, why this number of cancers is acceptable, particularly if the magnitude alone is judged as grounds for acceptance. Future persons affected by the waste will have little say in their contracting cancer, and they will have no possibility of exercising their due process rights. Indeed, there appears to be no adequate vehicle for compensating them. In the absence of such ethical and social considerations, the value judgment—that a given magnitude of risk or number of cancers caused by Yucca Mountain is acceptable—appears questionable.

In assuming that a given level of risk, or a given number of years of travel time of radioactive waste, is acceptable, risk assessors also appear to presuppose that low-probability events are very unlikely to occur. Over the long term, the likelihood of such events is not known with real accuracy, however, because there is no existing frequency record, and because we have no guarantee that the future will be like the past. If the future is not like the past, then allegedly rare events (like seismic activity) could shorten the hundreds of years required for radwaste migration to take place at repositories such as Yucca Mountain. As several USGS geologists put it, speaking of the Maxey Flats radioactive waste facility: extreme events of low frequency may perform the work of thousands of years of creep and slope wash. For example, an eight-hour deluge of 28 inches of rain may cause several thousand years' worth of "normal" erosion. Therefore, infrequent events threaten Maxcy Flats' integrity more than do continuous processes.[13] The same could be true at Yucca Mountain and at any other disposal site. Indeed, as we argued in the previous chapter, the DOE peer reviewers for the Yucca Mountain *Early Site Suitability Evaluation* warned that geology is an explanatory, not a predictive, science. They also argued that no reliable predictions regarding seismic or volcanic activity at the site were possible. If no reliable predictions are possible, then it is also not possible to know that a given level of risk is the case and that it is "low enough."

Another problem with the value judgment that given repository risks are low enough—for example, 10^{-6} or 10^{-9}—is that many risk estimates are subject to considerable uncertainty. As already mentioned, uncertainties of 6 orders of magnitude are "not unusual" in risk assessments characterized by incomplete data on long-term accident frequency.[14] If this is true, and if similar uncertainties are applicable to repository-risk figures, then an annual risk of 10^{-6} of an accident involving a radionuclide release might really lie between approximately 10^{-3} and 10^{-9}. An annual risk of 10^{-3} is arguably not a low risk; indeed, it is approximately 3 orders of magnitude higher than the risks that are normally regulated by government. Hence, one good reason for questioning the value judgment that a given level of risk—estimated for repositories like Yucca Mountain—is acceptable is that because of uncertainty in the estimates the real risk could be quite high. Indeed, the real risks associated with radioactive waste storage at past U.S. facilities have not been insignificant. According to government estimates for the Hanford facility, for example, just the normal radiation releases from this site could result in an annual exposure of 580 person-rem.[15] According to some of the lowest government estimates, this level of exposure from only one site could cause approximately 12 cases of cancer and 116 genetic deaths over a hundred-year period.[16] Given that exposures could go on for thousands of years, that other estimates for cancer and death are much higher, and that the risk is likely to accelerate, the magnitude of possible deaths and cancers becomes quite high. Admittedly, the Hanford facility is geologically and technologically quite different from the proposed Yucca Mountain repository and from other facilities likely to be used in Europe. Nevertheless, government projections of future Hanford leaks suggest either that there is no way to control the releases, or that they are too expensive to contain. Either of these suggestions could be quite damning for permanent geological disposal. If human error helped amplify the risk at Hanford, as was documented in the previous chapter, then human error could likewise help amplify the risk at other sites. For all these reasons it is not obvious that the magnitude of hazards predicted even for the newest proposed facilities, such as Yucca Mountain, is acceptable. Nor is it clear that the risk associated with previous radwaste facilities is acceptable.

Value Judgments that
Risk Reductions Are Sufficient

Yet another faulty methodological value judgment often present in evaluations of repository risks is that by using very conservative design techniques and by reducing uncertainties as much as possible, these reductions will be sufficient to insure safety.[17] One problem with such a judgment is that in a situation where uncertainty is very great, as at Yucca Mountain, it is often not possible to know whether a given strategy is "conservative enough." Obviousy, in a situation that is quite dangerous, even the most conservative strategy may not be conservative enough. The most conservative strategy for hang gliding, motorcycle riding, or bungee jumping, for example, may not be conservative enough to insure adequate safety. Hence, there may not be good scientific reasons to assume that because assessment strategies for a repository are conservative, they insure adequate safety. One reason they may not is that given the heterogeneity of values for basic hydrogeological parameters at many sites, it appears that experts often believe that their assessments are conservative when they are not.[18] For example, one official DOE document admits that "generally, categories of processes or events that have a small probability of occurrence at the site will be eliminated from consideration."[19] After this statement, the DOE policy document enjoins scientists to choose assessment values such that "the realistically conservative analyses might use a conservative value that is within one standard deviation of the mean value."[20]

However, choosing a value that is within one standard deviation on either side of a mean value (for an accident probability) would include only approximately 68 percent of all the cases in the frequency distribution. It is hardly conservative to have an analysis that takes account of only 68 percent of the cases, particularly if the problems likely to arise come from outliers, events associated with catastrophic failures of the repository. For example, we know that there are 8 orders of magnitude of variation in the saturated hydraulic conductivities of the various tuffs at Yucca Mountain.[21] If one takes a number—one standard deviation above the mean values—as a conservative estimate of the saturated hydraulic conductivity of the tuff, this might not take adequate account of repository safety. This allegedly conservative number might represent only 3 or 4 orders of magnitude of variation in the tuff. The remaining 32 percent of values that were not considered might include the tuffs for which saturated hydraulic conductivity was even 4 or 5 orders of magnitude higher. Hence, choosing an allegedly conservative value, up to one standard deviation above the mean, does not represent the extremes that could actually occur at Yucca Mountain and at other sites. And if not, then the methodological value judgment—that risk reductions and conservative techniques are sufficiently conservative—could lead to errors in the final assessment of several orders of magnitude.

It is especially difficult to know that a given repository design is conservative enough, or that a given risk reduction is large enough, because the DOE has contradictory "fundamental goals" in meeting regulatory requirements for safety at Yucca Mountain. Its allegedly conservative stance toward safety is undercut both by schedule constraints and by economics (see the next chapter for further discussion of this point). The DOE explicitly seeks to "minimize financial and other resource commitments" but also to "protect public health and safety."[22] Likewise, its two other (of four) goals are to "comply with applicable laws and regulations" and yet to "maintain an aggressive schedule." Obviously, short-term economy is at odds with health expenditures, and following health regulations is at odds with maintaining a tight schedule. The fact that these four goals conflict makes it less likely that assessors can make a reasonable methodological value judgment that designs are conservative enough or that risk reductions are great enough. Given these four goals, government officials could justify even contradictory policies. Moreover, much the same situation is likely to occur at permanent waste facilities in other nations. There is always a tension between safety and economic efficiency. Given this tension, it is questionable whether repository siting, design, and management will always reflect adequate risk reductions.

Of course, it is important to point out that, in some cases, actual risk assessments at Yucca Mountain have *not* been conservative. For example, in an assessment of seismic and faulting hazards,[23] scientists have based their designs on the assumption that the repository can withstand quakes that occur once every 10,000 years. Because moderate quakes are likely to occur during this period, and stronger quakes approximately once every 100,000 years, if the calculations were wrong by only 1 order of magnitude, then the repository might not be able to withstand a likely quake. Hence, such designs appear to need even more conservatism, more than allowing for an order of magnitude of error. Because risk assessments characterized by incomplete data on long-term accident frequency (see chapter 4) are typically wrong by 4 to 6 orders of magnitude,[24] it might be more reasonable to make the value judgment that allowing for errors of higher orders of magnitude represents a more conservative stance.

To some extent, the DOE itself is responsible for failure to design and perform repository assessments that are adequately conservative. After admitting that its Yucca Mountain approaches to geohydrology, geochemistry, and waste containers were not conservative, the DOE officially defended its "realism" by arguing that "evidence available" has been "sufficient to generate considerable, if not complete, confidence in the minds of responsible investigators."[25] In other words, the DOE simply appealed to its own authority to defend its lack of conservatism. Later in the volume, we shall discuss appeals to authority. For the present, it is sufficient to note that such appeals provide no empirical evidence to justify nonconservative quantitative risk assessment (QRA).

Value Judgments that Worst-case Hazards Are Not Credible

Another "nonconservative" methodological value judgment that occurs frequently in risk assessments like those being done at Yucca Mountain is that various worst-case hazards are not credible and need not be taken into account. For example, although a few scientists use models so conservative that they may overestimate the risk at Yucca Mountain,[26] many assessors fail to examine worst-case models. They postulate radioactive waste accidents, for example, none of which could result in violation of the radiation-dose limits set by the NRC. Likewise, they frequently claim that fracture flow of groundwater and volcanic activity are not credible at Yucca Mountain and, therefore, they need not take these events into account, even though both could rapidly increase the transport time of radioactive leachate; or, they claim that fracture flow predominates over matrix flow.[27] It is highly questionable, however, whether so many worst-case events can be dismissed as "not credible." Even Nuclear Regulatory Commission (NRC) officials note that a violation of regulations could occur at Yucca Mountain if fracture flow caused groundwater travel time, from the repository to the water table, of less than a thousand years.[28]

The reluctance of some individual assessors to consider worst cases follows in part from the position of the DOE. DOE researchers typically do not consider worst cases. In assessing the proposed Hanford site for high-level waste, the DOE assumed, for example, that a worst case involved a 50 percent, not a 100 percent, break of the Grand Coulee Dam, and that a hundred-year flood, rather than the maximum probable flood, was the worst case. The DOE also assumed no vertical fracture flow at Hanford. At Yucca Mountain, the DOE made the same value judgments in avoiding consideration of worst cases. Although weapons tests have caused fracturing and earthquakes at the proposed Yucca Mountain site, the DOE assumed that no worst-case radionuclide releases could occur, either because of these effects of testing, or because of interrupting repository activities in the future, whenever testing occurred. The DOE likewise assumed that radioactive waste at Yucca Mountain would be retrievable for fifty years, but not afterwards.[29] Facility managers could not prevent some worst-case radionuclide releases, however, if the waste is retrievable for only fifty years. Likewise, the DOE has assumed that the worst-case earthquake is one that might occur only once every ten thousand years, even though the site will be hazardous for much longer than ten thousand years.[30]

One apparent rationale for not considering worst cases is that, in general, the DOE claims that events whose probability is less than 10^{-5} per year are not credible.[31] However, an event having an annual probability of 10^{-5} obviously has a quite high probability of occurring, 10^{-2}, during the thousand years that the Yucca Mountain radwaste would be most lethal. Given such high probabilities, it appears that the DOE assumes not only that present persons have no right to be protected against worst-case accidents, but also that future generations may not have a right to be protected against even more likely catastrophes. Otherwise, DOE analyses would investigate worst-case accidents in the light of both present and future time periods. As we showed in the previous chapter, the DOE also fails to consider human-caused worst-case accidents by virtue of the fact that it subscribes to the value judgment that human error is not a significant contributor to risk. For all the reasons already discussed, there are grounds for believing that it is not credible to discount human-caused worst-case accidents. Moreover, for the DOE to claim that all military activities and terrorism related to Yucca Mountain are not credible is to beg the question, because there is no way of knowing what activities will be likely even one hundred years from now.

In situations like Yucca Mountain, failure to consider worst cases represents a very problematic value judgment, in part because some of the "worst cases" have actually occurred at U.S. radwaste facilities in the past. For example, at the Maxey Flats low-level radioactive waste facility already mentioned, risk assessors said that the shale was impermeable and that no migration of wastes would occur for thousands of years. They based their claim in part on the methodological value judgment that fracture flow was not possible at the site, and hence that the "worst case" of leachate migrating through fractures was not credible. However, there was flow through the hairline fractures, with consequent recharge to the groundwater at Maxey Flats, via precipitation, even though the entire system was shale and sandstone.[32] Hence, one of the "worst cases" happened at Maxey Flats. Analogously, as was already mentioned, there is a possibility that fracture flow and volcanism could occur at Yucca Mountain. These probabilities of occurrence seem high enough that it appears reasonable for anyone to consider them as part of a worst-case analysis.[33]

Even if the probabilities associated with parts of a worst-case analysis were not high, it might be reasonable to consider them at proposed facilities like Yucca Mountain simply because it is not possible to test the likelihood of a worst case and because the consequences of a worst-case repository incident could be so extreme. Often severity of consequences, not probability of occurrence, is so great that low-probability, high-consequence events merit detailed consideration.[34] And at possible sites like Yucca Mountain, the consequences could be severe. If there were little or no adsorption, thermally induced fractures, fracture flow, horizontal permeability, and significant seismic activity, catastrophic consequences could result; likewise, if there were no containment after two hundred years, if there were significant leaching at the repository, and if populations received hundreds to thousands of rems of radiation (either as a whole-body dose or as a bone dose), then catastrophic numbers of fatalities could occur.[35] These consequences—together with the uncertainties associated with long-term prediction and with the near worst cases that have occurred at places like Fernald and Maxey Flats—are arguably a sufficient basis for considering worst cases at permanent high-level repositories. And if so, then the value judgment—that worst cases are not credible—is highly questionable.

It is important to point out that even when assessors claim to be doing a worst-case analysis, often their methods are not sufficiently conservative to constitute a true worst case. For example, some analysts have claimed to be doing a worst-case analysis at Yucca Mountain, but then they have made assumptions that contradict the alleged severity of the case being considered. The DOE assumes, for instance, that in a worst-case transportation accident, no canisters will be breached and no release of radiation will occur.[36] In making such an assumption, the DOE assessors are again making the questionable methodological value judgment that a true worst case is not credible and does not need to be considered. In the case of waste canisters, in particular, the value judgment is highly suspect because, as was already mentioned, in some experiments all canisters of the required reference material exposed to a one-year test in groundwater and tuff at the expected 200 degrees Celsius have failed and showed stress-corrosion cracking.[37] Moreover, accidents worse than those predicted for catastrophic canister failure have already occurred.[38]

Ignoring worst cases is also questionable from an ethical point of view because it fails to guard against false negatives, against erroneously assuming something could cause no harm, even though it might do so. In pure science, it is often reasonable to guard against false positives, and to risk false negatives. To do so in cases like Yucca Mountain, however, is typically judged to be ethically wrong because it fails to take account of persons' rights to equal protection, due process, consent, and welfare.[39] In other words, it is arguable that in failing to guard against false negatives by considering worst cases, and in attempting primarily to avoid false positives, assessors at potential sites like Yucca Mountain incorrectly place the burden of risk on possible radwaste victims rather than on supporters of the repository.[40] Although there is no time to do so here, it can easily be shown that the public has the right to protection against uncertain risks; therefore, risk evaluators, in a situation of uncertainty, ought to risk false positives rather than false negatives. Any other procedure would fail to give the highest priority to protection of human welfare, and it would err ethically by using humans as means to short-term economic ends (see the previous note). Moreover, contrary to many repository-related methodological value judgments, members of the geology community recognize that the most protective prevention strategies for an aquifer are based on worst-case scenarios.[41] For all these reasons, the value judgment that one need not consider worst-case risks (at sites like Yucca Mountain) is questionable.

Value Judgments that Average Risks Are Acceptable

One of the most protective and conservative strategies for evaluating groundwater and radionuclide transport at permanent geological disposal sites is to avoid using mere average velocities for groundwater and instead to try to evaluate the risk of even the most pessimistic groundwater-transport cases. One of the most questionable methodological value judgments at Yucca Mountain, however, is that figures for average risks provide an acceptable measure of hazards. This value judgment about acceptability is questionable, even from an inductive or retroductive point of view, because averages hide some very high hazards among low ones and instead lump them all together. Even a small probability of a very great risk is cause for concern, apart from what the average probability is, because the averages themselves are often misleading. For example, as mentioned in the previous chapter, both the DOE and its risk assessors at Yucca Mountain have calculated the *average* or mean groundwater travel time from the repository to the water table yet noted that, because of uncertainties and heterogeneities in the data, the actual travel time of groundwater could be as much as 100 percent higher than the mean or average value.[42] Some Yucca Mountain risk assessors also claim, for example, that the groundwater travel time to the water table from the repository has a mean of 43,000 years.[43] This figure is misleadingly reassuring because approximately 1 percent of the calculated groundwater travel times are less than 10,000 years, and the travel times for some rock units are between 3,915 and 15,020 years.[44] Indeed, as was already mentioned, some assessors argue that the travel times could be less than 1,000 years.[45]

Given groundwater travel times on the order of 1,000, 3,000, and 15,000 years, it is misleading, if not incorrect, to argue that a *mean* or *average* groundwater travel time of 43,000 represents a meaningful or accurate figure. These shorter groundwater travel times could be enough to cause massive problems of cancer and contamination. In other words, the problem with using averages is that unless the values are clustered, the averages can mislead one about the allegedly long length of time for radwaste migration and about the allegedly high margin of safety.[46] In cases like Yucca Mountain, it is difficult to confirm that the values are clustered, as is required for legitimate use of averages, because there is no long frequency record for radwaste migration events. Also, because the length of time at issue is extraordinarily long, and because there is so much uncertainty in the numbers anyway, it is difficult to meet the conditions necessary for use of averages.

As has already been mentioned, the saturated hydraulic conductivities of the tuff vary by 8 orders of magnitude at Yucca Mountain,[47] and there are similar ranges of heterogeneities and uncertainties for other geological and hydraulic variables, both at the Yucca Mountain site and at proposed repository sites in other nations. The average hydraulic conductivity of different Yucca Mountain rock units such as the Tiva Canyon Unit and the Paintbrush Unit, for example, often varies by as much as 4 or 5 orders of magnitude.[48] Estimating saturated flow and aggregating units with such widely ranging values for hydraulic conductivity, in order to obtain average groundwater travel time from the repository to the water table, could be quite misleading, in part because solubility limits and retardation factors for radioactive leachate "are site and species dependent."[49] Hence, when a risk assessor or hydrologist claims that the travel time of groundwater from the repository to the water table could be from 3 years to 420,000 years,[50] using the average travel time makes no sense because the values are so widely dispersed. Likewise, when assessors claim, as they have at Yucca Mountain, that "no radioactivity from the repository will migrate even to the water table immediately beneath the repository for about

30,000 years,"[51] the term "about"—like the "average" groundwater travel time—is not useful because it obscures the shortest, easiest migration times, and these are the ones of greatest concern. If one is worrying about the easiest way to breach safety, or the quickest route for radwaste migration, both of which are necessary to protect public health and environmental welfare, then average travel times are meaningless. They give a false sense of security. Hence, it is highly questionable for assessors to use average risk figures as they have at Yucca Mountain. Averages do not kill people. Maverick events do so, however, and a number of maverick events are possible at proposed sites like Yucca Mountain.

Discussion of average travel times of groundwater and average percolation, precipitation, and infiltration was also a problem that helped to create the fiasco at the Maxey Flats low-level radwaste facility. The mean precipitation at the site is 45.4 inches per year, several times greater than that at Yucca Mountain. The mean figure is misleading, however, because massive rainfall over a short period, rather than the average annual rainfall, was the main contributor to the overflowing leachate and the contamination of groundwater at Maxey Flats. Extreme events of low frequency, such as a deluge of several inches of rain in several hours, perform the work of several thousand years of erosion, infiltration, and groundwater migration.[52] Hence, the value judgment that averages can accurately represent such extremes can lead to unpredicted groundwater or radionuclide migration at radioactive waste disposal sites.

Value Judgments that More Recent Assessments Are More Reliable

Yet another questionable methodological value judgment is that current state-of-the-art risk assessments, because of advances in hydrogeological modeling, are more reliable than those that have been done in the past. Indeed, DOE officials maintain "that it is unfair to judge past practices by today's more stringent environmental standards." Moreover, they say that the Yucca Mountain project has "many layers of external oversight, unlike the weapons facilities that were cloaked in secrecy from the start."[53] Admittedly, the DOE is correct in claiming that the latest risk studies, like the Yucca Mountain assessments, will be evaluated by the highest standards available; the

NAS says that the Yucca Mountain methodology is "state of the art."[54] For example, the Yucca Mountain assessments will be scrutinized by the Nuclear Waste Technical Review Board, a panel of experts recommended by the National Academy of Sciences and appointed by the president. Moreover, the facility will be licensed by the Nuclear Regulatory Commission. For all these reasons, both the DOE and their assessors maintain that the Yucca Mountain studies will be more reliable than those done in the past. They argue that the proposed Yucca Mountain facility will not fall victim to the same problems that have plagued other radioactive waste repositories, because the Nevada site is being assessed with more care than have the earlier installations such as Hanford, Idaho Falls, Fernald, Maxey Flats, and so on.

Optimistic value judgments about the reliability of current studies, like those at Yucca Mountain, are questionable in part, however, because even the best authorities often make errors. Indeed, if Cooke, Kahneman, Tversky, and others are correct, even highly trained mathematicians and scientists systematically underestimate risks and exhibit an overconfidence bias; moreover, many of the methods commonly used to generate 90-percent confidence bands fail to represent uncertainty adequately.[55] Methodological value judgments that risk assessments (like those done for Yucca Mountain) are sufficiently reliable likewise are questionable, even on inductive and retroductive grounds, because they ignore the pervasiveness of human error (see the previous chapter). There have been serious problems with most DOE assessments and with 1,061 other DOE facilities such as Fernald, Hanford, Idaho Falls, Maxey Flats, and Savannah River. Moreover, the period of time for which Yucca Mountain assessments must be done is longer than that for any other project ever assessed. There are also generally less data on radioactive waste risks than for other hazards (like those from nuclear fission reactors) commonly studied in the past.[56]

Another problem with even the best studies of contemporary repository risks is that many waste facility threats are already at or near the limit of acknowledged unacceptability. For example, after approximately one thousand years, the Yucca Mountain risk, as we shall discuss shortly, is supposed to be of the same order of magnitude as the radiological risk from unmined uranium ore. If this claim is in error by as much as some other probabilistic risk assessments have been—6 orders of magnitude—then Yucca Mountain might cause as many as 10^{13} to 10^{14} fatal cancers over a period of 100,000 years, or 100 million to 1 billion fatal cancers per year.[57] Although such figures may appear hyperbolic, they are consistent with the ranges of error typically found in QRA. Moreover, given that repository-risk numbers, like those supplied by the U.S. government for Yucca Mountain, have not been confirmed, it is highly questionable to assume that current assessments are much more reliable than those that have been done in the past. Besides, the consequences of over-optimism about the risk figures could lead to much human suffering and death.

Although the first and only permanent U.S. disposal site for high-level radwaste is supposed to be at Yucca Mountain, and although assessments there are presumably the best available anywhere, these studies may not be more reliable than other comparable risk assessments. In fact, contrary to the earlier NAS claim, they do not always employ the best available methodological techniques because the work is being done far more quickly than risk assessments of other proposed radwaste facilities throughout the world. Reviewers have spoken of the "potentially disastrous schedule" at Yucca Mountain, and DOE officials themselves have admitted that their "schedule is success oriented."[58] Also, the United States uses less conservative regulatory guidelines than do European countries (see sections earlier in this chapter). As a result, the United States has perhaps the most troubled radwaste program in the world. At least part of the reason for these troubles is that "U.S. rigorous time schedules [for assessment] are inconsistent with all other countries surveyed."[59] The United States has the earliest deadline for a high-level-radwaste repository opening, earlier than the deadline of France, the United Kingdom, Sweden, Japan, Canada, and Germany—and the United States also has the shortest in-situ research time.[60] All of these factors give one a basis for questioning the DOE's methodological value judgment that the Yucca Mountain risk assessments are/will be more reliable than other typical studies.

Value Judgments that Utilitarian Risk Theories Are Just

Risk assessors who assume that they need not consider worst-case risks and who judge the acceptability of risk on the basis of average hazards to persons—as a number of Yucca Mountain assessors have done—also make another important value judgment. This judgment is that utilitarian theories of risk distribution are just or acceptable. Risk assessors who use "efficient" (rather than the most reliable) sampling methods and simulations also subscribe to the value judgment that risk may be assessed and distributed on a utilitarian basis.[61] Utilitarian theories direct us to provide the greatest safety/welfare or the least risk for the greatest number of persons. To subscribe to utilitarian theories represents a questionable value judgment because utilitarianism has a number of significant flaws, such as ignoring the welfare of some minority of persons.[62] One could instead subscribe to a great many alternative ethical theories in order to allocate the risk at proposed permanent repositories like Yucca Mountain. One could follow, for instance, a stewardship ethic,[63] according to which risk was distributed so as to provide the greatest care for the earth and its inhabitants. Or, one could subscribe to a Rawlsian ethic,[64] according to which risk was distributed to benefit the least-well-off persons. Likewise, one could follow a Paretian ethic, or a libertarian ethic,[65] and so on.

Perhaps the most important alternative to the utilitarian value judgments exhibited in virtually all repository assessments, including the Yucca Mountain studies, is to espouse some version of egalitarian views. Egalitarians follow the ethical theory that one ought to treat persons equally with respect to distribution of social risks, costs, and benefits.[66] On the egalitarian view, members of future generations ought not bear more risk than present persons, and those who live near proposed sites like Yucca Mountain ought not bear more risk than those who live farther away from the facility. Indeed, according to egalitarian views, radioactive risk ought to be distributed equally with respect to states, nations, generations, and social groups. Egalitarian ethical theories require not only a substantive, equal distribution of risk, but they also require that risk decisions be made according to principles of procedural equity—so that all persons with a stake in the decisions have an equal voice, and so that democratic procedure does not violate the interests of any minority.[67]

Investigating the plausibility of the utilitarian—as opposed to egalitarian—value judgments evident in many repository risk assessments is important because substantive moral and political views provide guidance for the distribution of risks in a community.[68] Moreover, economists and philosophers have shown that policy decisions are highly sensitive to assumptions about what ethical theories ought to be employed. The same actions can be shown to be defensible, for example, given a benefit-cost analysis that presupposes Pareto value judgments, but indefensible given a benefit-cost analysis that presupposes Rawlsian ethical value judgments, and vice versa.[69] Hence, because policy conclusions—like decisions about the suitability of Yucca Mountain for a high-level radwaste repository—are highly sensitive to ethical assumptions and value judgments, it is important to assess those value judgments carefully.

The major flaw in utilitarian value judgments is that, on grounds of serving the good of some majority, they often permit some minority of persons to be hurt. They may allow various groups of persons to be treated inequitably, on grounds of utility, efficiency, or expediency. Egalitarian views, on the other hand, sanction equal treatment of all persons, rather than simply using persons—perhaps violating their rights—in order to achieve some alleged social goal. Applied to high-level radioactive-waste repositories, the utilitarian-versus-egalitarian issue focuses on distribution of risk. Fears about inequitable or utilitarian risk distributions are part of what drives the NIMBY (not in my back yard) syndrome.[70] Few persons want to be members of the minority (like Nevadans) bearing the risk for society as a whole. Because egalitarian theories emphasize providing equal protection, equal opportunity, and equal access to due process, it is arguable, from an ethical point of view, that they are preferable to utilitarian theories. The main inadequacy of utilitarian theories of justice and risk distribution is that they fail to provide equal justice and equal treatment to all victims of risk, especially persons likely to be harmed by radioactive waste. For this reason, egalitarians charge that utilitarian risk-distribution theories inequitably use persons merely as means to the ends of other persons.[71]

One of the main vehicles for utilitarian theories of risk distribution is benefit-cost analysis. This technique is particularly controversial when applied to environmental and public health issues like Yucca Mountain, because it is questionable whether utilitarians are correct in believing that benefits to a majority of persons are sometimes able to offset extreme harms to some minority of persons, perhaps those living in a certain place, such as near a hazardous waste facility. In other words, it is not clear that utilitarians are correct in presupposing either that "everyone has a price" or that it is morally acceptable to trade safety for efficiency or for monetary savings.[72] Typically it is cheaper, for example, to employ utilitarian risk-distribution theories in risk assessment and management because one need not worry about less likely "worst-case" situations against which it is more expensive to provide protection.[73]

An especially onerous aspect of benefit-cost and other utilitarian theories of evaluating risk is their implicit assumption that everyone does not have equal rights to protection against societal hazards, and that risk decisions ought to be made on grounds of efficiency or expediency. In other words, a central assumption implicit in utilitarian theories is that some minorities, some victims of risk, are expendable, provided that the group as a whole will benefit.[74] Although proponents of benefit-cost analysis and other utilitarian risk theories defend them as realistic and workable, opponents claim that they violate both justice as well as the Bill of Rights and the notion of equal treatment under law. Hence, the utilitarian presuppositions in risk evaluation are highly questionable,[75] especially insofar as they sanction violating the rights of some subset (or minority) of persons to protection against risks. Moreover, in the case of permanent geological disposal, it could well be that majority, as well as minority, rights are threatened. Members of future generations are likely to represent a majority of persons, and current beneficiaries of processes that have created radwastes may represent only a minority. If so, then repositories that threaten members of future generations may not be defensible even on utilitarian grounds.

Apart from the ethical basis for questioning utilitarian value judgments about risk acceptability at proposed repositories like Yucca Mountain, there are also practical, inductive reasons for questioning such judgments: they result in safety hazards. In the past, officials of government agencies like the DOE have used utilitarian value judgments of risk—for example, in failing to make safety improvements because of cost considerations—and these utilitarian judgments have resulted in severe radioactive contamination and threats to the public health and safety. In fact, this utilitarian evaluation of risks is exactly what occurred at the Fernald nuclear-feed-materials plant in Ohio. The top DOE officials told the managers of the plant to continue operating as they were, even though they were breaking environmental laws and threatening human life. The DOE rationale apparently was utilitarian: despite threats to nearby residents, it allegedly would have been too expensive to stop production, break the schedule, and correct the safety deficiencies.[76] The fact that utilitarian value judgments, like those apparently made at Fernald, have led to catastrophes in the past is arguably grounds for not subscribing to the same assumptions in current evaluations of repository risks. But if assessors ought not subscribe to utilitarian theories of distributing repository risk because such theories fail to provide equal treatment and equal justice to all persons, then it is difficult to see how assessors could justify permanent geological disposal of high-level radioactive wastes. Such disposal, especially after the radwaste canisters have been breached, clearly puts members of future generations at greater risk than present persons. Indeed, given the current regulations for canister lifetimes, for example, it appears that there is no way for permanent, high-level disposal *not* to place inequitable burdens on members of future generations. Hence, to the degree that such inequity is avoidable, through other means of managing high-level radwaste, permanent geological disposal is ethically questionable.

Value Judgments about Single-site Studies

Apart from the general ethical reasons that evaluations of all permanent repository risks are likely to be questionable, there are several specific reasons that evaluations of U.S. risks associated with permanent disposal are questionable. One problem is that U.S. assessors and policymakers have chosen to evaluate only one proposed high-level site. In late 1987, the U.S. Congress passed an amendment to the Nuclear Waste Policy Act of 1982. This amendment mandates that Yucca Mountain, Nevada is the only remaining potential site for the nation's first, commercial, high-level radioactive waste repository.[77] If Yucca Mountain is found to be unsuitable, then the Department of Energy is required to make recommendations to Congress within six months and then to take steps to negotiate with a state or an Indian nation willing to host a monitored retrievable storage facility.

One methodological value judgment underlying all the Yucca Mountain evaluations is that suitability of a site for high-level radwaste can be determined by assessing only one location (Yucca Mountain), rather than by comparative assessments of a number of sites. This value judgment is particularly problematic because it allows assessors and policymakers to decide upon a "suitable," rather than an "optimal," site.[78] Moreover, a number of researchers have charged that the Yucca Mountain location was chosen for evaluation from the nine original sites because of politico-economic expediency and manipulation, rather than because of demonstrated geological superiority.[79] At the very least, this methodological value judgment—about single-site studies—requires one to assume that an adequate risk assessment can be accomplished, even if there is no alternative for comparison. It requires one to assume that the political situation surrounding the one-site choice does not breed an undesirable consensus.[80] It could be, as R. R. Loux, director of the Nuclear Waste Project Office for the state of Nevada puts it: choosing only one site, Nevada, "sets the stage for a railroad job."[81] Other assessors say explicitly that the facility is being "forced" on the state of Nevada.[82] Also, as we have already noted in chapter 1, 80 percent of Nevadans oppose the repository.

Performing an adequate risk assessment, in the absence of alternative sites, is particularly problematic because there is no perfect location; because perfect containment of the waste, in perpetuity, is impossible; and because long-term predictions are quite uncertain. Hence, in the absence of perfect containment and certain predictions, conservative and comparative assessments surely are required. Following similar reasoning, members of the European nuclear community view the one-site strategy of the United States and Germany as "highly vulnerable."[83] Without comparative analyses of other sites, some assessors maintain that there is a declining confidence that permanent geological facilities for high-level radwaste will become available anytime in the near future. Availability is unlikely, since there are many problems associated with Yucca Mountain, even though it is the only proposed site.[84] Moreover, to study only one site appears to beg the question of site suitability and to "put the cart (the site decision) before the horse (the site evaluation)." As evaluators from the state of Nevada point out, assessing only one site appears to put the evaluation process backwards: selecting a site for nongeological reasons, then making the geological evaluations appear favorable.[85] Indeed, given DOE's inadequate analysis of proposed sites,[86] it is arguable that the question has already been begged.[87] In a one-site political environment, it is extraordinarily difficult to believe that assessors could discover that the site is not fit for a repository and then return to Congress for further instructions.[88] One reason why the assessors are unlikely to do so is that they will be able to define what is fit, and they will not be forced to answer the questions: "More fit than what other sites? More fit in what other respects?"[89] Hence, the single-site assessment is based on a methodological value judgment—and perhaps a political judgment—with questionable scientific, ethical, and policy assumptions and consequences.

There is also some evidence in the Maxey Flats case that once assessors get into the business of evaluating a single site—rather than doing comparative evaluation of several sites in order to determine which is best—the assessment inevitably becomes biased or misused by vested political interests. The fractured, heterogenous Kentucky site was chosen for political reasons,[90] in part because there was no open competition among alternative sites. It is arguable that the offsite migration might have been prevented, and another location chosen, were the Maxey Flats competition open to a variety of proposed sites. The same conclusion could hold true for the nation's first permanent high-level radwaste facility. It too ought to be part of an extensive study of a number of candidate sites.

Value Judgments that Full
Liability Does Not Promote Safety

Another questionable risk-evaluation judgment regarding proposed U.S. repositories is that the facilities should have liability limitations. In response to the states' recommendations for unlimited strict liability for any nuclear waste program or incident,[91] the DOE position is that "these activities should enjoy indemnity protection equivalent to other nuclear programs."[92] Other U.S. nuclear programs currently have a liability limit that is less than 3 percent of the government-calculated costs of the Chernobyl accident,[93] and Chernobyl was not a worst-case incident.[94]

The value judgment that Yucca Mountain liability should be severely limited, as it is for other aspects of the U.S. nuclear program, is highly questionable for at least five reasons. *First*, liability is a well-known incentive for behavior that is appropriate. If persons know that they are likely to be held responsible in full for their actions and their consequences, then they are more likely to behave in responsible ways. Not to tie responsibility to liability is analogous to not tying penalties or enforcement mechanisms to the law. Both situations, penalties and full liability, might help to generate behavior that is more socially acceptable. Hence, it is questionable for nuclear-related industries to enjoy a liability limit. Likewise, it is questionable for the 1988 Price-Anderson Amendments Act to exempt certain DOE contractors—those working on Yucca Mountain—from the $100,000 penalty for each violation of safety rules.[95] Without such a penalty, contractors have an incentive for violating safety rules.

Second, if the Yucca Mountain operations are as safe as risk assessors and the DOE proclaim, then the government and DOE have nothing to lose from full and strict liability. Hence, if Yucca Mountain is safe, then there is no compelling argument for limiting liability. Likewise, the main reason for limiting liability at Yucca Mountain is the belief that the facility would not be safe and that large damage actions are credible. But if large damage actions are credible, then Yucca Mountain is arguably not safe. This means that assessors cannot consistently argue both that Yucca Mountain would be safe and that a liability limit is needed. Of course, proponents of limited liability might respond that the limit is needed to deter nuisance lawsuits by irresponsible persons. This response is questionable, however, because protection against nuisance lawsuits argues against any liability whatsoever, and such an argument is clearly ethically and legally suspect, since persons ought to be liable for their actions.

Third, it is questionable whether government officials should have the right to limit persons' due process rights under the law. In arguing for limiting Yucca Mountain liability, the DOE is arguing for limiting due process rights to less than 3 percent of the known costs of nuclear accidents that have already occurred,[96] as was just mentioned. This means that most of the costs of a radwaste accident, by law (the Price-Anderson Act) likely would be borne by its victims rather than by its perpetrators. A maximum credible radioactive waste accident would greatly exceed $6 billion, the liability limit set in 1988 by U.S. law. The Chernobyl costs are expected to reach $283–358 billion. In fact, the Chernobyl costs may go higher, unless more persons are evacuated.[97] Although the 1988 Price-Anderson Amendments Act allows the liability limit to be adjusted for inflation and for the number of nuclear reactors, the adjustment formula insures that the figure will remain low. For example, for the 110 U.S. nuclear reactors existing in the United States in 1990, given a maximum charge of $63 million (annually adjusted for inflation) per licensee/reactor, the total U.S. liability limit for nuclear- or radiation-related incidents in 1990 was $7.2 billion, less than 5 percent of Chernobyl costs. Whether for nuclear accidents generally or for Yucca Mountain specifically, it is highly questionable whether the government has the right to limit liability and yet to maintain that all persons have a right to due process. In imposing the bulk of radwaste risks on victims and not on perpetrators, and in arguing that a citizen does not have a right to full redress of grievances, even when the source of the problem is the government itself, the DOE has made a highly questionable value judgment. Not to have the right to full redress seems both unconstitutional and inequitable. Moreover, it may also be imprudent, since the NAS has itself criticized the methods used in the DOE radwaste program.[98] Hence, there is reason to make the value judgment that there ought to be full, strict liability at Yucca Mountain. As one researcher put it, "coverage under the Price-Anderson Act is clearly inadequate. Congress must take another look at the matter."[99]

A *fourth* reason to question the value judgment that Yucca Mountain liability ought to be the same as that for other nuclear programs is that on the DOE's own admission, much more is known about risks associated with nuclear fission reactors than is known about high-level radioactive waste.[100] Indeed, the nuclear waste problem has been unsolved since the beginning of commercial fission reactors in the United States in 1956. It is not reasonable to argue that the liability provisions ought to be the same for two risks (nuclear reactors and radioactive waste), when one of the risks is much less well known than the other.

Fifth, as we have already mentioned, the DOE record of safety has been extremely poor in the past. It includes withholding information from Congress and the public, using biased assessors, avoiding competent peer review, violating environmental and safety laws and regulations, and failing to make corrections once serious environmental problems have been noted.[101] Given DOE's record, there appears to be a great need for full and strict liability in any DOE installation such as Yucca Mountain. This need for full liability is underscored by the fact that citizens in areas surrounding DOE facilities have repeatedly asked for full liability coverage, as have residents near the proposed DOE waste facilities. Moreover, there are grounds for such citizen requests. When the DOE nuclear materials plant in Fernald, Ohio was discovered to have serious, life-threatening problems of radioactive contamination and to have violated the law—causing worker deaths and cancers among nearby members of the public—DOE officials retreated behind the doctrine of sovereign immunity in order to obtain protection from direct legal action by citizens.[102] In part because of this precedent, there is a need for full liability at Yucca Mountain and for penalties for safety violations by all contractors. Hence, there are ethical, political, legal, practical, and scientific grounds for challenging the value judgment that full and strict liability is not needed at Yucca Mountain.

Value Judgments that
High-Level Waste Is as Safe as Ore

Another problematic risk-evaluation judgment made in Yucca Mountain assessments is that after a thousand years, if the risks from high-level waste are approximately the same as those from naturally occurring ore bodies, then the risks from Yucca Mountain are acceptably low.[103] Like the other value judgments discussed earlier, this methodological value judgment appears implausible, in part because conclusions about risk acceptability do not follow deductively from premises about the level of naturally occurring risks. Even from an inductive or retroductive view of scientific method, this value judgment is questionable because it presupposes that what is normal (the risk from ore) is acceptable. Many "normal" risks, however, such as those from background radiation that cause tens of thousands of U.S. cancers per year, are neither ethically nor socially acceptable. Rather, we put up with them because they are not preventable. To assume that a preventable risk (like that from Yucca Mountain) is acceptable because it is the same order of magnitude as a naturally occurring risk (like that from uranium ore) begs the question of ethical acceptability. This presupposition is highly debatable, in part because we typically try to avoid even naturally occurring hazards. Moreover, what is "natural" is also not a desirable norm for hazards created by technology, because natural disasters typically have less serious social impacts than do technological catastrophes causing the same number of fatalities.[104] Also, what is normal is not necessarily *morally acceptable*, as G. E. Moore showed.[105] Many dangerous and undesirable things are statistically normal, such as cruelty or unfairness, but their normalcy does not mean they are morally acceptable. Nor does their normalcy mean that governments can impose additional "normal" risks on persons, simply because they already occur.[106] It is not obvious that in all cases a "normal" magnitude of risk is acceptable, regardless of whether it is preventable, regardless of whether persons give their free, informed consent to it, and regardless of whether it results in inequitable risk burdens. Indeed, according to some moral philosophers, to say that a normal magnitude of risk is acceptable, regardless of such ethical considerations, is to commit the "naturalistic fallacy,"[107] a classic difficulty in ethics. Regardless of whether one chooses to use terminology such as the "naturalistic fallacy," however, there is a problem with the assumption of DOE officials that "normal" levels of risk are ethically acceptable simply by virtue of their magnitude. For example, justifying probable population exposures to radiation at the proposed Yucca Mountain facility, DOE officials argued that the facility would meet regulatory guidelines because such exposures "would be small compared to natural background sources" of radiation.[108] Such a defense is questionable, of course, both because natural background exposures are quite harmful, and because the existence of a hazard does not alone justify creating further hazards.

An additional problem with the "naturalistic" value judgment—that a repository risk of the same order of magnitude as that from uranium ore is ethically acceptable—is that the risk from uranium ore is arguably not low. Using Environmental Protection Agency dosimetry and environmental-pathway models, some assessors have calculated the hazard from the ore as causing 100 to 1,000 fatal cancers per year.[109] If these government assessors are correct, and if this hazard is present for only 100,000 years, it could cause approximately 10 million to 100 million fatal cancers during that time—hardly a low risk. Indeed, it is so high that we arguably should search for ways to reduce the risk. Hence, it is questionable whether one ought to make the value judgment that a repository risk of the same magnitude as that from uranium ore is acceptable.

Another difficulty with using the uranium ore criterion is that most assessors of the hazards associated with high-level radwaste admittedly underestimate the risk. They typically ignore, for example, the ingrowth of Ra-226 and other radionuclides in the long-lived decay schemes stemming from the uranium and plutonium in the wastes. Ra-226 has its maximum concentration 100,000 to 200,000 years after it has been removed from the reactor. In an ore deposit, however, the amount of Ra-226 initially present would be only that quantity produced by the decay of the U-238. From 30,000 years on, concentrations of Ra-226 in the high-level waste would be larger than those in the ore, because the waste contains large amounts of Pu-238 and U-234, both of which are parent nuclides of Ra-226. As these parent nuclides decay, they produce large quantities of Ra-226. In the ore, however, only U-238 creates Ra-226, which is removed rapidly because of solubility. This means that concentrations of Ra-226 from the ore would be similar to those from high-level wastes only during the first years of the repository and only about one mile from the site.[110] Hence, even if the risk from ore were an ethically acceptable touchstone for high-level sites like Yucca Mountain, it is not obvious that the Yucca Mountain risk would be even as low as that from ore. For all these reasons, the value judgment—that the Yucca Mountain risk is acceptable because it is likely to be of the same order of magnitude as that from ore—is questionable on both factual and ethical grounds.

Conclusion

Judgments about how to evaluate the risk posed by permanent geological disposal of high-level radioactive wastes are sometimes highly questionable, in part because they are judgments about methodological, political, social, and ethical values. To the degree that these value judgments are questionable, we in the United States should revise some of our notions about the desirability of single-site studies, the acceptability of limited liability for waste accidents, and the safety of repositories whose long-term hazards are roughly the same as those associated with uranium ore.

Other judgments about evaluating the risks of permanent disposal, however, do not call into question merely U.S. repository assessments and policies. Because such judgments appear unavoidable whenever one defends the permanent disposal option, the implausibility of these value judgments challenges the desirability of siting any permanent geological facilities for high-level nuclear waste. If any repository is assessed and sited on the basis of the value judgments that *magnitude* alone determines risk acceptability, that *average* groundwater-travel times define safety, and that *utilitarian* risk distributions are ethically defensible, then those assessments are likely to err because they tend to sanction unjust distributions of repository risks. Moreover, it appears impossible to site permanent geological facilities without thereby imposing a much greater, and therefore inequitable, risk burden on future generations. Because of this inequity, there are strong ethical grounds, at present, for arguing against permanent, geological disposal of high-level radioactive wastes. (In subsequent chapters, we shall argue that there are safer, more ethical alternatives—at least at present—to permanent disposal). Members of future generations have no direct way to exercise either their due process rights against earlier generations or their free consent to geological disposal. However, they might be able to exercise their rights to equal treatment and their rights to know the radwaste dangers facing them, provided that the wastes were perpetually monitored and retrievable rather than permanently geologically entombed. In any case, our repository policy ought not impose an inequitable risk burden on them. As members of future generations, they are almost completely vulnerable to whatever actions we in the present choose for them. The greater their vulnerability, the less defensible are the actions of those who could victimize them.

6

Problematic Inferences in
in Assessing Repository Risks

In 1962, scientists calculated the risks associated with a proposed U.S. site for shallow land burial of transuranics and low-level radioactive wastes. Representatives from industry and their consultants praised the (Maxey Flats) Kentucky location and calculated that if plutonium were buried there, it would take twenty-four thousand years to migrate one-half inch. They said that "the possibility of subsurface migration offsite is nonexistent."[1] More conservative assessors and geologists—from the U.S. Geological Survey and the Environmental Protection Agency—claimed that it would take many hundreds of years for the radionuclides to migrate offsite.[2] The migration rate is important, because Maxey Flats contains more plutonium (in curies) than any other commercial repository in the world,[3] and it has the second-highest total radioactivity in curies of all low-level sites in the United States.[4] Yet, only ten years after opening the facility, plutonium and other radionuclides were discovered two miles offsite,[5] causing the facility to be closed. The geological predictions of the site operators, Nuclear Engineering Company (NECO), now called U.S. Ecology, were wrong by as much as *6 orders of magnitude*.

One of the many questions raised by this case is what we can learn about methods of risk assessment on the basis of our mistakes at Maxey Flats and at other radwaste facilities. Although this analysis does not attempt to draw comparisons between two sites (like Maxey Flats and Yucca Mountain) with different physical attributes, missions, and types of radwastes, various sites can be compared with respect to their use of risk assessment. How risk assessors handle expert judgment, uncertainty, limited information, long time frames, and the process of evaluation at one site provides valuable comparative information for other sites. Can we do some Monday-morning quarterbacking about earlier assessments of nuclear waste repositories? Can we thereby learn how to improve both our risk assessments and our policies for dealing with high-level radioactive wastes? Although low-level sites like Maxey Flats might seem to have little to teach us about high-level facilities, as we argued in chapter 4 (see the section on modeling fractured media), there are a number of important lessons to be learned from failures like Maxey Flats. One of the most important of these lessons is that risk assessment, in general, and repository siting, in particular, exhibit a number of characteristic strengths and weaknesses. Knowing these strengths and weaknesses could help prevent errors like those that have occurred at Maxey Flats.

For phenomena for which the data, models, or probabilities are uncertain—as we mentioned in earlier chapters—scientists claim that uncertainties of 6 orders of magnitude are "not unusual" in quantitative risk assessment (QRA).[6] A famous study of the siting of LNG (liquefied natural gas) terminals in four countries showed that widely varying risk estimates for the same event are pervasive; in Oxnard, California, for instance, reputable hazard assessments (of the annual chance of dying in a liquefied natural gas accident) differed by 3 orders of magnitude.[7] Likewise, current U.S. government predictions for the likelihood of a Three-Mile-Island-type accident differ by 2 orders of magnitude.[8] Other cases are much the same; they suggest that scientific predictions and risk estimates are sometimes laden with enormous uncertainties. However, for phenomena characterized by accurate and more complete data, such as automobile accidents, QRA involves fewer uncertainties. For this reason, it provides extraordinarily valuable and objective information.

Our concern in this chapter is with situations in which QRA, used for permanent repository siting, is less valuable and less objective than it should be. Apart from difficulties associated with inaccurate data, there are three broad ways in which probabilistic risk assessments may go wrong: when assessors make methodological value judgments about *estimating* the magnitude of risks; when they make methodological and ethical value judgments about *evaluating* the acceptability of risks; or when they subscribe to false inferences in either estimating or evaluating risks. In chapters 4 and 5, we discussed examples of the first two ways that risk assessors may run into trouble. In this chapter, we shall show how scientists, engineers, and risk assessors (evaluating proposed high-level radwaste repositories) have employed inferences that are logically invalid. As in the two previous chapters, most of our examples are from state-of-the-art studies of Yucca Mountain, currently the only proposed U.S. site for permanent, high-level disposal. The assessors' problematic inferences and value judgments at Yucca Mountain are significant, both because of the alleged desirability of the Nevada site, and because many of the flaws that seem to be occurring there are paradigmatic of difficulties with permanent radwaste disposal elsewhere. Because legitimate and reliable science and risk assessment ought never to include logically invalid inferences, the presence of at least ten problematic inferences in the Yucca Mountain risk assessments renders the work highly questionable. Some of the more common of these inferences are discussed in this chapter. Indeed, at least three of the questionable inferences that we shall investigate appear unavoidable in *any* attempt to justify permanent, geological disposal of radwaste anywhere. The most important of these we discuss first.

The Appeal to Ignorance

One of the most problematic inferences that occurs in assessing long-term radwaste risks occurs when one assumes that because one does not know of a way for repository failure or radionuclide migration to occur, none will occur. Such inferences are examples of the appeal to ignorance. They are problematic because from ignorance, nothing follows. One's ignorance about potential problems—and admittedly such ignorance is always only partial—is not a sufficient condition for asserting that the problems are not significant. If there are fundamental uncertainties in one's premises, such that one is unable to conclude that "A" is the case, for example, then it is invalid to infer that "not-A" is the case. Of course, many conclusions in science are not based on deductively valid inferences. They rely instead on good reasons and on inductive support. The problem with assessors' use of the appeal to ignorance in Yucca Mountain analyses is that there are inadequate inductive grounds for many of their conclusions. For example, they have insufficient data regarding predictions of future volcanism or seismicity. Hence, in the face of incomplete data, the assessors often make an invalid inference, an appeal to ignorance. Repeatedly in its Yucca Mountain assessments, U.S. Department of Energy risk assessors have fallen victim to the appeal to ignorance. Department of Energy assessors have argued, for example, that

no mechanisms have been identified whereby the expected tectonic processes or events could lead to unacceptable radionuclide releases. Therefore . . . the evidence does not support a finding that the site is not likely to meet the qualifying condition for postclosure tectonics.[9]

Similarly, the DOE has argued that

the Yucca Mountain site has no known valuable natural resources . . . . Therefore, on the basis of the above evaluation, the evidence does not support a finding that the site is not likely to meet the qualifying condition for postclosure human interference.[10]

Likewise, as was mentioned earlier in our discussion of human error, the DOE has concluded that

no impediments to eventual complete ownership and control [of Yucca Mountain] by the DOE have been identified. Therefore, on the basis of the above evaluation, the evidence does not support a finding that the site is not likely to meet the qualifying condition for post-closure site ownership and control.[11]

Perhaps nowhere in the DOE literature is the appeal to ignorance as an invalid inference more apparent than in the DOE's 1992 *Early Site Suitability Evaluation* (ESSE) for Yucca Mountain.[12] Typically the DOE's ESSE team notes a variety of substantial uncertainties regarding a particular site condition, but then concludes that a site-suitability finding is justified. Indeed, the appeal to ignorance is one of the main inferences of the DOE's ESSE method, and the ESSE team admitted as much:

If . . . current information does not indicate that the site is unsuitable, then the consensus position was that at least a lower-level suitability finding could be supported.[13]

Accepting the ESSE inference—the appeal to ignorance—virtually guarantees that despite serious uncertainties regarding the site, the evaluators will judge it suitable. Indeed, only an invalid inference such as the appeal to ignorance could allow one to conclude that a site is suitable, despite massive and widespread uncertainties about it. The ESSE peer reviewers for the DOE warned that there was substantial, nonquantifiable uncertainty regarding "future geologic activity, future value of mineral deposits and mineral occurrence models . . . rates of tectonic activity and volcanism . . . natural resource occurrence and value."[14] Despite the facts (1) that there is uncertainty regarding crucial site factors (see above quotation), and (2) that this uncertainty precludes proving a disqualifying condition, the ESSE inference (the appeal to ignorance, that the absence of a disqualifying condition is sufficient to guarantee lower-level site suitability)[15] virtually guarantees that the site will be found suitable.

By assuming that the failure to prove unsuitability is sufficient to support a finding of lower-level site suitability,[16] the ESSE team not only appealed to ignorance but also placed the burden of proof on those arguing for site unsuitability. Placing the burden of proof on one side of a controversy is ethically questionable because it treats the two sides inequitably. On the contrary, it is arguable that Yucca Mountain decision making, like that in civil, or tort cases, ought to follow the decision rule of supporting the side having the greater weight of evidence on its side.[17] And if so, the burden of proof in the ESSE is both ethically inconsistent with standard civil case procedures and inequitable in its placement of evidentiary burdens. Hence, to the degree that the DOE's ESSE conclusions about site suitability are based on appeals to ignorance, they are problematic.

The difficulty with the ESSE is not merely that it falls victim to deductively invalid reasoning, such as appeals to ignorance. Much of science relies on induction. The real problem is that apart from deductive claims, scientists need to provide good inductive reasons for their conclusions. Instead of doing so, the DOE ESSE authors merely assumed that the absence of adequate evidence against site suitability, alone, provided sufficient grounds for concluding that the site was suitable. Therefore, their conclusions are questionable.

Even when risk assessors do not explicitly appeal to ignorance, often it is implicit in their arguments. One group of assessors, for example, claimed that there were "no significant technical obstacles to use of the world deserts as sites for a retrievable [radwaste] storage facility for 500 years."[18] Here the assessors inferred that their ignorance of obstacles constituted a sufficient condition for the assertion that there are no obstacles. Even Nuclear Regulatory Commission (NRC) officials affirmed that "spent [nuclear] fuel can be stored in a safe and environmentally acceptable manner until disposal facilities are available,"[19] and that it has been demonstrated "that safe and environmentally acceptable extended storage can be achieved."[20] On the basis of

claims that there are no known problems with such storage, risk assessors and policymakers often make the further inference that the desert
sites are acceptable, or that nuclear waste storage is demonstrably safe.
The problem with such inferences is not that they lack deductive validity, because much of science is not based on deduction. Rather, the
problem is that, lacking adequate inductive data, the assessors appeal
to an invalid inference.

In other words, assessors and policymakers often draw a specific
conclusion on the basis of the absence of evidence to the contrary.
They also often draw a specific conclusion, for example, about successful long-term waste storage, despite avowed (partial) ignorance of the
situation, or despite the fact that there are no comprehensive empirical
results that confirm their conclusion, or despite the fact that no adequate studies have been done. All these cases are instances of the appeal to ignorance.[21] Of course, in the light of comprehensive long-
term studies of particular phenomena, often it does make sense, for
pragmatic reasons, to draw a conclusion on the basis of searching
exhaustively for contrary evidence and finding none. In the Yucca
Mountain case, however, such appeals to ignorance are inductively
problematic because they are often based on studies that are neither as
fully representative nor as comprehensive as they reasonably could be.
For example, several risk assessors admitted that "measurement of infiltration [of water] into Yucca Mountain has not been performed."
They also admitted that they had not considered fracture flow, even
though it could cause rapid migration of radwaste at the site. Despite
these two significant areas of ignorance, the assessors decided that radioactivity releases at the site would be "significantly less" than those
imposed by government standards. They also concluded that there
would be less than one health effect every 1,400 years caused by Yucca
Mountain.[22]

Other DOE assessors, in a fashion typical of many of the Yucca
Mountain assessments, have used a computer model to simulate radionuclide transport. The computer model was based on a number of
conditions that were either unknown or counterfactual and unrealistic—such as that the flow was one-dimensional, the transport was dis-
persionless, the geologic medium was homogeneous, and the sorption
was in a constant velocity field. Despite these counterfactual and unknown conditions, the DOE assessors concluded that their model
"was found to be an effective tool for simulation of the performance
of the repository systems at Yucca Mountain."[23] How could a model—

especially a model based on highly unrealistic, counterfactual conditions not known to be applicable to the specific site—be found effective, short of some actual empirical testing? The same question arises for other Yucca Mountain risk assessors—DOE consultants—who write: "For the rock mass, it was assumed that nonlinear effects, including pore water migration and evaporation, could be ignored. In practice, nonlinear effects and the specific configuration of the canister, canister hole, and backfilling material would strongly influence very near field conditions."[24] Why did the DOE assessors assume counterfactual conditions known not to be applicable at Yucca Mountain in specifically doing a Yucca Mountain study? Clearly such implicit and explicit claims about repository and canister performance, in the absence of applicable evidence, constitute classic examples of an appeal to ignorance. Assessors would likely claim, in response to such charges, that they do have good reasons for their conclusions. The point of this analysis, however, is that good reasons often are not sufficient reasons.

Moreover, employing methodological value judgments that involve problematic inferences, such as the appeal to ignorance, are not limited to a few studies. Indeed, they are found throughout DOE assessments of many different repositories. When DOE assessors studied Hanford, Washington as a candidate for the first proposed permanent facility, for example, they made a number of problematic appeals to ignorance, including the following:

A final conclusion on the qualifying condition for preclosure radiological exposures cannot be made based on available data . . . it is concluded that the evidence does not support a finding that the reference repository location is disqualified.[25]

Making a similar appeal to ignorance, other DOE assessors, for example, claimed that the data were insufficient to allow them to state that offsite migration of radwaste would never occur, but then they concluded that there was only a small chance of contaminating public water supplies.[26] If they were ignorant about whether offsite migration would occur, how could they know that contamination of water was unlikely? Still other DOE assessors, after noting that changes in groundwater flow "are extremely sensitive to the fracture properties," concluded that they could simulate partially saturated, fractured, porous systems like Yucca Mountain "without taking fractures into account."[27] Not only does this admission appear inconsistent with their earlier claim about the importance of fracture flow, but the conclusion was based on no empirical work whatsoever and no application to the Yucca Mountain site. Instead, it was simply derived from capillarity theory and fracture-flow laws. Hence the conclusion is another classical example of an appeal to ignorance. Indeed, any conclusions that one can simulate adequately a fractured medium may rely on an appeal to ignorance, if some DOE assessors are right. They have claimed that their simulation models of transport in fractured porous tuff

demonstrate that the validity of the effective continuum approximation method cannot be ascertained in general terms. The approximation will break down for rapid transients in flow systems with low matrix permeability and/or large fracture spacing, so that its applicability needs to be carefully evaluated for the specific processes and conditions under study.[28]

Moreover, many of the experiments proposed for sites like Yucca Mountain have never been done before in an unsaturated, fractured medium.[29] Very little study of similar hydrogeologic systems has been done prior to selecting Yucca Mountain as the proposed permanent repository for U.S. high-level waste.[30] If the validity of the radwaste migration methods cannot be ascertained, and if most understanding of radioactive leaching and transport is based merely on laboratory experiments and simulations,[31] then it is impossible to guarantee that the repository will prevent dangerous offsite migration of radionuclides.

One of the areas of repository risk assessment that is most susceptible to use of the appeal to ignorance is evaluation of human interference at the site. In its 1992 *Early Site Suitability Evaluation* (ESSE), for example, the DOE admitted that

the performance analyses did not quantitatively evaluate the potential for adverse effects on repository performance by disruptive processes or events such as faulting or human intrusion.[32]

Instead, the authors said assessments that "address these processes 'uncovered no information that indicates that the Yucca Mountain site is . . . likely to be disqualified'."[33] Such a response is problematic, however, because the absence of information that the site is likely to be disqualified provides no justifiable inference that the site is suitable, particularly if no precise probabilistic studies have been done. Rather, reliance on the absence of some information, in evaluating the human-interference guidelines for Yucca Mountain, amounts to an invalid ap-

peal to ignorance. This appeal to ignorance is all the more questionable because some of the greatest uncertainties regarding a repository
have to do with future disruptive events and human interference. Indeed, when Golder Associates (1990) studied repository performance,
they found "that disruptive processes that cause direct releases to the
accessible environment provide the only conditions under which the
EPA standards might not be met."[34] This means that the one occurrence most likely to present a radiation hazard at Yucca Mountain is
precisely the threat that the DOE team did not (and likely could not)
evaluate quantitatively.

Moreover, in evaluating the human-interference guideline for postclosure site control, the ESSE authors admitted that they did not take
into account "the probability of occurrence of the senarios" when
they were "estimating the probability of exceeding the [radiation] release limits" set by the government.[35] If the probability of various oc-
currences was not taken into account, then how could one determine
whether radiation-release standards would be met? Likewise, because
the ESSE team admitted that it did not know the precise materials and
design for the waste containers,[36] it is not reasonable that the team
could validly conclude, as it did, that the waste package containment
will meet regulatory criteria for postclosure system performance. But
if not, then the ESSE conclusions regarding human interference are
based on an invalid inference, the appeal to ignorance.

Because future human behavior is so difficult to predict, it is easy to
see how assessors might rely on an appeal to ignorance. Often, however, use of this invalid inference occurs not only because certain activity is difficult to predict but also because assessors rely on assumptions
rather than evidence. For example, several DOE risk assessors listed
eleven assumptions that they had made about the Yucca Mountain
site, assumptions such as that the flow path from the repository to the
accessible environment would be vertically downward. (This is an assumption also made at Maxey Flats. It was found to be erroneous after
offsite radionuclide migration occurred through horizontal fractures
and bedding planes at the site.[37]) After making these eleven assumptions, some of which are quite questionable, the assessors concluded:

Given the general assumptions and boundary conditions listed above, it is
not necessary to use sophisticated groundwater flow models or complex con-
taminant-transport equations to estimate radionuclide transport times and
amounts at a repository site. . . . [E]ven without engineered barriers, Yucca
Mountain would comply with NRC requirements for slow release of wastes.[38]

This classic appeal to ignorance is based purely on the questionable assumptions made by the DOE risk assessors. It is impossible for any scientist to guarantee regulatory compliance for ten thousand years, as these assessors have done, because of possible climate change, volcanic activity, and so on, over the next several centuries. To make such a guarantee is either dishonest or an appeal to ignorance. The only way assessors could have formulated their conclusions in a nonproblematic way would have been to make an "if . . . then" claim, such as: "if our assumptions about Yucca Mountain are reliable for the centuries required, then Yucca Mountain would comply with NRC requirements."

The same DOE assessors also appeal to ignorance in estimating the failure rate of waste canisters[39]—even though the final canister design/composition has not been approved, even though there has been widespread canister failure in the past at DOE radwaste facilities, and even though (in some experiments) all canisters of the required reference material have failed (within a year) because of stress-corrosion cracking.[40] It is an appeal to ignorance to estimate the failure rate of a product whose final design is not determined. It is even more of an appeal to ignorance to estimate a low failure rate for an undesigned product when current prototype products fail rapidly (within one year) and seriously. From partial ignorance about the final design/composition of the canister, no conclusion about failure rate can be drawn. In particular, no valid conclusions about failure rate can be drawn on the basis of mere simulations. One group of DOE assessors, for example, used Monte Carlo simulation models for waste package reliability,[41] and then they concluded that the general method of probabilistic reliability analysis is "an acceptable framework to identify, organize, and convey the necessary information to satisfy the standard of reasonable assurance of waste-package performance according to the regulatory requirements during the containment and controlled release periods."[42] Immediately after drawing this positive conclusion about the acceptability of their nonexperimental simulation, however—a conclusion that appears to be an appeal to ignorance—the DOE assessors contradicted their own conclusion of acceptability. They wrote: "This document does not show how to address uncertainties in model applicability or degree of completeness of the analysis, which may require a survey of expert . . . opinions."[43] If the document does not address uncertainties in the model or the completeness of the analysis, how can the DOE authors conclude that the model used in the document is "an acceptable framework" for Yucca Mountain?

A similar inconsistency, combined with an appeal to ignorance, occurs in another important Yucca Mountain risk assessment. The DOE scientists admit that "in most cases, hydraulic data are insufficient for performing geostatistical analyses. Site-characterization studies should provide the hydrogeological data needed for modeling the groundwater travel time based on site statistics."[44] They also admit that they may "have underestimated cumulative releases of all nuclides during 100,000 years, by an amount that is unknown, but probably insignificant."[45] If the hydraulic data are insufficient, and if they have underestimated cumulative releases of nuclides by an unknown amount, then how can the same DOE assessors conclude that the "evidence indicates that the Yucca Mountain repository site would be in compliance with regulatory requirements"?[46] Likewise, DOE researchers say that deep tests for mineral and petroleum potential at the Nevada site are not necessary. Yet, despite their ignorance in this area, the DOE scientists concluded that the potential for petroleum or mineral reserves on site is low.[47]

Even when assessors attempt to avoid the appeal to ignorance, they often fall into another logical difficulty, inconsistency. For example, the same DOE assessors (whose conclusions were just discussed in the preceding paragraphs) admit: "Because data and understanding about water flow and contaminant transport in deep unsaturated fractured environments are just beginning to emerge, complete dismissal of the rapid-release scenarios is not possible at this time."[48] Yet this reasonable conclusion about rapid-release scenarios being possible is blatantly inconsistent with their earlier claim that "even without engineered barriers, Yucca Mountain would comply with NRC requirements for slow release of waste."[49] To be consistent, the assessors would have had to claim that there was a given *probability* that Yucca Mountain would comply with the requirements, or that there were strong grounds for believing that it would comply, not merely that it "would comply."

Drawing a positive conclusion about the safety and effectiveness of radwaste storage at repositories like Yucca Mountain—given a variety of unknowns regarding methodological value judgments, data, and hydrogeological theory—is not only logically invalid but empirically questionable. It is empirically questionable because assessors know that after high-level waste is placed in a repository, the radioactive fuel rods will be breached and eventually most of the cladding will corrode, exposing the fuel to oxidation that will split the cladding and expose additional fuel. Assessors admit that they have an "underlying uncertainty" about the rate of oxidation and that the oxidation data that they have gathered has an uncertainty (of which they know) of between 15 and 20 percent.[50] Moreover, experiments on stress corrosion cracking of spent fuel cladding in a tuff repository environment indicate that the cladding C-rings broke in 25 to 64 days when tested in water and in about 75 to 192 days in air.[51] Hence, assessors already know that the highly radioactive fuel is likely to be exposed rather soon after emplacement to the uncontained environment. Given such knowledge—as well as fundamental uncertainties, already discussed, about unsaturated fractured geological zones, about adsorption, about seismic activity, about volcanism, and about human amplification of risk at Yucca Mountain—it is questionable for anyone to claim that the radioisotopes at the site will be isolated from the environment for ten thousand years. Indeed, it seems questionable that anyone can guarantee the requisite integrity of any repository anywhere for more than a century or two, even though such integrity is a regulatory requirement of most governments pursuing permanent disposal. But if one cannot provide compelling evidence for site integrity for thousands of years, but merely argues that there is no evidence of serious site instability for this period, then such an argument in favor of permanent geological disposal of radwaste likely includes an implicit and questionable appeal to ignorance.

Two-Valued Epistemic Logic and the Appeal to Ignorance

Perhaps one of the reasons that Yucca Mountain assessors have appealed to ignorance is that they have been forced to employ a questionable two-valued epistemic logic for site evaluation. In the DOE's 1992 *Early Site Suitability Evaluation* (ESSE) for Yucca Mountain, for example, this two-valued logic is quite obvious. The DOE decided that all judgments regarding Yucca Mountain site suitability could be formulated in terms of only two options—that the site is either suitable or unsuitable. In so doing, they assumed that they did not need a three-valued logic, or a third option—such as "the data, at present, are inadequate to assess site suitability" or "the suitability decision, at present, is uncertain." As the ESSE report formulated this two-valued epistemic logic:

[C]onclusions about the site can be either that current information supports an unsuitability finding or that current information supports a suitability finding. . . . If . . . current information does not indicate that the site is unsuitable, then the consensus position was that at least a lower-level suitability finding could be supported.[52]

One important *consequence* of the DOE's mandating a two-valued epistemic logic in the ESSE is that if researchers find no disqualifying condition at the site, then their failure to do so is sufficient to produce a suitability finding for that condition. As the ESSE Peer Review Team put it: "A suitability finding means that (1) a disqualifying condition is not present, or (2) a qualifying condition is present."[53] There are at least six reasons, however, that this two-valued logic and its associated consequences are problematic for repository risk evaluation.

First, the most basic difficulty with the two-valued epistemic logic is that it is not typically used in scientific discovery and confirmation. In science we use a three-valued epistemic logic, according to which claims are either *falsified* (e.g., site is unsuitable), *confirmed* (e.g., site is suitable), or *uncertain* (e.g., we cannot determine suitability one way or the other). Because often we do not know whether a scientific claim is true or false, we say that it is uncertain.[54]

Moreover, in science we do not typically accept the consequence of the DOE's two-valued epistemic logic, that the absence of a falsification (or a disqualifying condition) is sufficient grounds for accepting an hypothesis (or claim about site suitability). In science we typically test an hypothesis, often by means of deduction, to see if it can be falsified. If, after testing, we have not falsified a hypothesis, we do not affirm its truth, but its uncertainty. It remains uncertain because, although we were unable to falsify it, it is possible that the hypothesis could be falsified by further testing.[55] Hence, in science, repeated failure to falsify an hypothesis is not alone sufficient grounds for confirming it, even though one falsification alone can be sufficient grounds for rejecting it. In science, confirmation and falsification of an hypothesis are not symmetrical; in situations of uncertainty, we often need a third option.

We are able to confirm an hypothesis (1) only after performing every relevant test on every relevant case, that is, only after completing all *representative* tests; (2) only after completing all *risky* tests, that is, attempting to falsify precise, predictive hypotheses; and (3) only after knowing that we have exhausted the set of representative and risky tests.[56] Yet in the Yucca Mountain case, obviously condition (1) cannot be met for long-term predictions (ca. 1,000 years or longer). At

Yucca Mountain, the most crucial hypotheses—about rates of volcanism, tectonics, and natural resource occurrence, for example—are, in practice, not susceptible to representative testing because of the long time frame.[57] Consider, for example, the hypothesis that fault displacement near Yucca Mountain over the next ten thousand years will not be adequate to interfere with total system performance of the repository. This hypothesis is obviously not in practice testable. Moreover, since Yucca Mountain provides little deterministic data, and even inadequate probabilistic and statistical data,[58] condition (2) cannot be met by current site studies. But if (1) and (2) cannot be satisfied, then neither can (3), since it is a function of them.

To claim that our inability to falsify an hypothesis (e.g., that the site is suitable) is sufficient grounds for confirming it—in the absence of meeting conditions (1), (2), and (3) above—is to affirm the consequent. Affirming the consequent is a classic form of invalid inference,[59] and we shall discuss it in more detail later in the chapter. Affirming the consequent is problematic, because even if one has not been able to falsify some hypothesis, it might still be possible to falsify it in the future; hence, our inability to falsify an hypothesis is never alone grounds for confirming it. Of course, failure to find a problem with an hypothesis may be sufficient grounds—in some nonscientific or pragmatic sense—for accepting it. Presumably, however, risk assessments of Yucca Mountain (such as the ESSE) are supposed to be accepted on scientific, rather than nonscientific or pragmatic, grounds. And if so, then it is arguable that the ESSE and other evaluations of proposed repository sites ought to follow a three-valued rather than a two-valued epistemic logic, just as scientific evaluation does. Moreover, by not following a three-valued epistemic logic for repository evaluation, assessors run the risk of begging the question in favor of site suitability. By framing the site-suitability question in terms of a two-valued epistemic logic, they control many of the answers to that question. Those who frame the questions control the answers.

Second, the use of two-valued epistemic logic in the ESSE and other repository assessments is also questionable because classical methods of Bayesian decision making typically employ three-valued logic, in the sense of including a category for events that are "uncertain" or about which we have inadequate information to make a decision. Bayesian decision theory recognizes that decisions are made under conditions of *certainty* (the outcome is known with probability 1); *risk* (the outcome is known with some probability less than 1); or *un-*

certainty (the outcome is known so little that we are unable to assign any exact probabilities to it).[60] Because Bayesian decision theory is the premier theory used in probabilistic risk assessments (such as those being performed at Yucca Mountain), and because Bayesian decision theory includes a third category for "uncertain" decisions, it is arguable that the Yucca Mountain evaluators ought not have used the two-valued epistemic logic.[61]

Third, apart from the fact that classical scientific and Bayesian methods employ a three-valued logic, it is reasonable to use such a logic in many situations.[62] Few events and decisions can be assessed in terms of two alternatives—either suitable or unsuitable—because often we do not have complete knowledge. Whenever we have less than perfect knowledge, or whenever there is not complete logical and factual closure on a problem, a particular resolution of it can never be either/or—in this case, either suitable or unsuitable. Later events could show that a judgment of suitability, for instance, was unsuitable.[63] Hence, many situations, because they are open-ended and imperfectly known, require a three-valued epistemic logic that reflects the category of uncertainty. For example, in earlier days, scientists might have claimed that vitrifying (incorporating within glass) highly radioactive liquids was suitable as a means of preventing them from escaping into the environment.[64] In 1992, however, scientists at Argonne National Laboratory learned that, contrary to previous scientific opinion, radioactive wastes may escape from glass via a new route.[65] They discovered a "previously unknown mechanism for directly generating colloids," particles too tiny to settle out of water.[66] By releasing only one drop of water per week over an inch-long, half-inch diameter glassy cylinder—containing neptunium, americium, and plutonium—scientists showed that exposure to slow dripping of water can change the largely nonreactive borosilicate glass into a form that facilitates the flaking of mineralized shards containing radionuclides. Hence, any claims about the suitability or unsuitability of vitrification for controlling radwastes depend on whether we have gained closure on the problems associated with vitrification. Likewise, in the absence of complete knowledge of, and closure on, numerous problems at Yucca Mountain, one can argue that scientists and policymakers ought to employ a three-valued, rather than a two-valued, epistemic logic for site evaluation.[67]

Fourth, a three-valued epistemic logic (that includes an alternative such as "uncertain at present") is also more reasonable than such a two-valued logic, because it is more consistent with the ESSE peer reviewers' judgments about the level of scientific knowledge at Yucca Mountain. In their "Consensus Position," the reviewers warned that the site was very poorly known. They said:

[M]any aspects of site suitability. . . predictions involving future geologic activity, future value of mineral deposits and mineral occurrence models . . . rates of tectonic activity and volcanism, as well as natural resource occurrence and value, will be fraught with substantial uncertainties that cannot be quantified using standard statistical methods.[68]

If many aspects of Yucca Mountain site suitability cannot be quantified and are uncertain, then the peer reviewers' own words appear to argue for a three-valued epistemic logic and against the two-valued logic that the DOE instructed them to use. Indeed, many of the ESSE peer reviewers—such as D. K. Kreamer, M. T. Einaudi, and W. J. Arabasz—complained that they "were given" only the choices of site suitability or site unsuitability, despite the fact that "there is . . . currently not enough defensible, site-specific information available to warrant acceptance or rejection of this site."[69] Hence, rejection of the two-valued epistemic logic appears consistent with the "Consensus Position" of the fourteen DOE peer reviewers for Yucca Mountain and with the comments of many individual reviewers of the ESSE.

Fifth, use of the two-valued epistemic logic in assessing repository risk also appears questionable because so many of the conclusions on which the Yucca Mountain ESSE rests are qualitative rather than quantitative and precise.[70] On the admission of the ESSE authors, many of their conclusions are not amenable even to probabilistic formulation and are based on subjective judgments.[71] For example, the qualifying and disqualifying conditions for the site repeatedly use qualitative language to speak of conditions that are "likely" or "unlikely," rather than conditions having a certain probability.[72] Such imprecise and qualitative language itself argues that a third decision option, such as "data inadequate at present to support a conclusion," be used.

Sixth, the two-valued epistemic logic—for decisions that the proposed repository site is suitable or unsuitable—is also questionable because it ignores the category (uncertainty) applicable to most controversial siting decisions. Many experts, including the U.S. National Academy of Sciences, have indicated that virtually all questions involving technological controversy are Bayesian cases of *uncertainty*, not cases of risk or certainty; the fact that they involve significant factual or probabilistic uncertainties is one of the reasons that they generate controversy.[73] Hence, to ignore the third decision option ("uncertainty") is to ignore the one category that, according to experts, is most likely to be applicable to Yucca Mountain.

Of course, the obvious objection to the claim—that the major DOE evaluation of Yucca Mountain, predicated on a two-valued epistemic logic, is inadequate in ignoring the decision finding of "uncertain"—is that the peer reviewers approved the 1992 ESSE. Most of the peer reviewers signed a statement acknowledging that (1) "the conclusions about the status of lower- and higher-level findings on the siting guidelines are balanced and defensible," and (2) "the revised ESSE Integrated Evaluation Package adequately addresses my comments."[74] If there were problems with the two-valued epistemic logic—including the absence of the "uncertain" option regarding site suitability—then why did most of the peer reviewers agree to statements (1) and (2)? The answer appears to be, in the words of the ESSE Core Team, that the

DOE General Siting Guidelines (10 CFR Part 960) do not allow a "no decision" finding. . . . Thus the ESSE Core Team [of peer reviewers] followed the intent of the guidelines.[75]

In other words, the DOE evaluation team and the DOE peer evaluators for Yucca Mountain appear to have answered the questions in the two-valued epistemic logic that the DOE told them to use. They employed this logic despite the fact that their own words (see reason four earlier) indicate that use of such a two-valued logic is questionable in the Yucca Mountain situation.

The two-valued epistemic logic used to assess the Yucca Mountain site is questionable, however, not only because it ignores the third alternative of uncertainty but also because the two options (site suitability and site unsuitability) are not treated consistently. For example, the DOE interpretation of repository requirements makes it more difficult to disqualify a site than to qualify it, because only one time frame, the *present*, is defined as sufficient for *disqualification*, whereas either time frame, *present or future*, is sufficient for *qualification*. That is, the site may be disqualified only if "present day activities" or the search for "presently economic resources" will jeopardize waste isolation onsite.[76] On this criterion, future events are unable to disqualify the site, although they are sufficient to qualify it. That is, the site may be qualified on the basis of "the natural resource potential for both those resources that are presently valuable and those resources that . . . may be valuable in the foreseeable future."[77]

The DOE interpretation makes it more difficult to disqualify (than to qualify) a site with respect to the natural resources guidelines, in part because a shorter time frame (the present) is applicable to disqualification than to qualification. Also, the two-valued epistemic logic (see the earlier discussion) places the burden of proof, generally, on the disqualifier side. As we argued earlier, the ESSE assumes that failure to disqualify a site counts as its being qualified. Hence, because of this assumption, if there is a shorter time period applicable to disqualification questions and, as a result, if one does not disqualify the site, then the site will be qualified. Such a situation obviously places a heavier evidentiary burden on the disqualifier side of the site controversy. This inequitable burden suggests that there may be problems with the ESSE interpretations and findings and with repository risk assessment at Yucca Mountain.

Placing a heavier burden on the disqualifier side of the controversy also renders the "logic" of qualification and disqualification inconsistent, because the same time frames are not applicable to both sides. The inconsistency is obvious because the DOE defines suitability as the absence of a disqualifying condition.[78] Yet in the case of the natural resources guidelines the absence of a disqualifying condition, regarding the *present*—as required by the ESSE[79]—does not argue for suitability for both *present and future* time periods. Hence, the DOE interpretations of time periods relevant to natural resources are clearly inconsistent with the DOE claim that suitability may be defined as the absence of a disqualifying condition. From inconsistency, no valid (or sound) conclusions can be drawn.

Arguments over the long-term stability of the Yucca Mountain repository for thousands of years seem not merely based on a questionable appeal to a two-valued epistemic logic and on attempting to draw a certain conclusion from partial ignorance. Rather, they also fail in attempting to draw a certain conclusion from strong evidence to the contrary. This is part of the reason that some DOE evaluators have charged that the scientific integrity of the site-characterization at Yucca Mountain is not acceptable.[80] The questionable character of numerous fallacious appeals to ignorance, in the case of Yucca Mountain, is even more apparent when one considers that most existing U.S. nuclear waste facilities have leaked in the past and continue to leak. Despite the improvements in the new high-level technologies, past inductive evidence about radwaste migration after only short periods suggests that radwaste migration may also occur at Yucca Mountain— and facilities like it—for centuries. This past inductive evidence, already mentioned in earlier chapters, includes the facts that all existing means of managing nuclear wastes have resulted in major leaks of radioactivity into the biosphere. Plutonium, for example, has traveled offsite from both high- and low-level storage facilities.[81]

At Hanford, the largest commercial storage site for high-level waste, over 500,000 gallons of high-level waste have leaked from their containers.[82] Officials from the U.S. Environmental Protection Agency have indicated that because of migration patterns of radioactivity released directly to the soil and water at Hanford, normal annual radiation releases from this facility "could result in a yearly impact of 580 man-rem total body exposure."[83] In fact, more than 50 percent of the radioactivity released directly to the soil at certain Hanford sites reaches the Columbia River (via groundwater) in four to ten days.[84] Based on the great number of radioactive leaks from high-level storage tanks, government officials have stated that "extrapolation of past data would indicate that future leaks may occur at a rate of 2 to 3 per year."[85] In addition to the Hanford leaks, extensive radioactive migration also has occurred at 1,061 DOE sites, such as the waste disposal areas at Savannah River and at Idaho National Laboratory. These problems include widespread plutonium contamination in the groundwater.[86] If government officials did not prevent these leaks in the past, over a decade or two, and if they even project them into the future (suggesting that not enough is being done to prevent them), then it is questionable whether government officials can and will prevent leaks in the thousands of years to come at Yucca Mountain. This past inductive evidence about radioactive contamination provides even further reasons for criticizing risk assessors' appeals to ignorance in evaluating future potential risks at sites such as Yucca Mountain. Indeed, EPA researchers have warned that it is in practice impossible to predict beyond the next one hundred years what the institutional conditions and costs associated with such storage or management will be, or whether storage or management will even be possible.[87]

Begging the Question

In many instances of the appeal to ignorance, the reasoning also presents classical examples of another logical problem, begging the question. Begging the question occurs whenever one assumes, in the face of incomplete data, what one is trying to prove. In such a case one often has some evidence to support one's conclusion, but the evidence is neither sufficient nor compelling. Hence, instead of drawing a modest or tentative conclusion, one often overstates the case and thereby begs the question. For example, if one assumes that the health effects of Yucca Mountain will be minimal, or that the facility will comply with government radiation standards for thousands of years in the future, then one begs the question. Likewise, if one assumes that a counterfactual model—one that cannot in principle be tested conclusively because of the centuries requiring confirmation—provides an "effective" simulation of Yucca Mountain,[88] then one begs the question. Indeed, to assume the conclusion, as these DOE assessors did, in the absence of adequate inductive evidence necessary for drawing a conclusion one way or the other is a classical example of begging the question, an invalid inference. Although much of science does not rely on deductive inferences, reliable science avoids invalid inferences such as begging the question. Rather than using this questionable inference, assessors ought instead to attempt to show that there is some *probability* that their conclusions are true, instead of to conclude, invalidly, that their conclusions are true. In other words, they ought to employ good probabilistic, inductive, or retroductive reasoning. Examples of begging the question occur throughout many repository risk assessments, including the Yucca Mountain literature. When Hanford was a candidate site for the first permanent, high-level repository, for example, DOE assessors expressed confidence that it could meet the requirement "that activities by future generations at or near the site will not be likely to affect waste containment and location." Even though there are no data that establish that such a specification can be met for ten thousand years, the DOE assessors begged the question and merely assumed that the requirement could be met:

The evidence does not support a finding that the reference repository location on the Hanford site is not likely to meet the . . . qualifying condition related to human interference. . . . There is little uncertainty associated with this conclusion.[89]

Just as risk assessors and government agencies often beg the question that a permanent repository will be safe for ten thousand years, so also they beg related questions about their ability to construct such a facility. As one assessor put it: "DOE has the confidence that the capability will exist to . . . conduct the assessments required for near-term site evaluation and repository-design activities."[90] How could the DOE be confident of some capability whose existence could only be established in the future? At best, the capability appears to have only a certain *probability* of being satisfied. Indeed, one of the major reviewers of the DOE risk-assessment work at Yucca Mountain concluded: "Much of the data is assumed and not field measured."[91] For example, the repository design is still indeterminate, and there are many uncertainties regarding fracturing and radionuclide transport. Yet, DOE assessors repeatedly maintain that "evidence indicates that the Yucca Mountain repository site would be in compliance with regulatory requirements."[92]

Assessors also make claims such as the following: "The subsurface radar profiling system has been demonstrated in the field to be an effective tool in the arsenal of remote sensing devices that can be applied to the location and identification of subsurface disturbances."[93] Likewise they claim that "the method [used at Yucca Mountain] can be applied . . . providing credibility and documentation for decisions regarding the acceptability of any particular site when substantial uncertainties are present." And, "there is no technical obstacle to applying methodology of this type on a larger scale . . . This application will lead to realistic (rather than simply demonstrative) results."[94] How could one possibly claim that an unknown application will lead to realistic results? Obviously such an assertion begs the question. Likewise, how could a DOE assessor claim, for example, that continuum models of the site are "probably sufficient for analysis of the thermomechanical response of excavations in welded tuff"?[95] Clearly such conclusions assume what they need to prove. Although the Nuclear Regulatory Commission's regulations require "use of verifiable and tested scientific models,"[96] these citations indicate that at least some DOE assessors nevertheless draw conclusions that beg the question.

Not only the individual assessors but government agencies themselves and official government documents may be guilty of begging the question. Members of both the U.S. Congress and representatives of the state of Nevada have charged that the site-characterization plan of the DOE makes the implicit assumption that the Yucca Mountain site is acceptable and that the DOE officials have adopted a site-advocacy approach,[97] especially because they address the question of whether or not the DOE has met licensing requirements, rather than whether or not the site is suitable.[98] State officials warn that the DOE's approach "is more one designed to confirm its own preconceived notion of a simplified site model than it is to determine through site investigations the most likely conceptual model for the site that can be supported by objective and comprehensive data collection and analysis."[99] For example, the DOE concluded in the ESSE that "estimates of expected releases from the NTS [Nevada Test Site] can be predicted."[100] Nevertheless, the authors of the document admit that "no specific evaluation has been done for a repository at Yucca Mountain for expected releases, since design details are not yet available."[101] But if there is neither a design nor an evaluation regarding expected releases, then it begs the question to claim that releases can be predicted.

Similar cases of begging the question occur throughout the ESSE, the ESSE response to peer reviewers, and the Yucca Mountain literature.[102] For instance, the DOE authors of the ESSE conclude that no "significant amount of radionuclides will be released from the proposed Yucca Mountain repository."[103] Yet, when peer reviewer J. H. Bell inquired, "What method of analysis [was used] to determine 'significant amount'?", the ESSE team responded:

The potential release of radionuclides, design factors, release of radionuclides to unrestricted areas, weather, that amount less than allowable under the regulations, and many more parameters are all related through a comprehensive dose-assesment model and calculations for the site, yet to be completed. Such an effort will be accomplished and discussed as part of the system guideline for radiological safety.[104]

If the dose-assessment model and site calculations have not been completed, however, then one begs the question to claim that the studies show no significant amounts of radioactivity will be released. Likewise, when the ESSE team concludes that "radionuclides released from the proposed facility are expected to be minimal," yet admits that "a site dispersion model has not been developed,"[105] they also beg the question.

One of the main ways in which repository risk assessors appear to beg the question of site suitability is by failing to offer a second-order analysis of various issues. For example, as a first-order analysis, the ESSE for Yucca Mountain surveyed the controversy over climate-induced repository flooding.[106] In order to resolve the disagreement at this first level, however, we need second-order arguments—a rationale for deciding which side of the controversy is more correct. There is no such rationale in the ESSE. After admitting controversy and uncertainty in the first-order analysis of the flooding issue, the ESSE authors merely jumped to a conclusion about site suitability.

In the case of the climate issue and possible repository flooding, the

ESSE authors agree with the experts who argue against flooding induced by climate change.[107] They fail, however, to explain why they find their arguments more compelling than those that predict possible repository flooding.[108] Of course, the ESSE position is consistent with that of a recent panel of the National Academy of Sciences.[109] Nevertheless, the ESSE authors fail to provide a second-order analysis of arguments that explain how to account for a number of anomalous events, such as the existence of fossils of several different "wet species" near Yucca Mountain.[110]

The failure to provide a second-order analysis of the climate issue in the ESSE is all the more puzzling because the authors claim that the lower-level finding of suitability has been strengthened by evidence obtained since the environmental analysis.[111] At a minimum, the authors' second-order analysis would need to explain how and why the evidence is stronger for site suitability, even though they admit (1) that they have ignored certain issues,[112] (2) that the quantitative model needed to predict future climate is problematic and incomplete,[113] and (3) that there are large uncertainties in their data.[114] In the absence of a second-order analysis, the conclusion about Yucca Mountain site suitability appears to beg the question of climate-induced flooding.

It is surprising that logical problems, like begging the question, have occurred in what purports to be excellent scientific work. One explanation for such faulty inferences has been offered by state of Nevada officials. Nevada charged that the same risk assessors who performed the various scientific and engineering studies and environmental assessments for site suitability would be those used by the DOE to do further research, both before and after the site is accepted. Hence, members of the U.S. Congress and state officials have argued that risk assessors have vested interests. If they wish further employment at a particular location, they must present an optimistic picture of the proposed site.[115] This suggests why some assessors might beg the question. Similar claims about the DOE managers pushing the schedule and being more interested in production and siting than in risk assessment—if true—could also explain assessors' apparent tendencies to draw invalid conclusions. Yucca Mountain is a "unique, first-ever effort" to site a permanent U.S. geological repository. Given that it is the sole proposed site and that there was virtually no baseline work on it prior to the Yucca Mountain investigations,[116] it is not surprising that assessors often do not have the evidence that they seek. When they do not, however, the proper solution ought to be to admit such deficiencies, to rely on inductive or retroductive reasoning, and not to beg the question. Some DOE assessors, of course, have been careful to admit what they do not know. By avoiding any begging of the question, their conclusions can serve as a model for future QRA. One government report, for example, claimed that a repository "would meet the U.S. Environmental Protection Agency standards . . . if present hydrologic, geologic, and geochemical conditions (as presently understood) persist for the next 10,000 years."[117] Using "if" avoids begging the question.

Another way to avoid begging the question is to develop several alternative conceptual models, as the Nuclear Regulatory Commission said ought to be done at Yucca Mountain.[118] That way, assessors would be less likely to assume that a model was adequate just because it was consistent with the available data. Instead, they would be forced to determine which of a variety of models were better substantiated by empirical results. Several examples of the sort of honesty required by the assessors who face major uncertainties in the data and theory relevant to repository sites are the following:

Objective estimates of probabilities for future resource exploration beyond more than a few years are not possible now; this probably will remain true indefinitely because resource estimates contain a large component . . . that cannot be predicted realistically.[119]

No method is adequate to quantitatively assess, with a high degree of certainty, the probability of tectonic activity at the Yucca Mountain site.[120]

There are no good probabilities of volcanism at Yucca Mountain because of the uncertainties owing to limited numbers of events; a statistically good sample population does not exist.[121]

It is impossible to predict volcanic eruptions because there is too much uncertainty.[122]

If assessors followed the procedures of developing alternative models and attempting to test them, or of admitting uncertainties that make their predictions and probabilities unknown, then they could avoid begging the question. They could also avoid the criticism that the tone of the DOE Yucca Mountain work conveys the conclusion that few problems exist. If the jury is "still out" regarding the suitability of proposed sites like Yucca Mountain, then it is impossible to conclude, without begging the question, that few problems exist.

The Expertise Inference

Another important way in which some risk assessors, including those at Yucca Mountain, draw problematic conclusions is in inferring that their calculations and assessments are more reliable than they are. They often assume that it is possible for experts alone to distinguish "actual risk"—as a property of a technology, policy, or action—from so-called "perceived risk" postulated by laypersons. Once they make the distinction between actual and perceived risk, some assessors assume that the (misguided) perceived risks of laypeople cause most controversy over technology and environmental impacts.[123] As a consequence, they work on how to mitigate the impact of risk *perceptions* (which they assume to be erroneous), rather than on how to mitigate the impact of the (actual) *risk* itself. They assume that public relations, "risk communication," is their only problem.[124] They assume that they—scientists, engineers, and risk assessors—understand risk, and that those who disagree with them are the victims of faulty perceptions. DOE assessors, for example, make precisely this assumption when they reject lay views of risk acceptability, without evidence, and appeal to their own "professional judgment."[125]

Contrary to the expertise inference, however, one cannot completely separate risks and risk perceptions.[126] All known risks are perceived and for at least nine reasons. Before explaining why we cannot completely separate risks and perceived risks, however, it is important to emphasize that we can sometimes distinguish risks from risk perceptions. That they cannot be completely separated, however, does not force us into a complete relativism regarding risk. Even though a risk is perceived, it need not be biased or unreal. The risk of death, for example, although real, is not certain because it is in part a probability. The *risk* of death is merely perceived, theoretical, or estimated *until* death becomes a certainty. Indeed, the occurrence of death in a particular case reveals how accurate our perceptions or estimates of the risk of death were. But if this reasoning is correct, then (more generally) although all risks of some X occurring are real, the exact degree and nature of these risks are not, in principle, confirmable until X actually occurs. Prior to this occurrence, risk perceptions can be judged as more or less accurate only on the basis of nonempirical and theoretical criteria like explanatory power, simplicity, internal coherence, and so on. Nevertheless, risk perceptions are often *real* and *objective*, at least in the sense that empirical evidence, such as accident frequency, is relevant to them and is capable of providing grounds for amending them. This means that at least some risks (the probability p that some X will occur) are both *perceived* and *real*. They are objective because empirical data are often relevant to them, but they are partially subjective—a function of one's beliefs—because their formulation always involves methodological value judgments. Their exact nature and magnitude become more fully knowable, however, insofar as more instances of X occur. Therefore, because a risk can be both perceived and real, avoiding the expertise inference does not commit us to complete relativism.

Avoiding the expertise inference instead commits us to the belief that we cannot completely separate risks and risk perceptions, even though we can often distinguish them. Why is a complete separation of risks and risk perceptions not possible? *First*, there is a problem with *causality*. One cannot establish that a perception about a risk (and not the risk itself) caused a particular impact. It is not enough to establish correlations between particular impacts (e.g., aversion to a particular danger) and specific risk perceptions, because this would not show that the perceptions caused the alleged effects. For example, there might be a correlation between catastrophic risks and the impact of high risk aversion. Yet this correlation might be accidental. Instead, the real cause of high risk aversion might be the lack of control over the hazard, not its catastrophic nature. If so, then it may be difficult to separate completely the impacts of risks and the impacts of risk perceptions.

Second, risk *probabilities* often do not reflect risk *frequencies*. This is in part because there are numerous difficulties of hazard estimation that do not admit of analytical, probabilistic resolution by experts. Often the risk problem is not well enough understood to allow accurate predictions, as the use of techniques like fault-tree analysis shows. Hence, assessors are forced to rely on subjective or perceived risk probabilities, instead of on actual, empirical accident frequencies established over a long period of trial. Even if assessors based their notions of probability on actual, empirical accident frequencies, this move would not always deliver their estimates of risk from the charge of being "perceived." Because there are reliable frequencies only for events that have had a long recorded history, use of historical accident/hazard data for new technologies can result in an underestimating of the danger; this is because certain events may not have occurred between the inception of a technology and the end of the period for which the risk information is compiled. Moreover, low accident frequency does not prove low accident probability. Only when the period of observing accident frequency approaches infinity would the two, frequency and probability, converge.

A *third* reason why one cannot completely separate actual from perceived risk in any wholly accurate way is that actual risk estimates are sometimes very rough and imprecise. For some phenomena (see the beginning of this chapter), assessments typically vary from 2 to 6 orders of magnitude. Indeed, some level of imprecision is unavoidable, whether the estimates are based on probabilistic calculations or on actual experience. On the one hand, if they are based on probabilities, then assessors are forced to employ a number of value-laden theoretical assumptions and mathematical models. On the other hand, if the risk estimates are based on actual experience, or accident frequency, they are likewise "perceived" because probability does not equal frequency, as has already been argued. Moreover, even actual frequencies do not provide a precise measure of a particular risk, because this number is typically formulated as an *average*, and such averages, by definition, do not take particular, perhaps site-specific, deviations into account.

Fourth, some of the most important aspects of hazards, whether real or perceived, are *not amenable to quantification*. For example, (what some risk assessors call) "actual" risk estimates are based on the presupposition that risk is measured by probability and consequences and that both can be quantified. Yet most laypeople would probably claim that what makes a thing most unacceptable are factors that are not susceptible to quantification, factors such as a risk's being imposed without consent, or being unknown, or posing a threat to civil liberties or to rights of future generations.[127]

Fifth, completely separating risks and risk perceptions is likewise impossible because both are *theoretical concepts* and hence not completely amenable to precise empirical prediction or confirmation. In *general*, "risk" is defined in terms of expected utility theory, and hence it is a theoretical concept carrying with it all the baggage of this specific decision theory.[128] In *particular* applications, "risk" is always defined on the basis of a whole host of theoretical assumptions, many of which are often controversial. For example, a number of incompatible "cancer models" (dose-response models), each with attendant assumptions, has been used to estimate the incidence of tumors in populations exposed to formaldehyde. In 1987, EPA researchers called formaldehyde a "probable human carcinogen." They said that those exposed to formaldehyde-treated pressed wood could face a cancer risk, over ten years, of 2 in 10,000. Scientists at the Harvard School of Public Health, however, criticized the Environmental Protection Agency (EPA) risk assessment as premature and said the true formaldehyde risk was uncertain. Still other risk assessors, including scientists at the American Cancer Society and the Consumer Product Safety Commission, argued that the EPA models were incorrect, but in the opposite direction. They said EPA findings underestimated the cancer risk.[129] The formaldehyde case, as well as those of EDB, dioxin, and methylene chloride, all illustrate that even as late as the 1980s, particular accounts of risk are highly controversial and theory-laden. But if risk is known in terms of the categories of a particular scientific or modeling *theory*, then there is no actual hazard that is completely separable from some particular theoretical account of it. Hence, there is no uncontroversial way to completely separate "actual" from "perceived" risk.

Sixth, because risk perceptions often affect risk probabilities, and vice versa, it is frequently impossible to completely separate hazards from perceptions of them. This is well known to social scientists as part of the "self-fulfilling prophecy." For example, if I perceive my chances of getting cancer to be high, then my perceptions can exacerbate stress and therefore increase the probability that I actually do become a cancer victim. Hence, it is often impossible to separate actual and perceived risk.

Seventh, there are also a number of reasons for arguing that the complete separation of actual and perceived risk cannot be based on the alleged *objectivity* of *expert* estimates, as opposed to the alleged *subjectivity* of *lay* risk estimates. Admittedly, laypersons typically overestimate the severity of many technological hazards. However, even if it could be established that the public exaggerates the accident probabilities associated with some technology, for example, liquified natural gas (LNG), this fact alone would be a necessary, but not a sufficient, condition for establishing the thesis that laypersons erroneously overestimate risks. This is because even though laypersons' perceived probabilities may be erroneous, they may not completely explain their risk aversion. The public might view risks as high not only because of their accident probabilities but also because their consequences are potentially catastrophic, or involuntarily imposed, or for some other reason.

Eighth, apart from whether probabilities alone explain risk judgments, there is reason to believe that, at least in some areas, scientists', engineers', and risk assessors' estimates of probabilities are not necessarily superior to those of laypeople. In their classic studies of the heuristic judgmental strategies that often lead to error in probability estimates, authors such as Kahneman and Tversky concluded that experts were just as prone as laypeople to judgmental error regarding probabilities whenever they had merely statistical data. Highly trained mathematicians, scientists, and engineers are particularly susceptible, for example, to the fallacy known as representativeness, the gratuitous assumption that a particular sample is similar in relevant respects to its parent population and that it represents the salient features of the process by which it was generated. Kahneman and Tversky showed not only that experts were just as prone to this probabilistic bias as laypeople but also that, even after the error was explained to the experts, the bias could not be "unlearned."[130] Another common judgmental error of mathematically trained professionals is overconfidence; this occurs because experts' trust in their probability estimates is typically a function of how much information they have gathered, rather than a function of its accuracy or its predictive success. Because everyone, even those highly trained in probability and statistics, must make simplifying assumptions in estimating probabilities, and because those trained in probability and statistics are just as prone as laypeople to these judgmental errors, there is little reason to believe that experts are always able to calculate actual or *real* risk, whereas laypeople are merely able only to construct perceived or *subjective* risk.[131]

A *ninth* difficulty is that those who attempt to separate "actual risk" and "perceived risk" are wrong to assume that the latter is merely an erroneous understanding of the former.[132] They are wrong because there is no universal definition of risk underlying the two concepts. For one thing, assessors disagree as to whether (and when) to employ concepts such as "individual risk," "relative risk," "population risk," and "absolute risk."[133] Moreover, as was already suggested, the term "risk" in "actual risk" and "perceived risk" has neither the same referent nor the same meaning. What Hafele, Okrent, Jones-Lee, Morgan, and others[134] call "actual risk" is the probability of a particular hazard occurring times the magnitude of its consequences. What they call "perceived risk," alleging that it is an incorrect view of actual risk, however, is not merely (an incorrect) *perception* of probability times consequences. Rather, most laypeople would claim that (what typical risk assessors call) "perceived risk" includes *more* than mere probability. Hence when laypeople say that something is a "high risk" they do not necessarily mean only that it has a high probability of causing death. (See the next chapter for further discussion of this point.) And if so, then "actual risk" is not mere probability times fatality, and "perceived risks" are not merely perceptions of probability times fatality. In sum, no complete separation is possible between perceived risks and actual risks. If there were hazards that were not perceived, then we would not know them. Because we know them, in some sense, proves that risks are perceived. Even real risks must be known via categories and perceptions. This is related to the earlier point that all known risks are, *in part*, theoretical constructs, not completely empirical, not wholly capable of confirmation.

Some Yucca Mountain assessors have fallen victim to the expertise inference, assuming that a complete separation is possible between actual risk calculated by risk assessors, mathematicians, and scientists, and perceived risk estimated by laypersons.[135] They have ignored the fact that all known risks are perceived and hence value-laden, and they have assumed that risks calculated by experts are free of subjective perceptions. For example, one industry assessor argued that public concern over radwaste was caused primarily by the absence of a structured, scheduled waste-management program, rather than by real concern over long-term safety.[136] In other words, the assessor assumed that he understood the risk objectively, that the "real" risk was minimal, and that the problem with laypersons was merely their misperception of the risk. However, there is no known "real" risk that is not structured by assessors' value judgments about it. Thus there is no easy assurance that the allegedly "real" radiation risk is minimal. Hence, those who make the expertise inference typically beg the question of risk acceptability.

Dismissals of lay risk perceptions regarding radwaste are all the more questionable because Congress has reported that 80 percent of Nevadans oppose the repository and believe that the state should do everything in its power to stop the Yucca Mountain facility.[137] Such statistics suggest that something more is at issue than merely faulty perceptions of an allegedly "real" risk that is minimal. Instead, in cases like that at Yucca Mountain, there is a quantitative "expert" definition of *risk*, as opposed to a qualitative, allegedly subjective notion of lay *risk perception*. Those who fall victim to the expertise inference typically assume that risk can be defined purely probabilistically, for example, as an average annual probability of fatality.[138] They likewise assume that anyone (e.g., a layperson concerned about consent, equity, etc.) who does not subscribe to this purely probabilistic definition has an erroneous *risk perception*, rather than an accurate, alternative risk perception. It will not do, however, to stipulatively define one type of risk (that of laypeople) merely as a misperception of another type of risk (that of scientists, engineers, and risk assessors). All known risks are perceived, and all risk judgments involve methodological value judgments. There are no perception-free risks that are known, and hence there are neither wholly objective risk assessors nor wholly accurate risk perceptions.

The important thing about lay risk perceptions is that most laypeople would probably claim that what makes a thing most unacceptable are factors that are not susceptible to quantification, factors such as a risk's being imposed without consent, or being unknown, or posing a threat to civil liberties or to the welfare of members of future generations. Such factors are part of the reason why consideration of potential human error and the social amplification of risk is so important at sites like Yucca Mountain, even though most probabilistic risk assessment ignores the social amplification of risk.[139] Moreover, if laypersons have perceptions of mismanagement or managerial incompetence at repositories like Yucca Mountain, then this perception is likely to influence their response to the hazardous facility. Perceived risks are often good predictors of socioeconomic impacts and of people's reactions to them.[140] Hence, no complete separation may be possible between actual and perceived risk. Admittedly, at Yucca Mountain there is a large gap between expert and lay perceptions of the risks associated with the repository.[141] Even if it could be established, however, that the public exaggerates the threatening probabilities associated with some facility, such as Yucca Mountain, this alleged exaggeration might not be the main reason for opposition to it. The opposition could be based, for example, on potential threats to future generations or on future socioeconomic impacts. Hence, the lay risk perceptions might not be so much *wrong*, compared to those of experts, as they are based on *different* values about risk.

Apart from the fact that it is not possible to completely separate risk from risk perceptions, if policymakers assume that there is a perceived risk/real risk distinction, and that only scientists or assessors can describe "real" risk, then at least two undesirable consequences could occur. One consequence is that there would be less reason for policymakers/experts to take account of lay views because they would be viewed as erroneous. ("Error has no rights.") The expertise inference also could lead to disenfranchising democratic decisionmakers. This appears to be one of the causes of concern at proposed radioactive waste sites such as Yucca Mountain. As our earlier discussion of human error (see chapter 4) suggested, Nevadans are worried about being disenfranchised and about decisions being made that are not in their interests. Hence, it behooves all risk assessors not to employ the expertise inference but, instead, to attempt to understand lay risk perceptions. They are important at least because of the lack of trust that often lies behind them.[142]

The Linearity Inference

Another common difficulty to which repository risk assessors sometimes fall victim is the linearity inference. This is the belief that for any rational and informed person there is a linear relationship between a risk (defined as an annual probability of fatality) and the value of avoiding the risk.[143] Following this strategy, many hazard assessors "explain" societal aversion to certain low-probability technological risks by alleging that the public does not know the accident probabilities in question. They maintain that, given knowledge of the actual likelihood of death, rational persons always are more averse to high-probability risks than to low-probability ones. Indeed, assessors who rely on this inference frequently are correct: persons often are more averse to higher-probability risks. In general, however, the inference is not true.

In employing the linearity inference, risk analysts likely err, in part, because the restriction of risk to "probability of fatality" is highly questionable. There are no compelling inductive reasons for relying on the linearity inference because there are obviously many other cost burdens, such as "decreasing the GNP by a given amount," whose probability also determines the value of avoiding a given risk. Another problem is that the value of avoiding a given risk is often a function of the benefits to be gained from it, or whether it is distributed inequitably.[144] In fact, if Fischhoff and other assessors who employ psychometric surveys are correct, then risk acceptability is more closely correlated with equity than any other factors.[145] Catastrophic potential and the fact that low-probability/high-consequence situations are often the product of *public* (societally imposed) risks, as opposed to *private* (individually chosen) risks, may also explain risk aversion; there is evidence that the psychological trauma (feelings of impotence, depression, rage) associated with the imposition of a *public* hazard (like a nuclear power plant) is greater than that associated with the choice of a *private* risk (like smoking a certain number of cigarettes) of the same probability. One author even suggests that widespread despair and an increasing suicide rate may be attributable to the hazards and fatalities caused by "industrial cannibalism."[146] If so, then there may be good reason why society's risk aversion is not proportional to probability of fatality. Moreover, although according to utility theory, a high-probability/low-consequence event (10,000 accidents, each killing 1 person) and a low-probability/high-consequence situation (1 accident killing 10,000 persons) may have the same expected value, reasonable persons are typically more averse to the low-probability/high-consequence situation. One explanation may be that the high-consequence events, like nuclear accidents or catastrophic global warming, are often more difficult to quantify.[147] Regardless of the reason, however, it is clear that many rational people do not believe that the value of risk aversion is directly proportional to the probability of fatality associated with it. And if not, then to infer this proportionality is to employ the linearity inference.

A number of assessors who argue for permanent repositories use the linearity inference. Indeed, even DOE assessors do so. In one assessment, for example, the DOE dismissed radiological hazards associated with a proposed high-level facility, because the exposures were expected by the DOE to be below those from background radiation.[148] In thus dismissing the facility-induced hazards, it is clear that DOE researchers employed the linearity inference. They assumed that the hazards were insignificant, merely because the probability of fatality associated with them was lower, on a linear scale, than the probability of fatality associated with background exposures. In other assessments, DOE assessors have likewise fallen victim to the linearity inference by virtue of dismissing allegedly "small" radiological risks, on the grounds that the public is exposed to much larger risks in other areas of life.[149]

Often risk assessors employ the linearity inference when they wish to dismiss some safety improvement as "insignificant," given the costs required to make such an improvement. For example, one Yucca

Mountain quantitative risk assessment (QRA) argued that it was too expensive to fabricate a 10,000-year waste package merely to meet Environmental Protection Agency and Nuclear Regulatory Commission standards for carbon-14 dioxide because the numbers of persons likely to be benefited were quite small.[150] The assumptions underlying this questionable inference are that only large risks to the general population, not smaller risks to a restricted population, are worth expensive controls. Another faulty value judgment here is that equity in risk distribution is not important, only the overall magnitude of risk. Likewise the problematic inference is based on the presupposition that the value of risk avoidance is proportional to the probability of fatality.

Whenever they fall victim to the linearity inference, assessors err because they discount the importance of the cumulative nature of radiation risks (mentioned in chapter 2), the inequities imposed by "average" standards, and the necessity of consent and compensation for all those on whom risks are involuntarily imposed. In ignoring all these social and ethical determinants of risk acceptability, assessors who employ the linearity inference likewise make a number of questionable utilitarian value judgments (see the previous chapter), such as that the rights of some (geographical or temporal) minority to protection from risk can be ignored. They also err in reducing risk to purely "physical" impacts. Similarly, they err in ignoring the fact that low-probability, high-consequence risks—such as a worst-case leaching of radwaste from Yucca Mountain—could be unacceptable. For all these reasons, the linearity inference ought to be avoided in assessing radwaste repositories.

The De Minimis Inference

Another problem that frequently occurs at the third, or risk-evaluation, stage of assessment is the faulty inference that because a particular exposure to risk is below a certain threshold or consistent with a particular standard, therefore the exposure is harmless or acceptable. This inference is questionable, even on inductive grounds, especially in the case of radiation, because exposures are cumulative. Hence, numerous allegedly small exposures to radiation could yield a cumulative dose that causes injury or death. The inference is also questionable because it is inconsistent and dangerous to condone sub-threshold hazards but to condemn the deaths caused by the aggregate of these sub-threshold harms. It is irrational for risk assessors to say both that each sub-threshold exposure to a cumulative hazard is harmless and yet that the sum of these doses causes great harm. If they claim that each of the sub-threshold risks is *unacceptable*, however, then they face the undesirable consequence that government officials must somehow regulate or compensate for such risks, an extraordinarily difficult and expensive task, since attaining zero risk is technically and practically impossible. If they claim that sub-threshold risks are *acceptable*, then they must admit that although it is immoral to murder fellow citizens, it is moral to impose an increased risk of death on some persons, little by little, by hazards such as radiation. The only consistent path is to admit that even small exposures to a cumulative hazard are harmful.[151]

A related difficulty occurs because society must declare some threshold below which a hazard is judged to be negligible. Often this de minimis level for a given risk is set at what would cause less than a 10^{-6} increase in one's average annual probability of fatality.[152] The reasoning behind setting such a level is that a zero-risk society is impossible and that some standard needs to be set, especially to determine pollution control expenditures. Choosing the 10^{-6} standard also appears reasonable, both because society must attempt to reduce larger risks first, and because 10^{-6} is the natural-hazards death rate.[153] The erroneous inference arises because no de minimis standard is able to provide equal protection from harm to all citizens. On the one hand, if one rejects the de minimis standard, then pollution control requirements would be difficult to determine. On the other hand, if one accepts the de minimis standard, then citizen protection would be based on some *average* annual probability of fatality, not on *equal* protection for all.

Because the 10^{-6} threshold seems acceptable, on the average, does not mean that it is acceptable to each individual. Most civil rights, for example, are not accorded on the basis of the *average* needs of persons, but on the basis of *individual* characteristics. For instance, I have a right to free speech, as defined by societal standards and as interpreted on the basis of the *individual* characteristics of my speech (whether it is slanderous or not, and so on). My right to free speech is not limited to my making the sorts of statements made, on *average*, by persons. Hence, why is a 10^{-6} average threshold for societal risk accepted for everyone, without compensation, when adopting it poses risks higher than 10^{-6} for the elderly, for children, for persons with previous exposures to carcinogens, for those with allergies, for persons who lead sedentary lives, and for the poor? Presumably society also needs to take account of the *individual* needs of the elderly, children, and so on, and not merely *average* risk levels. If risk assessors make the de minimis inference and claim that average exposure data or average levels of risk are harmless or acceptable, then they err. To use such average levels requires somehow that persons consent to possible additional risk that they may bear and/or that they be compensated for possible risk that exceeds the average level.[154]

One of the clearest examples of using the de minimis inference in repository assessment occurs in a DOE document stating that: "the rule of thumb is that scenario classes in which combinations of processes and events have less than 1 chance in 10,000 of occurring during the period of interest are generally excluded from further consideration."[155] The judgment is questionable on all the grounds already considered, as well as problematic for a number of other reasons. One reason is that DOE officials claim that the department regulates Yucca Mountain consistent with other nuclear facilities. Yet the regulations governing other nuclear facilities specifically require consideration of all risks greater than 10^{-6} per year.[156] This means that the DOE is being inconsistent in allowing Yucca Mountain risks to be 2 orders of magnitude higher (than other nuclear risks) before they are subject to analysis and potential regulation. The more serious problem, however, is that DOE managers appear to use the de minimis inference. That is, they assume that some level of risk, below 10^{-4}, is acceptable merely because it is of a certain magnitude.[157] As we have already explained, low magnitude alone does not make a risk acceptable; one must take account of factors such as accuracy of the estimates, equity, consent, compensation, due process, and so on.

Similar de minimis assumptions and problematic value judgments have also been made by some Yucca Mountain assessors when they concluded that risk from transport of radioactive materials to and from Yucca Mountain was "small" merely because they predicted it to be below the level of natural background risks already occurring in the United States.[158] (The researchers predicted Yucca Mountain truck, rail, and radiological fatalities to be as high, respectively, as 38, 8, and 12 deaths during the first 26 years of the operation of the repository.) Their judgment of smallness, in turn, carries with it a presupposition of the acceptability of the Yucca Mountain risk. However, no risk arguably is small enough if it is avoidable, or not necessary, or unfair, or inequitably distributed. Hence, it is questionable to infer that some de minimis risk level is acceptable purely because of its magnitude.

The Consent Inference

Another risk-evaluation problem occurs whenever assessors forget that, all things being equal, rational persons are more averse to risks to which they have not consented than to those voluntarily accepted. As a consequence of human rights to free, informed consent, imposition of certain risks is ethically legitimate only after consent is obtained from the affected parties. Questions of consent pose problems for risk evaluation (of facilities like proposed repositories) because all those genuinely able to give legitimate consent to a particular risk are precisely those who—very likely—will never do so, whereas those alleged to have given consent to a particular risk are often those who are unable to do so. A good example of this arises in workplace situations. Here there is an alleged compensating wage differential, noted both by economists and risk assessors. According to the theory behind the differential, the riskier the occupation, the higher the wage required to compensate the worker for bearing the risk, all things being equal.[159]

Moreover, imposition of these higher workplace hazards is legitimate apparently only after the worker consents, with knowledge of the risks involved, to perform the work for the agreed-upon wage. Yet who is most likely to give legitimate informed consent to a workplace hazard? It is a person who is well educated and possesses a reasonable understanding of the risk, especially its long term and probabilistic effects. It is a person who is not forced, under dire financial constraints, to take a job that he knows is likely to harm him. Yet sociological data reveal that as education and income rise, persons are less willing to take risky jobs or to tolerate hazardous facilities in their communities; those who do so are primarily those who are poorly educated or financially strapped.[160] If these sociological data about situations of consent are accurate, and if one does not wish to sacrifice either workers or citizens who have not given free informed consent to the risks that they face, then risk assessors ought to evaluate involuntarily imposed hazards more negatively. Or, risks ought to be evaluated as less acceptable, all things being equal, to the degree that potential victims are less likely to have given genuine free informed consent. Otherwise, assessors employ the consent inference.[161] Frequently, however, assessors do not evaluate involuntary risks more negatively, and hence they fall victim to this difficulty.

In the work associated with various candidate repositories, virtually none of the DOE assessments are dedicated to evaluating whether the facilities might jeopardize citizens' rights to free, informed consent and thus impose an undesirable ethical and social burden on the public. Indeed, one of the ways in which the Yucca Mountain assessments have encouraged use of a consent inference is in failing to provide adequate information to citizens about the nature of the possible risks that they might face because of the proposed facility. The reluctance of DOE assessors to consider worst cases and to assess possible events having a probability lower than 10^{-4} per year indicates that the site studies will provide only limited information about the repository risk. Other causes of limited information at Yucca Mountain are the insistence of DOE officials on meeting the schedule for completion of assessments[162]—rather than on assessing the risks in a comprehensive way—and the secrecy and bias that have pervaded DOE repository activities.[163] Indeed, until the Nevada attorney general sued the DOE, the DOE refused to fund Nevada requests for independent experts to study the site.[164] As a result, Nevadans have charged the DOE with not consulting adequately regarding the evaluation of the site.[165] Affected citizens from Nevada, Texas, Washington, and Mississippi also have argued that DOE officials have withheld data regarding the proposed radioactive waste facilities in their respective states.[166] As a result, General Accounting Office (GAO) researchers concluded that the "DOE has not allowed them (states and Indian tribes) to participate in the program to the extent intended by the [Nuclear Waste Policy] Act [of 1982]."[167] Dozens of lawsuits have been brought against the DOE regarding its handling of the waste program.[168] Because DOE officials have made it difficult for the public to obtain adequate information about Yucca Mountain, citizens cannot exercise their rights to free informed consent to the risk. And if the assessment process has jeopardized the public's exercise of free informed consent to the Yucca Mountain risk, then that process is flawed—by a consent inference.

Indeed, it is likely that any attempted justification for siting a permanent, high-level radioactive waste facility will fall victim to the consent inference. By virtue of the fact that permanent, high-level geological disposal imposes its greatest risks on members of future generations, it is impossible for current policymakers to obtain the free informed consent of the very persons most likely to be harmed seriously by permanent disposal. In order to do a better job of providing free informed consent to future generations, we shall argue in chapter 8 that geological disposal ought to be avoided, at least for the foreseeable future (the next century). In chapter 9, we shall argue that monitored retrievable storage of the wastes would provide more information (through monitoring) about the risk and hence more opportunity for citizens to exercise free informed consent regarding its storage or management.

Specious Accuracy

In addition to their difficulties regarding free informed consent, repository risk assessors also often fall victim to an inference of specious accuracy, confusing the precision of their quantitative results with their applicability in a specific situation. For example, economists use "price" to stand for "value." They then infer that, because the substituted concept has predictive and explanatory power, therefore they have captured the original phenomenon. In inferring that they have captured the original phenomenon, as Morgenstern explains, they fall victim to "specious accuracy,"[169] to confusing precision with applicability. They confuse precise but irrelevant and inapplicable results with real explanation. In so doing, they simplify the situation, but in a way that misrepresents or falsifies it, or that renders objective risk assessment impossible. They become like the drunk who looks for his watch under the street light, not because he lost it there, but because it is the only place he can see. Likewise, repository risk assessors often calculate results that are available rather than those that are relevant.

Exhibiting the inference of specious accuracy, some DOE assessors evaluated the test-selection process for Yucca Mountain and outlined information needs but then asserted that determination of acceptable levels of confidence was outside the scope of their investigations.[170] Yet without determination of an acceptable confidence level, results are not obviously applicable or reliable. Other DOE assessors likewise calculated rates of radionuclide discharge at Yucca Mountain by using methods that presupposed that transport was of a single radionuclide, that the rock contained uniform parallel fractures, or that the flow was one-dimensional.[171] By making all these (and other) assumptions, repository risk assessors were able to get precise quantitative results. Without the assumptions, no calculations would have been possible. Nevertheless, the precise results were not applicable to the situation because the assumptions were counterfactual, at least in the Yucca Mountain case. Hence, the results exhibited a specious accuracy.

Such specious accuracy has caused problems at radwaste repositories in the past. Consider, for example, the counterfactual assumption in many of the Yucca Mountain groundwater models, that the flow is one-dimensional or vertical.[172] Because this assumption was made at the Maxey Flats low-level radioactive waste site, assessors missed the lateral components of flow that appear to have been one of the main vehicles for release of the radioactive leachate. This particular methodological value judgment (about one-dimensional flow at Yucca Mountain) should be scrutinized all the more carefully because some researchers have indicated that there is great potential for lateral flow through faults and fractures at Yucca Mountain.[173] If so, we could repeat Maxey Flats' mistakes in studies of other proposed waste facilities. Assessors should continue to model multidimensional vertical and lateral flow and not merely one-dimensional vertical flow.[174]

Some researchers have recognized and avoided the inference of specious accuracy. They have specifically noted that their conclusions are based on the "best scientific judgment" but that they may not be applicable to specific sites given the disanalogies between the general models and the heterogeneous field situations.[175] Nevertheless, a number of repository risk assessors appear to have forgotten the limits on reliability imposed by particular methodological value judgments and inferences.

The Inference of the Multiple Maximand

Another problematic value judgment that occurs frequently in assessing repository risks is the inference that it is possible to maximize both safety and efficiency in storing high-level radioactive waste. DOE documents mandate Yucca Mountain repository performance, for example, that is both safe and efficient.[176] This mandate to maximize both safety and efficiency presupposes a questionable value judgment because it is impossible to observe. Greater safety is more expensive, and greater efficiency of time and money results in less safe radwaste management. The value judgment that one can maximize these two variables is clearly problematic because only a priority ranking is mathematically possible, with one or the other being maximized at a time. Admittedly, one can employ differential equations, for example, that provide "multiple objective analyses," but such analyses do not genuinely maximize more than one variable at a time.

Apart from the mathematical impossibility of maximizing two variables, like safety and efficiency, there is also a practical reason for doubting the claim that one can maximize safety and efficiency at sites like Yucca Mountain. This practical reason is that DOE managers are in charge of both production and safety at its installations. United States Representative Tom Luken calls this the "big similarity" between Chernobyl and DOE facilities, and Representative Ron Wyden has talked about the fox (the DOE) guarding the henhouse, the nuclear facilities.[177] As another member of Congress put it: "The DOE system of virtual self-regulation is incompatible with the built in pressures for production."[178] As a result of such self-regulation, at DOE radiation-related facilities like the feed-materials plant at Fernald, Ohio, efficiency and production have always had the highest priority. According to Representative Philip Sharp and representatives of the Fernald labor union—and as DOE officials themselves admit—the tradeoffs between safety and production have been very pronounced and the source of many difficulties at DOE installations, including the Ohio facility. Production and "meeting the schedule" have always come first.[179] Indeed, as we already mentioned in the previous chapter, the competition between safety and production, according to Representative Tom Luken, caused government officials either to ignore reports of health and safety violations or to retaliate against the whistleblowers.[180]

K. O. Fultz of the Government Accounting Office confirmed that because of the push to meet production schedules (efficiency), DOE managers have repeatedly allowed safety to be compromised in the name of alleged efficiency. Fernald, Lawrence Livermore, Savannah River, Rocky Flats, Hanford, Oak Ridge, and Idaho Falls all have extensive soil and water contamination caused by pressure to meet the schedule and to work cost effectively. Moreover, officials from Washington, Nevada, Mississippi, Minnesota, and other states have complained about DOE's pushing its schedule above all else. As Representative Tom Luken put it: "In many cases the DOE decided the costs [of removing safety violations] were prohibitive and therefore the health [of workers and the public] would be sacrificed."[181] In 1985 the DOE issued the Kane Report and said that the Department's environmental, health, and safety program was a "toothless watchdog . . . a disgrace."[182] Such 1985 criticisms of the DOE apparently did little to accomplish reform because, in 1989, every nuclear-materials reactor in the United States was shut down because of safety problems.[183] Luken has claimed that the DOE record of inductive evidence on safety indicates that short-term efficiency often is allowed to take precedence over environmental and human welfare. Hence, there is a strong empirical base for doubting that DOE managers at Yucca Mountain, or any similar repository, would be likely to maximize safety considerations if they got in the way of efficiency. Indeed, reviewers have already charged that, at Yucca Mountain, "the schedule constraint appears to be driving the heavy reliance on analytical models in determining site suitability, rather than determining suitability through the use of empirical findings."[184]

Part of the reason for the DOE's being "schedule-driven" is not only that it is attempting to maximize efficiency at the expense of safety, but also that it is receiving pressure from U.S. nuclear utilities needing a repository for storing radioactive waste. According to the utilities, they have paid more than $4 billion into the Nuclear Waste Fund.[185] Yet despite their payments to DOE under the Nuclear Waste Policy Act, they have no facility operative for spent fuel. Hence, part of the schedule-pushing by DOE officials could be in response to the accumulation of spent reactor fuel at plants throughout the United States.

Regardless of the factors causing DOE managers to push the repository schedule, the consequences of the pressure are contributing to poor science in the repository assessments. Risk assessors themselves have claimed that tight schedules for producing final versions of environmental assessments for Yucca Mountain have prevented their using developed equations for estimating releases of radionuclides into groundwater.[186] Other assessors have claimed that they chose particular models of the Yucca Mountain site because they were easier and more efficient to use.[187] Hence, it is not surprising that representatives for the state of Nevada have argued before Congress that the DOE is "driven by schedule" rather than by safety considerations and that the environmental assessment of Yucca Mountain is based on "incomplete, inaccurate, and sometimes manipulated data."[188] Representatives of citizens affected by DOE facilities in other states—Ohio, Washington, and Texas, for example—have made similar charges.[189] If schedule efficiency has already compromised state-of-the-art risk studies, then there is reason to believe that other considerations of alleged efficiency likewise might compromise safety at future repositories, just as they have at other DOE facilities, and as they appear to have done already at Yucca Mountain. And if so, then there are additional social, political, and practical grounds for believing that it is impossible to maximize both safety and efficiency at radwaste repositories, including Yucca Mountain.

Affirming the Consequent

Yet another difficulty that occurs frequently in repository risk assessments is the inference of affirming the consequent. This inference occurs whenever one postulates that a hypothesis is true or accurate, merely because some test result—predicted to follow from the hypothesis—actually occurs. In fact, however, failure of predictions can only falsify theories, but success of predictions can only tend to confirm (but not verify) theories. A particular test result's occurring never establishes the truth of the hypothesis from which it follows, because "h entails r" is not the same as "r entails h." All that can be validly inferred from a test is that the results are consistent with the hypothesis or that the results have falsified the hypothesis, h, because of the failure of r. In other words, from "h entails r," one can infer "*not r* entails *not h*." To assume that one can infer "r entails h" from "h entails r" is to affirm the consequent. Of course, it is very important to test one's hypotheses in order to determine whether the data falsify them or tend to confirm them. Moreover, the greater the number of tests, and the more representative they are, the greater is the assurance that the data are consistent with the hypotheses. Indeed, one of the repeatedly acknowledged failures of the Yucca Mountain assessments is that the models often are not tested.[190] It is important to test the models, to attempt to falsify them, and to determine the degree to which they are consistent with the data. If the models do turn out to be consistent with the data, however, it is wrong to assume that they have been absolutely "verified" or "validated" because, short of affirming the consequent, it is impossible to verify or validate any model. It is possible merely to achieve higher degrees of confirmation or probability—through testing—that the hypothesis or model has been confirmed to this or that degree.

At the proposed Yucca Mountain repository, risk assessors have repeatedly proposed to test some *h*, some hypothesis, such as that the number of calculated groundwater travel times are less than ten thousand years. When the calculations, data, and models are shown to be *consistent* with the hypothesis, then the assessors have erroneously assumed that the hypothesis has predictive power or has been "verified." For example, one group of assessors, studying groundwater travel time, concluded: "This evidence indicates that the Yucca Mountain repository site would be in compliance with regulatory requirements."[191] Many other risk assessors speak of "verifying" their models and "validating" them. For instance, one group of assessors concluded that the tools they used demonstrated "verification of engineering software used to solve thermomechanical problems" at Yucca Mountain.[192]

Admittedly, software and systems engineers speak of computer models' being "validated" and "verified." Yet, such "validation" language obscures the fact that the alleged validation really only guarantees that certain test results are consistent with a model or hypothesis; it does not validate or verify the model or hypothesis because affirming the consequent prevents legitimate validation or verification. Hence, when computer scientists speak of "program verification,"[193] at best they are making a problematic inference in affirming the consequent. At worst, they are trading on an equivocation between "algorithms" and "programs." As Fetzer argues,[194] algorithms, as logical structures, are appropriate subjects for deductive verification. As such, *algorithms* occur in pure mathematics and pure logic. They are subject to demonstration or verification because they characterize claims that are always true as a function of the meanings assigned to the specific symbols used to express them. *Programs*, however, as causal models of logical structures, are not verifiable because the premises are not true merely as a function of their meaning. "The discontinuous nature of programming"—with its holes and caverns, its patchwork of ad hoc, informal structures, and its cumulative complexity—is not the problem. The problem is that *encodings* of algorithms that can be compiled and/or executed by a machine, as opposed to the performance of an abstract machine, cannot be conclusively verified. The performance of an abstract machine can be conclusively verified, but it possesses no significance for the performance of a physical system. As Einstein put it, insofar as the laws of mathematics refer to reality, they are not certain; insofar as they are certain, they do not refer to reality.

In using "verification" and "validation" language, both official

DOE documents and individual risk assessments for repositories like Yucca Mountain are systematically misleading as to whether the studies are reliable. For example, explicitly affirming the consequent, the DOE affirmed:

Validation . . . is a demonstration that a model as embodied in a computer code is an adequate representation of the process or system for which it is intended. The most common method of validation involves a comparison of the measured response from in-situ testing, lab testing, or natural analogs with the results of computational models that embody the model assumptions that are being tested.[195]

Authors of the same official DOE document, used to provide standards for Yucca Mountain risk assessments, also talk about the need to verify computational models of the waste site. They say:

Verification, according to the guidelines in NUREG-0856 . . . is the provision of assurance that a code correctly performs the operations it specifies. A common method of verification is the comparison of a code's results with solutions obtained analytically. . . . Benchmarking is a useful method that consists of using two or more codes to solve related problems and then comparing the results.[196]

Although the term "verification"—as used by DOE assessors—suggests that the computer models or codes accurately represent the phenomena they seek to predict, it is merely a misleading euphemism for "benchmarking," comparing the results of two different codes (computer models) for simulating an identical problem. On this scheme, one "verifies" a model of Yucca Mountain against another model. What is required in the real world, however, is validating a model against reality. This validation or confirmation can be accomplished only by repeated testing of the code or model against the real world, against field conditions.

Even with repeated field testing, however, compliance can never be confirmed, short of full testing of all cases throughout all time periods. Classic studies of the problem of induction show that complete testing is impossible. Therefore, the shorter the time of testing and the fewer the cases considered, the less reliable and the less confirmed are allegedly "validated" computer models or codes. The tests can only falsify or confirm a hypothesis, not validate it. To assume otherwise is to affirm the consequent. Hence, every conclusion of compliance with government regulations or every conclusion of repository safety, on the basis of "verified" or "validated" test or simulation results, is an example of affirming the consequent. Program *verification*, in other words, "is not even a theoretical possibility."[197] One cannot *prove* safety. One can only demonstrate that one has attempted to falsify one's results and either has failed in doing so or has done so. Therefore, both the DOE risk documents and risk assessors at Yucca Mountain are misleading in speaking of "validation" and "verification" at Yucca Mountain:

1. Real validation and verification is impossible because of the problems of induction and affirming the consequent. Only falsification of an hypothesis, or determining that the data are consistent with it, is possible. In the latter case, when one obtains repeated results indicating that the data are consistent with the model or hypothesis, one is able merely to increase the probability that the model or hypothesis has been confirmed.

2. The DOE's and assessors' use of the terms "verification" and "validation" misleads the public about the reliability of studies allegedly guaranteeing repository safety.

3. Use of the term "verification" by DOE assessors is, in particular, misleading because they typically only compare different computer codes or models with no reference to the real world, and because any model can be tuned or calibrated to fit any pattern of data, even when the model is not well confirmed.

4. It is arguable that most useful programs are not merely unverifiable but incorrect; that even programs that function correctly in isolation may not do so in combination; and that most of the important requirements of real programs are not formalizable.[198]

Given these four difficulties with "verifying" programs used in real-world situations, as in the case of repository modeling, there are both prudential and ethical problems with risk assessors' continuing to use the language of "program verification" in connection with modeling causal relationships. The *prudential* problem is that aiming at "verification" does not tell us what we most want to know—about complex relationships in the physical world. The more complex the system, the less likely it is to perform as desired and the less reliable is inductive testing of it. Moreover, by emphasizing verification, theorists have increased the expense of achieving "transparent software upgrades," and they have decreased software reliability because of their emphasis on "misplaced advocacy of formal analysis."[199] The *ethical* problem is that by encouraging confidence in the operational performance of a complex causal system, claims of "verification" oversell the reliability of software and undersell the importance of design failures in safety-critical applications like waste repositories. Such overselling and underselling not only expose the safety of the public to the dangerous consequences of risk assessors' "groupthink,"[200] but also risk misunderstanding of software in cases where the risks are greatest. To avoid affirming the consequent, the invalid inference that repository safety models can be "verified," repository risk assessors need to refrain from the claim that their results "indicate" or "show" or "prove" compliance with government regulations or with some standard of safety. They also would do well, when they have not checked the models against field data, to avoid misleading claims that they have "verified" or "validated" the mathematical models at Yucca Mountain and elsewhere.[201] Such terms suggest a level of reliability and predictive power which, because of the long time periods involved, is impossible in practice at Yucca Mountain. Instead, assessors might do better to speak in terms of *probabilities* that a given model or hypothesis has been *confirmed* and to avoid misleading claims about verification.

The Appeal to Authority

If it is impossible to "verify" or "validate" either the safety of any permanent facility for high-level radioactive waste or its future compliance with government regulations, then what is the basis for risk assessors' claims of safety and compliance? For one thing, more testing and modeling—especially "risky" testing designed to falsify erroneous hypotheses—could help to provide a basis for sound conclusions regarding Yucca Mountain and other proposed repositories. It also could help to increase the probability that the reliability of certain models or hypotheses is confirmed. Apart from such safeguards, however, much of repository risk assessors' basis for their conclusions is often mere opinion. But the use of expert opinion sometimes involves assessors in another difficulty, the appeal to authority. An appeal to an authority is no foolproof logical basis for a conclusion because authorities can be wrong and because only data and logic force a conclusion to be true. An authority's guarantee, alone, is not sufficient to cause a conclusion to be true. Rather, if a conclusion is true (because of the data and logic supporting it), then an authority will be correct in supporting it. The reverse is not true. Hence, in the absence of correct inferences and adequate data, when risk assessors merely appeal to authority to support their conclusions, they exhibit an invalid inference.

Of course, in many areas of science we are forced to rely on the judgments of authorities. Typically such reliance on expert opinion is plausible to the degree that (1) it represents scientific consensus, (2) we are able to test the claims and confirm them, and (3) the appeals to authority are not substitutes for sound reasoning and adequate evidence. The appeals to authority in the Yucca Mountain case are problematic because conditions 1–3 typically are not satisfied. In other words, such appeals (in Yucca Mountain studies) are troublesome not primarily because they are invalid inferences, but because they take the place of *inductive* studies that need to be more comprehensive.

Appeals to authority are particularly damaging in cases like Yucca Mountain because they intimidate citizens and laypersons who have neither the power nor the position to influence repository risk-assessment outcomes as they—potential victims likely to be affected by the disposal facility—would like to do. As several Yucca Mountain researchers put it: even when the data do not support the optimistic conclusions, the tone of the DOE risk-assessment work conveys the attitude that few problems exist at Yucca Mountain.[202] Such a tone and attitude is part of an appeal to authority that has no logical relationship to empirical confirmation of the scientific conclusions. Specific examples of appeals to authority on the part of Yucca Mountain risk assessors include the claims that radioactive releases at the site would be "significantly less" than those imposed by government standards, and that there would be less than one health effect every 1,400 years caused by Yucca Mountain.[203] The assessors gave these assurances after noting that they had not measured water infiltration into Yucca Mountain and that they had not considered fracture flow.[204] Hence, the appeal to authority was used here as a substitute for comprehensive testing and for gathering additional inductive data. Other assessors, in a fashion typical of some repository assessments, used a computer model to simulate radionuclide transport at Yucca Mountain. The computer model was based on a number of counterfactual and unknown conditions, yet the DOE assessors concluded that their model "was found to be an effective tool for simulation of the performance of the repository systems at Yucca Mountain."[205] Assertions such as these indicate not only that risk assessors are sometimes guilty of an appeal to ignorance (see earlier parts of this chapter) but also that, in the absence of data, the assessors often simply appeal to their own authority. Again, the main problem with such an inferential appeal is not its deductive invalidity but the fact that the appeal, atypical of its use in other areas of science, is employed as a substitute for actual testing and inductive confirmation.

In the case of the proposed Yucca Mountain repository, the assessors' appeal to authority appears to be generated in part by DOE adherence to the same invalid inference. In response to reviewers' questions, for example, DOE officials often defend repository risk assessments with mere appeals to their own expertise. For instance, when questioners pressed DOE authorities on their use of uncertain geological data and nonconservative site models, the DOE simply responded that the "evidence available" was

sufficient to generate considerable, if not complete, confidence in the minds of responsible investigators that the Yucca Mountain site could be shown to meet the post closure system guidelines.[206]

Likewise, instead of explaining or defending its use of specific scientific evidence for its conclusions, when the DOE officials were questioned by reviewers they simply appealed to their "professional judgment" and their "technical judgment."[207]

One problem with the DOE's appealing to its professional or technical judgment is that often such judgment is exercised in a very subjective way. For example, in the 1992 *Early Site Suitability Evaluation* (ESSE) for Yucca Mountain, the DOE admitted repeatedly that subjective judgments have played a "significant" and a "critical" role in site determinations, given the inadequacy of the data and the inability of assessors to quantify many site risks.[208] There are a number of reasons, however, for believing that this reliance on subjective judgments is highly problematic. For one thing, for the DOE to assume the adequacy of nonquantifiable, subjective judgments is inconsistent with the repeated ESSE claim that "the content of the ESSE Integrated Evaluation Package provides an unbiased and objective presentation of information relevant to the suitability issues covered by each guideline."[209] How can the DOE ESSE Core Team admit its repeated reliance on nonquantified "subjective" judgments and yet claim that its presentation is "objective"? How can the DOE ESSE Core Team itself admit that its judgments are subjective,[210] and yet claim that the purpose of the peer review was "to determine whether the ESSE report presents an objective and technically defensible view" of the site suitability issue?[211] If the DOE team admitted its reliance on subjective decisions, then it already knows the answer to its own question.

A second problem with accepting the adequacy of subjective judgments for site suitability is that, as one reviewer (J. H. Bell) of the 1992 ESSE put it, if some data are "subjectively" determined, "why couldn't it [the decision that the site is 'suitable'] just as well be an unsuitable [site decision]?"[212] More precisely, if the ESSE decision is based in part on subjectivity, as both the DOE team and the peer evaluators admit, then presumably there is no clear, purely objective procedure for deciding whether the site is suitable or not. But if there is no purely objective procedure for deciding whether the site is suitable or not, then it cannot be a purely objective decision to say that the site is suitable rather than unsuitable.

A third problem with the assumption—that nonquantifiable and subjective judgments about risk are adequate for determining site suitability—is that at least one of the peer reviewers for the 1992 ESSE of Yucca Mountain appears to disagree with this judgment. W. J. Arabasz signed a statement denying that the ESSE, in final form, was "unbiased" and "objective." He also denied that the site suitability conclusions were balanced and objective.[213] Another peer reviewer (T. Webb) simply did not sign the statement affirming that the ESSE was unbiased and objective.[214] Moreover, three other reviewers (M. T. Einaudi, D. K. Kreamer, and W. G. Pariseau) noted on their statements that, provided that the original ESSE document was revised along the lines they suggested, it would be unbiased and objective.[215] This means that more than one-third of the peer reviewers apparently believed that at least the original ESSE for Yucca Mountain was not unbiased and objective. Also, several of the fourteen reviewers maintained that even the final version of the DOE ESSE document was not unbiased and objective. Because of all these difficulties with risk assessors' reliance on subjective judgments, the inference—that assessors can reliably appeal to (their own) authority in repository assessment—is questionable.

Some of the most problematic appeals to authority have occurred when DOE officials and risk assessors were questioned about their commitment to safety. They responded, for example, that

in the past 35 years, the Department [of Energy] and its predecessor agencies have accumulated thousands of man years of experience in managing radioactive wastes at various sites around the country. During this time, active health and safety programs have been maintained to reduce industrial and radiological accidents to levels as low as reasonably achievable. Accidents and releases of radioactive materials have occurred, but there have been no injuries to members of the public or serious environmental damage as a result of these operations.[216]

Such a claim contradicts the explicit statements of both the General Accounting Office (GAO), and the DOE's own Kane Report (1985), as well as the conclusions of many members of Congress who have investigated DOE facilities.[217] Hence, the DOE assertion appears to be merely an appeal to authority. DOE officials likewise claimed, after a particularly damaging set of criticisms of the DOE health and safety record, that "these reviews [of radioactive materials/waste facilities], while identifying possible improvements, have shown that the Department's operations have not and do not present a significant hazard."[218] Given the earlier discussions of bias, coverup, retaliation against whistleblowers, and GAO criticism of DOE environmental and safety standards (see chapter 4 and earlier sections in this chapter), such claims seem to be little more than appeals to DOE authority.

Appeals to authority in cases like Yucca Mountain are especially suspect because of the disastrous consequences that have resulted from appeals to authority in the past. As already mentioned at the beginning of this chapter, when hydrogeologists had inadequate data about possible radwaste migration at the proposed Maxey Flats site, they merely did some well and pumping tests, then relied on their own opinion to claim that the waste would not migrate for centuries. As already noted, their expert predictions erred by 6 orders of magnitude. Given short-term tests of the Maxey Flats site and inadequate knowledge of the fractured, unsaturated zones, the earlier assessors' optimistic appeals to authority regarding site suitability have obviously been proved wrong. Moreover, despite ten years of public outcry against conditions at the (now closed) Maxey Flats facility, current levels of radioactive pollution (tritium) outside the burial trenches are 5 orders of magnitude above the Environmental Protection Agency (EPA) limits for groundwater pollution.[219] Radionuclide migration at the site is getting worse, not better. When the facility was opened, authorities not only denied that any problem would exist in the future, but when they were proved wrong, the same authorities did little to resolve the problems of radioactive contamination. This means that government managers and risk experts have not merely erred in the past when they were predicting future events about which they should have shown more care, but they also have erred in not correcting dangerous conditions at radioactive facilities, even after managers and whistleblowers got their attention. At the Fernald uranium feed-materials plant, for example, the engineers and scientists on site made "no attempt to monitor these kinds of releases [illegal uranium emissions to the air and water], take corrective measures or give estimates of what these releases might have been."[220] Indeed, safety conditions were so serious at the DOE plant that the plant manager, fearing worker deaths and legal liability, informed DOE that he would shut down the plant unless DOE authorities told him in writing to continue operating. The DOE site manager said to keep operating.[221]

One of the reasons why some risk assessments (dealing with low-frequency events or with untested technologies, e.g., for high-level radwaste disposal) probably err by 2 to 6 orders of magnitude is that, in the absence of complete data, assessors often extrapolate or use their own subjective opinions and methodological value judgments as a basis for prediction. For example, when scientists and engineers completed the most famous and allegedly best risk assessment ever performed, WASH 1400,[222] it was used as a basis for U.S. policy and standards regarding commercial nuclear reactor safety. Much of the assessment was based on mere appeals to authority, however, in the absence of data.[223] Later, when Dutch researchers compared the subjective risk estimates and opinions in WASH 1400 to the actual data, they discovered a severe overconfidence bias in the study. The assessors in the Netherlands used actual empirical frequencies obtained from Oak Ridge National Laboratories to calibrate some of the more testable subjective probabilities employed in WASH 1400. Obtained as part of an evaluation of operating experience at nuclear installations, the frequencies were of various types of mishaps involving nuclear reactor subsystems.

The Dutch study of Oak Ridge data uses operating experience to determine the failure probabilities for seven reactor subsystems (loss-of-coolant accidents, auxiliary feedwater-system failures, high-pressure injection failures, long-term core-cooling failures, and automatic de-pressurization-system failures for both pressurized and boiling-water reactors). Amazingly, *all* the values from operating experience fall *outside* the 90 percent confidence bands in the WASH 1400 study. However, there is only a subjective probability of 10 percent that the true value should fall outside these bands. This means that if the authors' subjective probabilities were well calibrated, we should expect that approximately 10 percent of the true values should lie outside their respective bands. The fact that all the quantities fall outside them means that WASH 1400, the most famous and allegedly best risk assessment, is very poorly calibrated. It also exhibits a number of flaws, including an overconfidence bias on the part of the authorities or experts.

Appeals to authority and resultant invalid inferences do not occur merely in risk assessments like those done for commercial nuclear fission (for example, WASH 1400) or for existing or proposed radwaste repositories (for example, Maxey Flats or Yucca Mountain). Rather, errors as a result of an appeal to authority are predictable any time even a well-trained scientist or engineer goes beyond the data and substitutes mere opinion for a probabilistic or scientific analysis of the facts. As we argued earlier, during the discussion of the expertise inference, Kahneman, Tversky, and others have discovered that even statisticians typically fall victim to a number of errors of overconfidence and representativeness. Indeed, they err in many of the same ways as do laypersons whenever they are conjecturing beyond the level of their data. Hence, on the grounds of the work of Kahneman, Tversky, and others, there are strong reasons to question any appeal to authority, any expert "opinion" whenever the data is limited, as in cases like the evaluation of Yucca Mountain and other proposed repositories.

Yet another reason to avoid the appeal to authority, in assessing repository risk, is that most radwaste authorities (to which government and other officials often appeal) typically have a vested interest in siting a nuclear waste repository. In the United States, for example, they frequently work for DOE or obtain their funding from DOE, both conditions that could influence the outcome of their opinions and conclusions. Indeed, National Academy of Sciences panelists expressed concern that DOE's using only its own experts would "mask the degree of real uncertainty" in repository risk studies.[224] Moreover, as we have emphasized throughout this volume—and as many government hearings[225] and independent scientists[226] have confirmed—numerous incidents have compromised the integrity of the siting process (including risk assessment) and the reputation of the DOE. A 1986 study by the GAO found that 90 percent of DOE's 127 nuclear facilities had contaminated groundwater that exceeded regulatory standards by a factor of up to 1,000.[227] Moreover, officials from various states (in which repositories have been proposed) have criticized the DOE for failing to provide adequate funding for independent studies and monitoring at the possible radwaste sites. This failure suggests that the DOE has relied on an invalid appeal to its own authorities[228] rather than on a comprehensive, empirical substantiation of its claims. The failure of the DOE to provide adequate funding for external review, as recommended by the National Academy of Sciences,[229] until it was forced to do so by the courts[230] also suggests that the claims of DOE officials, regarding repository assessment, might not stand up to independent review. Indeed, if the conclusions of DOE scientists and risk assessors would stand up to empirical and logical scrutiny and were not based on questionable appeals to authority, one wonders whether the DOE would have dozens of lawsuits pending against it.[231]

Apart from all the logical reasons for faulting risk assessments (like those done at Yucca Mountain) because of their appeal to authority, an additional problem with use of this inference, in the absence of conditions 1–3 mentioned at the beginning of this section, is that it encourages employment of the expertise inference (see earlier sections of this chapter). As a consequence, it also encourages assessors to ignore public views of risk and the social amplification of risk. As the accidents at Three Mile Island,[232] Goiania, Brazil,[233] and Gorleben, Germany reveal,[234] public perception and risk evaluation are just as important, if not more important, in determining socioeconomic impacts as the physical magnitude of the accidents themselves. Hence, whatever diminishes our understanding of these impacts—as the appeal to authority is likely to do—diminishes the quality of risk assessment. Moreover, expert appeals to authority sometimes are as much examples of faulty risk perceptions as are the views of laypersons.

In summary, there are at least four reasons why assessors at Yucca Mountain have seriously erred when they have appealed to authority, rather than to logic and to actual empirical or probabilistic studies, to justify their conclusions.

1. The appeal to authority is an invalid logical inference.
2. Appeals to authority in the past have repeatedly been wrong, especially in the case of risk assessments of radwaste facilities like Maxey Flats and Fernald and in the QRAs of commercial nuclear reactors, such as WASH 1400.
3. Appeals to authority, in cases like Yucca Mountain, sometimes are not even based on the considered opinion of most of the relevant experts in the field; rather they may be biased by political considerations and by a desire to promote a particular technology or repository site.

4. Appeals to authority, as in the Yucca Mountain case, are likely to prejudice assessors and decisionmakers against lay perceptions of risk. This prejudice, in turn, is likely to harm the democratic foundations of risk assessment and public policy regarding radioactive waste management.

Conclusion

Despite the billions of dollars being spent to evaluate a single, proposed, high-level site[235] (like Yucca Mountain) for permanent radwaste disposal, even the best assessment efforts are beset with empirical problems and logical difficulties. In order to improve the scientific methodology of the Yucca Mountain QRAs we recommend that assessors admit the methodological uncertainties in their work and that they attempt to take account of probabilistic bias, human error, inappropriate use of probabilistic language, social amplification of risk, and the lack of public trust in the DOE. We also recommend that assessors employ null models to test their results; that they provide ranges of values (rather than averages) for parameters such as rates of radionuclide transport; that they analyze social impacts such as threats to due process, equal treatment, informed consent, full liability protection, and full compensation; that they obtain independent reviews of their work; and that they employ successful assessment procedures used in other nations.[236]

Arguing in favor of the desirability of certain sites, DOE researchers have begged the question and employed questionable reasoning such as the expertise inference, the linearity inference, the de minimis inference, the inference of specious accuracy, the inference of the multiple maximand, and the appeal to ignorance. Of course, any one of these problematic inferences can be found committed somewhere in the history of science. And, of course, it is possible to assess the risks of permanent radwaste disposal without employing most of these particular inferences. However, if one admits that sanctioning permanent geological disposal requires (1) meeting precise, existing U.S. regulations, and (2) affirming disposal-site stability for at least ten thousand years, then it is impossible to avoid several invalid inferences. If one sanctions disposal on the grounds that there is no evidence that conditions (1) and (2) cannot be met over ten thousand years, then it is impossible to avoid at least two implicit, but fundamentally questionable logical inferences, the appeal to ignorance and affirming the consequent. These two invalid inferences are unavoidable in such a situation because, when one argues for permanent geological disposal, there is no precise, predictive scientific evidence at present that disposal will work and that we can meet U.S. government regulations. Scientists are able merely to point to an absence of evidence that permanent disposal will not work and that regulations will not be violated. Scientists do not have precise and predictive evidence for the success of a repository ten thousand years from now. As we argued in chapter 4, geology is an explanatory—not a predictive—science, and precise predictions about factors such as volcanism and seismicity are currently impossible, as the 1992 DOE peer reviewers for the ESSE affirmed. Hence, if assessors are to argue that a site is suitable, by virtue of meeting conditions (1) and (2), then they must appeal to ignorance. Also, because they are forced to rely only on past and present evidence relevant to repository safety, scientists cannot, in principle, avoid affirming the consequent if they use this evidence to argue that a proposed repository will meet specific, quantitative government regulations for permanent geological disposal of high-level radwaste. They are forced either to conclude (on the basis of affirming the consequent) that a permanent repository would meet very precise, quantitative U.S. safety standards ten thousand years from now, or to refrain from drawing such a conclusion. Of course, one could argue for a permanent repository on pragmatic grounds, or on the grounds that it was more desirable than some other option. The problem with DOE risk assessments, however, is that they claim to have a *precise, scientific* foundation that is undercut both by the appeal to ignorance and by affirming the consequent.

Science can often give us precise, confirmed predictions. In the case of Yucca Mountain, however, we do not have the data to develop or to test such predictions. Moreover, given the warnings of the scientists who served as DOE peer reviewers for the 1992 Yucca Mountain *Early Site Suitability Evaluation*, it is clear that the scientific foundations of any argument for a permanent repository are, at present, inadequate. In their "Consensus Position," the DOE peer reviewers claimed that

many aspects of site suitability are not well suited for quantitative risk assessment. . . . Any projections of the rates of tectonic activity and volcanism, as well as natural resource occurrence and value, will be fraught with substantial uncertainties that cannot be quantified using standard statistical methods.[237]

In the face of "substantial uncertainties," assessors are able to affirm that Yucca Mountain will meet precise government regulations and be secure for ten thousand years only if they affirm the consequent or appeal to ignorance. Hence, proponents of permanent repositories need either to support them on grounds other than precise, scientific predictions, or to reconsider their position. Science can give us precise predictions, but it is not yet clear that, at present, it can do so for permanent repositories at locations such as Yucca Mountain.

Likewise, it is impossible to argue for permanent, geological disposal (which precludes monitoring and retrievability after fifty years) and to avoid the consent inference. By virtue of arguing for radioactive waste policy that prevents *monitoring* of leaks, one thereby deprives future generations of information regarding the radwaste risks that they face. Without such information, future persons are not able to give free, informed consent to a permanent repository. Also, by virtue of arguing for policy that precludes *retrievability* of the wastes beyond fifty years, the DOE has thereby preempted future generations from exercising an effective choice regarding how best to safeguard themselves against the hazards of radionuclides. By preempting future persons' information and choices, proponents of permanent geological disposal thereby deny their rights to free, informed consent to the risks they face.

If the reasoning in this chapter is correct, then it is impossible, at present, with our current data base, for proponents of permanent, geological disposal to avoid three invalid inferences in scientific and ethical reasoning: the appeal to ignorance, affirming the consequent, and the consent inference. Consequently, our conclusion dictates a change in policy regarding radioactive waste, provided that there is an alternative waste strategy that is superior with respect to both scientific and ethical considerations. In the remaining three chapters of this volume, we shall argue that such an alternative exists.

7

Uncertainty: An Obstacle to Geological Disposal

The authors of a recent U.S. Geological Survey study of the Yucca Mountain site, proposed as the first permanent high-level radwaste repository in both the United States and the world, warned that site "data are not sufficient to predict accurately rates of [ground]-water movement and travel times."[1] One question raised by the USGS warning is whether the Yucca Mountain predictions, although inaccurate, are *accurate enough* for us to build the repository. Indeed, this is the same question raised by the three previous chapters. Are the controversial methodological value judgments and questionable inferences in the repository risk estimates and evaluations significant? Or are the risk assessments nevertheless accurate enough to justify permanent geological disposal of high-level radwaste?

If no scientific result is ever certain or completely objective, and if no policy is ever perfectly just, a reasonable person ought fault neither science nor policy merely for uncertainty, subjectivity, or incomplete justice. The real issue is the significance of the apparent problems. How objective is objective enough? How certain is certain enough? How just is just enough? How ought one to interpret the revelations and accusations of the last three chapters? In this chapter, we argue (1) that, in the paradigm case of Yucca Mountain, the sensitivity and the precision of the risk assessments of the site are not adequate for existing, precise regulation; therefore, the facility ought not be sited anytime in the foreseeable future (the next century). Moreover, building on the analyses of the last three chapters, we argue (2) that scientific uncertainties associated with any proposed site anywhere are so extensive and problematic that we ought not adopt permanent geological disposal any time in the foreseeable future.

We Cannot Adequately Guarantee
Yucca Mountain Safety

Given the questionable methodological value judgments and inferences made in Yucca Mountain risk assessments (see chapters 4 through 6), as well as the knowledge that similar judgments appear to have contributed to problems at other DOE radioactive waste facilities (such as Maxey Flats, Fernald, Savannah River, Hanford, Idaho Falls, and Rocky Flats), an obvious question is whether the Yucca Mountain site itself is known well enough to guarantee long-term isolation of radionuclides and compliance with government regulations. Do the available data and site characteristics lead one to believe that QRAs of Yucca Mountain can be done with sensitivity and precision adequate to insure credible regulation and long-term safety?

Many risk assessors believe that the data and the site are adequate to insure excellent regulation and safety. They say that Yucca Mountain would comply with the regulations.[2] This methodological value judgment, however, is quite controversial given all the ways in which incomplete data, inadequate theory, uncertainty, and site heterogeneity threaten accurate knowledge of Yucca Mountain (see chapters 4 through 6). Even DOE assessors use language that suggests their largely qualitative and imprecise knowledge of the site is a problem. Note, for example, the DOE's use of the terms "estimate," "likely," and "significant" in the following claim:

[E]stimates of groundwater travel time along any path of likely and significant radionuclide travel from the disturbed zone to the accessible environment are more than 1,000 years. Therefore, the evidence does not support a finding that the site is disqualified.[3]

Presumably, if DOE officials were more certain about Yucca Mountain safety, they would speak of "calculations" or definite "probabilities" of given groundwater travel times and not of "estimates." Likewise, if their data were more accurate, presumably they would speak of threats posed by "any path of radionuclide travel," rather than of threats "along any path of likely and significant radionuclide travel." As the

DOE's own words illustrate, its claims of safety are laden with vague statements, with methodological value judgments, and with language that avoids assigning any probabilities to regulatory compliance. The DOE officially admits, for example:

The characteristics of the Yucca Mountain site and the processes operating there permit, and probably ensure, compliance with the limits on radionuclide release to the accessible environment.[4]

When one is considering a potentially catastrophic threat to health and safety, however, one requires a very high probability that the site in question will comply with regulations.

One of the main reasons why the methodological value judgment—that site knowledge is adequate for regulation and for safety—is questionable is that the various DOE probabilities allegedly associated with site characteristics are already very close to the limits of regulatory acceptability. Hence, given a variety of questionable inferences, assumptions, and value judgments made by assessors,[5] actual site characteristics might not comply with regulations. Changes of only 1 order of magnitude in some of the parameters dealing with fracture flow, infiltration, precipitation, or volcanic and seismic activity could initiate disastrous changes—such as flooding or unacceptably rapid groundwater transport—in the Yucca Mountain repository. As Amory Lovins warned, an error factor of 2 at each stage of a 20-step methodology permits a possible millionfold mistake.[6] For example, increasing the alleged percolation rate by only 1 order of magnitude could initiate fracture flow and speed groundwater travel time.[7] Such sensitive numbers, together with the 2 to 6 orders of uncertainty characterizing many risk assessments (see chapters 4 through 6), show that the margin for error at Yucca Mountain may be too slim to insure adequate government regulation and safety. Even the NAS noted that the DOE assumes, incorrectly, "that the properties and future behavior of a geological repository can be determined and specified with a very high degree of certainty." "In reality," said the U.S. National Academy of Sciences (NAS), "the inherent variability of the geological environment will necessitate frequent changes in the specifications."[8] But if geological variability necessitates changes in repository specifications, then there is question whether a facility like Yucca Mountain can meet the predetermined U.S. safety regulations.

As we already mentioned in chapter 4, porous flow alone would mean leachate could reach the water table at Yucca Mountain in ten to twenty thousand years.[9] Fracture flow, however, could enhance transport of water and radioactive leachate, above the flux at Yucca Mountain, by as much as 5 orders of magnitude.[10] Assessors have confirmed that "fractures do exist of sufficient width to allow significant water flow in the unsaturated region."[11] Moreover, with a large fracture-flow rate, ^{99}C, ^{238}U, and ^{237}Np could get through to the water table in less than ten thousand years.[12] Hence, understanding fracture flow is a crucial determinant of site safety. Yet knowledge of fractured zones, particularly for unsaturated regions, is very limited. Likewise, the seismicity at Yucca Mountain, prior to 1960, is virtually unknown even though seismic failure is possible.[13] One wonders how a possibly seismic, fractured site, even in an arid climate like Yucca Mountain, could be acceptable if volcanism, intruding water, and seismic activity were not highly improbable during the life of the repository.[14] At Yucca Mountain, these conditions do not appear to be highly improbable.

A person who makes the value judgment that site knowledge is sufficient for regulation and for safety is in the questionable position of knowing that significant problems could occur with fracture flow, seismicity, and volcanism, yet not being able to predict any of them accurately—because of all the difficulties with modeling, sampling, extrapolation, and so on, already discussed. Even the Nuclear Regulatory Commission (NRC) officials recognized some of these problems when they complained that the Yucca Mountain risk assessments fail to recognize adequately the uncertainty in the data. Likewise, the NAS warned that "uncertainty is treated inappropriately" in the Yucca Mountain assessments.[15] Indeed, the NRC said that the environmental assessments of the DOE for its proposed radwaste facilities are, in general, "overly optimistic."[16] Such optimism often appears almost gratuitous, because it is not based on precise, quantitative predictions. For example, an official DOE document claims that the site can protect the safety of all future generations from radiological hazards:

The quality of the environment during this and future generations can be adequately protected. Estimates of radiation releases during normal operation and worst-case accident scenarios provide confidence that the public and the environment can be adequately protected from the potential hazards of radioactive-waste disposal.[17]

Equally gratuitous is the DOE claim that *no* future groundwater conditions will disrupt the site:

Currently available engineering measures are considered more than adequate to guarantee that no disruption of construction and operation will occur because of groundwater conditions at Yucca Mountain.[18]

Such assurances are highly questionable, given present uncertainties about basic hydrological and geological conditions at the site. For example, at Yucca Mountain "in most cases, hydraulic data are insufficient for performing geostatistical analyses,"[19] and "traditional flow path chemical evaluation does not directly apply to tuffaceous volcanic environments."[20] Likewise, there is "no known mechanical model that describes nonuniform corrosion well enough to use in performance assessment" of the waste canisters.[21] In areas of hydrology, geology, canister security, climate, volcanism, and seismicity, no techniques exist, at the present time, that are adequate for removing the uncertainties at Yucca Mountain or even for quantifying them.[22] Basic questions concerning the reliability of the studies remain unanswered.[23] Indeed, how could significant uncertainties be removed if one required precise predictive power and regulatory guarantees regarding the site for ten thousand years?

The long time period of storage is one reason that Yucca Mountain reviewers have claimed that "compliance with U.S. [radiation-dose] limits cannot be shown objectively by PRA [probabilistic risk assessment] methods."[24] One reason for this problem is that the precise, probabilistic standards of the Environmental Protection Agency for the management of spent fuel and high-level and transuranic radioactive wastes cannot be confirmed with current data. The standards set limits for releases when events have more than a 1 in 10 chance of occurring over the ten thousand years.[25] Such precise probabilistic standards cannot be guaranteed for so long a time, however. As one reviewer put it: "No assurance can be given that all significant factors have been examined here."[26] Other reviewers maintain that it is doubtful whether we can model or predict long-term behavior at all, given the heterogeneities and uncertainties at the site.[27] Still other evaluators, including those from the utility industry and the NAS, have proclaimed that the limits of environmental science have been exceeded by the goals set by the nation's radioactive waste program.[28] Perhaps the most significant analysis of how scientific uncertainties undercut assurances of repository safety is that of the DOE team of fourteen peer reviewers who in 1992 analyzed the DOE's *Early Site Suitability Evaluation* for Yucca Mountain. The "consensus position" of the fourteen DOE-selected peer reviewers is telling:

It is the opinion of the panel that many aspects of site suitability are not well suited for quantitative risk assessment. In particular are predictions involving future geological activity, future value of mineral deposits and mineral occurrence models. Any projections of the rates of tectonic activity and volcanism, as well as natural resource occurrence and value, will be fraught with substantial uncertainties that cannot be quantified using standard statistical methods.[29]

Because of all the uncertainties in the Yucca Mountain data and methods, assessors typically are not able to determine the degree of accuracy in their models.[30] They are able, for example, merely to say that there is a "high level of probability" that groundwater travel time to the water table will exceed ten thousand years.[31] In other words, the degree of uncertainty regarding groundwater travel time is very great. Likewise, the margin of safety necessary to prevent significant problems, such as fracture flow, is quite slim. Yet, despite this narrow "window," some persons appear to believe that Yucca Mountain will be predictably safe or in compliance with government regulations requiring a groundwater travel time greater than one thousand years.[32] There is also only a "narrow window," or slim margin, of safety because groundwater travel time is extremely sensitive to fracture flow, and fracture flow is extremely sensitive to percolation rate. If either fracture flow or percolation increase by even a small amount, then the travel time of leachate from the waste will increase significantly.[33] In the world of groundwater flow, where risk assessments "are highly uncertain,"[34] a factor of 10 as a window of safety is quite small. Indeed, in some of the simulated cases, water travel time from the repository to the water table is less than one thousand years.[35] Hence, the methodological value judgment that current and near-future knowledge about Yucca Mountain can guarantee safety and compliance with government regulations—for example, requiring groundwater travel time of more than one thousand years—may be questionable.

The value judgment about travel time is not only factually questionable but also inconsistent. One well-known group of assessors, for example, found that, according to their models, some calculated groundwater travel times are less than ten thousand years. They also admitted that hydraulic data were insufficient and that there has not been enough time to estimate cumulative radioactive releases.[36] Nevertheless, they concluded that the "evidence indicates that the Yucca Mountain repository site would be in compliance with regulatory requirements"[37] and that "no radioactivity from the repository will migrate even to the water table immediately beneath the repository for about 30,000 years."[38] How do some migration values of less than ten thousand years translate to a migration time of "about" thirty thousand years? How can the same DOE assessors claim that the repository will be in compliance with government regulations[39] when they also assert that low flux "will probably limit flow velocities to the extent that no leachate will reach the water table for tens to hundreds of thousands of years"?[40] Such poorly grounded "probable" knowledge of something that may occur within tens to hundreds of thousands of years (a wide range) is hardly consistent with precise claims about safety and regulatory compliance! Likewise, how can the same DOE assessors conclude, with confidence, that no radioactivity will migrate to the water table for at least thirty thousand years,[41] and yet claim: "Because data and understanding about water flow and contaminant transport in deep unsaturated fractured environments are just beginning to emerge, complete dismissal of the rapid-release scenarios is not possible at this time"?[42] How is the thirty-thousand-year claim consistent with the assertion about not dismissing the rapid-release scenarios?

Assessors investigating the uncertainties in the Yucca Mountain hydrogeological data also have admitted that, for the unsaturated zone, uncertainties in groundwater velocities may be as much as 100 percent above or below the mean value.[43] They likewise claim that a change in percolation of a factor of only 10 is sufficient to initiate fracture flow, that groundwater travel time is extremely sensitive to fracture flow,[44] and that heat from the waste could cause fractures.[45] Given such admissions, how can the same DOE assessors consistently claim that fracture flow is not a credible process,[46] and that groundwater flow will be "well within the limits set by the NRC"?[47] Similar inconsistencies appear when the same assessors, after acknowledging (1) that they have incomplete data,[48] (2) that they had no time to estimate cumulative radioactive releases,[49] and (3) that they may "have underestimated the cumulative releases of all nuclides during 100,000 years, by an amount that is unknown,"[50] nevertheless draw a contradictory conclusion. They conclude that only one ten-millionth of allowable releases of radionuclides will reach the water table.[51]

Likewise, Yucca Mountain assessors admit that solubility limits and retardation factors are site- and (radioactive) species-dependent.[52] They also claim that they may have underestimated radioactive releases.[53] If the same DOE assessors *do not know* the degree to which they may have underestimated radioactive releases,[54] how do they know so precisely that only one ten-millionth of allowable releases will occur? Similar inconsistencies and unsupported extrapolations occur throughout the Yucca Mountain analyses, with DOE assessors confidently affirming that there will be "less than one health effect every 1,400 years."[55] A more precise and consistent appraisal, given the problems with the data and models at Yucca Mountain, might be that of the assessors who concluded: "Even though we have tried to use the best data and models available at this time, we make no claims that these results have any value in the performance assessment of the Yucca Mountain repository site."[56]

Instead of using such precise language, however, the DOE's final 1992 *Early Site Suitability Evaluation* (ESSE) for Yucca Mountain continues to formulate site risks in terms of words such as "likely" and "unlikely" rather than by using numerical probabilities.[57] Similarly, when DOE reviewer M. T. Einaudi complained that the ESSE had vaguely defined the "foreseeable future" as "the next few years to 10 years, and occasionally as long as 30 years,"[58] the DOE ESSE team responded by removing from the document all language mentioning the number of years. Next the team noted:

The evaluation and definition of the terms, such as "reasonable projections" and "likely future activities" will receive considerable attention in the future and is likely to utilize the review of a panel of experts.[59]

This response, however, does not solve the problem with vague language, both because the DOE team uses the language to argue for site suitability, and presumably such usage must have implications. Indeed, if the language did not have certain implications regarding future time periods, then it would not be part of an effective argument for site suitability. Hence, if the terms are used effectively, they must have some precise, implicit meaning. If they do not have a precise, implicit meaning, then it is arguable that they are not effective in supporting the site-suitability conclusions and ought not be used. Indeed, by using indefinable terms to defend conclusions about site suitability, the ESSE renders its conclusions nonfalsifiable and therefore ineffective, because vague claims cannot be falsified. And if the ESSE site-suitability claims are not falsifiable, then this suggests that they are a priori rather than empirical and scientific.

Another reviewer (of the 1992 ESSE), J. I. Drever, also complained about the failure of the ESSE to provide rigorous definitions of words such as "likely" and "significant."[60] Again, the final ESSE document did not alleviate the difficulty. Instead the ESSE Core Team responded to Drever's criticism:

The terms 'likely' and 'significant' should be defined in the context of the overall postclosure performance objectives. Because the evaluations of system performance cannot be definitive at this time, the ESSE Core Team believed it inappropriate to define those terms precisely for this evaluation.[61]

This response by the DOE team, however, creates more questions than it answers. For one thing, to say that terms like "likely" should be defined in terms of overall postclosure performance is not coherent, because the term "likely," for example, is rarely if ever used in the context of "total system performance." Rather, it is used in radically different but specific contexts, such as probability of human interference at the site or the probability of a route of radionuclide transport.[62] Hence, terms like "likely" not only do not refer to "overall performance," as the DOE team claimed, but, *second*, they are not univocal. They clearly mean different things in different ESSE contexts. *Third*, although the ESSE team says that such terms cannot be defined precisely because the system evaluations are incomplete, this response is puzzling because the ESSE team obviously has already used the terms to mean something. *Fourth*, if the system-performance evaluations are not definitive enough to allow the ESSE team to define the very terms that it uses, then it is unclear why the system-performance evaluations are definitive enough to support a lower-level suitability finding, rather than an unsuitability finding, for Yucca Mountain. *Fifth*, contrary to the response of the DOE ESSE Core Team, the terms used by the team clearly presuppose some precise meanings, because words like "likely" are often used in precise *regulatory* contexts, such as "not likely to exceed a small fraction of [radiation dose] limits."[63] If such terms were not used somewhat precisely, then it would be impossible for the claims in which they are imbedded not to be false. Likewise, the ESSE Core Team claims, for example, that "although confidence is substantial, it is not yet sufficient to support the higher-level suitability finding for this qualifying condition."[64] Such a claim appears to presuppose some precise level or cutoff of confidence or likelihood. It appears to presuppose that lower-level findings are justified below this level, and that higher-level findings are justified above it. For all these reasons, there appears to be a mismatch between the science and the regulations discussed in DOE assessments such as the ESSE. Because of this mismatch, it is questionable whether the science discussed in repository assessments is adequate to the regulatory task.

Previous experiences at the Maxey Flats low-level radwaste facility show that similar problems with value judgments about hydrogeological accuracy—and the ability of QRA to meet regulatory guidelines—may have occurred there. Environmental Protection Agency (EPA) assessors believed that the knowledge of the Maxey Flats site was adequate to insure containment, credible regulation, and safety largely because "the general soil characteristics" at the facility have been "very impermeable."[65] Yet such general assurances failed to address the problem of leachate migration with sufficient precision and accuracy. Other EPA geologists noted that precise determination of hydraulic conductivity is impossible at a site such as Maxey Flats, which has fractures.[66] United States Geological Survey scientists claimed that the Maxey Flats hydrogeology, because of the fractures, was "too complex for accurate quantitative description."[67] Given the complexity and uncertainty associated with much information about Yucca Mountain, there is reason to believe that optimistic value judgments about the accuracy of site studies may err just as they did at Maxey Flats. Because inaccurate knowledge of the Yucca Mountain facility prevents scientists from being able to predict precisely migration rates of the waste thousands of years into the future, it also prevents them from guaranteeing that the proposed repository will comply with very specific U.S. radiation dose limits. Because compliance with government regulations is unknown, and because the consequences of repository failure could be catastrophic, it is arguable that the Yucca Mountain facility ought not be built, at least not until there is significantly more knowledge about the future risks likely to be associated with the installation.

Extensive, Nonquantifiable Uncertainty at Yucca Mountain Argues against Disposal

United States National Academy of Sciences panelists said that perhaps the United States should delay closing any permanent radwaste facility until we have more knowledge about long-term repository behavior. Likewise, a major U.S. government commission, studying policy for dealing with high-level radioactive waste, concluded recently that Congress should reconsider the subject of interim [rather than permanent] high-level radwaste storage by the year 2000 so as to "take into account uncertainties that exist today and which might be resolved or clarified within 10 years." Indeed, said the commission, "despite the considerable time and money already expended to site a repository, none has been sited yet, and the date by which a permanent repository will be available is uncertain. . . . the most notable uncertainty" is the "date of opening a permanent repository" in the United States.[68]

At least some of the reasons for the commission's worries, it appears, are the scientific uncertainties associated with the proposed facility at Yucca Mountain, many of which have been outlined in the preceding section and in chapters 4 through 6. Moreover, to the degree that this nonquantifiable uncertainty precludes assurance that precise radiation-control standards can be met during the thousands of years of operation of the proposed Nevada repository, to that extent it is arguable that we cannot yet guarantee the safety of permanent waste disposal. And if we cannot guarantee the long-term safety of proposed repositories like Yucca Mountain, then the "dig now, pay later" approach of repository supporters is highly questionable. Part of the rationale for delay or avoidance of a permanent U.S. repository is a basic legal premise: *res inter alios acta alteri nocere non debet,* that is, no one ought to suffer from what others have done.[69] Unless we can guarantee that many others in the future will not suffer unreasonably from what we have done in building a permanent repository, then our scientific uncertainty may be sufficient to argue against building the Yucca Mountain permanent repository.

Why does our uncertainty about whether Yucca Mountain will lead to catastrophe in the future argue against the facility? Although later we shall say more on this point, Brian Barry has provided one of the simplest rationales for the claim that the possibility of causing future catastrophe is a decisive reason for not acting in the present. He argues that (1) in the case of an individual making a possibly lethal choice that affects only himself, we should regard anyone who chooses the potentially fatal action—who claims that uncertainty makes it premature to decide against the action—as crazy. Likewise, says Barry, (2) when we change the case to one that involves millions of people and extends over many centuries, the same reasoning applies with increased force. Barry's rationale for (1) is that no rational person gambles with his own life except to gain a comparable benefit, to save it. Rock climbers, sky divers, and other risk enthusiasts, however, might claim that they are skilled and well trained and hence not gambling with their lives since the probability of death for such a skilled person is low. Risk enthusiasts probably would also argue that they gain great benefits from their activities. Both Barry and these enthusiasts would likely agree, however, that as the benefits decreased and as the probability of death increased, the risky actions become more foolish. Hence, (1) is reasonable. Barry's rationale for (2) is that because the numbers of persons potentially at risk of death are larger, the impetus for choosing against the risk is likewise even greater. Despite reasoning such as Barry's, official DOE documents have argued for permanent repositories on exactly the grounds that Barry says are most questionable. He claims that anyone in this position—who argues that uncertainty makes it premature to decide against a potentially catastrophic action—is "crazy." Yet, the DOE repeatedly has argued for such a claim, for example:

A final conclusion on the qualifying condition for climatic changes cannot be made based on available data. However, the evidence does not support a finding that the reference repository location is not likely to meet the qualifying condition.[70]

In other words, DOE officials have used uncertainty about climatic changes as an argument for the thesis that the repository ought not be disqualified. Such an argument, like the many appeals to ignorance documented earlier in this volume, is problematic on both logical grounds and for the ethical reasons outlined by Barry. Moreover, in cases of future catastrophic risk, Barry's reasons (1) and (2) likewise are compelling because a repository catastrophe presumably could wipe out an entire culture, not just many persons, and destroying a culture may be worse than merely killing many people. Also, in the case of our threatening future generations, the repository risk is imposed without the consent of the possible victims, and it is not confined to the beneficiaries—a point that we shall discuss in more detail in the next chapter. For all these reasons, scientific uncertainty argues against siting permanent radwaste facilities like Yucca Mountain.[71]

Uncertainty and Permanent Disposal

Because Yucca Mountain has been proposed as the first permanent geological repository for high-level radioactive waste anywhere in the world, the United States is spending billions of dollars to study and engineer the site. Indeed, as of 1991, more than $2.5 billion has already been spent in the formalities of site study and selection,[72] and the U.S. government was nowhere close to final approval of a single site. Because of the scientific and financial preeminence of Yucca Mountain, it provides a paradigm case of the risks and benefits associated with permanent disposal. Hence, if there are fundamental uncertainties associated with Yucca Mountain, the focus of the most ambitious and expensive permanent disposal program in the world, then unless there is a geologically more suitable site somewhere, there are likely to be similar uncertainties associated with other sites—and hence potential problems with building any permanent high-level repository in the foreseeable future.

Indeed, the earliest date that the United States could have a permanent geological facility for storage of high-level radioactive waste is 2010.[73] That deadline has already been moved forward many times. No other country is moving so quickly to permanent repositories. Officials in other nations have openly admitted that they are proceeding more slowly with high-level radioactive waste disposal, precisely because of the scientific uncertainties involved. As the Board on Radioactive Waste Management of the National Research Council of the U.S. National Academy of Sciences put it:

The U.S. program is unique among those of all nations in its rigid schedule, in its insistence on defining in advance the technical requirements for every part of the multibarrier system, and in its major emphasis on the geological component of the barrier as detailed in 10 CFR 60. Because one is predicting the fate of the HLW into the distant future, the undertaking is necessarily full of uncertainties. . . . It may even turn out to be appropriate to delay permanent closure of a waste repository until adequate assurances concerning its long-term behavior can be obtained through continued in-situ geological studies. . . . There are scientific reasons to think that a satisfactory HLW repository can be built and licensed. But for the reasons described earlier, the current U.S. program seems unlikely to achieve that desirable goal.[74]

What can we learn about the likelihood of success in permanent geological disposal on the basis of activities in the various countries considering the repository option?

Uncertainty and Permanent Disposal: Other Countries

In eight of the nations with the most radioactive waste, uncertainties have forced the countries to postpone permanent geological disposal. In Canada, for example, although nuclear reactors supply about 13 percent of the country's electricity, there has been no decision about spent reactor fuel, even though Canada will have approximately 34,000 MTU by the end of the century. Because Canada has made no decision about permanent disposal, the earliest Canadians could have such a repository is 2010, even assuming that it wanted one.[75]

Similarly, the French plan to use interim storage for a minimum of twenty years before moving to permanent disposal. Nuclear reactors currently supply more than 70 percent of French electricity. The earliest a permanent facility could be ready in France is 2010. The French rationale for delaying decisions about permanent storage is that cooling the waste would reduce the thermal impact on the host rock where it might be stored. (See chapter 9 for discussion of cooling the waste, as a U.S. option.) In the Yucca Mountain studies, many problems have arisen because of the ability of the high-temperature wastes to induce thermal fractures in the host rock, thereby increasing the probability of fracture flow of the leachate. Given such difficulties, "the French believe that the period [of interim storage] could be extended as long as needed because of the safety of monitored storage."[76]

Nuclear reactors supply approximately 40 percent of electricity in Germany. Like France, Germany is building interim storage facilities for high-level radioactive wastes, although the Germans hope to use deep geological disposal at the Gorleben salt dome. Even if the German plans are not delayed, the earliest a permanent repository could be ready is 2008. The Gorleben facility was licensed in 1983, but litigation concerning safety and scientific uncertainty has, so far, prevented its use as a repository for spent fuel.[77] In Japan, approximately 32 percent of the nation's electricity is supplied by nuclear reactors. Despite this fact, the Japanese appear to be quite concerned about a premature leap to an inadequately tested technology for permanent waste disposal. They plan to store their vitrified waste for thirty to fifty years before considering deep geological emplacement. In fact, the Japanese do not plan even to try to develop regulations for siting a permanent repository until after the year 2000. Hence, if approved, the earliest date at which a Japanese repository could operate is 2030.[78]

Spain is following a strategy similar to that of its European neighbors. With 36 percent of its electricity supplied by nuclear reactors, the Spaniards plan to store spent fuel at the reactors for ten years and then to use interim storage for another forty years. Sometime around the turn of the century, they plan to consider possible candidate sites for permanent geological disposal. Their explicit strategy is to gain more experience dealing with the wastes before deciding what to do with them.[79]

In Sweden, approximately 50 percent of electricity is supplied by nuclear reactors. Because of scientific uncertainties and because they want to achieve a tenfold reduction in radiation and heat output from the waste, the Swedes are storing their spent fuel for thirty to forty years in centralized interim storage facilities. They do not expect to have a permanent facility available until some time after 2020.[80] Like the Swedes, the Swiss plan to store their spent fuel in interim facilities for forty years. Approximately 38 percent of electricity in Switzerland is supplied by nuclear reactors. The earliest a permanent repository could be available in Switzerland is sometime after 2025. Like the Swedes, the Swiss have laws and regulations that make it impossible to site a new commercial nuclear plant unless operators can demonstrate safe disposal of spent fuel. As a result, no new plants have been sited in either country.[81]

The United Kingdom, with 17 percent of its electricity coming from nuclear reactors, has one of the longest periods of interim storage of spent fuel, fifty years. Using interim storage at Sellafield has been necessary, in part, because of opposition in the U.K. to permanent disposal and because of scientific uncertainties associated with deep geological facilities. The earliest date by which the British could have a permanent repository ready is 2030, although they have not begun the siting process.[82]

Although all eight countries just surveyed are some of the world's major users of nuclear electricity, and even though all of them plan to use permanent geological disposal of spent fuel in the future, none of them expects to do so as quickly as the United States. Indeed, the preferred alternative is to reduce uncertainties about behavior of the waste. As the U.S. review commission put it: "In general, deferred disposal is viewed as beneficial because it reduces the heat output of the wastes." As a result, centralized, monitored, interim storage facilities have been built or planned in all but one country, Canada, which intends to use at-reactor interim storage.[83] If the experience of eight major nuclear countries is correct, then one powerful argument for not pursuing permanent disposal at present and for postponing a decision about a geological repository is that no nation, except the United States, has plans for rapid permanent disposal of nuclear waste. If the plans of most countries reflect a scientific consensus about our inability at present to handle the uncertainties associated with permanent disposal of high-level nuclear waste, then these uncertainties may undercut arguments for permanent disposal anywhere at present.

Uncertainty and Permanent Disposal: Faulty Inferences

But what is the nature of the uncertainties that argue against permanent disposal anywhere at present? As we mentioned earlier, the uncertainties are so extensive that they are not even quantifiable. The Consensus Position of the 1992 DOE peer reviewers for the Yucca Mountain *Early Site Suitability Evaluation* is:

Any projections of the rates of tectonic activity and volcanism, as well as natural resource occurrence and value, will be fraught with substantial uncertainties that cannot be quantified using standard statistical models.[84]

If uncertainties at any proposed site are so severe that they cannot be quantified, then it is arguable that they force those who favor a permanent repository, at present, into either begging the question or appealing to ignorance in defending site suitability. Indeed, as chapter 1 argued, anyone who maintains that there is at present a compelling scientific basis for permanent geological disposal is unavoidably forced to use incomplete and short-term data (on seismicity, volcanism, hydrogeology, and so on) as a basis for extraordinarily precise long-term predictions—tens of thousands of years—about site suitability. We are able to make general predictions about the future, of course, and geologists do so all the time. Precise predictions, however, are a problem. Because of the imprecision of our hydrogeological and climate models, we are at present unable to predict the geological and hydrological situation at Yucca Mountain with any degree of reliability and precision ten thousand years into the future. As a result, we cannot quantify the claim that we shall be able to meet current U.S. repository standards for safety ten thousand years from now. We cannot be reasonably assured that a permanent repository might not cause catastrophe hundreds or thousands of years into the future. Indeed, to claim the ability to predict very precise geological events ten thousand years into the future when one's precise, site-specific evidential base for doing so covers only tens of years has little scientific justification.

As we argued in chapter 4, to assume that incomplete, short-term data enable one to make specific and reliable long-term predictions is, in general, an uncertain methodological value judgment. Although we can reconstruct geological histories spanning millions of years, geology is primarily an explanatory and not a predictive science, as we argued earlier. Hence, it seems prima facie evident that one ought not base arguments for the safety of a permanent repository on an uncertain methodological value judgment about our ability to make precise geological predictions.

Another reason that it is difficult to know the distant future in great detail is that we humans and our institutions are not precisely predictable. Anyone who argues for permanent geological disposal must discount the effects (on repository safety) of human error and the social amplification of risk that might occur in thousands of years. Discounting these effects is problematic, as the Chair of the U.S. National Academy's overview committee (for the WIPP project for storage of weapons-related radwaste in New Mexico) noted before Congress:

[C]urrent feeling is that the WIPP site could probably meet EPA standards with the exception of the so-called "human-intrusion" scenario. This is the idea that sometime in the future somebody comes and drills directly into a repository.[85]

As we argued in chapter 4, dismissing the effects of human activities such as terrorism, sabotage, or ignorance tens of thousands of years into the future is highly problematic. Indeed, given the prevalence of flaws in humans and their institutions, it might be more reasonable to assume that terrorism or ignorance would be a major problem for a facility storing radiotoxic materials. As we argued in chapter 4, whether about climate and hydrogeology, or about human errors and institutions, precise predictions about the long-term future are highly questionable, at least at present, because our generalizations are built on such a limited empirical base.

Scientific uncertainty further undercuts the case for permanent high-level radwaste disposal because, as we argued in chapter 6, anyone who claims that geological repositories will be safe for tens of thousands of years is probably using at least two logically invalid inferences, the appeal to ignorance and affirming the consequent. If it is impossible to know the long-term future with great precision, then any claims to precision (as U.S. radwaste regulations require) about the long-term future must rely in part on ignorance. Yet, from ignorance about a particular claim, it is logically invalid to conclude that the claim is either true or false. From our ignorance about long-term repository safety, it is logically invalid to conclude that a repository would be either safe or unsafe. Like many scientific claims, conclusions about the safety of repositories—tens of thousands of years into the future—are uncertain. Based on data from the present or even from several decades, there can be no empirically compelling argument for the safety of such repositories in the distant future. The best our experiments can do is to confirm that if permanent repositories meet certain safety standards in the future, then our current experiments are likely to exhibit these same features. Because affirming the consequent (see chapter 6) does not invariably lead to valid conclusions, however, the reverse is not true. We cannot infer that because of the success of current short-term experiments, therefore repositories will avoid catastrophic releases of radionuclides and will meet safety standards thousands of years from now.

In summary, in addition to Barry's intuitive argument about reasonable persons avoiding uncertain situations with the potential for catastrophe (see the earlier sections of this chapter), there appear to be at least four compelling arguments, all related to scientific uncertainty, against permanent geological disposal of high-level radwaste anywhere at present. These arguments include (1) the scientific uncertainties, including lack of data, associated with Yucca Mountain (see chapters 4 through 6); (2) the reluctance of other countries to move rapidly into programs of permanent geological disposal; (3) the presence of highly questionable methodological value judgments in scientific or empirical arguments in favor of the safety of permanent geological repositories; and (4) the presence of logically invalid inferences (the appeal to ignorance and affirming the consequent) in official arguments in favor of the safety of permanent geological repositories.

Uncertainty and Permanent Disposal: An Objection

In response to these arguments about the scientific uncertainty associated with the safety of permanent geological disposal, a proponent of the repositories could argue that no science is ever certain and that scientific *certainty* is not always required before one acts. In other words, one could argue that *reasonable assurance* of safety, not scientific certainty, is a precondition for ethically defensible behavior. On this view, one could argue that certainty is impossible and therefore that one need merely follow the best available scientific opinion or the course of action leading to the best estimated results.

The heart of this objection to our analysis is correct. One does not need certainty before one acts, because certainty is unattainable. Our argument, however, is not that permanent disposal requires certainty. Rather, the argument is that permanent disposal requires more certainty than we have now and that, at present, the uncertainties associated with permanent disposal are extreme. In subsequent chapters we shall also argue that the uncertainties associated with permanent disposal are more extensive and more threatening than those associated with other radwaste options. For now, we wish to raise the issue of what behavior is ethically defensible under conditions of uncertainty. Following Barry's insights, already mentioned, our presupposition is that, in cases of extensive scientific and probabilistic uncertainty—like those concerning precise geological predictions ten thousand years from now or like those concerning events whose uncertainty cannot be quantified—we ought to behave in an ethically conservative way. But what is ethically conservative behavior? On one view, ethically conservative behavior in a situation of uncertainty is behavior that does not reject the null (no-effect) hypothesis. That is, if we are uncertain about a catastrophic event in the future, for example, ethical conservatives do not assume there will be no effect. In other words, we ought to minimize type-II statistical errors. Although we shall not take the time to provide the arguments in full here,[86] there are a number of reasons for minimizing type-II error in situations of uncertainty, like those associated with permanent geological disposal of radioactive waste.

Uncertainty and Permanent Disposal: Type-II Error

In a situation of uncertainty, errors of type I occur when one rejects a null hypothesis that is true; errors of type II occur when one fails to reject a null hypothesis that is false. (One null hypothesis might be, for example: "The proposed Yucca Mountain repository will secure high-level radwastes so that only one ten-millionth of allowable releases of radionuclides will reach the water table over 100,000 years.")[87]

Given a situation of uncertainty, which is the more serious error, type I or type II? An analogous issue arises in law. Is the more serious error to acquit a guilty person or to convict an innocent person? Ought one to run the risk of rejecting a true null hypothesis, of not using the Yucca Mountain technology that is really acceptable and safe? Or, ought one to run the risk of not rejecting a false null hypothesis, of employing the Yucca Mountain technology that is really unacceptable and unsafe? The basic problem is that to decrease type-I risk might hurt the public, especially members of future generations, and to decrease type-II risk might hurt both present persons and especially those dependent on the industries promoting the permanent repository.

In the area of pure science and statistics, most persons believe that in a situation of uncertainty one ought to minimize type-I risks, so as to limit false positives, assertions of effects where there are none. Pure scientists often attach a greater loss to accepting a falsehood than to failing to acknowledge a truth.[88] Societal decision making under uncertainty, as in cases involving siting permanent radwaste facilities, however, is arguably not analogous to decision making in pure science. Societal decision making involves rights, duties, and ethical consequences that affect the welfare of persons, whereas purely scientific decision making involves largely epistemological consequences. For this reason, it is not clear that in societal cases under uncertainty one ought to minimize type-I risks. Instead, there are a number of prima facie reasons for minimizing type-II errors. For one thing, it is arguably more important to protect the public from harm (from possible catastrophic radwaste releases) than to provide, in some positive sense, for welfare (building permanent repositories), because protecting from harm seems to be a necessary condition for enjoying other freedoms.[89] Admittedly, it is difficult to draw the line between providing benefits and protecting from harm, between positive and negative laws or duties. Nevertheless, just as there is a basic distinction between welfare rights and negative rights,[90] so there is an analogous distinction between welfare policies (that provide some good) and protective policies (that prohibit some infringement). Moral philosophers continue to honor related distinctions, such as that between letting die and killing someone. It therefore seems more important to protect citizens from public hazards, like a catastrophic leak at a permanent radwaste facility, than to attempt to enhance their welfare, over the short term, by implementing a technology such as permanent geological disposal of radwaste.[91]

A second reason for minimizing type-II errors under uncertainty is that the public typically needs more risk protection than do the industry or government proponents of the risky technology, like Yucca Mountain. The public usually has fewer financial resources and less information to deal with societal hazards that affect it, and laypersons are often faced with bureaucratic denials of public danger. Certainly members of future generations are likely to have less information to deal with a permanent repository since, by definition (U.S. regulations), it will not be monitored. Hence, their needs for protection seem larger, and the importance of minimizing type-II errors appears greater.[92]

Third, it is more important to minimize type-II error, especially in cases of great uncertainty, because laypersons ought to be accorded legal rights to protection against technological decisions that could threaten their health and physical security. These legal rights arise out of the considerations that everyone has both due process rights and rights to bodily security. In cases where those responsible or liable cannot redress the harm done to others by their faulty decisions—as they cannot in the case of repositories' harming future generations—there are strong arguments for minimizing the public risk. Industrial and technological decisionmakers cannot adequately compensate or insure their potential victims from bad consequences in the case of permanent disposal because the risks involve death. Therefore, they are what Judith Jarvis Thomson calls "incompensable." Surely incompensable risks ought to be minimized for those who do not have the opportunity to give free, informed consent to them. Whenever risks are incompensable, (e.g., imposing a significant probability of death on another), failure to minimize the risks is typically morally unjustifiable without the free, informed consent of the victim.[93] In the next chapter, we shall discuss the problem of free informed consent in more detail.

A final reason for minimizing type-II error in cases of uncertainty is that failure to do so would result in using members of future generations as means to the ends of present persons. It would result in their bearing a significantly higher risk from radwaste than members of present generations, despite the fact that present persons have received most of the benefits associated with generating the waste. Such discrimination (in this case, against future persons), as Frankena has pointed out, is justified only if it would work to the advantage of everyone, including those discriminated against. Any other attempt to justify discrimination fails because it would amount to sanctioning the use of some humans as means to the ends of other humans.[94]

In the next chapter, we shall give detailed arguments that discrimination against future persons would not work to the advantage of everyone. Because it would not, discrimination against members of future generations is not justified. And if it is not justified, then failure to minimize type-II errors, which cause such discrimination, is also not justified. Hence, in situations of uncertainty, such as those concerned with permanent radwaste disposal, the ethically preferable course of action is to minimize type-II, rather than type-I, error. This course of action, in a situation of uncertainty, requires us to run the risk of rejecting the null hypothesis, to run the risk of not using permanent high-level radwaste repositories, at least not until significant uncertainties are removed.

Conclusion

If the arguments of this chapter are correct, then permanent geological disposal of radwaste is highly questionable on both epistemological and methodological grounds. The *epistemological* grounds are the tremendous uncertainties associated with permanent disposal, uncertainties arising because of the ten-thousand-year time frame, the precision of safety predictions required by existing regulations, and our inability even to quantify these uncertainties. The *methodological* grounds are the imprecision of the methods currently available for assessment of proposed radwaste sites, some of which have been outlined in chapters 4 through 7.

Moreover, as chapter 6 argued, it is impossible to justify building a permanent radwaste repository, at present, without employing at least two logically invalid inferences: the appeal to ignorance and affirming the consequent. Policy based on questionable logical and scientific inferences is highly problematic. Hence, all those who support using permanent radwaste repositories at present appear to err in some of the same ways as DOE assessors. They appear to have abandoned conservative scientific assumptions and value judgments and, instead, to have "embraced with enthusiasm an unwarranted optimism."[95]

8

Equity: An Obstacle
to Geological Disposal

Nuclear proponent Alvin Weinberg described the problem of radioactive wastes as a "Faustian bargain." In return for the present benefits of atomic energy, we must export the risks of nuclear waste to future generations.[1] Since we have already made the Faustian bargain, we cannot turn back; we cannot avoid dealing with radioactive waste already generated. We can, however, choose better or worse ways to live out the consequences of our pact with Mephistopheles. Is permanent geological disposal of radwaste our best option? The National Research Council of the United States National Academy of Sciences affirmed in 1990 that it is, stating:

There is a strong worldwide consensus that the best, safest long-term option for dealing with HLW [high-level radwaste] is geological isolation.[2]

As the statement of the National Academy board reveals, arguments for permanent disposal of spent nuclear fuel often come down to safety. Regardless of the admitted uncertainties about the future performance of a radwaste repository, nevertheless, we need to isolate the waste so that it cannot affect present and future persons adversely. If this chapter is correct, however, the safety rationale for permanent disposal is highly questionable. In subsequent paragraphs, we explain that such an argument, indeed any argument for permanent geological disposal, is likely to violate considerations of equity, consent, and due process.[3]

Equity and Permanent Geological Disposal

In chapter 5, we argued that a number of Yucca Mountain risk assessments are highly questionable because they are based on the implicit ethical value judgment that utilitarian risk distributions are acceptable. Likewise, in chapter 6, we argued that some Yucca Mountain assessments are also problematic because they are based on the implicit ethical value judgment that consent is not a necessary condition for imposition of a serious threat to the health and well-being of an innocent person. Now we wish to argue both (1) that these questionable value judgments about utility and consent are unavoidable if one supports a permanent geological repository, and (2) that because they are unavoidable, therefore the permanent repositories themselves are ethically suspect.

Whenever assessors make ethical or methodological value judgments, such as that they need not consider worst cases, or that average risk determines risk acceptability, we argued in chapter 5 that they presuppose utilitarian value judgments. Such utilitarian judgments are ethically suspect mainly because they presuppose that risks need not be distributed in an egalitarian, but only in an efficient, manner. They are also open to criticism because they sanction using members of some geographical or temporal minority who are most at risk so as to benefit the majority, and because they sanction using persons as means to the ends of other persons.[4] Because permanent geological disposal of radwaste is premised on the knowledge that complete, perpetual containment of the waste will not be achieved,[5] that the canisters will remain intact for several hundred years, and that no significant levels of waste likely will escape for several generations,[6] it is clear that permanent disposal places the greatest health and safety risks on members of future generations. Because it places the greatest burdens on future victims, permanent disposal implicitly sanctions an inequitable risk distribution. This distribution is particularly onerous not only because future persons will face the greatest hazards but also, as we shall argue in this chapter, because they appear to receive the fewest benefits from the generation and disposal of radwaste. Present persons, however, receive the greatest benefits. Because of the inequity of the risk distribution, permanent disposal likewise sanctions using some future persons so as to benefit present persons. Hence, permanent disposal sanctions using future persons as means to the ends of other persons.

Most moral philosophers have argued that it is ethically unacceptable to use other persons as means to our ends, and so we shall not repeat their reasoning here.[7] We accept it as a truism that all persons ought to be treated as ends, not merely as means to satisfy the desires of other persons, not merely as objects. There are also good grounds for believing that all persons ought to receive equal treatment with respect to societal risk, equal consideration of their interests. Some of these reasons are that the comparison class, present and future persons, is all humans, and all humans have the same capacity for a happy life.[8] Another reason for egalitarian risk distributions is that free, informed, rational people would likely agree to principles of equal rights or equal protection.[9] Moreover, principles of equal treatment provide the basic justifications for other important concepts of ethics and are presuppositions of all schemes involving consistency, justice, fairness, rights, and autonomy.[10] Finally, equality of rights is presupposed by the idea of law; "law itself embodies an ideal of equal treatment for persons similarly situated."[11]

If all persons in all generations have an equal, prima facie right to life and therefore to bodily security, as the most basic of human rights, then allowing one group of persons to be put at greater risk—without adequate compensation and for no overriding, morally relevant reason—amounts to violating their rights to life and to bodily security. Indeed, if there were no obligations to equalize the burden of risk imposed on one generation or segment of society for the benefit of another generation or segment of society, then there could be no authentic bodily security and no legal rights. Using a utilitarian justification, one group or one generation could simply do whatever it wished to any victimized minority or generation. This is why justice, at its most fundamental level, is fairness.[12] Of course, treating everyone the same is impossible; hence, one cannot be ethically required to provide precisely the same treatment to all persons. Moreover, arguing that equal treatment of all persons is morally required, in the name of fairness, does not mean guaranteeing all persons the *same* treatment, but rather treatment that is proportional to their merits or to the strength of their claims. Hence, we may treat persons differently but equally as a result of a number of factors, for example: as a reward for merit, as compensation, as an incentive, or as a provision for special needs.[13] In other words, although there is no ethical requirement always to treat everyone the same, one needs to have *relevant moral grounds* for treating persons differently.[14]

Equity and Permanent Geological Disposal: Objections Based on Utility

Proponents of permanent geological disposal might argue, however, that there are relevant moral grounds for treating present and future persons differently. They might claim that utility, efficiency, or the greater good requires building permanent geological repositories. In response to this objection, we shall argue that there do not appear to be relevant moral grounds for treating present and future persons differently with respect to risk, for discriminating against subsequent generations on the basis of utility or efficiency. One reason for denying the legitimacy of this discrimination is that because we accept prima facie principles of political equality (see the previous paragraphs) and equal treatment under the law, equal treatment of persons and generations requires no justification, since it is presumed defensible. Only unequal (different) treatment of different generations or different communities requires defense.[15] Therefore, because we accept prima facie principles of political equality, the burden of proof is on the person who wishes to discriminate, who wishes to provide unequal treatment to different communities, persons, or generations. Indeed, the NAS affirmed an even stronger position regarding our duties to future generations: "Moral intuition tells us that our descendants deserve a world that we have tried to make better."[16]

In response, proponents of utilitarian distributions of radwaste risk could claim that nuclear generation of electricity benefits everyone, even future generations. They could also respond that commercial nuclear power (with its byproduct of spent fuel) serves a higher good, economic welfare that makes everyone better off as a result, even members of future generations. For example, they might argue that nuclear electricity and the generation of radwaste have prevented further use of nonrenewable resources, such as fossil fuels. Or, they might respond that nuclear electricity, with its associated waste, has prevented a significant amount of global warming that would have been caused by our using coal instead of nuclear power. Hence, they might argue that nuclear fission and its wastes benefit future persons as well as present ones; therefore, they might conclude that imposing risks on the future is a justifiable "discrimination" and, as a result, not inequitable.[17]

There are at least two problems, however, with the claims that nuclear electricity and its associated wastes will benefit future persons and that permanent geological disposal of the wastes would not impose inequitable burdens on distant generations. One problem is that even on narrow economic criteria, the costs of nuclear electricity and permanent disposal exceed the benefits, provided that members of all generations are treated equitably, and provided that we do not discount future deaths from the facility. The costs exceed the benefits because economists believe that future generations do not benefit significantly from nuclear power. Only if future deaths (from radwaste storage or disposal) are discounted, however, is it possible to argue that nuclear benefits exceed the costs. Hence, nuclear electricity and permanent disposal are cost effective only for members of present generations, if at all, and only if we do not treat future deaths the same as those of present persons.[18]

Even if one believes that future generations have received as many benefits from nuclear technology as present persons have, and even if one claims that the overall benefits of nuclear fission and permanent radwaste storage are worth the risks,[19] these two admissions would not resolve the equity problem with future generations. The inequity remains, despite these two admissions, because—regardless of the equity of *benefit* distribution—future generations will bear extraordinarily disproportionate *risks* from permanent geological disposal. In other words, even if the benefits are worth the risks, nuclear-related risks and benefits need to be distributed equitably. Permanent repositories do not distribute the risks equitably across generations. In the next chapter, we shall argue for an alternative to permanent geological disposal that distributes radwaste risks more equitably across generations.

A second reason why the alleged benefits (received by future generations from nuclear fission) do not resolve the problems of intergenerational equity raised by geological disposal is that permanent repositories do not serve the overall interests of everyone in an equal way, even though they do bring many benefits. For a utilitarian decision to be truly successful in serving the overall interest of everyone, it must be "required for the promotion of equality in the long run." Any other interpretation of "serving the overall interest" would be open to the charge that it was built upon using some humans (future persons) as means to the ends of others (present persons), rather than treating them as ends in themselves.[20] Therefore, we must ask whether allegedly efficient or utilitarian decisions, per se—for example, building permanent repositories, or avoiding more expensive, longer-lived radwaste canisters—lead to the promotion of equality in the long run.

Given the history of technology and environmental welfare, there is little basis for believing that efficiency or utilitarian policy judgments will help promote a more equitable distribution of wealth and therefore more political equality.[21] In the United States, for example, although there has been an absolute increase in the standard of living in the past thirty-five years, the relative shares of wealth held by various groups have not changed. The poorest 20 percent of persons still receive 5 percent of the wealth, while the richest 20 percent still hold 41 percent; the share of the middle three quintiles also has remained fairly constant.[22] These figures suggest that economic and technological growth, coupled with efficiency or utility in the form of inequity of risk abatement, have not promoted economic equality. Because of the close relationship between wealth and the ability to utilize equal opportunities,[23] it is unlikely that such efficiency, economic expansion, and utility have promoted equal political treatment.[24] If anything, they have probably made inequities even worse.[25]

Efficient or utilitarian risk distributions, even accompanied by technological progress, likewise typically fail to remove distributive inequities because the poor usually bear the brunt of technological hazards. Most environmental policies, for example, including risk policies, "distribute the costs of controls in a regressive pattern while providing disproportionate benefits for the educated and wealthy, who can better afford to indulge an acquired taste" for environmental quality and risk mitigation.[26] This means that for the poor, whatever risk abatement and environmental quality cannot be paid for cannot be had.[27] Hence, for all these reasons, it is doubtful that efficient or utilitarian risk distributions will help promote overall political equality. If not, then it is likewise doubtful that efficient or utilitarian distributions of radwaste risks, as a result of a permanent geological repository, will help promote overall political equality. And if utilitarian distributions do not do so, then there appear to be no morally justified grounds for discriminating against members of future generations by virtue of imposing a greater radwaste risk on them.

Even if there are no *morally* relevant justifications for the allegedly utilitarian risk judgments presupposed by policies favoring permanent radwaste disposal, someone might object that there are practical justifications for the inequity. They might object, for example, that imposing a greater radwaste risk on future generations is justified because permanent disposal is safer than any other means of dealing with the waste. They might claim, for example, that because permanent disposal is safer for everyone, present and future, than above-ground monitored storage, therefore we ought to proceed with geological disposal. The safety objection just given, however, does not provide a compelling argument for defending the inequities associated with permanent geological disposal, because several of its main premises are highly questionable. It is not clear, for example, that permanent disposal is safer than other means of dealing with radwaste because there are so many uncertainties associated with predicting future events. Indeed, the whole point of chapters 4 through 7 is to outline the numerous ways in which judgments about future repository safety are highly uncertain. Hence, it is not obvious that geological disposal is safer than other methods of waste management. It may well be safer for several generations, but if this is the argument, then it begs the very question at issue, namely, whether inequitable risk distributions are justified by overall considerations of safety. One could always ask: "Safer for whom?" "Safer for which generation?"

Of course, radwaste does seem to be safer from hazards such as terrorist attacks when it is deep underground rather than stored and monitored above ground. Admittedly, the risk of foul play and human error decreases with permanent disposal, as does the need for some paramilitary force to guard the waste. Unfortunately, however, the risk of leakage increases with permanent disposal. Hence, the safety argument for permanent waste disposal is at best an argument for trading one risk (terrorism) for another (leakage). It also is not obvious that permanent disposal is safer than monitored above-ground storage, both because permanent repository waste will not be monitored and because it will be retrievable only for the first fifty years. Moreover, most countries are currently pursuing a policy of long-term (thirty to fifty years) interim storage. If above-ground storage were extraordinarily risky compared to geological disposal, then presumably most countries would now be storing their radwastes in permanent geological repositories. The fact that no one is yet doing so suggests that perhaps permanent disposal is not currently known to be the safest means of managing the wastes.

Another reason why there do not appear to be relevant practical grounds for imposing different radwaste risks on present and future persons is that we already recognize the importance of equity in risk distribution. Indeed, the U.S. government is currently following schemes to compensate persons and regions that bear a higher risk as a result of permanent radwaste disposal. The government recognizes the principle that persons and regions ought to be treated equally and that, if they are not, then they ought to be compensated. For example, extensive 1987 amendments to the U.S. Nuclear Waste Policy Act of 1982 authorized compensating a U.S. state, locality, or Native American tribe willing to accept either a monitored retrievable storage facility (MRS) for radwaste or a permanent geological repository. According to the benefits provision of the 1987 Amendments, annual payments to the locale hosting such a facility could range from $5 to $20 million, payable upon execution of a benefits agreement.[28] The existence of such compensation schemes in current U.S. law dealing with high-level radioactive waste indicates that we as a society recognize the importance of geographical or regional equity. We recognize that Nevadans, for example, ought to be compensated by the citizens of the rest of the country if the state agrees to take on the burden of disposing of spent reactor fuel. If we recognize the requirements of geographical equity, however, then we ought to be consistent and recognize the importance of temporal or intergenerational equity. Moreover, recognizing intergenerational equity would lead to the consequence that we ought not impose higher risks from nuclear waste on future generations without compensating them in full.

Equity and Permanent Geological Disposal: Are There Duties to Future Generations?

At this point, proponents of permanent radwaste repositories might object that although there are principles of regional or geographical equity, recognized in current law, there are no comparable principles of intergenerational equity. They might argue that we have no obvious duties to members of future generations. After all, they might object, even human fetuses do not have legal rights until they are a number of months old. Moreover, they might argue, future persons are even more "potential" than fetuses; following this argument, they cannot be said to be holders of legal rights, and we cannot be said to have duties to them. Therefore, the objectors might conclude, we have neither any clear obligations to members of future generations nor any obligations to avoid permanent geological disposal so as to protect the interests of future generations.

Scholars have offered many reasons for our failure to have any duties to members of future generations. Derek Parfit has made one of the most famous of such attacks, arguing that justifications based on how our decisions will affect the interests of future individuals cannot succeed. They cannot, says Parfit, because the policy choices that we make now will not only determine the circumstances of those later individuals, but also so alter social patterns that *different* individuals will come into existence as a result of different choices. Thus, whatever choice we make cannot be said to harm future individuals, or make them worse off than they might otherwise be, says Parfit, because different choices will mean that different persons will exist. Hence, he concludes that whatever our duties toward future generations, they cannot be justified by appeals to how our actions will affect the individuals of later generations.[29]

Some of the other arguments against duties to members of future generations are the following:

1. We are unable to predict the course of the future and hence unable to predict the consequences of our actions.
2. We are unable to insure that the needs or wants of our descendants can be met, since intervening generations might not take account of them.
3. Future persons are indeterminate or unknowable to us as individuals.
4. Future persons are contingent, not actual.
5. We are ignorant of the needs or desires of future persons.
6. We are ignorant of the number of future people and hence, unable to make utility calculations regarding them.
7. We are unable to determine whether future persons will share our social ideals or be members of our moral community.
8. We are uncertain as to whether we share a social contract with future persons, because we have no reciprocal relationship with them; possibly we can affect their welfare, but they cannot affect ours.[30]

In response to the previous arguments against the existence of duties to members of future generations, philosophers have provided a variety of counterarguments.[31] Because a number of scholars, such as Douglas MacLean,[32] have seen the Parfit argument as compelling, it may be most important to defuse it. Both Parfit and Maclean appear to err when they allege that because different individuals will come into being as a result of different policy choices in the present, therefore we cannot be said to harm future persons (or to make them worse off) because different choices will mean that different persons will exist. Our choices, they claim, cannot make the same person worse off; rather, they note that our choices will cause a different person to exist. The main problem with the Parfit and MacLean response is that the identity problem should not matter to the ethical evaluation of an act, as Joel Feinberg and others have recognized.[33] If someone is murdered, for example, or if an innocent person is killed without provocation, we know that the act is wrong regardless of the identity of the victim. Likewise, who the members of future generations turn out to be should not matter to the ethical assessment of our acts that will affect them. Those who bear the consequences of our reckless actions, regardless of who they are, have grounds for complaint. For example, if an airplane steward negligently fails to close the rear cabin door properly, then persons hurt in the event of depressurization have grounds for complaint. Indeed, there are grounds for complaint even if, when the door is improperly shut, we are not certain who will occupy the plane and what their identities will be.

Another important response to those who argue against duties to members of future generations is that some of the claims—on which the arguments against duties to future persons are based—are false. For example, it is false to claim that we cannot predict the future. Indeed, many precise aspects of the future are uncertain. For example, the precise climate and hydrogeology at Yucca Mountain ten thousand years from now are uncertain, as chapters 4 through 7 argued. We do have a reasonable probability of knowing other, more general, aspects of the future, however. We know, for example, that future persons are likely to need clean air and water. Some arguments against our duties to members of future generations also fail because they contradict ethical principles that we already hold. For example, as we argued earlier, we believe that murder is wrong regardless of whether the victim is knowable to us an individual, or whether she has the same needs and interests as we. Hence, if knowing the victim as an individual or knowing her tastes and interests is not a necessary condition for asserting the wrongness of murder, knowing both these characteristics is likewise not a necessary condition for asserting the wrongness of jeopardizing the safety of members of future generations. Just as it is ethically improper to place an unknown living person in possible jeopardy, it is likewise ethically improper, all things being equal, to place some unknown future person in possible jeopardy.

One of the most significant recent philosophical discussions of our duties to members of future generations is that of Harvard philosopher John Rawls. He argues that any reasonable person—who did not know to which generation, social class, intelligence bracket, and so on he belongs—would accept the principle of equal apportionment of risks, resources, and goods as the distribution that is fair. Although there is no time to discuss Rawls' elaborate scheme in detail,[34] we can outline his main points. Rawls, Barry, and other moral philosophers argue that principles of equality in the distribution of opportunity are intuitively obvious and fair. If we accept such principles of egalitarianism, says Rawls, we have a threefold task: (1) to preserve the gains of our civilization; (2) to maintain intact our just institutions; and (3) to hand over to posterity an accumulation of capital and technology greater than we received from our ancestors, so as to compensate for resource depletion.[35]

Less abstract and theoretical than that of John Rawls, Daniel Callahan's arguments for a social contract among all generations is also quite persuasive.[36] According to Callahan, social contracts exist even when there is no prearranged plan of explicit reciprocity. In the parent-child relationship, says Callahan, there is indeed a social contract, but it is not brought about by reciprocity. Rather, he says, the contract is brought about because one party (the parents) chooses to accept an obligation. Children are not asked whether they wish to be born, says Callahan, but their parents' taking on the obligation of children nevertheless initiates a social contract among them. The contract exists, in part, says Callahan, because the children owe their parents a debt in return for their life. Moreover, says Callahan, the parents' duty is not contingent on the child's reciprocity. The parent has a duty, regardless of whether he is ever reciprocated, regardless of whether the children are asked if they wish to be born, and regardless of whether the parents know the needs of the children. Likewise, one can argue that members of present generations—as recipients of benefits from their ancestors—have duties to future persons, regardless of whether or not the future persons are asked if they wish to receive benefits, regardless of whether or not the future persons can reciprocate their giving, and regardless of the degree to which the present persons know the needs of future generations. As Feinberg points out,[37] regardless of our ignorance about the needs of future persons, we know that they will have an interest in living space, fertile soil, fresh air, and so on. Because present persons can affect the interests of future persons, and because we have some general ideas about what they will need, it is reasonable to claim that opportunities ought to be distributed equitably, even across generations. Hence, it is reasonable to claim that we have duties to future persons.[38]

Moreover, as we shall argue later in the chapter, both national and international laws explicitly drafted by legislators and accepted by policymakers are based on the notion that present persons have duties to members of future generations. Such laws suggest that our strong intuitions about our duties to members of future generations have received support in numerous ways. Even skeptics admit that "most people would agree that a total disregard for the future is unreasonable."[39] Equally importantly, some of our most distinguished ethical thinkers have presented compelling cases for our duties to future generations.[40] In addition, there appear to be no morally relevant grounds for discriminating against members of future generations and treating them unequally. For all these reasons, it makes sense to assume that we do have duties to future persons. If we do have such duties, then the burden of proof, as in all cases of alleged discrimination, is on the person who favors discrimination, the person who is willing to treat future persons less equitably than present persons. But what does it mean to treat future persons less equitably than present persons? What does it mean *not* to discriminate against members of future generations? What is equal treatment? At the simplest level, as Barry points out,[41] each person's or each generation's being treated equitably means that each person or generation will have the same opportunity to use resources (oil, clean air, soil, and water) as another. Each person deserves the same opportunity, rather than the same level of resources, because factors like merit and effort also ought to determine the level of one's resources. For example, the level of resources ought not always be the same for all persons if the effort expended to obtain the resources is different for different persons.

Obviously, however, each person and generation cannot have the same opportunity to use resources if some of them are finite and if persons are to use them and leave the rest for others. Therefore, equal opportunity to use resources must mean that persons in different spatial and temporal groups (in different countries and different generations) will be treated equally by virtue of being compensated (via increased capital investment and improved technology) for the depletion of resources. In other words, we are bound in equity to do whatever is necessary to provide future generations with the same level of opportunity as they would have had if we had not depleted some resources or polluted their environment. Obviously, however, not all losses of opportunity are compensable, so fairness and equity dictate that one person not diminish opportunities for another in a way that is not compensable. Otherwise, there would be no way to correct unequal opportunity.

In the case of making decisions about pollution from radioactive waste, insuring that future generations have equal opportunity presumably means that the risks imposed on future persons ought to be no greater than those they would otherwise have faced if no radioactive wastes had been produced.[42] If they were not produced, future persons would face no radioactive risk greater than that of naturally occurring uranium. Hence, one provides equal opportunity to members of subsequent generations (with respect to radioactive waste) by insuring that future risks from nuclear waste are no greater than those that arise from naturally occurring uranium. Indeed, the uranium criterion is exactly the one used in U.S. laws and regulations. It assumes that radwaste risks are acceptable, provided that they create no more risk than natural uranium would cause.[43]

Because federal laws and regulations are based on the equal opportunity criterion for nuclear risks, claiming that they are acceptable if they cause no more injuries or fatalities than would be induced by naturally occurring uranium, this criterion may be ethically appropriate for repositories. Several problems arise, however, with its application and interpretation. One difficulty is that naturally occurring uranium is a dangerous material, although not nearly so dangerous as spent fuel. Because those who generate radioactive waste are creating *more* of a dangerous substance, it is not clear that once spent fuel has decayed to the level at which it is like naturally occurring uranium, the equal opportunity criterion has been met. It may not have been satisfied because, as a result of our creating radwaste, we impose a greater *volume* of dangerous material on future generations, material that is as hazardous as naturally occurring uranium. Hence, although spent fuel may one day be no more hazardous than naturally occurring uranium, it is not obvious that as a result of its creation future generations will bear no risks greater than they otherwise would have faced. A second problem with the natural-uranium, or "neutrality," criterion is that there is no guarantee that any repository, including Yucca Mountain, could meet it. If some of the worries articulated in chapters 4 through 7 are correct, then the canisters may be breached, and the waste may leach out long before it decays to a level where it is no more harmful than naturally occurring uranium.

The uranium criterion is also questionable because in the centuries prior to the time that the high-level radwaste decays to the level of hazard of uranium, the risk would presumably be higher than that caused by natural uranium. Hence, at least three difficulties face the U.S. government's interpretation of the natural-uranium, or "neutrality," criterion for equity: (1) we would be imposing a greater volume of hazardous material, not the same amount that future generations would otherwise have faced; (2) we cannot reasonably guarantee that no repositories will leak before the spent fuel has become only as hazardous as naturally occurring uranium; and (3) for the first several hundred years of the repository life, the risk is clearly greater than that posed by natural uranium. Because of these three difficulties with the equal opportunity, or neutrality, criterion, future generations clearly bear a disproportionate radwaste risk from permanent repositories. Because future persons will not receive correspondingly great benefits, permanent disposal of nuclear waste is inequitable. And, as we have already argued in chapter 7, because the risks imposed on future persons by geological repositories are at best highly uncertain and at worst higher than those imposed on present persons, it appears that they are greater than the risks that future persons otherwise would have faced. Moreover, for the reasons given earlier in this chapter, there do not seem to be any morally compelling grounds for claiming that future persons would be adequately compensated for the inequities associated with geological repositories. Hence, permanent disposal is inequitable and therefore ethically unacceptable.

Consent and Permanent Disposal

Installations for permanent storage of nuclear waste are not merely problematic on grounds of equity, however. They are also questionable because it is unlikely that future persons would consent to them. Members of future generations obviously have no opportunity, *in practice*, to consent to the additional radwaste risk these facilities would impose on them. Moreover, as we shall argue shortly, it is unlikely *in principle* that future persons would consent to such risks. Yet some form of consent, either implicit or explicit, appears to be a precondition of most just laws and policies—indeed a precondition of the power of government over persons.[44] When the delegates to the first Continental Congress met in 1774, for example, they affirmed this point:

[T]he inhabitants of the English colonies in North America . . . have the following RIGHTS: . . . life, liberty, and property: and that they never ceded to any power whatever, a right to dispose of either without their consent.[45]

When they met two years later, they proclaimed in the "Declaration of Independence" that

> to secure these rights, Governments are instituted among Men, deriving their just powers from the consent of the governed,—that whenever any Form of Government becomes destructive of these ends, it is the Right of the People to alter or abolish it, and to institute new Government.[46]

Moreover, early in American history, the federal judiciary, in justifying judicial review of legislation, recognized that consent is required to abrogate natural rights, such as the right to life:

> There are certain vital principles in our free Republican government, which will determine and overrule an apparent and flagrant abuse of legislative power; as to authorize manifest injustice by positive law.[47]

Our founding leaders may also have recognized that the duty to insure free, informed consent extended even to future generations. As Thomas Paine wrote:

> Every age and generation must be as free to act for itself, in all cases as the ages and generations which preceded it. The vanity and presumption of governing beyond the grave is the most ridiculous and insolent of all tyrannies. Man has no property in man; neither has any generation a property in the generations which are to follow.[48]

Those who favor permanent geological disposal of radioactive waste probably would agree that government actions in this regard are premised on citizen consent. After all, governmental authority depends on the consent of the governed, in a political sense. Also, in an ethical sense, no one has the right to impose an avoidable and serious risk of harm on another without his consent. Therefore, in the case of permanent repositories, supporters of the facilities would likely argue (1) that future generations have given second-party consent[49] by virtue of present persons acting as proxy decisionmakers for them via representative democracy, or (2) that serving the common good outweighs considerations of whether future persons have consented to the radwaste risk. In other words, proponents of permanent repositories probably would not deny the importance of free, informed consent, but they would likely say either that some form of consent has been given, or that other considerations—such as serving the common good or the necessity of practicing a politics of sacrifice—outweigh considerations of consent.[50] Do either of the defenses, 1 or 2, justify our failure

to obtain explicit informed consent from future persons before sub-
jecting them to the risks of permanent radwaste disposal? Earlier in
the chapter, we argued against thesis 2, showing that discrimination
against members of future generations appeared to be unjustified because there were no morally compelling grounds for treating them unequally. We also argued that utilitarian considerations did not outweigh the inequities imposed on future persons. Hence, thesis 2 does
not provide grounds for discrimination against future persons because
there are no greater-good factors that outweigh the significance of
their consent in justifying a permanent repository.

The more important issue, however, is 1, whether one could reasonably argue that second-party consent justifies exposing future generations to the effects of a permanent radwaste facility. Such second-
party consent is at least prima facie plausible because, in a democracy,
we recognize that all citizens must make some concessions to one another to operate a constitutional government. At least one of these
concessions could be that our representatives can make decisions for
us, and therefore that the representatives of future persons could make
decisions for them. Hence, it is arguable that second-party consent
justifies building permanent repositories that will affect future persons,
just as second-party consent justifies many of our other actions that
will impact our descendants. In other words, something like second-
party consent may provide reasonable grounds for our policies implementing permanent disposal because everyone recognizes that there
must be some concessions to majority rule if one is to gain the advantages of democratic government: "There is no other way to manage a
democratic regime."[51]

Is the affirmation of second party consent regarding future persons
one concession that we ought to make to majority rule? In the case of
a permanent radwaste repository there seem to be at least three reasons that future generations ought not be said to have given consent
via a second party. The *first* and most obvious reason is that it is not
clear that a majority of persons, across time, supports permanent radwaste disposal. Yet foregoing explicit consent and accepting the duty
to comply with government rules and regulations presupposes at least
that the rules and regulations are the product of authentic and informed majority rule. Of course, a policy's being chosen/sanctioned
by an authentic and informed majority is not a sufficient condition for
the policy's being just, but it is arguably a necessary condition.[52] And
if so, then the next question is whether the policy of employing per-

manent radwaste repositories meets this necessary condition. Is it a policy that would be sanctioned by an authentic and informed majority?

Using permanent radwaste disposal is the policy pursued by a minority. It is the policy chosen by representatives of the two or three generations living now who have benefited from atomic power and who see commercial nuclear energy and radwaste disposal as part of a cost-effective way of generating electricity for them.[53] These two or three generations are not a majority, historically speaking. Indeed, they are probably a minority, whereas members of future generations (likely to be affected by stored radwaste) are truly a "silent majority." Hence, it is not clear that the imposition of permanent disposal represents anything but a minority decision based on relatively short-term economic interests. Indeed, some authors have argued that because of factors such as the proliferation problem, present use of nuclear electricity provides little benefit to future persons.[54] To the degree that the policy of permanent disposal does not represent a decision to which an authentic informed *majority* of persons, present and future, would theoretically agree, to that extent current policy and law sanctioning geological repositories do not outweigh considerations requiring the consent of future persons. Presumably there are times that one can dispense with explicit consent, but only when the greater good— as recognized by an authentic informed majority—defines this dispensation as a greater good. It is not clear that a majority of persons would support dispensing with informed consent in the case of permanent geological disposal.

A second reason why future persons have probably not given consent, via second parties, to permanent radwaste disposal is that even a majority of present persons cannot be said to have given any form of consent to geological disposal. Polls indicate that a majority of persons believes that radioactive waste disposal is not safe.[55] Indeed, the NIMBY (Not In My Back Yard) syndrome is pervasive. In Nevada, for example, 80 percent of the population is opposed to a permanent repository in the state.[56] If one makes the reasonable assumption that the preferences of present persons indicate something about the preferences of future persons, then the opposition of this generation to permanent disposal provides grounds for arguing that subsequent generations would not likely consent either, since they would face an even greater risk from facilities built now. And if they would not consent, then no theory of second-party consent will likely justify the repositories.

A third reason why future persons cannot reasonably be said to have given consent, via second parties, to permanent radwaste disposal is that "putting up with" unjust or undesirable policies or laws is reasonable only if the burden of injustice is evenly distributed. As Rawls puts it,

> when they adopt the majority principle the parties agree to put up with unjust laws only on certain conditions. Roughly speaking, in the long run the burden of injustice should be more or less evenly distributed over different groups in the society, and the hardship of unjust policies should not weigh too heavily in any particular case . . . Instead we submit our conduct to democratic authority only to the extent necessary to share equitably in the inevitable imperfections of a constitutional system.[57]

But, as we argued earlier in this chapter, the burden of radwaste risk from permanent repositories is not equitably distributed. Hence, one of the apparently necessary conditions for affirming the (second-party) consent of future persons—that the consent is to a scheme that evenly distributes societal risks, costs, and benefits—cannot be met. Therefore, because permanent disposal represents neither a policy to which a majority of all persons would agree, nor a policy to which present persons agree, nor a policy in terms of which risks and costs are evenly distributed, permanent disposal is very likely not something to which future persons could be said to have given some sort of implicit political consent via second parties. If they were able to act in their own behalf, future persons would very likely withhold consent, perhaps in part for these three reasons. They might also reason that, given the uncertainties surrounding permanent disposal, consenting to it would amount to their agreeing to be experimental guinea pigs.

Moreover, the traditional doctrine of free informed consent (as employed in other cases of risk) provides additional reasons for claiming that future persons cannot easily be said to have given consent, via second parties, to permanent radwaste disposal. To see why they would be unlikely to consent, we need to understand the history of the doctrine of free, informed consent. It began to receive attention shortly after the Nuremburg trials in which horrifying accounts of Nazi experimentation led persons to examine the issue of experimental subjects who might not have consented to the procedures that they underwent. The term, "informed consent," arose roughly a decade after the trials, and the issue began to receive substantial consideration in the literature ever since at least 1972. Very little of this consideration, however, has focused on free, informed consent to technological or environmental risk.[58] Most of the discussion has been directed at consent in cases of medical ethics.[59] The main *motive* behind interest in free informed consent appears to have been reduction of risk, avoidance of unfairness, and elimination of exploitation. The main *justification* for supporting the necessity of free informed consent, however, has been the protection of individual human autonomy. Some persons have also appealed to beneficence and to nonmaleficence as grounds for justifying the necessity of recognizing persons' rights to free informed consent.[60]

To determine whether possible future persons affected by a permanent radwaste repository can be said to have given second-party consent to such a facility, we must know exactly what notions are imbedded in the concept of "informed consent." According to historians of the concept, it is best analyzed as "autonomous authorization" and may be broken down in terms of four analytical components: disclosure, understanding, voluntariness, and competence. Disclosure, the main component from an institutional point of view, refers to the necessity of professionals' passing on facts or information to decisionmakers and possible victims. For example, medical doctors need to disclose information to patients, and government scientists studying a repository need to disclose information to citizens making a decision about such a facility. This obligation regarding disclosure includes: facts that the subjects believe are relevant to the decision about consenting to a proposal; information the professionals believe to be material; the professionals' recommendation; the purpose of seeking consent; and the nature of consent as an act of authorization.[61] Obviously full disclosure of effects is impossible—at least in part because professionals may not know all the effects. The requirement of disclosure therefore means, at a minimum, that professionals not withhold information relevant to a decision about risk and, especially, that they not withhold information about areas of uncertainty.

Understanding, the second element in the process of obtaining free informed consent, may be the most important. In order for subjects to give free informed consent, professionals have a duty to help them overcome illness, irrationality, immaturity, distorted information, or other factors that can limit their grasp of the situation to which they have the right to give or withhold consent. Often communication of information necessary to understanding can be accomplished by means of analogies between such information and more familiar or ordinary events. Understanding of choices among risky alternatives also can be helped if various options can be understood in terms of projected benefits or opportunities as well as risks. In some cases, however, many scholars doubt that the genuine understanding requisite for informed consent is possible, as in the case of a fourteen-year-old girl consenting to a risky procedure in order to help her mother,[62] or a poorly educated immigrant consenting to take a risky job in order to support his family.

Voluntariness, or being free to act in giving consent, usually means that the subjects are acting in a way that is free of manipulation and coercion by other persons. Whenever significant influence is exerted by professionals through their roles, authority, or power, then consent is not truly voluntary. For example, some of the best-known obstacles to voluntariness of consent have involved giving subjects irresistible offers, such as rewards of early parole for prisoners becoming medical-research subjects. Very attractive offers, such as extra money, can leave some needy persons "without any real choice other than to accept the offer."[63] Competence, the last element of the process of obtaining free, informed consent, is the ability to perform a task. In the case of consent, it is the ability to give autonomous authorization to some act, like building a repository. Although the notion of competence is value-laden, it includes the ability to make a decision based on rational grounds.[64]

Given the elements that scholars acknowledge as necessary for informed consent—disclosure, understanding, voluntariness, and competence—is it reasonable to claim that future persons can be said to have given a form of second-party consent to the risk of permanent radwaste repositories? If one examines each of the four elements and applies it to the repository issue, the answer appears to be "no." With respect to disclosure, for example, because it is so difficult to project the effects of a repository for ten thousand years into the future (see chapters 4 through 7), it is likewise difficult to believe that the disclosure condition can be met. One cannot consent to a situation when so many vital factors (like safety) regarding it are uncertain. Hence, even if one assumes that second-party consent is legitimate in the case of geological disposal, the scientific uncertainty about the relevant repository risks appears to jeopardize the conditions necessary for disclosure. Hence, it appears to jeopardize the free informed consent of future generations. Likewise, if uncertainty blocks conditions necessary for disclosure, it probably also blocks conditions necessary for understanding the situation to which one is free to give or withhold consent. If the arguments in chapters 4 through 7 are correct, then there are major uncertainties regarding permanent disposal. One cannot understand adequately a risk that is largely uncertain. Hence, lack of understanding likewise appears to block the free informed consent of future generations to a permanent repository. Members of future generations also seem unable to meet the condition of voluntariness because they are victims of coercion at its most extreme. It is impossible for our descendants to exercise control over present persons' making decisions that will affect them. Their lack of control is absolute. Because it is absolute, it appears impossible for future generations to be said to meet the "voluntariness" condition of free informed consent to a permanent radwaste repository.

Even if one responds that present persons can act as guardians or proxies for future persons, and that present persons are not being coerced or manipulated if they choose the repository, this response is doubtful. It is questionable in part because of the coercive tactics and the withholding of information practiced by U.S. Department of Energy officials (see chapters 4 through 7). Indeed, even the general counsel of the DOE noted that the department has acted unlawfully in not carrying out the mandates for siting repositories as specified in the Nuclear Waste Policy Act.[65] The U.S. National Research Council, in a recent position statement on radioactive waste disposal, noted that because of such activities, the "DOE lacked credibility" in the siting process.[66] At least in the United States, even the laws governing high-level radioactive waste disposal appear to interfere in part with the voluntariness of the alleged consent of present persons. According to the provisions of the Nuclear Waste Policy Act (NWPA), for example, a state or Indian tribe hosting a high-level radwaste repository can obtain millions of dollars per year to compensate it for the social costs of the facility; to obtain the money, however, the state must waive its right to veto the repository. Hence, the NWPA requires citizens living near a proposed repository to "sign a blank check" in favor of the repository and to forego reimbursement of all costs of investigating the site or legally challenging the federal government's site-selection process, unless they sign the "blank check." Citizens can hardly claim that their decision about a particular site is voluntary when they must bear the heavy costs of scientific investigation and legal challenges alone, as the price paid for their not consenting.[67]

It is also questionable whether present persons are being coerced or manipulated into consenting to permanent disposal because of the tactics currently being practiced by those attempting to build repositories, as they are at Yucca Mountain. Allen Keesler, president of Florida Power and chair of the utility industry's American Committee on Radwaste Disposal, revealed (in a confidential letter, leaked to the press) in late 1991, for example, that the nuclear utilities in the United States were about to begin a $9 million "advertising blitz in Nevada designed to overcome its resistance to serving as the dumping ground for other states' nuclear wastes."[68] Keesler also revealed, in his letter to other nuclear utility executives, that the federal waste disposal program is progressing only "because of the active support, guidance, and involvement of our industry" in "re-educating" the people of Nevada. According to Keesler's plan, each utility owning a nuclear unit in the United States would be assessed $50,000 per unit, per year, for the cost of the Nevada advertising. For 112 U.S. reactors, this assessment comes to $5.6 million annually. Keesler called the campaign "sensitive," and he "asked utility executives to keep it confidential," especially because "Keesler expects all costs for the utility campaign to be charged to [utility] customers, not stockholders."[69]

Given the nuclear advertising blitz designed to change the minds of the 80 percent of current Nevadans who oppose the Yucca Mountain permanent repository,[70] there is strong evidence of coercion of present persons who might allegedly consent to the disposal. Moreover, without equal funding and education efforts being provided on behalf of opponents of the facility, it appears highly manipulative for the U.S. public to pay for one-sided "information" provided by the nuclear industry. Hence, it is difficult to argue that such behavior—as that exemplified by utilities interested in siting Yucca Mountain—does not compromise conditions necessary for the voluntariness of consent to the proposed Nevada facility.

Even if one argues that present individuals are competent to give second-party consent (on behalf of future persons) to a permanent geological repository, this does not solve the problem of consent. Preceding paragraphs have argued that there are strong obstacles, in the case of permanent disposal, to meeting the other three criteria for informed consent—disclosure, understanding, and voluntariness. Because second-party consent on behalf of future generations cannot satisfy these three other criteria, second-party consent cannot be said to justify building permanent repositories like the one proposed at Yucca Mountain. Indeed, because of the nature of the problems with the criteria of disclosure and understanding, these two criteria appear to block the conditions for free informed consent to any permanent radwaste repository anywhere at present.

In response to these arguments that a permanent repository for nuclear waste cannot satisfy requirements for the free informed consent—even second-party consent—of future persons, there are likely to be a number of objections. One objection is that because future generations will be compensated for the risk that they bear, they are not treated unfairly even if they do not give consent to repositories like Yucca Mountain. In fact, claim the objectors, the 1987 Amendments to the Nuclear Waste Policy Act call for affected states or Indian tribes (hosting a permanent repository or a monitored retrievable storage facility) to receive payments ranging from $5 to $20 million per annum payable upon execution of a benefits agreement.[71] In the Yucca Mountain case, the compensation argument, however, is unconvincing as grounds for ignoring consent to a permanent repository. For one thing, the compensation might compromise the conditions for the voluntariness of the consent (see the discussion in preceding paragraphs). A second difficulty is that it is not clear that one ought to allow compensation for risks to life and bodily security. Indeed, there are a number of telling arguments against the ethics implicit in the so-called "compensating wage differential" used to compensate workers who bear higher risks.[72] These objections raise questions about the compensation of future persons in exchange for imposing higher repository risks on them.

The most damning reply to arguments that compensation justifies imposing higher radwaste risks on future generations, however, is that despite hefty compensation offers, even present generations appear to be rejecting permanent disposal. As we mentioned earlier, 80 percent of Nevadans do not want the Yucca Mountain site.[73] A 1986 poll showed that a majority of Americans do not believe that nuclear waste can be disposed of safely.[74] Hence, if compensation is inadequate grounds for present persons to consent to a permanent radwaste repository, then compensation is also likely to be inadequate grounds for future persons to consent to an even larger risk posed by the same repository.

Another problem with compensating future generations is that it is impossible for them to agree in advance to an acceptable level of compensation, even assuming such compensation is in principle ethically acceptable. Moreover, as we have already mentioned, it is possible that the level of compensation will not be acceptable because it is limited by law. The difficulty here is both (1) that it is impossible for future generations to exercise their due process rights by consenting to some level of compensation, and (2) that it is unlikely the compensation will be adequate, given the magnitude of possible consequences and the legal limits set on compensation. If members of future generations have been injured because of a repository built by earlier generations, then the problem is not merely that it is impossible for them to collect damages from their ancestors. To deal with this difficulty, the government could set up a public trust—as we shall argue in the next chapter. With current legal restrictions on levels of compensation, however, it would be impossible to know if the amount of money were adequate to compensate future persons for whatever harms they might suffer because of radioactive contamination. Hence, the real problem is that it would be impossible to guarantee that the due process rights of future persons could be recognized in full, and impossible to guarantee that they could be compensated in full. These guarantees would be particularly difficult because even large or unlimited compensatory sums may not be adequate to win the consent of present persons who have lost trust in either the siting process or its outcome. If current residents of Nevada near the proposed Yucca Mountain permanent facility would not consent to it, regardless of the level of compensation, then future persons may not do so either.

One difficulty with alleging that future persons can be compensated for the repository-related risks that they bear is that at least in the United States, Canada, and several other countries, the law guarantees only partial compensation for repository-related accidents and radioactive contamination. As we argued in chapter 5, in response to the states' recommendation for unlimited, strict liability for any nuclear waste program or incident,[75] the DOE position has been that "these activities should enjoy indemnity protection equivalent to other nuclear programs." Other U.S. nuclear programs, as mentioned in chapter 5, currently have a liability limit of just over $7 billion, a limit less than 5 percent of government-calculated costs—$358 billion—of the Chernobyl accident.[76] Because Chernobyl was not a worst-case accident, future accidents at reactors or repositories conceivably could run even higher. Since they were given in chapter 5, we shall not repeat here the arguments against limiting liability for permanent geological repositories. What is important, however, is that if compensation is needed to offset the effects of future generations' not being able to give free informed consent to a proposed radwaste site, then limiting liability for repository accidents is doubly questionable: first, on the grounds of violating the due process rights of future persons and second, on the grounds of not providing adequate compensation for future persons' foregoing their consent.

Perhaps the most significant objection to the claim that a permanent geological repository cannot satisfy the standard requirements for free informed consent is that the conditions for consent are rarely, if ever, met in real life. Therefore, according to repository proponents, it may be inappropriate to hold permanent radwaste disposal hostage to conditions for consent that other technological activities likewise cannot satisfy. Moreover, the objector might claim that in many situations, the standard for free informed consent is current professional practice,[77] and such practice admittedly sanctions many decisions—for example, decisions about production of toxic chemicals—that will affect future generations. Hence it is not clear, according to the objector, that facilities like Yucca Mountain present more of an obstacle for free informed consent than do some other current policies or activities. To the degree that such an objection claims that no consent is perfect, it is correct. However, the objection errs both in affirming that permanent geological repositories are no worse than other situations (in terms of free informed consent) and in alleging that "current professional practice" provides the consent norm for permanent repositories. The professional practice norm errs, in part, because for 60 percent of states the current norm is the "reasonable person," not professional practice.[78] The "reasonable person" norm asks what a reasonable person would do, confronted with a situation requiring free informed consent. Because 80 percent of Nevadans oppose the proposed Yucca Mountain facility,[79] it is likely that, on the "reasonable person" standard, current citizens would not consent to a permanent repository.

Even classical doctrines of implicit consent would require that if present persons (proxies for future persons) do not agree to the repository, then they cannot be said to have given implicit consent to it on behalf of future persons. As a number of theorists have pointed out, "it is not plausible to appeal to implicit consent to override current express refusals."[80] Moreover, actual or predicted future consent, according to most scholars, is also not likely to override the express refusals of present persons. Future consent does not satisfy the requirement for free informed consent because it does not respect the autonomy of future persons at present. In other words, "predicted future ratification does not transform the current intervention" into respect for persons' autonomy:[81] "Future or retroactive approval is not a substitute for the exercise of autonomy in giving informed consent or refusal at the outset."[82] If it were, then any activity or process to which present persons had refused consent could simply be said to be justified on the grounds of future consent, and the whole doctrine of free informed consent—in the present—would be undermined.

Repositories like Yucca Mountain are also not likely to provide opportunities for the free informed consent of future persons because they concern risks that are both significantly greater and substantially more unknown than most other situations involving free informed consent. Obviously information and consent need not be perfect, because they cannot be, but the possibility of free informed consent diminishes in proportion to the degree to which the activity in question is more risky or more uncertain. As leading theorists of informed consent put it: as substantial risk is added to a research project, justification that the norms of consent have been met becomes progressively more difficult.[83] Hence, although consent is never perfect because Yucca Mountain and other repositories involve such high uncertainties and high risks[84]—possibly thousands of deaths over thousands of years—the case for informed consent to geological disposal becomes even more difficult to make than for facilities that involve fewer uncertainties and less catastrophic possible consequences.

Practical and Legal
Considerations against Disposal

Although a conclusive case against permanent geological disposal of radwaste can be made on the basis of uncertainty, inequity, and lack of free informed consent of affected persons, there are additional grounds for believing that the repositories are difficult to defend. One set of reasons is legal. Both national and international law sanction our duties to future persons and hence provide a basis for questioning the effects of a permanent repository on future persons. The Charter of the United Nations, for example, drafted after World War II, speaks of saving "succeeding generations from the scourge of war." The 1972 preamble to the Stockholm Declaration on the Human Environment affirms the objective of protecting the welfare of future generations, and its first principle is that humans have "a solemn responsibility to protect and improve the environment for present and future generations." Explicit cases in both public and private international law likewise appeal to the notion of duties to future generations.[85]

In the United States, the first stated goal of the 1969 U.S. National Environmental Policy Act (NEPA) is to "fulfill the responsibilities of each generation as trustee of the environment for succeeding generations."[86] NEPA also proclaims that present persons should not impose risks on "a future generation . . . greater than those acceptable to the current generation."[87] Likewise, the Environmental Protection Agency (EPA) has affirmed that permissible levels of danger that may be imposed on future generations can be defined by referring to the acceptability of risks among the present generation.[88] The EPA also has indicated that, under its approach to regulating permanent repositories, the residual risk to future generations should be "no greater than the risks from an equivalent amount of unmined uranium ore."[89]

Admittedly, however, because the EPA has issued specific standards for high-level radwaste disposal, it appears that the agency sanctions some level of radioactive contamination of future persons that is higher than that to which present persons are subject. For example, the EPA requires the nuclear waste disposal system to ensure that the maximum annual dose equivalent to any individual member of the public in the "accessible environment" will be no greater than 25 mrem to the whole body or 75 mrem to any critical organ for one thousand years after disposal. For the period after one thousand years, the EPA has set limits—for the contamination of drinking-water aquifers—on some sources of radioactive contamination, for example, such that the annual dose equivalent to the total body or any organ is not greater than 4 mrem.[90] Because the one thousand-year EPA rules allow significant radioactive exposure above background levels, it appears that future generations are certain to face higher risks than present persons if there are permanent repositories. Also, because uranium ore is normally deep underground and does not typically expose persons above ground to contamination, it is likewise not evident that the one thousand-year rules allow exposure to future persons on the same level as that received from ore. Hence, the EPA repository standards appear to be consistent neither with the agency's desire to impose future risks that are no greater than those imposed on present persons, nor with its apparent aim to impose future risks that are not greater than those arising from uranium ore. Nevertheless, apart from whether EPA standards do what they are claimed to do, the EPA has affirmed its commitment to protecting members of future generations. If one takes the EPA at its word, to impose neither risks greater than those faced by present persons nor risks greater than those presented by uranium ore, then it appears impossible both to build permanent repositories and to meet these two EPA objectives.

Another legal obstacle to permanent disposal of radwaste may be the Safe Drinking Water Act (SDWA), a law that regulates, among other things, underground injections of radioactive contaminants.[91] In effect, the SDWA states a nondegradation policy for aquifers with respect to potential carcinogens. Provided that spent fuel and its emplacement fit the SDWA definitions, respectively, of "fluid" and "well," as they appear to do,[92] then the SDWA prohibits the "endangerment" of aquifers by underground injection. However, because permanent radwaste repositories will one day leak, it seems unavoidable that their long-lived wastes will, at some point, endanger aquifers. The SDWA also prohibits disposal of hazardous waste into or above a formation within one-quarter mile of an underground source of drinking water. Likewise the act prohibits well injection of any substance that will "allow . . . the movement of fluid containing any contaminant into underground sources of drinking water."[93] Hence, it appears that the SDWA prohibits a permanent high-level radwaste repository unless it is in a location free of aquifers.

Admittedly, however, there appears to be an inconsistency between the EPA high-level waste disposal standards and the SDWA, because the latter appears to prohibit any contamination of drinking water, whereas the former seems to allow radioactive contamination of aquifers provided that the dose, for example, does not exceed 4 mrem per year. Again, if one takes the wording of the SDWA at face value, regardless of the EPA standards, then the SDWA appears to prevent the permanent, geological disposal of radwaste.[94]

In addition to the statements of the EPA and laws like NEPA and the SDWA, there are approximately fifty federal statutes in the United States that contain explicit reference to future generations. Most of these references purport to create or preserve benefits accruing in the short-term future to members of the current generation and future generations. However, no public or private attorney general is authorized to bring suit on behalf of future persons who might be injured by violations of any provisions in current law.[95] Legal limits on public indebtedness reflect, nevertheless, an awareness of the intergenerational implications of borrowing against the credit of the public. Hence, such limits are intended to circumscribe the current generation's opportunity to disregard the financial burdens that it imposes on future generations. Debt limitations appear in both state and municipal codes.[96]

Within the Anglo-American legal system, property law also provides one of the best examples of restraints on present generations who might impair the opportunities of future persons. Many of the rules concerning property determine the extent to which society will allow the current generation owning private property to dictate the configuration of property ownership for subsequent generations. The rule against perpetuities, for instance, prohibits creating interests in property that take it out of trade for a period exceeding that fixed by law. Another rule prohibits suspension of the power of alienation, that is, it prohibits conditions that restrict the owners' ability to use or dispose of property in the future. Although both rules have exceptions, nevertheless they preserve the transferability of property and hence the possibility of its redistribution for the future.[97] Likewise, whenever unborn persons are identified by law as beneficiaries of a trust, this creates an enforceable entitlement in some members of a future generation. Hence, in any action to alter the terms of a trust, equity requires the court to appoint a guardian to represent the interests of future beneficiaries. In fact, the protection given to unborn beneficiaries under private trusts has suggested to some legal commentators that an expanded law of public trusts might provide a response to problems of intergenerational equity.[98] We shall say more about this issue in the next chapter.

Despite all these provisions in international and current U.S. law designed to protect future generations, assessors freely admit that the risks to our descendants caused by repositories such as Yucca Mountain will be greater than those imposed on present persons. This is because following U.S. Nuclear Regulatory Commission standards, scientists expect the waste containment in the canisters to be "substantially complete" for at least three hundred years and no radionuclide to migrate to the accessible environment for at least one thousand years.[99] Hence, assessors already admit that the Yucca Mountain facility will impose risks on the future that are both higher than those actually imposed on present persons and higher than those acceptable to present persons. Both the state of Nevada and 80 percent of Nevadans oppose the repository, as we have already mentioned,[100] just as residents of New Mexico have opposed the WIPP repository for defense waste contaminated by plutonium and other radioactive nuclides.[101] Such opposition indicates that even current repository risks are not acceptable to many persons in this generation. Therefore, it is arguable that even larger risks, by virtue of the legal and regulatory constraints of NEPA and the EPA, ought not be said to be acceptable to members of future generations.

Indeed, because of the obvious commitment of NEPA and the EPA to future generations, several scholars have argued that the Nuclear Waste Policy Act (NWPA) of 1982 and the Nuclear Waste Policy Amendments Act (NWPAA) of 1987 are inconsistent with the goals of NEPA. At least part of the argument is that because the two waste acts commit the nation to permanent geological high-level radwaste disposal, they take inadequate account of our responsibilities as trustees for future generations.[102] Therefore, according to this reasoning, there are strong grounds, especially in the United States, for arguing that any permanent geological disposal of radwaste contradicts some provisions of existing U.S. laws and regulatory policy.

Permanent geological disposal of high-level radwaste may also be questionable on practical grounds. Because the disposal is permanent, there are no plans to monitor the waste. Not monitoring the waste is highly impractical, however, if one wishes to protect oneself from its contamination. Given the leaks (see chapters 4 through 6) already documented at other radwaste facilities, building a repository, presuming it can be permanent, and then losing the ability to monitor its contents appear to be highly impractical. It may be cheaper to avoid monitoring a facility, but it is not safer, especially not safer over the long term. What we don't see could hurt us.

Conclusion

If the arguments in this chapter are correct, then permanent geological disposal of radwaste is highly questionable on ethical grounds. These ethical grounds include the inequities of risks and benefits, across generations; the inability to obtain free, informed consent—even second-party consent—from members of future generations or their representatives; and failure to guarantee that the due process rights of future persons will be recognized.

In response to these ethical obstacles to permanent disposal, the main objections are that permanent disposal is safer than other options, or that it is more resistant to terrorist attack, or that it is cheaper than other options. Many of these objections will be discussed in more detail in the next chapter. We have argued in this chapter that all of them fail in general because they presuppose that some utilitarian goal (safety, avoiding terrorism, economic efficiency) justifies extreme distributive inequities, placing severe burdens on innocent persons in the future. This presupposition errs because the end does not justify the means. It also errs because we do not now allow ourselves to place severe burdens on innocent persons and thus ought not allow such burdens in the future. Hence, in response to arguments that permanent disposal is cheaper or safer, the appropriate response is: "Cheaper for whom?" "Safer for whom?" Certainly not for members of future generations.

Obviously, permanent disposal is cheaper and safer for this generation, the beneficiaries of commercial nuclear fission. As we argued, permanent disposal is not cheaper or safer for future generations. The radwaste is certain to leak some day, and it is certain to cause some fatalities.[103] Hence, even on classical utilitarian grounds—the greatest good for the greatest number—it is difficult to justify permanent radioactive waste disposal. Geological repositories represent, perhaps, the greatest good for the *present* number of persons, but not the greatest good for the *greatest* number of all persons, present and future. Hence, building permanent repositories is justified, if at all, primarily on the grounds of the narrow self-interest of us in the twentieth and twenty-first centuries. Analogous to racism and sexism, the narrow self-interest of this generation might be called "generationism." Though whites, in general, have more political and economic power than blacks, this does not give them the right to do to blacks whatever they wish. Though men, in general, have more political and economic power than women, this does not give them the right to do to women whatever they wish. Likewise, our power over future persons does not give us the right to do to them whatever we wish. Might does not make right.

9

An Alternative to Permanent Geological Disposal

In 1952, four years before the United States began commercial generation of electricity by nuclear fission, James Conant—Roosevelt's wartime advisor on atomic energy and later president of Harvard University—predicted that the world would turn away from nuclear power because the problem of waste disposal would prove to be intractable. In 1957, a U.S. National Academy of Sciences (NAS) panel issued a similar warning: "Unlike the disposal of any other type of waste, the hazard related to radioactive wastes is so great that no element of doubt should be allowed to exist regarding safety."[1] Another NAS panel expressed reservations about solving the radwaste problem in 1960. Again in 1983, NAS scientists continued to express doubts about nuclear waste disposal when they warned that flooding a permanent radwaste repository, with subsequent "exposures after many thousands of years considerably higher than background . . . could not be absolutely ruled out."[2]

Conant's prediction, that the world would turn away from nuclear power, appears to be coming true—although perhaps not for the reasons he suggested. Indeed, as the first chapters of this volume have argued, the development of nuclear power is slowing down worldwide. Although this slowdown could change, perhaps because of global warming, no new commercial reactors have been ordered in the United States, for example, since 1974. Moreover, as we argued in chapter 2, the commercial nuclear programs in every developed nation, with the exception of France, have been either halted or cut back. Centralized and government owned, the French nuclear program has not proved economical and is billions of dollars in debt. Throughout the world, cost overruns, public opposition, and safety concerns—such as the 475,000 fatal cancers likely caused by the Chernobyl accident—have all caused utilities and citizens to turn away from nuclear-generated electricity.[3] The availability of cleaner, sustainable, alternative energy technologies,[4] such as solar power (which U.S. government studies claim can now supply 40 percent of U.S. energy needs at competitive prices and little risk),[5] and continuing difficulties with radioactive waste have also caused a growing rejection of commercial nuclear power. As Nobel prize-winning physicist Henry Kendall puts it, using atomic energy to generate electricity is "one of the largest-scale technological failures that has ever occurred in a major nation."[6] Despite this failure, however, we still need to deal with the problem of the wastes created by our use of commercial nuclear fission. For more than half a century, nations throughout the world have been generating radioactive waste. Even if all commercial and military nuclear programs came to an immediate halt, there would still be at least 86,000 metric tons of high-level waste (HLW) requiring permanent isolation, in addition to the low- and intermediate-level wastes and transuranics. As one author put it, the nuclear installment plan has already been rung up on the register of time.[7]

Because the catastrophic-radwaste-exposure scenario of the 1983 NAS panel cannot be ruled out, at least under current U.S. plans for permanent waste disposal, Alvin Weinberg recently made a proposal to Congress. He recommended that the Department of Energy (DOE) follow the example of Sweden and exert "more effort than it is now to develop . . . inherently safe waste disposal schemes . . . waste packages, waste forms, canisters, and overpack, that are completely resistant even if the repository is invaded by water, for much longer than . . . 300,000 years."[8] Since the U.S. government requires the HLW package to last for only three hundred years, Weinberg's recommendation calls for 3 orders of magnitude improvement in the longevity of U.S. canisters. To employ Weinberg's scheme, he says we would have to cool the wastes for up to one hundred years above ground, rather than the planned ten years. After one hundred years, Weinberg claims, the heat generated per minute by the waste would be only one-fourth of that produced after ten years; this temporary storage would increase safety and reduce the later probability of leaks from the canisters. Storage for only fifty years would also enable the wastes to be packed

1.5 times more densely; it would simplify repository design and cut facility costs by more than a billion dollars.[9]

Although Weinberg favors permanent HLW storage, he is a proponent of temporary, monitored, retrievable storage for the first one hundred years that the waste exists. Hence, his position is significantly opposed to that of U.S. government officials who are pursuing immediate permanent disposal. Believing that Weinberg's proposal has more merit than that of the DOE and the NRC, we argue in this chapter for above-ground, temporary management of HLW in negotiated, monitored, retrievable storage (NMRS) facilities for approximately one hundred years. At the end of that time, we can reexamine the uncertainty and inequity issues (discussed in earlier chapters of this volume) associated with permanent repositories. We argue, therefore, for using NMRS for a century, then making a decision about geological disposal. This is a wait-and-see position. Wait and see if we can develop more resistant copper canisters. Wait and see if we can prevent water from generating colloids and leaching waste from borosilicate glass.[10] Wait and see if we can devise a way to render radioactive materials less harmful. Wait and see if we can resolve some of the uncertainty and inequity problems treated earlier in this volume. At least part of the rationale for our "wait-and-see" attitude is the belief that science, especially science in the public interest, ought to be conservative. Conservative science, as I. S. Roxburgh put it, makes it prudent to assume that if high-level radwastes are buried, then groundwater will eventually come into contact with them.[11] And if groundwater will come into contact with them, then it makes sense to use the long-term copper canisters, as the Swedes do, and to defer permanent disposal until we are certain that we can deal with the problem of groundwater intrusion.

Knowing the uncertainties and inequities involved in our imposing nuclear wastes on future generations (see the previous chapters), the most rational and ethical course of action is to strive to limit both the uncertainty and the damage resulting from our actions. As A. Bates puts it: "Having recognized the fundamental unfairness of inflicting injury upon the innocent and unrepresented people of the future, we can only, in fairness, strive to limit the damage to the full extent of our natural abilities."[12] This chapter presents one option for limiting the uncertainty and damage from high-level radioactive waste: NMRS.[13] Our discussion of NMRS is not comprehensive, because the focus of this volume is to evaluate the current policy of geological disposal. Nevertheless, our argument is developed enough to show that there are probable alternatives to permanent disposal. After presenting a summary of one important alternative means of high-level waste management, negotiated monitored retrievable storage facilities (NMRS), the chapter outlines the basic arguments in favor of NMRS. The third and final section of the chapter evaluates some of the main objections that can be raised against NMRS.

Basic Principles

If our criticisms of the methodological and ethical flaws in current programs to develop permanent geological repositories are relevant to contemporary decisionmaking, then these criticisms ought to provide some suggestions for improving our public policy regarding nuclear waste. On the basis of the analyses in the eight preceding chapters, we have seven basic suggestions for alternative policies regarding high-level radioactive waste (HLW).[14] Following our conclusions (in chapters 3 through 6) regarding uncertainty, human error, value judgments, social amplification of risk, and questionable inferences, we have three proposals for reforming these aspects of current policy regarding HLW:

1. Minimize scientific uncertainty by delaying the decision about permanent disposal and by creating technically qualified, multiple NMRS facilities. Each of these will begin accepting spent fuel, for temporary storage, with storage periods and amounts set by legal limit.
2. Maximize methodological soundness in NMRS site studies and maximize disclosure, understanding, and consent by funding and creating independent technical and financial capabilities, as well as independent review committees in host communities. All these independent groups should be funded by the beneficiaries of nuclear power and be able to help the host community negotiate with government officials regarding HLW site selection, operation, monitoring, and maintenance.
3. Minimize human and institutional errors in site selection by using a lottery to eliminate qualified NMRS sites.

Following the discussion of risk distribution in chapters 5 and 8, we have two suggestions for alleviating inequity.

4. Spread the geographical risk and maximize regional equity by developing a number of regional NMRS facilities.

5. Spread the temporal risk and maximize intergenerational equity by funding a "public defender for the future," equipped with an independent technical staff and capable of challenging laws, policies, and regulations regarding HLW.

Following the discussion of liability limits, compensation, and consent in chapters 5 and 8, we have two proposals for beginning to address these problems:

6. Guarantee full liability, now and in the future, for all nuclear and waste-related accidents, deaths, and injuries.

7. Maximize voluntariness and consent by compensating proposed host communities for the NMRS, even before the communities begin negotiating regarding the terms under which they might accept the NMRS facilities.

The NMRS Option

The first proposal, developed in response to the criticisms of existing plans for permanent HLW repositories, is to plan and build NMRS facilities. We could minimize scientific uncertainty by delaying the decision about permanent disposal for one hundred years and by creating technically qualified, multiple NMRS facilities, each of which will begin accepting spent fuel, for temporary storage, with storage periods and amounts set by legal limit.[15] The main rationale for NMRS is scientific. As Alvin Weinberg says, U.S. waste management has been like a football game. We were trying for a touchdown pass (permanent disposal), and we fumbled. Now, says Weinberg, we must try for a first down. The first down is successfully handling waste through a monitored retrievable storage facility.[16]

In proposing facilities that are negotiated, monitored, retrievable forms of temporary storage, it is important to examine and defend each of the four components of the NMRS. Because the siting, operation, and management of the NMRS will be *negotiated*, the host communities will be better able to exercise free, informed consent over the siting process. Indeed, as we shall discuss later, a number of communities have already offered to be sites for NMRS facilities. In addition to being negotiated, another reason why NMRS installations are likely to be easier to site (than permanent repositories) is that they will be continually *monitored* and hence as secure as possible. They will be designed so as not to contaminate either the present or future environment. Conceivably the canisters at an NMRS site could leak, just as they might at a permanent repository. Monitoring should enable us not merely to detect and correct such leaks as rapidly as possible. Better still, monitoring should enable us to detect weak or corroding containers and replace or repair them even before they begin to leak. It is also important for HLW policy to keep open options for the future, to preserve flexibility, and to enable us to respond to mistakes. Hence, to correct gaps in our knowledge, it is important for the NMRS sites to be *retrievable* facilities. Later, in perhaps one hundred years, society may be better able to deal with HLW in a way that ensures long-term predictability and containment; the waste will be cooler then, and there will be safer, easier methods of permanent disposal, if that is the option we choose.[17] Retrievability simply "buys time" until our science and ethics develop to the degree that we can decide whether to continue to use the NMRS facilities or move to permanent disposal. Because there will be several NMRS installations serving as temporary *storage* sites for HLW, they will avoid the geographic and temporal inequities of having only one or two permanent facilities. A key component of the regional inequities associated with permanent disposal are those caused by transportation routes from reactors to the geological repositories. By having a number of NMRS facilities operating at a time, the transportation risks to states not benefiting from nuclear power would be decreased, both because the routes would be shorter and because the reactor-NMRS route would be more direct. The multiple-site argument could also be used for permanent repositories, but it is likely to be unsuccessful, both because of the greater cost of permanent sites and because of extreme public opposition to them.

Historical Context

The concept of a federal monitored retrievable storage facility for HLW is not new. It first was proposed in 1972 by Floyd Cullers after the U.S. Atomic Energy Commission abandoned the plan to build a permanent repository near Lyons, Kansas. To provide for the waste needing to be stored when this proposal was rejected,

Cullers suggested above-ground radwaste structures, called "Retrievable Surface Storage Facilities" (RSSFs) for interim storage until a permanent repository became available. After U.S. Environmental Protection Agency scientists criticized the RSSF concept, saying it was dangerous because it could become a cheap permanent repository, the AEC withdrew the proposal in 1975.[18] (In subsequent pages, we shall explain proposals for avoiding this EPA objection to NMRS.)

Because of President Carter's decision not to reprocess spent fuel, the need for interim storage became greater. In his 1980 waste-policy announcement, Carter proposed a method for interim storage called the "away-from-reactor" (AFR) facility. In 1981, the Reagan administration lifted the reprocessing deferral and withdrew the AFR proposal. In the Nuclear Waste Policy Act of 1982, the U.S. Congress gave the highest priority to permanent geological radwaste disposal but also called for the Department of Energy to study the need for one or more monitored retrievable storage (MRS) facilities. In 1985, DOE officials proposed that the MRS be used for consolidating, repackaging, and storing the radwaste until the permanent repository was ready. The DOE officials suggested three MRS sites, all in Tennessee. Tennessee authorities tried to block these selections in court, but they were unsuccessful, and the DOE gave its proposals to the U.S. Congress. Congress responded by passing the Nuclear Waste Policy Amendments Act of 1987. The Act revoked DOE's proposal to site the three Tennessee facilities, and it directed the DOE to study only the Yucca Mountain site for a permanent repository.[19] Nevertheless, the Act authorized the MRS concept, but only after the MRS Review Commission had presented its report to Congress and only with the provision that MRS planning could be linked to the permanent repository completion schedule. Hence, under current U.S. law, the MRS is tied to the permanent repository so that the former cannot become an unintended, inexpensive (therefore unsafe) permanent repository.[20]

Independent Technical and Review Committees

The second proposal, developed in response to the criticisms of existing plans for permanent HLW repositories, is to tax the beneficiaries of nuclear power so as to fund independent technical and review committees (committees whose members are not employed by the DOE or nuclear-related industries) in the proposed host communities for the NMRS facilities. The purpose of such funding is to maximize the methodological soundness and objectivity of site studies, to counteract some of the negative effects of possible DOE bias and utility advertisement campaigns, and to provide persons in host communities with material that enables them to negotiate with the government regarding site selection. Meeting all three of these goals should increase both the technical quality of site studies and the disclosure, understanding, voluntariness, and competence that are essential to the free informed consent of the host NMRS communities. Moreover, by funding alternative studies and committees, we would explicitly recognize that the process of science, as exemplified in chapters 3 through 6, is unavoidably bound up with methodological value judgments. Alternative studies and committees could be expected to present opposing sides of an issue and to espouse different methodological value judgments and inferences regarding whether, how, and where to build NMRS facilities.

Calling for the beneficiaries of nuclear power to pay for actions related to waste storage is already a part of the national consensus regarding radwaste equity. Current national policy, in fact, requires that all costs of waste management be recovered through fees paid by utilities and the users of the services, those who benefit from the activities generating the wastes.[21] Some persons, however, claim that taxpayers still currently cover too great a portion of the waste-management bill. Nobel prize-winning physicist Henry Kendall of MIT claims, for example, that taxpayer subsidies of the nuclear industry are $20 billion per year and that the cost of nuclear-generated electricity would double if these subsidies were removed.[22] In the area of waste management, government officials have collected a total of $3 billion from U.S. ratepayers for radwaste management/disposal,[23] although they have spent many times that figure on activities related to caring for the nuclear wastes. Hence, requiring the beneficiaries of commercial fission (investors, industrialists, utility employees, and ratepayers) to pay for alternative studies regarding NMRS sites is justifiable by virtue of current radwaste policy. It is also justifiable in terms of the principle that all persons in this society have a right to legal representation when their interests are at stake, as they are in a siting decision.

Perhaps the core value underlying the call for alternative review committees and negotiation regarding the siting and management of NMRS facilities is democracy. In the context of high-level radioactive waste, democracy means, in part, that the people must come to understand and to have a say in accepting the risks and uncertainties associated with various radwaste management or disposal policies.[24] If democratic principles become a part of policymaking regarding high-level nuclear waste management, then government officials, scientists, engineers, and industrialists alone will not be able to exercise all of the decisionmaking prerogatives. Instead, all the people will have a role in determining how we manage societal risks.

There are a number of models of negotiated, adversarial, and mediated decisionmaking regarding hazardous technologies. Because such models of community negotiation have been explained and evaluated elsewhere,[25] we shall not repeat here the relevant proposals and arguments. The basic idea behind having members of communities negotiate with government and industry regarding siting facilities (like those for NMRS) is that such decisions should be made in a context of participatory government, constitutional choice, and social equity. As the U.S. National Academy of Sciences put it: "Technical analysis alone cannot substitute for decisions about the degree of risk that is acceptable."[26] Because existing federal and legal frameworks for decisionmaking risks have not kept pace with the constraints of equity and citizen consent, we need to develop new concepts involving cooperative or voluntary approaches to developing risk policies. For example, H. Inhaber proposed a "reverse Dutch auction" concept that replaces technical coercion with an offer of benefits and rewards for the community where a potentially hazardous facility is sited.[27] Obviously, however, regardless of the benefits and rewards, some sorts of facilities ought never exist. Likewise, there need to be restrictions—independent of financial rewards—that enable the poor of the world to retain their rights to self-determination and to avoid their being bribed by those who would provide great incentives for acceptance of hazardous waste. There are a number of legal and regulatory vehicles for protecting the poor in such a situation.[28] Nevertheless, a necessary condition for acceptable construction and siting of repository projects should probably be that benefits and rewards be used to provide incentives for the voluntary participation of the host community. Such participation would enhance flexibility, attention to public concerns, compensation for community sacrifices, and acceptability to the persons who are impacted. In other words, by negotiating regarding NMRS sites, we would move from a context of confrontation and coercion to one of cooperation in siting controversial facilities.[29]

In order for the negotiation regarding NMRS site selection and management to avoid some of the problems (mentioned in the previous chapter) with consent, compensation, and equity of risk distribution, residents of the proposed host community need to negotiate with government and industry officials to be certain that both their technical worries and their ethical, social, and political concerns are addressed. Part of the negotiating process will need to be designed to minimize the possibility of violations of equity, due process, and the free informed consent that are owed all citizens. This minimization is probably best achieved by giving persons in the host communities control of funding for siting studies, monitoring, and adversary assessment, as well as for whatever compensatory schemes can be worked out through the negotiation. A quasi-judicial process designed to call forth the best arguments and objections associated with alternative points of view on a particular position, adversary assessment is one important way to provide the information that is essential to informed consent.[30] The point of negotiation among different groups, by means of adversary assessment, is in part to weigh the merits of alternative site studies, each with different methodological value judgments and points of view. Negotiation should help insure that decisionmaking about radwaste policy does not allow politicians and industrialists to use that policy to coopt individuals who have rights to equal protection, due process, and self-determination. Negotiation should help insure that DOE officials alone do not define the constraints of justice. In a democracy, only the people themselves can determine the fairness of the burdens imposed on them.

Although U.S. National Academy of Sciences researchers did not go so far as to suggest adversary assessment in their recent report, they did recommend that the DOE include "publicly negotiated relicensing agreements" on how to deal with uncertainties, improved performance assessment, and the precise goals of programs of the EPA and the NRC.[31] Hence, although the Academy stopped short of recommending a precise form of negotiation, it is clear, from its report, that members of the NAS recognize that democracy must ultimately determine our radwaste policy. As they put it themselves: "These decisions belong to the citizenry of a democratic society."[32]

A Lottery to Determine NMRS Rotations

The third principle, developed in response to our earlier criticisms of existing plans for permanent HLW repositories, is to minimize human and institutional errors in site selection by using a lottery to eliminate qualified NMRS locations. Because geology is not the main consideration in siting NMRS facilities, and because the waste would be monitored and retrievable, virtually every area that uses nuclear-generated electricity could have a potential repository for NMRS. A lottery to determine which proposed NMRS facilities ought to be developed would be desirable, in part because it would help avoid placing the entire NMRS burden on the dry, less populous, western states, instead of using the northeastern states, for exámple, where many of the producers and users of HLW are located. With a greater number of possible NMRS sites, there also would be a greater opportunity for the nuclear beneficiaries to share the costs and risks of radwaste storage rather than to impose them on people in areas not benefiting from nuclear power. Regional NMRS facilities likewise would provide for greater geographical and temporal equity. Geographically, the radwaste risk would be spread among the beneficiaries of nuclear energy. Because the facilities would be temporary, monitored, and compensated in full, they also would present less risk to members of future generations. An additional benefit of the lottery proposal would be to reduce unnecessary tensions over siting. It would guarantee persons in a host state that the HLW risk would actually be shared, and that they would not be alone in a dangerous situation. By providing a lottery to determine actual NMRS sites among those already judged suitable in various states, it would also be possible to reduce the fear of persons in host communities who want to avoid becoming the site for a permanent repository. In the absence of other approved facilities, for example, New Mexico residents fear the consequences of their hosting the WIPP repository for defense transuranic waste. Their worry is that persons in other states will refuse the wastes and that more radioactive materials will be stored there than have been agreed.[33] Multiple NMRS sites, determined in part by a lottery and by negotiation, would help to alleviate such fears.

Regional and Temporary NMRS

The fourth proposal, developed in response to our earlier criticisms of existing plans for permanent HLW repositories, is to spread the geographical risk of radwaste management and to maximize regional equity by developing a number of NMRS facilities. The main rationale for the multiple sites would be to achieve more equity through risk sharing and to simplify the transport system, making it more efficient. With regional NMRS facilities, fewer states and communities would be involved in waste transport, although more of them would host the facilities. Of course, as Kasperson, Derr, and Kates point out,[34] a HLW system that is too highly decentralized could enlarge the aggregate risks of spent-fuel storage and increase social conflicts and costs. Nevertheless, a recent National Academy of Sciences panel found that achieving regional equity in radwaste management may be essential to a social consensus on nuclear policy. Moreover, the panel members wrote, by moving from a single federal repository in the United States to two or three regional repositories, the annual transportation costs would decrease from about $171 million to about $71 million. The panel also concluded that having two or three regional facilities would decrease not only transportation costs but also accidents by at least a factor of 2 below those associated with a single repository.[35]

Currently, there are about 20,000 MTU (equivalent to metric tons of uranium) of spent fuel needing storage and 87,000 MTU total of spent fuel likely needing to be stored for all U.S. nuclear reactors in the future. As the earlier sections of this chapter revealed, military and commercial HLW, taken together, are now about 100,000 MTU. The MRS Review Commission in 1989 recommended 5,000 MTU-capacity facilities for interim storage of high-level radwaste and spent fuel, and 2,000 MTU-capacity facilities for emergency storage facilities. The commission's rationale for these two MRS sizes is that 1,000 MTU of capacity is needed to empty a large, full, storage pool at a reactor; that dry, spent-fuel storage technology, by its nature, is modular; that significant economies of scale do not appear beyond about 2,000 MTU; and that smaller facilities are easier to site because there is less probability that they would turn into de facto permanent repositories.[36] On this basis, if each regional NMRS facility were built for a capacity of 5,000 MTU, it would take approximately four MRS facilities to store existing spent fuel now onsite at seventy reactors, and a total of approximately eighteen MRS facilities to store all present and future spent fuel from U.S. reactors. Presumably, Congress and the DOE, through the democratic process, could help determine what number and size of facilities—between four and eighteen sites—would maximize MRS safety, regional equity, economies of scale, and ease of siting and yet would minimize transportation and facility accidents.

One advantage of the regional NMRS installations is that they would probably be easier to site than permanent repositories. This is because the facilities would operate—by law—only for a specified number of years, perhaps several decades, only according to a prescribed schedule, and only for a predetermined amount of waste. Because the NMRS facilities would not be permanent, persons in the host communities would not have to make as great a commitment to waste management as they would if the waste were to be permanently stored within their jurisdictions. Also, because the waste would be monitored and would remain stored in casks that prevented pollution, there would conceivably be no onsite permanent contamination. The casks could be reinforced or replaced, on a regular schedule, that could prevent leakage. Hence, community concerns about safety would probably be less for a temporary, monitored facility than for a permanent one. Also, since a specific, limited amount of waste would be stored in an engineered, monitored vault for only a given number of years, one would not have to worry as much about the geological environment of the host community. One would need to consider only factors such as earthquakes and erosion, for example.[37] Leakage could be more easily detected than in a permanent facility, and any accidents would not be likely to affect a whole region, as they might in the case of a permanent geological facility. If it were unlikely that an entire region would be permanently affected by leakage from a monitored facility, then presumably it would be easier to find host communities such as Nye County, Nevada. Persons in this county support the location of a nuclear waste site in their backyard,[38] but because of the regional effects of a permanent repository, the opposition of the rest of Nevada will likely keep Nye County from having its way. This county might be a good candidate for an NMRS site, however, if it could be shown that the effects of such a facility would likely be localized and relatively short term. Also, state of Nevada officials have argued for using several NMRS facilities, rather than a permanent repository, for high-level waste.[39]

Morgan County, Tennessee, and Yakima Indian Nation (in Washington state) also have both expressed an explicit interest in being a site for NMRS.[40] Their willingness to host such installations suggests that public opposition to temporary storage might be significantly less than opposition to a permanent facility, perhaps in part because the sites would be temporary, monitored, and negotiated with the host communities. Because some communities have offered to be NMRS sites, it appears that the policy of temporary storage of radwaste may be easier to implement—avoiding the NIMBY (Not in My Backyard) syndrome—than the policy of permanent geological disposal. Admittedly, however, in the case of one "volunteer NMRS site," state of Tennessee officials do not appear to agree with officials in Morgan County. And, admittedly, both a permanent repository and a NMRS facility face the same difficulty: the persons most likely to accept either of them would proba-bly live in communities that face great poverty and unemployment. Residents of such towns would likely see the facility as an economic boon for them. In Morgan County, Tennessee, for example, unemployment is about 14 percent, and income is small. About half of the tax rate is needed merely to service the bonded indebtedness of the county. Schools and other services are poor. In offering to be a host community for a radwaste facility, the representatives of the county made it clear that they wanted annual incentive payments from the repository to equal the total of all state and local taxes and that the facility owners should take over its obligations of bonded indebtedness.[41] Hence, it appears that the residents of Morgan County welcome a radwaste facility largely because they seek a way out of poverty. In such a situation, however, serious questions about the free informed consent of the citizens are appropriate (see chapter 8), and the negotiation process would need to be designed so as to maximize free informed consent, equity, and due process.[42]

One step toward maximizing values such as equity and due process would be to guarantee the temporary nature of the NMRS facility. With only temporary NMRS sites, no community could be forced to bear permanently the HLW burden for the rest of the nation. Moreover, guaranteeing short-term NMRS facilities would also likely encourage greater safety and accountability, since few communities in the future would be willing to accept NMRS installations that had already proved unsafe. Having NMRS for only a century also would enable us to delay the decision about permanent radwaste disposal. It would provide more time for laboratory and field experiments in order to determine the reliability of permanent storage, and it would give us a firmer basis for long-term predictions. It could also happen that progress in medicine might make it possible to counteract the more damaging effects of radiation on the human body, so that some of our fears about release of radionuclides from repositories would be lessened. After all, this is the sort of reasoning that underlies Sweden's intention to keep the waste in surface storage for forty years and England's and France's goal of storing it for fifty years before attempting underground disposal.[43]

Public Defender for the Future

The fifth proposal, developed in response to the criticisms of existing plans for permanent HLW repositories, is to avoid all unmonitored permanent geological disposal for the time being and to spread both the spatial and temporal risk of radwaste management. One way to help spread, and therefore equalize, the temporal risk is to maximize intergenerational equity by funding a "public defender for the future."[44] Such a person would be equipped with an independent technical staff and capable of challenging laws, policies, and regulations regarding the selection, operation, and management of NMRS facilities. The rationale for the public defender, a concept developed by Kasperson, Derr, and Kates,[45] is that most of those who will bear the risk of spent fuel cannot participate in the decision-making process regarding it. Hence, maximizing the free informed consent of future persons, via a second-party public defender, is essential to mitigating some of the ethical problems associated with equity, consent, and due process that we discussed earlier in the volume.

Full Liability

The sixth proposal, developed in response to our criticisms of existing plans for permanent HLW repositories, is to guarantee full liability for all nuclear- and waste-related accidents, deaths, and injuries. Full liability is ethically required for all the reasons already noted earlier in chapter 5. In fact, citizens living in areas where there are existing or proposed radwaste repositories have repeatedly requested full indemnification against the nuclear risk. In every case, DOE officials have denied these requests.[46] The main rationale for our demanding full liability for potential victims of any waste facility is that, consistent with the earlier discussion of types I and II risk in chapter 7, we need to place the burden of proof, in cases of technological uncertainty, on those who benefit from a technology, rather than on those who are its potential victims. For NMRS repositories and for nuclear power, the beneficiaries are largely in this, the preceding, and the next, generation, whereas the potential victims are mainly members of distant generations. In order to equalize the burden of radioactive wastes and other environmental hazards, we need to reform our procedures for siting dangerous facilities. We also need to change our manner of dealing with legal actions like "toxic torts," so that the burden of proof and liability is not placed so heavily on environmental victims.[47]

Currently, even for a minor radiation-related accident involving no medical or personal injury expenses, the greatest part of the cost is borne by persons in the general public, not those individuals responsible for the injuries and damages. In such cases, accident costs are typically displaced. A recent sensitivity analysis of the Three Mile Island nuclear accident, done by the U.S. Federal Insurance Administration (FIA), for example, revealed that innocent members of the public bore substantial, uncompensated costs because of the accident. The FIA showed that even with no medical or personal injury expenses, a more severe accident involving evacuation would have caused an average Harrisburg family to lose $67,000—with only $2,247 recoverable from the millions of dollars in the Price-Anderson pool of benefits.[48]

Moreover, the 1983 U.S. Supreme Court decision on Three Mile Island (*Metropolitan Edison Co.* v. *People Against Nuclear Power*) held that it would be almost impossible to distinguish between persons suffering genuine psychological stress, as a result of the accident, and those who merely opposed the facility. Hence, even if there were psychological (medical) costs as a result of a nuclear or radwaste accident, it would be difficult for victims to recover these damages. The problem with such a situation is not only that potential victims are likely to go uncompensated, but also that, as a factual claim, the Supreme Court decision was probably wrong. As William Freudenburg and T. Jones have demonstrated,[49] if the Supreme Court hypothesis were correct, then attitudes toward dangerous facilities would be almost perfectly correlated with stress symptomatology. They tested this correlation, using the only other nuclear host community known to have experienced as much opposition as Three Mile Island, and found it was false. In fact, the strongest attitude-stress correlation in this community was −.096, even though simple, sociodemographic variables showed far stronger correlations with the stress measures. Freudenburg and Jones have argued that there is support for an alternative hypothesis: that the risk of technological accidents is a significant predictor of psychological stress. If this hypothesis is true, then it provides additional grounds for arguing that the burden of proof and liability, in all technological situations, including NMRS and HLW facilities, ought not be on the potential victims. And if not, then there ought to be full liability for all those harmed by hazards related to such facilities. Full liability would also provide an incentive for siting the regional facilities.

Compensation from the Beginning

The seventh proposal, developed in response to our earlier criticisms of existing plans for permanent HLW repositories, is to maximize voluntariness and consent by compensating members of proposed host communities for NMRS site studies, feasibility plans, and so on, even before the citizens make a final decision as to whether they will accept the facilities. Currently under the 1987 Nuclear Waste Policy Amendments Act, as already mentioned earlier in the volume, members of communities hosting either a permanent repository or an NMRS site would receive $5 million per year until the facility began operating, and $10 million for every year thereafter. Since Congress could approve a larger amount of compensation for the host community,[50] the level of compensation ought to be raised, if necessary, in order to meet the needs of persons in the host community as expressed in negotiation about the NMRS. These needs can best be determined by means of ethical, political, and legal analysis designed to maximize consent, equity, and due process. A number of legal and ethical scholars have analyzed some of the considerations that ought to be brought to bear in determining whether, how much, and when to compensate communities for the technological risks that they bear.[51] Some members of Congress have proposed that $50 million, for example, is an appropriate level of annual compensation.[52] Under current law, the NMRS facility and the increased compensation for it could be financed by the Nuclear Waste Fund, to which utilities pay on the basis of the amount of nuclear electricity they generate. Ultimately, however, persons in the host communities themselves ought to have the right to negotiate appropriate levels of compensation for being an NMRS site.

Negotiated Compensation

The eighth proposal, developed in response to our earlier criticisms of existing plans for permanent HLW repositories, is to maximize citizens' understanding of, and consent to, NMRS by negotiating with persons in proposed host communities. A major part of the negotiation would be the degree of citizen control over safety at the site and the level of compensation appropriate for persons in the community to receive in exchange for hosting the NMRS facility. Negotiation is important to the NMRS concept because there is neither zero risk nor perfect, free informed consent. Hence, the way to reduce risk and to heighten consent is to negotiate with persons regarding actual and potential hazards they face and to compensate them for the risks they bear. As we mentioned earlier, we shall not review here the framework for achieving negotiation and compensation, because that has been accomplished elsewhere.[53]

Negotiation is necessary to the success of NMRS because a purely voluntary system, complete with state or regional veto power, would not work. Despite the fact that there are NMRS "voluteer sites," already mentioned, persons in some potential host communities might not voluntarily accept the burden of temporary storage of radioactive waste, even with great incentives and compensation.[54] Moreover, there are a number of communities that have benefited from commercial nuclear fission, and it is arguable that they ought to bear some of the costs of using this technology by hosting an NMRS site. Regardless of whether we ought to have generated the waste, we now must devise a safe and equitable means of dealing with it. Giving members of a proposed NMRS host community veto power over the facility might seem reasonable from the point of view of equity and consent— if the community were not a nuclear beneficiary. However, a veto would not be feasible. One plausible alternative to such a veto might be to maximize consent and equity by placing the burden of gaining community acceptance on the government or scientific group siting the proposed NMRS facility. This burden would mean that persons other than the builder/developer of the site would have the duty to inform the community and to achieve consent through negotiation. Both goals could be accomplished by meeting the objections and concerns of the potential victims of the NMRS. Meeting these objections and concerns, in turn, could be facilitated by improving public participation in siting decisions and by committing resources to develop alternative technical and review committees in the host communities, as was already suggested in connection with the second proposal.

As with full liability (already discussed), full compensation is especially important for members of the host community, as Kasperson, Derr, and Kates point out,[55] because of the difficulties associated with defining the pool of compensation according to a burden of uncertain risks. To accomplish full compensation, government officials could offer host NMRS communities a "rental fee" for the period during which they served as one of the sites for the HLW. This rental fee would provide an additional incentive for members of the community to accept the waste, and it would take account of the fact that many damages are unanticipated, incalculable, and often underestimated. The rental fund also could serve, in part, as an escrow fund to ameliorate the consequences of future accidents.[56]

A Public-legacy Trust

The ninth proposal, developed in response to the criticisms of existing plans for permanent HLW repositories, is to maximize intergenerational equity by a public-legacy trust that is fully funded by the beneficiaries (utilities, industrialists, investors, and ratepayers) of nuclear electricity. The fund could be used for site mitigation and for compensation of future NMRS impacts. The trust could be funded by a mill rate on nuclear electricity use and by general taxes. A trust for the future is especially needed because of the likelihood of potentially poorer or delayed site management in the later years of operation of the NMRS facilities. We need an institutional mechanism, such as a public-legacy trust, both to compensate future persons and to serve the ethical principles of distributive equity, consent, and compensation.[57] Moreover, however successful we are in the future in reducing radwaste risks, we shall nevertheless have accidents, make questionable siting decisions, fall into management mistakes and human errors, and impose inequitable risk burdens. To alleviate all of these problems that we have discussed earlier in the volume, we must provide now for full compensation for those risks that cannot be mitigated. The trust might be likened to a perpetual Superfund pool, except that the main beneficiaries of nuclear power will be responsible for contributing to the fund, so that they can compensate for nuclear-waste-related harms far into the future.[58]

Benefits of NMRS Facilities

Even though the outline of several proposals essential to our NMRS plan is quite brief, it is clear that the plan provides for a reallocation of a number of radwaste-related benefits and costs. This reallocation is directed both at reducing the uncertainties and inequities that might victimize members of future generations and at minimizing the effects of scientific and ethical problems associated with current plans for perpetual geological disposal of radwaste. In general, our re-allocation of waste-related costs and benefits is aimed at increasing the degree to which beneficiaries of nuclear waste also bear its risks and costs. As such, our NMRS plan has a number of distinct advantages, each of which we shall discuss in subsequent paragraphs.

Because our plan calls for several NMRS facilities to operate at one time during the next one hundred years rather than for one permanent repository, such as Yucca Mountain, the radwaste risk would be spread more equitably among different states and regions. Also, by delaying the decision on a permanent repository and building several NMRS facilities, each lasting one hundred years or less, the radwaste burden would be spread more equitably across those generations benefiting from the waste, rather than imposed largely on future persons. Indeed, by waiting for one hundred years, the heat of the wastes will be reduced, making either continued NMRS or permanent repositories safer for future generations.[59] Likewise, by having the beneficiaries of nuclear power (e.g., the recipients of nuclear-generated electricity) pay for NMRS, this proposal would also have the benefit of achieving greater ratepayer equity, as well as more regional and intergenerational equity.[60]

Another important benefit of having NMRS facilities is that they would provide storage for emergency purposes, in case of difficulties at a reactor or at other waste sites. Because there would be a number of NMRS installations, there would be considerable redundancy in the NMRS system, which is good in the event of unforeseen circumstances. Indeed, the U.S. Monitored Retrievable Storage Review Commission concluded that "some interim storage facilities . . . are in the national interest to provide for emergencies and other contingencies."[61] One such contingency could be a reactor core melt that would require us to remove the fuel and store it elsewhere, perhaps in a NMRS facility. Indeed, even the U.S. government admits that for one hundred reactors over a twenty-year period, there would be a 10 percent chance of a core melt. If the Lewis Report of the American Physical Society is correct, then the core-melt probability for this same period could be as high as 100 percent or as low as 1 percent.[62] Another contingency conceivably could be a permanent repository's being delayed or scrapped. Also, if there is no facility ready to accept spent reactor fuel, substantial amounts of it will begin to accumulate at shutdown U.S. reactors after 2015. Since fuel stored at shutdown reactors could pose a safety problem, it would be preferable to have NMRS facilities.[63]

Because NMRS sites would replace planned permanent repositories, at least for the next one hundred years, using a system of regional storage facilities also would give decisionmakers more flexibility in deciding how best to manage/dispose of high-level nuclear waste.[64] Such flexibility is in short supply in the existing U.S. nuclear waste program. As the National Academy of Sciences put it:

> This approach [of the US toward permanent disposal] is poorly matched to the technical task at hand. It assumes that the properties and future behavior of a geological repository can be determined and specified with a very high degree of certainty. In reality, however, the inherent variability of the geological environment will necessitate frequent changes in the specifications, with resultant delays, frustration, and loss of public confidence. The current program is not sufficiently flexible or exploratory to accommodate such changes.[65]

By storing high-level radwaste in NMRS facilities for the next century, we could leave open future options that might include such programs as permanent geological disposal, continued surface storage, or subseabed disposal.[66]

Yet another benefit of regional NMRS sites is that they would avoid delays in handling spent reactor fuel and would enable utilities to keep onsite fuel-storage pools empty, for use in case of emergencies. Many persons associated with the current permanent repository program of the United States have argued that it is at a standstill, largely because of opposition to geological disposal.[67] Even the NAS has argued that "It may be appropriate to delay the licensing application or even the scheduled opening of the [permanent] repository, until more of the uncertainties can be resolved."[68] Such assertions suggest that the opening of the world's first permanent repository may well be delayed beyond the year 2010. Yet it appears that some communities are ready now to accept NMRS facilities, as we have already mentioned. Apart from how the question of geological disposal ultimately is answered, using NMRS would enable dangerous radwastes not to be subject to the vagaries of the "uncertainties regarding the availability of a repository."[69] Most utility officials favor NMRS facilities because they would enable the government to begin accepting the high-level radwaste and spent fuel at the earliest possible time. Moreover, because the owners of utilities have been paying fees into the Nuclear Waste Fund, they argue that the DOE has strong contractual obligations to accept the spent fuel as soon as possible.[70]

By accepting the waste, placing it in NMRS facilities, and delaying (for a century) the decision on whether to use a permanent repository, we might gain another benefit. Scientists in the future would be better able to design a safer repository.[71] They would also be able to take advantage of the waste having cooled, so that it could be stored more easily, efficiently, cheaply, and safely in the future. In other words, part of the rationale for delaying the decision on a permanent repository, so as to allow more time for better waste technology to develop, is that we would avoid the problematic current policy of the DOE, namely, "Get it right the first time." As the National Academy of Sciences put it: "The geological environment will always produce surprises . . . No matter what technical approach is initially adopted, the design can be improved by matching it with specific features of the site." Waste technology needs to be "robust in the face of newly discovered uncertainties in the geology."[72] One way to achieve this robustness is to move step by step, taking advantage of new scientific developments as we move.

One scientific development that might make radioactive waste storage or disposal easier and safer in the future could be transmutation. Transmutation involves showering the waste with neutrons to convert fission products to stable or short-lived radioactive isotopes. Although transmutation would not entirely neutralize the radioactivity, some scientists and engineers claim that it would be possible to store transmuted materials for several centuries in near-surface facilities, rather than having to store the original wastes for tens of thousands of years. If the volume of transmuted wastes were significantly reduced, and if the time required for isolation were cut to hundreds of years, then some scientists at Los Alamos believe that permanent disposal might become politically acceptable. Critics of transmutation, however, claim that the process is "modern alchemy": it creates more wastes than those it neutralizes, it is extraordinarily expensive and dangerous over the short term, especially to workers, and it increases the risk of proliferation.[73] Apart from whether transmutation turns out to be feasible, nonetheless, it provides an illustration of the sort of scientific development that, in the future, might make storing radioactive wastes cheaper, easier, and safer. Another development that could increase the safety and efficiency of permanent storage is improving our techniques of vitrification—storing the wastes in borosilicate glass—so that leaching of dangerous radionuclides does not occur (see note 10 in this chapter). Both transmutation and improved vitrification provide illustrations of possible scientific reasons for deferring the decision about permanent disposal of high-level nuclear wastes.

Using NMRS facilities is also reasonable on grounds of avoiding uncertainty. There are many unknowns associated with geological repositories. Earlier in the volume we outlined, for example, some of the hydrological, geological, and seismic uncertainties associated with the proposed Yucca Mountain facility, and we questioned some of the methodological and ethical value judgments used to deal with these uncertainties. Indeed, even an NAS panel concluded recently that there was "an incomplete and inadequate body of social science knowledge available to guide the formulation and implementation of an effective radioactive waste management system."[74] Because of such inadequacies and uncertainties, an important benefit of NMRS facilities is that one would not need to beg the question about a number of unknowns many years into the future. Instead, one could sidestep these uncertainties by developing NMRS sites and by continuing research into permanent repositories.[75] In fact, a reasonable principle is that HLW should be retrievable for the period of uncertainty about its effects and behavior. Something similar to this principle was articulated recently by the National Academy of Sciences: "It may even turn out to be appropriate to delay permanent closure of a waste repository until adequate assurances concerning its long-term behavior can be obtained through continued on-site geological studies."[76] Such a principle also was extremely influential in Swedish arguments for an NMRS program.[77] Not to accept this principle would be to avoid precautions against harm from what is unknown and uncertain. NMRS facilities are one such precaution.

Another benefit of using NMRS facilities is that we could learn, in stages, how best to store high-level radwaste safely, rather than having to build a permanent repository with which we would be forced to live in perpetuity.[78] If some dangerous technologies—like those for disposal of high-level nuclear waste—are unforgiving, then it makes sense to lengthen our scientific, institutional, and regulatory "learning curves" about them for as long as possible. By lengthening our learning process, we might avoid making uncorrectable mistakes with permanent repositories. Developing NMRS sites thus would provide valuable experience in siting, licensing, and operating a large-scale waste disposal facility. This experience would also enable us to learn more about the technology needed for safe disposal.[79] Indeed, when a recent panel of the NAS criticized the U.S. program of permanent waste disposal, one of its emphases was that we need to learn from experience rather than to rely on "predetermined specifications." Otherwise, we shall not learn to deal appropriately with uncertainty.[80] Although the NAS did not specifically recommend using NMRS facilities instead of permanent repositories, the NAS criticisms of the existing radwaste program—its manner of handling uncertainty and its failure to provide ways to learn from experience—suggest that building NMRS facilities might be an alternative means of achieving one of the ends promoted by the NAS.

Another benefit of using several NMRS facilities is that transportation routes from reactors would be shorter in many cases than would routes from reactors to a single, permanent repository. Also, routes to NMRS sites would more often avoid passing through states without commitments to nuclear power than would routes to a permanent repository.[81] Hence, NMRS facilities would help achieve more geographical and temporal equity than would permanent geological disposal. Obviously, however, U.S. government officials do not seem compelled by the equity argument. The United States is not following the policy of using NMRS for one hundred years. The United States is not deferring the decision on permanent geological disposal of radioactive wastes. Therefore, to understand U.S. policy, we need to understand the arguments against NMRS facilities. What are some of the main objections to use of NMRS for at least a century? And what responses can be made to them?

Objections to NMRS Facilities

Perhaps the most obvious objection to NMRS sites, proposed for at least the next one hundred years, is that the facilities are unsafe, that they are targets for terrorist attacks, and that they contribute to the proliferation problem. They may be especially vulnerable because of their not being permanent and their being retrievable facilities. This is precisely the objection to temporary facilities that has been formulated, for example, by representatives of the Sierra Club.[82] Other persons also argue against NMRS on the grounds that at-reactor storage is acceptable. They claim that NMRS sites would require additional handling of the waste and a subsequent increase in the risk.[83] In response to these safety objections, it is important to point out that, as earlier chapters of this volume have argued, permanent geological disposal is also highly questionable with respect to safety. Indeed, as D. Deere, chair of the NAS Nuclear Waste Technical Review Board, expressed it: "Many in the technical community are currently concerned about our ability to construct and license a repository in accordance with present Federal standards and regulations."[84] It is also important to note that the one-hundred-year NMRS facility locates many of the major risks of radwaste with members of the very groups that have benefited most from it. Hence, NMRS appears to be a more equitable solution to the problem of HLW than is permanent storage. Moreover, current Nuclear Regulatory Commission requirements mandate that the HLW must be retrievable for at least 110 years any-way.[85] Hence, government officials have already implicitly addressed the safety issue and decided that one-hundred-year NMRS facilities are acceptable. The Nuclear Regulatory Commission and the U.S. Monitored Retrievable Storage Review Commission also have affirmed that "spent fuel can be stored safely at reactor sites for as long as 100 years" if an extended period of reactor operations is included, and for at least 30 years onsite, beyond the expiration of a reactor's operat-ing license.[86] The MRS Commission affirmed that "MRS options are safe," and members of Congress specifically found that "long term storage of high-level radioactive waste or spent nuclear fuel in monitored retrievable storage facilities is an option for providing safe and reliable management of such waste or spent fuel."[87] The French have gone so far as to claim that the period of NMRS storage could be extended as long as needed,[88] and U.S. study groups at sites wishing to host NMRS facilities have argued that they are safe.[89]

The MRS Review Commission has supported its arguments for NMRS safety with detailed calculations. The Commission estimated, for example, that the total radiation doses, both to the public and to workers, would be less in the case of an NMRS facility not linked to a repository than for a permanent facility handling the same amount of waste; the group indicated, however, that it did not believe that the safety differences were great between the two options. The Commission likewise emphasized that the MRS option was safer than onsite storage at reactors, in part because the MRS facility would employ experienced fuel handlers and would have a full staff available.[90] Onsite storage is also more expensive ($2 to $3 million per site) than NMRS.[91]

If government authorities are correct that onsite reactor storage for one hundred years is safe, then there is reason to believe, as they note, that an NMRS facility is safer yet, because the latter involves more precautions and safeguards than does onsite storage. Admittedly, however, NMRS would likely involve more transportation risks than onsite storage, but onsite storage is not a feasible alternative to NMRS because storage space at reactors is already scarce and is soon to be nonexistent. Also, because permanent disposal is now being questioned so widely, and because persons in no region appear to want a permanent facility, onsite storage cannot provide the space needed for spent fuel over the next one hundred years. Moreover, because onsite storage is not meant to be permanent, it will involve some sort of transportation risks in the future, either to NMRS sites or to a permanent repository. Thus, it is not clear that onsite storage is advantageous because of its avoiding current risks associated with transportation. The MRS Review Commission also concluded that "the estimates of the radiological effects of transporting spent fuel are small, and the difference between the estimates for different alternatives is not large enough to make transportation effects significant in choosing between alternatives [no MRS versus MRS plus repository]."[92]

Another safety consideration that argues for NMRS is the fact that most government authorities admit that human intrusion into a permanent repository is the event most likely to cause a significant release of radiation in the future.[93] Even the National Academy of Sciences (NAS) indicates that human intrusion is the main reason that permanent repositories may not be able to meet EPA safety standards.[94] In fact, this NAS conclusion is consistent with our earlier worries, in previous chapters, about human error and the social amplification of risk. If the concerns of the NAS, the EPA, and our earlier chapters are correct, then permanent disposal underground makes it more likely that a future person would inadvertently drill into the site. With aboveground or vaulted storage via NMRS, inadvertent drilling seems less likely, since the facility would be easy to see, not hidden underground. Moreover, continued monitoring and management of NMRS sites also argues against inadvertent intrusion. Admittedly, temporary storage facilities may be more susceptible to terrorism and sabotage than are permanent installations, but the monitoring and management of NMRS sites might make them better able to resist such attacks, once they occurred. Also, given examples like the pyramids, it should be possible to build surface structures that are extremely protective.

In response to all these safety-related arguments for NMRS, someone could object that calculations about NMRS safety and cost are just as problematic as analogous DOE estimates (for permanent repositories) that we have criticized earlier in the volume. Such an objection could be correct, because we have devoted six previous chapters to evaluating current HLW policy and only one chapter to the NMRS alternative to that policy. Nevertheless, there are several reasons for believing that the NMRS calculations are probably more accurate than those for permanent repositories: (1) The MRS Commission that performed the NMRS calculations has not come under serious attack for bias, withholding information, and so on, as has the DOE, the department responsible for QRAs of proposed permanent repositories; (2) Because the NMRS estimates of safety and cost cover a period only up to one hundred years, whereas analogous estimates for permanent repositories cover one thousand to ten thousand years, it is arguable that the shorter-term estimates are closer to being correct. Indeed, much of the methodological uncertainty in the DOE estimates arises from the attempt to make precise long-term predictions. Moreover, in earlier chapters we noted that methodological value judgments about precise long-term predictions were a fundamental problem at Yucca Mountain. Even if the NMRS estimates of safety were no better than those for permanent repositories, however, NMRS installations would reduce problems with temporal and intergenerational equity, with due process, and with free, informed consent—three difficulties that present serious obstacles to permanent geological disposal. NMRS facilities also would not encourage us to subscribe to the belief that what we cannot see cannot hurt us.

Is a Hundred-year NMRS More Expensive?

Yet another objection to deferring the decision about a permanent repository and instead storing the HLW in NMRS facilities for a century is that such storage would be more expensive than permanent disposal over the long term.[95] The main reason why NMRS sites are viewed as more expensive, however, is that permanent disposal does not achieve the same level of pollution control. Disposal is premised on a philosophy of "dilute and disperse" the radioactivity. Dilution and dispersal of some hazardous substance is always cheaper than containment of it. Because NMRS storage is typically premised on a philosophy of containment, however, it is more expensive than allowing some eventual dispersal of the waste from a geological repository.[96]

The main problem with the economic objection to NMRS sites is that economics, although an important policy determinant, ought not be the only or the primary determinant of nuclear waste policy. After all, if cost were the sole criterion for a reasonable choice, one might be able to use a purely economic criterion to argue for dumping radioactive materials into the sea or for using shallow land burial. Such a criterion is not acceptable, in part because it ignores the value of containment. Using narrow economic criteria for waste management is also undesirable because persons in this generation have produced the waste. Hence, as the waste producers, we have an obligation to do as much as is necessary and possible to protect subsequent generations. To argue that economics ought to be the sole determinant of waste policy would be to use an expediency criterion for recognition or denial of basic human rights to equal protection and to bodily security. In the Bill of Rights, for example, we do not say that we have rights to life, liberty, or the pursuit of happiness provided that it is economical to recognize them. Rather, we say that we have inalienable rights. If our nuclear waste policy is to be consistent with existing philosophical, legal, and political doctrines about human rights, then expediency ought not be our primary guide.

Apart from equity considerations, however, it is not clear that NMRS is more expensive than permanent storage, even on narrow economic criteria. A single NMRS facility is projected to cost from approximately $530 to $907 million, with an additional $73 million needed annually to operate the plant.[97] Total costs for an NMRS facility for one hundred years would be from about $7.3 billion to about $8.2 billion. A site characterization study for one permanent repository costs $1 to $3 billion dollars,[98] and there is no guarantee that other studies costing the same amount would not need to be done in order to obtain a suitable site. Even if one assumes that only one study would need to be done, one permanent repository would likely cost in the neighborhood of $13 billion, with total life-cycle costs, including burial, running from $40 billion to $51,077 billion for 100,000 MTU of spent fuel.[99] Hence, for about six or seven facilities for NMRS, the one-hundred-year costs are comparable to those for a permanent repository. Using similar reasoning, the DOE maintains that one NMRS facility represents about 5 percent of the total permanent repository waste-system costs.[100] If this is accurate, then it appears that one could build six or seven such facilities for NMRS and still have spent only one-third of the amount needed for permanent geological disposal. It is true that after one hundred years of operation of NMRS sites, one would still face the question of whether to continue using NMRS plants or to opt for a permanent repository, both of which would require additional funds. However, choosing the NMRS option, for at least one hundred years, even if we subsequently opt for permanent disposal, seems reasonable from an economic point of view. It is reasonable because once the waste is cooled the canisters would have reduced thermal requirements and thus would cost less to store than if they had been permanently stored at the outset. Reduced thermal requirements would thus make it possible to dispose of more spent fuel per unit area, given the lowered temperature.[101] Also, as the MRS Review Commission stated in its 1989 report, if a permanent repository is delayed beyond the year 2013, then it may not be more expensive to build one NMRS facility plus a permanent repository than it would be to construct merely a permanent repository. Once there is a delay in permanent disposal, the economics of NMRS appear to improve even more, because delaying a geological repository increases the price of at-reactor storage for utilities. NMRS sites could reduce these at-reactor storage costs.[102]

Another factor that could drive up the costs of a permanent repository, relative to those of NMRS facilities, is that a number of authorities have claimed that, given the current impasse in the U.S. radwaste program, no amount of money alone is enough to provide an incentive for members of a community to accept a permanent repository.[103] And if no amount of money would provide enough incentive for a facility for geological disposal, then provided community acceptance is a necessary condition for the installation, permanent repository costs would be so high as to render the facility impossible to build. Hence, compensation for members of the local community could be a significant factor that might drive costs of permanent repositories far above those for NMRS.

Discounting Underestimates Repository Risks

One reason that a permanent, unmonitored, nonretrievable facility may appear to be less expensive than one for NMRS is that although the unmonitored facility is likely to cause more deaths and cancers from normal operation than is a monitored facility, these greater numbers of fatalities are typically minimized because assessors use a discount rate to calculate future costs. Economists traditionally discount costs or risks that occur in the future, especially when they are evaluating long-term environmental impacts. For example, if a radioactive waste facility is responsible for killing one person this year, and that person's life is economically counted as $40,000 in the benefit-cost analysis, then at a 6 percent discount rate, one death thirteen years from now is economically counted as approximately $20,000 today. Likewise, at a 6 percent discount rate, if one death now is counted at $60,000, then one death twenty years later is counted now as $20,000. In other words, future costs—like death or environmental pollution—are counted by economists in the present as the amount of money (e.g., $20,000) needed to be invested now at some percent (for example, 6 percent) in order to yield approximately $40,000 in thirteen years and approximately $60,000 in twenty years. In the example just given, economists assume that the value of human life, at a 6 percent discount rate, is worth half as much in thirteen years, and one-third as much in twenty years. Using a higher discount rate would increase the discrepancies between the present and future value of human life. After several hundred years at a 6 percent discount rate, a human life would be counted as worth less than one-millionth of what it is worth now.

Because classical economists use social-discounting techniques for future risks and costs, they do not assume that the lives of future persons are as valuable as our own. They also make it appear that future risks, like those from a permanent repository, are less serious than they truly are because they have discounted them. Moreover, for exceedingly long-term environmental hazards, like storing high-level radioactive wastes, economists effectively count the risks as zero. This is because only a small sum—less than a dollar—invested at some traditional rate over thousands of years would be necessary to yield an amount that is valued later at billions of dollars. Philosophers such as Derek Parfit have argued that although there are reasons for economic discounting (technological progress, opportunity costs), there is no justification for temporal discounting. The moral importance of future events, he claims, does not decline at some n percent per year. As he puts it, unlike merit or compensation, there is no moral relevance in time alone.[104] Moreover, if the arguments in chapter 8 are correct, then members of future generations deserve to be treated equitably, not to have their costs and risks discounted by present generations. Because present and future persons are arguably members of the same moral community,[105] future persons ought not have permanent un-monitored radwaste facilities imposed on them if their risks will be higher than those borne by members of the present generation. Like-wise, future persons ought not bear the additional risk of having their hazards discounted relative to our own. And if not, then NMRS facilities may be the best way of achieving both these demands of equity.

Does NMRS Unrealistically Seek Zero Risk?

Some experts on radioactive wastes nevertheless claim that we ought to pursue permanent disposal immediately, because the uncertainties associated with the wastes will never be removed, given the longevity of the HLW. Moreover, they say, achieving a risk-free situation is impossible. Therefore, they argue, one ought not recommend NMRS facilities on the grounds that they are safer or better than permanent disposal, because permanent disposal is "safe enough."[106]

Rejecting NMRS facilities on the grounds that their proponents seek an unattainable goal of safety, however, is highly questionable. For one thing, NMRS does not mitigate all risks. As the previous dis-cussion made clear, even NMRS sites are susceptible to threats such as terrorism. Part of what NMRS facilities do is to reduce the long-term radwaste risk and to place it on the shoulders of those who have prof-ited from nuclear energy, instead of imposing it disproportionately on members of future generations. Second, it is ethically inappropriate to object to NMRS risks on the grounds that permanent disposal is "safe enough." Safe enough for whom? Safe enough for what generation? The problem with the "safe enough" objection is that it ignores the fact that several generations have benefited and are benefiting from nuclear waste, whereas quite different generations, under plans for permanent disposal, will bear the most significant risks and costs of the waste. It is self-serving and unjust for the beneficiaries of an in-equitable and unsafe system to presuppose that the system is "safe enough" because they themselves are not harmed by the inequity and the danger. Because the "safe enough" objection contains this presupposition, it is obviously wrong. It ignores whose ox is getting gored. The "safe enough" objection is also ethically questionable because it presupposes that some ways of dealing with radwaste are safe enough, even though there are safer alternatives, and even though many of the risks of permanent disposal are avoidable, for example, through monitoring. Not to avoid imposing our risks on others is ethically questionable, especially if we might be able to reduce the risks. Situations are only "safe enough" when we have fulfilled our ethical obligations with respect to fairness, equal treatment, and safety. It is not clear that, with permanent geological disposal, we have done so.

Would NMRS Burden the Future?

Still other proponents of a permanent repository argue that we should not pursue NMRS sites because leaving the HLW in temporary facilities would burden future generations, forcing them to deal with a problem that we have imposed on them. Permanent disposal, however, might free them from this burden.[107] Indeed, this is the official position of the Sierra Club, a conservation organization that opposes NMRS and supports permanent disposal.[108]

In response to the objection about burdening future persons, one important reply is that the objection begs the question. If the issue is whether or not NMRS burdens the future persons more than permanent disposal does, then to argue that NMRS poses a greater future burden is to assume that permanent disposal presents less of a burden. However, this conclusion is assumed because for permanent disposal to present less of a burden, we would need to have a reasonable guarantee that the disposal was safe, and that the canisters and site geology provided protection for many centuries. Because we do not have this reasonable guarantee, and because the permanent repository will not be monitored forever, there are strong grounds for believing that it could present a great burden to future persons. Also, if "the devil you don't know is worse than the devil you know," then unmonitored permanent facilities could be a worse burden than monitored temporary facilities. Otherwise, one would be committed to the problematic assumption that what you don't know couldn't hurt you. Indeed, what you don't know is probably more likely to hurt you. Hence, the greater future burden may lie with permanent disposal. Moreover, provided that NMRS facilities are associated with a permanent public trust to defray costs of monitoring and accidents, then the burden on future persons is likely to be minimized, or at least minimized more than a burden for which there is no permanent monitoring, no complete retrievability, no complete compensation, and no complete trust funds available. Also, because our NMRS proposal provides for retrievability and monitoring of the waste, future generations could lessen their burden through scientific developments or through a plan for ultimate geological disposal. If one pursues the permanent repository option now, however, then that decision will be, practically speaking, irreversible. Hence, NMRS repositories reduce the irreversibility burden. They reduce the burden of involuntary imposition of risks and waste-management choices on the future. Our NMRS proposal maximizes the choices of future generations more than permanent disposal does, provided that there is adequate funding to compensate future persons for caring for the waste. Our plan also leaves future options open more than does permanent disposal. For this reason it appears to maximize the consent, equity, due process, and autonomy of future persons more than permanent disposal does.

Would NMRS Facilities Become De Facto Permanent?

Just as officials of the Environmental Protection Agency warned in 1974, another objection to the NMRS concept is that in the event of scientific or political problems with permanent radwaste disposal or with some future NMRS site, any existing NMRS installations could become inexpensive, de facto permanent repositories. Indeed, this is one of the main arguments used by state of Tennessee officials when they opposed the MRS facilities proposed for the state a decade ago.[109] Critics of NMRS also fear that interest in permanent disposal will erode once an interim storage facility is available.

In response to the objection that NMRS facilities could become permanent, it is important to point out that by continuing research on geological disposal (as the Swedes are doing), we would decrease the chance of an NMRS site becoming permanent. Also, according to the plan already discussed, there would be legally enforceable maximum storage capacities and time limits set for each NMRS site. In the face of such legal constraints, it would be difficult for a nation to force a host community to use an NMRS facility as a permanent geological repository. Even if this did happen, however, the preceding plan for NMRS calls for monitoring of the waste and for compensation of members of the host community. The monitoring would protect persons in the community, and the compensation would counterbalance some of the inequities that might be associated with using an NMRS site as a permanent repository. Admittedly, the permanent repository objection is a difficult one to answer, because it presupposes that there is strong political sentiment against permanent repositories. If so, then permanent repositories will not be possible. In a situation in which no one will accept a permanent repository, the best that can be done is to use regional NMRS facilities and to site them so as to maximize regional equity and safety.

NMRS Uncertainties

Still other arguments against NMRS facilities are based on uncertainties associated with siting and developing them, just as there are unknowns in the area of permanent repositories. Because of these uncertainties, some critics have argued that the NMRS schedule might be as uncertain as the permanent-repository schedule. Hence, they say, there might be no clear advantage to attempting to site NMRS installations.[110] Arguing that NMRS is as problematic as permanent disposal, however, seems questionable because it is well known that less permanent facilities are more politically acceptable.[111] NMRS sites also are more acceptable because they are monitored, because the wastes can be retrieved in the event of a difficulty, because they provide for regional equity achieved through a number of facilities, and because they are not as dependent as permanent repositories on underlying geology for their safety. Even if difficulties arise with siting NMRS facilities, the plan outlined here calls for increasing the level of citizen participation and compensation available to the host communities. If these devices do not work to achieve acceptance, then the problem of storing or disposing of nuclear waste is likely insolvable. Given the extremely complex nature of the radwaste issue, and given the reasons surveyed earlier in this chapter and in the entire volume, the best of many bad options—and likely the least undesirable of political solutions—appears to be our NMRS proposal. The NMRS proposal is not a perfect solution. Our argument is that there are no perfect solutions to the problem of radioactive waste. NMRS is, however, the best available solution.

Do Several Sites for
NMRS Create Too Much Anxiety?

Although the merit of using a number of NMRS facilities is that the risk burden is distributed more equitably, one problem with such a distribution may be, as Luther Carter says,[112] that it creates too much anxiety among possible host states. In other words, the objection is that the more sites for NMRS, the greater is the potential for political unrest. Although the objection that NMRS may create anxiety is correct, it is in part beside the point. The anxiety is acceptable in part because the NMRS sites likely will be located in states whose citizens have benefited from nuclear electricity. Hence, although the equity of this distribution of anxiety does not resolve it, considerations of equity make it clear that causing anxiety among those who are not beneficiaries of nuclear energy is more reprehensible than causing anxiety among those who are beneficiaries. Also, to site noxious facilities purely on the grounds of what decreases overall anxiety may itself be an ethically suspect criterion. It may reduce overall anxiety to have one permanent repository, but imposing one permanent repository on citizens who do not want it and who have not benefited from nuclear power may be a decision made on grounds of expediency. It always may be expedient to impose a risk on a geographical minority of persons who do not deserve a particular risk, but such an imposition does not minimize inequity just because it minimizes anxiety. Indeed, it may maximize inequity. Hence, it does not appear ethically acceptable to avoid NMRS facilities purely on the grounds of avoiding anxiety. The question is whether the anxiety deserves to be avoided, and whether there is an option that does not sacrifice equity for a reduction in overall anxiety. Moreover, inequitable distribution of radwaste risks might also create anxiety.

Does the Quantity of
Waste Require Permanent Disposal?

Yet another argument against NMRS installations and in favor of permanent repositories is that because of the amounts of nuclear waste already generated, plus the quantities likely to be created in the future, permanent repositories are a virtual necessity.[113] Indeed, for the spent fuel already existing at nuclear reactors, we need at least four NMRS facilities, each with a capacity of 5,000 MTU, as earlier sections of this chapter have suggested. To handle the projected spent fuel for existing U.S. reactors, we are likely to need eighteen NMRS facilities, each with a capacity of 5,000 MTU, or six NMRS facilities, each with a capacity of 15,000 MTU, if we follow the Tennessee model.[114]

The "volume objection" to NMRS is reasonable because, as the number of NMRS sites multiplies, although distributive equity increases, so also does the risk factor. There are some indications, however, that the risk factor may not need to increase, because we may not need eighteen NMRS facilities. If the nuclear reactors now in existence are abandoned—for some of the reasons surveyed in chapter 2—and if the nuclear weapons program is cut back or halted, then the amounts of high-level wastes needing storage would be drastically reduced. Such cutbacks are plausible assumptions in part because of the recent breakup of the former Soviet Union, because of the apparent turn away from the Cold War, and because, as discussed in earlier chapters, commercial nuclear electricity is being abandoned throughout the world, with the exception of perhaps France and Japan. Indeed, if some scientists and policymakers are correct, then "true progress on the waste issue may only come about once human society turns decisively away from nuclear power,"[115] as has occurred in Sweden. One of the priorities of an independent Ukraine, for example, is the immediate closure of the Chernobyl reactors.[116] Faced with the massive deaths (up to 475,000) and high costs ($358 billion) of the Chernobyl accident,[117] citizens of the former Soviet Union are not likely to support further development of commercial reactors. Likewise, members of the U.K. trade unions voted for a nuclear phase-out on the grounds that men, women, and children are dying as a result of nuclear-induced cancers and leukemias.[118] Even in the United States, reactors are closing down ahead of schedule, suggesting that high-level radioactive wastes may not be as voluminous as expected. Of the 126 U.S. reactors put into commercial operation thus far, 16 have been abandoned short of their fortieth year, the lifespan originally planned. Indian Point-1 in New York, for example, was closed down in 1974 after only twelve years because of problems with its emergency core cooling system. Dresden-1 in Illinois closed in 1978 after nineteen years because of contamination problems, and the Rancho Seco plant in California was closed after thirteen years because a citizens' referendum rejected it. Likewise, the Yankee Rowe in Massachusetts was closed, despite reliability, because of petitions initiated by the Union of Concerned Scientists. Its owners had planned to apply for a twenty-year renewal of its license.[119] All these nuclear failures suggest that the public may be coming to accept the description of commercial nuclear fission offered by MIT Nobel-prize winner and physicist, Henry Kendall. Kendall calls it a "dead-end technology . . . a loser in competition with such things as wind power."[120]

Even if reactors are not shut down ahead of schedule, thus reducing the expected volume of HLW and spent fuel, another reason why the volume of nuclear waste might not require permanent disposal is that the public appears to be militantly opposed to geological repositories.[121] As previous chapters of this volume have argued, the DOE has lost much of its credibility, and the primary author of the U.S. Nuclear Waste Policy Act—that mandates permanent disposal—has concluded that the U.S. repository program needs to be scrapped. "The only fair thing to do might be to start over," said U.S. Representative Morris Udall.[122] Indeed, the discussion over siting a federal repository in some states is so extreme that even the NAS concluded that there "exists no effective means for overcoming such [state vs. federal] impasses."[123] Lawmakers throughout the country have called for an end to the permanent repository program, and some governors have explicitly demanded that we "remove DOE from the process and replace it with a new entity."[124] If the people will accept neither permanent disposal nor DOE management of the repository wastes, then regardless of the volumes of waste needing to be managed, permanent disposal may not be a solution.

Conclusion

If the conclusions in this chapter are correct, then they are consistent with those of the 1989 MRS Review Commission. Commission members concluded that an MRS facility linked to a permanent repository, as required by current law and as proposed by DOE, "could not be justified." Commission members affirmed, however, that a variety of reasons (flexibility, redundancy, and so on) together "justify a [MRS] facility not limited in capacity or linked to the repository schedule and operation."[125] Hence, they have argued for the desirability of an MRS, independent of a permanent repository, just as we have done. To argue for delaying the decision about permanent geological disposal is to part company with overall U.S. policy. It is consistent, at least in part, however, with the scientific recommendations of Alvin Weinberg, mentioned earlier in this chapter, and with the recommendations of several other authorities.[126] Moving to an NMRS system and deferring the decision about permanent disposal would also make U.S. radwaste policy consistent with that of most other countries in the world. As the MRS Review Commission put it: "In general deferred disposal is viewed [by most nuclear nations] as beneficial because it reduces the heat output of the waste. Only . . . Germany plans to have a repository before 2010 and that country has no plans for rapid disposal."[127]

Part of the purpose of this chapter has been to spell out the main lines of one possible NMRS proposal without, at the same time, taking the time to defend the particulars of the system. Such a defense would require a longer treatment than this volume can give, and it can be accomplished better by those whose specialized knowledge enables them to analyze the details of the politics, science, and sociology of radwaste management. We have offered our considerations as one response to the problems created by geological uncertainty and by regional and temporal inequity. Because our solution calls for at least one hundred years of NMRS, it is not a permanent solution to the problem of radwaste. It is a solution based on our ability to learn from our experience. Permanent waste disposal may work in the future, but before we try to make it work, we need to learn from our mistakes, to leave our options open, and to bear our own burdens, imposing on others as little of them as possible.

Even if the uncertainty and inequity surrounding permanent disposal were not sufficient grounds for arguing in favor of NMRS facilities, the political difficulties with geological repositories might be. As this volume argued earlier, people apparently do not believe that permanent disposal is safe and, even if they are wrong, the people have the right to be wrong. Officials ought not coopt democracy. As Daniel Koshland, chair of the General Advisory Committee of the National Academy of Sciences put it: "The ultimate power in a democracy rests with the people . . . the Nuclear Regulatory Commission cannot impose something that the voters really don't want."[128] And in the case of permanent repositories, the voters apparently do not want them. If many social scientists are correct, moreover, the voters also may not want geological repositories for the future. Social scientists have shown that it is much easier to lose people's trust than to regain it, once lost. Because citizen opposition to permanent disposal is, in large part, a result of lack of trust in the federal government and in the DOE, it is questionable whether the government and its repository program can ever regain public support.[129] And if they cannot, then it may be time to stop expecting the DOE to do what may be impossible: safely store high-level wastes in perpetuity. Indeed, DOE officials may have failed us only because we asked them to perform an impossible task. Given two risky options, permanent burial or NMRS, there is no easy solution to the problem of managing radioactive wastes. NMRS has its associated problems, as this chapter has revealed. At least it does not misrepresent our scientific uncertainties or misappropriate our ethical burdens. Proponents of NMRS realize that minimal fairness requires us to clean up after ourselves or to pay our descendants, in full, to do it for us. Leaving a potential catastrophe for the future is not an ethically defensible option.

Notes

Notes to Chapter One

1. P. Z. Grossman and E. S. Cassedy, "Cost Benefit Analysis of Nuclear Waste Disposal," *Science, Technology, and Human Values* 10, no. 4 (Fall 1985): 49.

2. D. J. Evans, U.S. Senator, State of Washington, "Statement," in *Nuclear Waste Program*, Hearings before the Committee on Energy and Natural Resources, U.S. Senate, 100th Congress, 29 April and 7 May 1987, part 3 (Washington, D.C.: U.S. Government Printing Office, 1987), 17; hereafter cited as: U.S. Congress, NWP.

3. D. Hawkins, Assistant Administrator for Air and Waste Management, *Considerations of Environmental Protection Criteria for Radioactive Waste* (Washington, D.C.: U.S. EPA, February 1978), 1. The half-life is the amount of time it takes for 50 percent of the original radioactivity to decay. After ten half-lives, one one-thousandth of the original radioactivity remains. See N. Lenssen, "Confronting Nuclear Waste," in *State of the World 1992*, ed. L. Brown (New York: Norton, 1992), 50.

4. J. R. R. Tolkien, *The Fellowship of the Ring* (New York: Ballantine Books, 1965), 349–350. Other persons have also used Tolkien's Ring as a symbol of nuclear waste, notably A. Lovins, in an unpublished paper, and A. Blowers, D. Lowry, and B. Solomon, *The International Politics of Nuclear Waste* (New York: St. Martin's Press, 1991), xvii; hereafter cited as: Blowers et al., *International Politics*.

5. One possibility for rendering the nuclear wastes less harmful is transmutation, a process proposed by Los Alamos researchers that would transform dangerous radionuclides into less harmful elements. Later in the volume, we discuss transmutation research. See Lee D. Gibson, "Can Alchemy Solve the Nuclear Waste Problem?", *The Bulletin of the Atomic Scientists* (July/August 1991): 12–17.

6. Richard Watson has pointed out (private communication) that Floyd Cullers of the U.S. Nuclear Regulatory Commission first proposed the idea of retrievable surface storage facilities (RSSFs) for high-level radwaste.

7. C. Fairhurst, National Research Council and National Academy of Sciences, "Statement," in *The Federal Program for the Disposal of Spent Nuclear Fuel and High-Level Radioactive Waste*, Hearing before the Subcommittee on Nuclear Regulation of the Committee on Environment and Public Works, U.S. Senate, 101st Congress, Second Session, 2 October 1990 (Washington, D.C.: U.S. Government Printing Office, 1990), 18; hereafter cited as: U.S. Congress, *Federal Waste*.

8. D. Deere, U.S. Nuclear Waste Technical Review Board, "Statement," in U.S. Congress, *Federal Waste*, 18. The position in favor of permanent geological disposal is also confirmed by Blowers et al., *International Politics*, 318, and by the U.S. National Academy of Sciences Commission on Geosciences, Environment, and Resources, National Research Council, *Rethinking High-Level Radioactive Waste Disposal* (Washington, D.C.: National Academy Press, 1990), v, 6. See Waste Isolation Systems Panel, Board on Radioactive Waste Management, *A Study of the Isolation System for Geologic Disposal of Radioactive Wastes* (Washington, D.C.: National Academy Press, 1983). See also note 17.

9. Blowers et al., *International Politics*, 318–319.

10. R. Murray, *Understanding Radioactive Waste* (Columbus: Batelle, 1989), 127, 142; Blowers et al., *International Politics*, 318.

11. See, for example, J. Raloff, "Nuclear Waste Still Homeless," *Science News* 136, no. 3 (15 July 1989): 47; R. Monastersky, "More Questions Plague Nuclear Waste Dump," *Science News* 135, no. 25 (24 June 1989): 389; R. Monastersky, "Opening Delayed for Nuclear Waste Site," *Science News* 134, no. 13 (24 September 1988): 199. For the Soviet disaster, see Z. Medvedev, *Disaster in the Urals* (London: Angus and Robertson, 1979).

12. U.S. ERDA, *Final Environmental Statement: Waste Management Operations, Hanford Reservation, Richland, Washington*, ERDA-1538, vol. 1 (Springfield, Va.: National Technical Information Service, October 1975), x–28. See also A. B. Benson and L. Shook, "Statement," in *High-Level Radioactive Waste Disposal at Hanford Reservation*, Oversight Hearings before the Subcommittee on General Oversight, Northwest Power, and Forest Management of the Committee on Interior and Insular Affairs, U.S. House of Representatives, 99th Congress, First and Second Sessions, 15 April 1985 (Washington, D.C.: U.S. Government Printing Office, 1986), 230ff.

13. U.S. Congress, *Safety of DOE Nuclear Facilities*. Hearing before the Subcommittee on Energy and Power of the Committee on Energy and Commerce, House of Representatives, 101st Congress, First Session, 22 February 1989, Serial No. 101–1 (Washington, D.C.: U.S. Government Printing Office, 1989); U.S. Congress, *Nuclear Waste Policy Act*, Hearings before the Subcommittee on Energy and Environment of the Committee on Interior and Insular Affairs, House of Representatives, 100th Congress, First Session, 18 September 1989 (Washington, D.C.: U.S. Government Printing Office, 1988), 3ff., 45ff., 46–47, 97, 211ff., 393; U.S. Congress, NWP, 31, 73, 41ff., 185. For costs of the DOE facility cleanup, see U.S. Congress, *Federal*

Facility Compliance with Hazardous Waste Laws, Hearing before the Subcommittee on Superfund and Environmental Oversight of the Committee
on Environment and Public Works, U.S. Senate, 100th Congress, Second
Session, 4 August 1988 (Washington, D.C.: U.S. Government Printing Office, 1988), esp. 2–3, 160–161. See also U.S. Congress, *DOE: Pollution
at Fernald, Ohio.* Hearing before the Subcommittee on Transportation and
Tourism, House of Representatives, 100th Congress, Second Session on H.R.
3783, H.R. 3784, and H.R. 3785, 14 October 1988, Serial No. 100–236
(Washington, D.C.: U.S. Government Printing Office, 1988); U.S. Congress,
DOE Nuclear Facility at Fernald, Ohio. Hearing before the Subcommittee on
Energy Conservation and Power of the Committee on Energy and Com-
merce, House of Representatives, 99th Congress, Second Session, 13 August
1986, Serial No. 99–163 (Washington, D.C.: U.S. Government Printing Of-
fice, 1986), 2ff., 9ff.; J. Emel et al., *Risk Management and Organization
Systems for High-Level Radioactive Waste Disposal: Issues and Priorities,* NWPO-
SE-008-88 (Carson City: State of Nevada, Agency for Nuclear Projects/
Nuclear Waste Projects Office, September 1988), 68–74. See note 48, chapter
2, this volume, for the $300 billion Congressional estimate for cleanup.

14. J. Neel, "Statement," in *Low-Level Radioactive Waste Disposal,* Hear-
ings before a Subcommittee of the Committee on Government Operations,
House of Representatives, 94th Congress, Second Session, 23 February, 12
March, and 6 April 1976 (Washington, D.C.: U.S. Government Printing
Office, 1976), 245; EMCON Associates and J. McCollough, "Geotechnical
Investigation and Waste Management Studies, Nuclear Waste Disposal Site,
Fleming County, Kentucky, Project 108-5.2" (unpublished report, 1975).
Available from EMCON, 326 Commercial Street, San Jose, California.

15. U.S. Geological Survey, "Memo, 1 July 1962," vertical file, "Maxey
Flats: Correspondence and Phone Conversations" (Louisville: U.S. Department of the Interior, USGS, Water Resources Division, 1962); G. Meyer,
"Maxey Flats Radioactive Waste Burial Site: Status Report," unpublished re-
port, Advanced Science and Technology Branch, U.S. Environmental Protec-
tion Agency, 1975, 9; Pacific Northwest Laboratory et al., *Research Pro-
gram at Maxey Flats and Consideration of Other Shallow Land Burial Sites,*
NUREG/CR-1832 (Washington, D.C.: U.S. NRC, 1980), esp. v, I-1, I-2,
I-14, IV-6, IV-9, V-7ff. See also Neel, "Statement," 245, and A. Weiss
and P. Columbo, *Evaluation of Isotope Migration—Land Burial,* NUREG/
CR-1289 BNL-NUREG-51143 (Washington, D.C.: U.S. NRC, 1980), 5.
For more discussion of problems at Maxey Flats and other sites, see L. Carter,
Nuclear Imperatives and Public Trust (Washington, D.C.: Resources for the
Future, 1987), 73ff.

16. The DOE quote is taken from R. Monastersky, "The 10,000-Year
Test," *Science News* 133, no. 9 (27 February 1988): 139–141. See also
G. Hart, "Address to the Forum," U.S. Environmental Protection Agency,
*Proceedings of a Public Forum on Environmental Protection Criteria for
Radioactive Wastes,* ORP/CSD-78-2 (Washington, D.C.: U.S. Government
Printing Office, May 1978), 6.

17. U.S. ERDA, ERDA-1538, pp. X-74, II-1–II-57; U.S. AEC, *Comparative Risk-Cost-Benefit Study of Alternative Sources of Electrical Energy,*

WASH-1224 (Washington, D.C.: U.S. Government Printing Office, December 1974), 3–83; see also I. Amato, "Dangerous Dirt: An Eye on DOE," *Science News* 130, no. 14 (4 October 1986): 221.

18. For some of the problems with poor management practices see, for example, W. Freudenburg, *Organizational Management of Long-Term Risks: Implications for Risk and Safety in the Transportation of Nuclear Wastes,* NWPO-TN-013-91 (Carson City: State of Nevada, Agency for Nuclear Projects/Nuclear Waste Project Office, 1991).

19. For an excellent early discussion that emphasizes the socioeconomic and political problems associated with disposal of high-level radwaste, see W. Bishop, I. Hoos, N. Hilberry, D. Metlay, and R. Watson, *Essays on Issues Relevant to the Regulation of Radioactive Waste Management,* NUREG-0412 (Washington, D.C.: U.S. Government Printing Office, 1978). By the same authors, see *Proposed Goals for Radioactive Waste Management,* NUREG-0300 (Washington, D.C.: U.S. Government Printing Office, 1978).

20. See, for example, D. S. Baron, "The Abuses of Risk Assessment," in *Risk and Society,* ed. M. Waterstone (Boston: Kluwer, 1992), 173–178.

21. F. Parker, National Research Council/National Academy of Sciences, "Letter," in *Nuclear Waste Program,* Hearings before the Committee on Energy and Natural Resources, U.S. Senate, 100th Congress, First Session, 29 January, 4–5 February 1987 (Washington, D.C.: U.S. Government Printing Office, 1987), 445–449.

22. R. Monastersky, "Quake Nuclear-Waste Space," *Science News* 141, no. 3 (18 January 1992): 44. For information on the WIPP facility, see U.S. DOE, *Final Environmental Impact Statement, Waste Isolation Pilot Plant,* 2 vols. (Washington, D.C.: U.S. Department of Energy, 1980); and U.S. Congress, *Waste Isolation Pilot Plant Land Withdrawal,* Hearings before the Committee on Energy and Natural Resources, U.S. Senate, 101st Congress, Second Session, 3 and 26 April 1990 (Washington, D.C.: U.S. Government Printing Office, 1990); and Panel on the Waste Isolation Pilot Plant, U.S. National Academy of Sciences/National Research Council, *Review Comments on DOE Document DOE/WIPP 89-011* (Washington, D.C.: U.S. National Academy of Sciences, 1990). See also note 7.

23. Quoted in U.S. Energy Research and Development Agency, Draft Environmental Statement, *Waste Management Operations: Savannah River Plant, Aiken, South Carolina,* ERDA-1537 (Washington, D.C.: U.S. Government Printing Office, October 1976), p. K-62.

Notes to Chapter Two

1. See, for example, A. Lowry et al., "Taiwan Aboriginal Tribes Protest Use of Island for Waste Site," *World Information Service on Energy (WISE) News Communique* 356 (10 July 1991): 4–5. C. C. Aveline, "Argentine Activist Receives Death Threats," *World Information Service on Energy (WISE) News Communique* 344 (21 December 1990): 4–5. J. Kalanti, "Finnish Waste

to USSR," *World Information Service on Energy (WISE) News Communique* 325 (19 January 1990): 5. For one example of the NIMBY syndrome in the United States, see R. L. Goldsteen and J. K. Schorr, *Demanding Democracy after Three Mile Island* (Gainesville: University of Florida, 1991), chap. 8.

2. See, for example, R. Monastersky, "First Nuclear Waste Dump Finally Ready," *Science News* 140, no. 15 (12 October 1991), 228, and J. Raloff and I. Peterson, "Trouble With EPA's Radwaste Rules," *Science News* 132, no. 5 (1 August 1987): 73. See also R. E. Dunlap, M. E. Draft, and E. A. Rosa, (eds.), *The Public and Nuclear Waste: Citizens' Views of Repository Siting* (Durham, N.C.: Duke University Press, 1992). For some of the groups that oppose the U.S. repository program and some of the bills proposing to suspend or abandon the program, see U.S. Congress, *Nuclear Waste Program,* Hearings before the Committee on Energy and Natural Resources, U.S. Senate, 100th Congress, 29 April and 7 May 1987, part 3 (Washington, D.C.: U.S. Government Printing Office, 1987); hereafter cited as: U.S. Congress, NWP. See also U.S. Congress, *Nuclear Waste Policy Act,* Hearing before the Subcommittee on Energy and the Environment of the Committee on Interior and Insular Affairs, House of Representatives, 100th Congress, First Session, 18 September 1987 (Washington, D.C.: U.S. Government Printing Office, 1988), and L. Carter, "Nuclear Waste Policy and Politics," *Forum for Applied Research and Public Policy* 4, no. 3 (1989): 5–18.

3. A. Blowers, D. Lowry, and B. Solomon, *The International Politics of Nuclear Waste* (New York: St. Martin's Press, 1991), 1, 4, and N. Lenssen, "Confronting Nuclear Waste," in *State of the World 1992,* ed. L. Brown (New York: Norton, 1992), 50.

4. P. L. Joskow, "Commercial Impossibility, The Uranium Market, and the Westinghouse Case," *Journal of Legal Studies* 6, no. 1 (January 1977): 165. Information on the one-thousand-plant prediction may be found in H. R. Price, "The Current Approach to Licensing Nuclear Power Plants," *Atomic Energy Law Journal* 15, no. 6 (Winter 1974): 230; L. M. Muntzing, "Standardization in Nuclear Power," *Atomic Energy Law Journal* 15, no. 3 (Spring 1973): 22.

5. M. Batten, "The Challenge of Chernobyl," *Calypso Log* 18, no. 6 (October 1991): 5. For another scientist and policymaker who supports the 475,500 figure for Chernobyl cancer deaths, see Lenssen, 49 (note 3).

6. H. Kendall, "Calling Nuclear Power to Account," *Calypso Log* 18, no. 5 (October 1991): 8.

7. C. Flavin, *Nuclear Power: The Market Test* (Washington, D.C.: Worldwatch Institute, December 1983), 33. See also J. K. Asselstine, S. Eden, M. Waterstone, "The Future of the Nuclear Power Industry in the United States," in *Risk and Society,* ed. M. Waterstone (Boston: Kluwer, 1992), 101–120.

8. C. Polluck, *Decommissioning: Nuclear Power's Missing Link* (Washington, D.C.: Worldwatch Institute, April 1986), 27; Flavin, *Nuclear Power,* 45–47. See also P. Diehl, "Leaked Internal Documents Critical of French Nuclear Establishment," *World Information Service on Energy (WISE) News Communique* 330 (6 April 1990): 8–9.

9. Public Citizen, *Critical Mass Energy Project* (Washington, D.C.: Public

Citizen, 1990). See also A. Lowry, "A Decade of Decline for U.S. Nuclear Power," *World Information Service on Energy (WISE) News Communique* 325 (19 January 1990): 3.

10. For an overview of nuclear technology and effects of radiation, see Blowers et al., *International Politics*, 1ff.; and R. Murray, *Understanding Radioactive Waste* (Columbus: Batelle Press, 1989). See also R. Bertell, *No Immediate Danger: Prognosis for a Radioactive Earth* (Summertown, Tenn.: The Book Publishing Company, 1985), 19, and R. D. Lipschutz, *Radioactive Waste* (Cambridge, Mass.: Ballinger, 1980). See also Office of Radiation Programs, U.S. EPA, *Draft Environmental Impact Statement for 40 CFR 191: Environmental Standards for Management and Disposal of Spent Nuclear Fuel, High-Level and Transuranic Radioactive Wastes*, EPA 5201102025 (Washington, D.C.: U.S. EPA, 1982).

11. The U.S. Atomic Energy Commission, the U.S. Nuclear Regulatory Commission, the U.S. Public Health Service, and the U.S. Federal Radiation Council have all admitted that radiation risk has no threshold and that it is cumulative. See 10 CFR 20 and 10 CFR 50 and K. Shrader-Frechette, *Nuclear Power and Public Policy* (Boston: Kluwer, 1983), chap. 2, esp. p. 45.

12. N. Lenssen, "Confronting Nuclear Waste," in Brown, *State of the World 1992*, 49.

13. J. P. Murray, J. J. Harrington, and R. Wilson, "Chemical and Nuclear Waste Disposal," *The Cato Journal* 2, no. 2 (Fall 1982), 569. Sierra Club, *Low-Level Nuclear Waste: Options for Storage* (Buffalo: Sierra Club Radioactive Waste Campaign, 1984), 2. For summary data on high-level waste, see Office of Civilian Radioactive Waste Management, DOE, *Characteristics of Spent Fuel, High-Level Waste, and Other Radioactive Wastes Which May Require Long-Term Isolation*, DOE/RW-0184, vol. 1 (Washington, D.C.: U.S. DOE, 1987), p. 1. 3ff.

14. J. M. Deutch and the Interagency Review Group on Nuclear Waste Management, *Report to the President*, T1D-2817 (Springfield, Va.: Technical Information Service, October 1978), pp. D-11, D-12, D-14, D-19.

15. D. MacLean, "Introduction," to D. Bodde and T. Cochran, "Conflicting Views on a Neutrality Criterion for Radioactive Waste Management" (College Park, Md.: University of Maryland, Center for Philosophy and Public Policy, 23 February 1981), 3; J. M. Deutch, *Report to the President*, pp. D-11, D-12, D-14, D-19. See also K. B. Krauskopf, *Radioactive Waste Disposal and Geology* (London: Chapman and Hall, 1988).

16. W. S. Caldwell et al., "The 'Extraordinary Nuclear Occurrence' Threshold and Uncompensated Injury under the Price-Anderson Act," *Rutgers-Camden Law Journal* 6, no. 2 (Fall 1974): 379; K. S. Shrader-Frechette, *Nuclear Power and Public Policy* (Boston: Kluwer, 1983), 10–11.

17. S. Novick, *The Electric War* (San Francisco: Sierra, 1976), 32–33; Shrader-Frechette, *Nuclear Power*, 8–9.

18. Shrader-Frechette, *Nuclear Power*, 75–81. See also A. Lowry, "Canadian Nuclear Liability Act Challenged," *World Information Service on Energy (WISE) News Communique* 329 (9 March 1990): 329. For current U.S. nuclear-liability limits see Price-Anderson Amendments Act of 1988, P.L. 100–408, Stat 102, pp. 1066–1085. For estimates of the cost of Cher-

nobyl, see M. Koryakin, "State of the Soviet Nuclear Industry," *World Information Service on Energy (WISE) News Communique* 332 (18 May 1990): 2 (P.O. Box 5627, NL-1007, AP Amsterdam, The Netherlands). See note 38.

19. Flavin, *Nuclear Power*, 33, 45–47. See also C. Polluck, *Decommissioning: Nuclear Power's Missing Link* (Washington, D.C.: Worldwatch Institute, April 1986), 27.

20. K. S. Shrader-Frechette, "Nuclear Arms and Nuclear Power: Philosophical Connections," in *Nuclear War: Philosophical Perspectives*, ed. M. A. Fox and L. Groarke (New York: Peter Lang, 1985). See also S. M. Cohen, *Arms and Judgment* (Boulder, Colo.: Westview, 1989); and K. Kipnis and D. Meyers (eds.), *Political Realism and International Morality* (Boulder, Colo.: Westview, 1987). For a discussion of the problems associated with use of commercial nuclear fission in developing countries, see, for example, A. del Callar, "The Impact and Safety of Commercial Nuclear Energy: Perspectives from the Philippines," in *Nuclear Energy and Ethics*, ed. K. S. Shrader-Frechette (Geneva: World Council of Churches, 1991), 66–71. See also note 19.

21. E. Winchester, "Nuclear Wastes," *Sierra* (July–August 1979). Office of Civilian Radioactive Waste Management, *Characteristics of Spent Fuel, High-Level Waste, and Other Radioactive Wastes which May Require Long-Term Isolation*, DOE/RW-0184 (Washington, D.C.: U.S. DOE, 1987).

22. P. Z. Grossman and E. S. Cassedy, "Cost Benefit Analysis of Nuclear Waste Disposal," *Science, Technology, and Human Values* 10, no. 4 (Fall 1985): 48.

23. Murray, Harrington, and Wilson, "Chemical and Nuclear Waste Disposal," 586.

24. D. Hawkins, Assistant Administrator for Air and Waste Management, *Considerations of Environmental Protection Criteria for Radioactive Waste* (Washington, D.C.: U.S. EPA, February 1978), 27–29.

25. See note 10, this chapter. See also Novick, *The Electric War,* and Shrader-Frechette, *Nuclear Power.*

26. For discussion of the secrecy and radiological experiments conducted on the local persons around Hanford, Washington, see Blowers et al., *International Politics*, 34–39. See also note 10, chap. 1.

27. Cited by Novick, *The Electric War*, 32–33, in a taped interview with Walske. For discussion of the "Atoms for Peace" program, see L. Carter, *Nuclear Imperatives and Public Trust* (Washington, D.C.: Resources for the Future, 1987), 47ff.; hereafter cited as Carter, NIPT.

28. Kendall, "Calling Nuclear Power," 9. If the costs of nuclear power doubled, it would be considerably more expensive than coal. See Shrader-Frechette, *Nuclear Power*, 57ff. and references cited. Given global warming, however, coal is not obviously a desirable energy option.

29. See Shrader-Frechette, *Nuclear Power*, chap. 1.

30. Murray, *Understanding Radioactive Waste*, 45, and Blowers et al., *International Politics*, 4ff. See also note 28.

31. Blowers et al., *International Politics*, 10ff. See also note 1 and Nils-Axel Morner, "High-Level Waste Site Cracked/Sweden," *World Information*

Service on Energy (WISE) News Communique 326/7 (9 February 1990): 10–12; Nenig, "UK Dump Plan: Sellafield Dangers as Great at Dounreay," *World Information Service on Energy (WISE) News Communique* 355 (28 June 1991): 7; Nenig, "UK Waste Dump Site Chosen," *World Information Service on Energy (WISE) News Communique* 357 (22 August 1991): 3; E. Mealey, "London Dumping Convention," *World Information Service on Energy (WISE) News Communique* 357 (22 August 1991): 3; E. Mealey, "London Dumping Convention," *World Information Service on Energy (WISE) News Communique* 343 (7 December 1990): 5; A. Lowry, "International Controls on Nuclear Waste Dumps Needed," *World Information Service on Energy (WISE) News Communique* 331 (27 April 1990): 8–9.

32. Blowers et al., *International Politics*, 12ff.

33. Regarding the WIPP site, see note 2, this chapter, and note 17, chap. 1. See also U.S. Congress, *Waste Isolation Pilot Plant Land Withdrawal*, Hearings before the Committee on Energy and Natural Resources, U.S. Senate, 101st Congress, Second Session, 3 and 26 April 1990 (Washington, D.C.: U.S. Government Printing Office, 1990).

34. See C. Eid (ed.), *Incineration of Radioactive Waste* (London: Graham and Trotman, 1985). See also A. Lowry, "Radwaste Incineration in the U.S.," *World Information Service on Energy (WISE) News Communique* 326/7 (9 February 1990): 10–11. For discussion of Sellafield pollution, see Carter, NIPT, 251ff.

35. See Blowers et al., *International Politics*, 41ff., and L. Scheinman, *The International Atomic Energy Agency and World Nuclear Order* (Washington, D.C.: Resources for the Future, 1987).

36. See the previous note.

37. Quoted by Blowers et al., *International Politics*, 44.

38. For discussion of the Price-Anderson Act and the catastrophic consequences of nuclear accidents, see Shrader-Frechette, *Risk and Rationality* (Berkeley, Los Angeles, London: University of California Press, 1991), 25ff., 88ff.; hereafter cited as *Risk*; Shrader-Frechette, *Nuclear Power*, chap. 4; J. Marrone, "The Price-Anderson Act: The Insurance Industry's View" *Forum* 12, no. 2 (Winter 1977): 607; W. S. Caldwell et al., "Nuclear Occurrence," 379; J. R. Brydon, "Slaying the Nuclear Giants," *Pacific Law Journal* 8, no. 2 (July 1977): 781; "AEC Staff Study of the Price-Anderson Act, Part I," *Atomic Energy Law Journal* 16, no. 3 (Fall 1974): 220. See also note 18. The 1988 amendments to the Price-Anderson Act (P.L. 100–408; Stat 102, pp. 1066–1085) set the liability limit at $63 million times the number of reactors. For one hundred reactors, the limit would be $6.3 billion. Each year, the $63 million is adjusted for inflation.

39. The Energy Reorganization Act, as a response to government problems regarding the AEC's pro-industry bias, is discussed in M. A. Rowden, "Nuclear Power Regulation in the United States: A Current Domestic and International Perspective," *Atomic Energy Law Journal* 17, no. 2 (Summer 1975): 102ff. See also Novick, *Electric War*, 354–355; Brydon, "Nuclear Giants," 771; V. McKim, "Social and Environmental Values in Power Plant Licensing," in *Values in the Electric Power Industry*, ed. K. M. Sayre (Notre

Dame: University Press, 1977), 38–40; G. B. Karpinski, "Federal Preemption of State Laws Controlling Nuclear Power," *Georgetown Law Journal* 64, no. 6 (July 1976): 1336; and J. G. Palfrey, "Energy and the Environment: The Special Case of Nuclear Power," *Columbia Law Review* 74, no. 8 (December 1974): 1380.

40. L. Carter, NIPT, 64–65. For further discussion of the AEC coverup, see the previous note.

41. For discussion of the 1982 Nuclear Waste Policy Act, see Carter, NIPT; note 12, chap. 1; note 2, (this) chap. 2; and U.S. Congress, *High-Level Nuclear Waste Issues*, Hearings before the Subcommittee on Nuclear Regulation of the Committee on Environment and Public Works, U.S. Senate, 100th Congress, First Session, 23 April, 2, 3, 18 June 1987 (Washington, D.C.: U.S. Government Printing Office, 1987). See also *Radioactive Waste Legislation*, Hearings before the Subcommittee on Energy and Environment of the Committee on Interior and Insular Affairs, House of Representatives, 97th Congress, First Session, 23, 25 June, 9 July 1981 (Washington, D.C.: U.S. Government Printing Office, 1981).

42. For discussion of the 1987 Act, see J. D. Raeber, "Federal Nuclear Waste Policy as Defined by the Nuclear Waste Policy Amendments Act of 1987," *Saint Louis University Law Journal* 34, no. 1 (Fall 1989): 111–131.

43. U.S. DOE, *Site Characterization Progress Report: Yucca Mountain, Nevada*, DOE/RW-0307P (Washington, D.C.: U.S. DOE, 1991), xiv.

44. H. W. Swainston, "Yucca Mountain. A Study of Conflicts in Federalism," *Inter Alia* 57, no. 1 (October 1992): 11–16. Grant Sawyer and the State of Nevada Commission on Nuclear Projects, *Report of the Nevada Commission on Nuclear Projects* (Carson City: Nuclear Waste Project Office, 1992), 47–48. See also U.S. Congress, *Nuclear Waste Policy Amendments Act of 1991*, Report of Mr. Johnston (Washington, D.C.: U.S. Government Printing Office, 1991), 1–5.

45. R. H. Bryan, Governor of Nevada, "Statement," in U.S. Congress, NWP, 41, provides the 80-percent figure. See also M. Yates, "DOE Reassesses Civilian Radioactive Waste Management Program," *Public Utilities Fortnightly* (15 February 1990): 36–38, esp. 36; R. Loux, "Will the Nation's Nuclear Waste Policy Succeed at Yucca Mountain?" *Public Utilities Fortnightly* (22 November 1990): 27, 52.

46. For discussion of sub-seabed disposal, see, for example, R. A. Kaplan, "Into the Abyss: International Regulation of Sub-seabed Nuclear Waste Disposal," *University of Pennsylvania Law Review*, no. 3 (January 1991): 769–800; and U.S. Congress, *Civilian Radioactive Waste Disposal*, Hearings before the Committee on Energy and Natural Resources, 100th Congress, First Session, 16, 17 July 1987 (Washington, D.C.: U.S. Government Printing Office, 1987), 244ff., 309ff.

47. See Murray, *Understanding Radioactive Waste*, for a discussion of laws and regulations regarding nuclear waste.

48. Lenssen (note 3), 53. Blowers et al., *International Politics*, 36ff. See also U.S. Congress, *Federal Facility Compliance with Hazardous Waste Laws*, Hearing before the Subcommittee on Superfund and Environmental Over-

sight of the Committee on Environment and Public Works, U.S. Senate, 100th Congress, Second Session, 4 August 1988 (Washington, D.C.: U.S. Government Printing Office, 1988).

Notes to Chapter Three

1. I. S. Roxburgh, *Geology of High-Level Nuclear Waste Disposal* (New York: Chapman and Hall, 1987), 189.

2. See E. Nagel, *The Structure of Science* (New York: Hartcourt, Brace, and World, 1961), 13–105.

3. C. Hempel and P. Oppenheim, "Studies in the Logic of Explanation," *Philosophy of Science* 15 (1948): 135–175. R. B. Braithwaite, *Scientific Explanation* (Cambridge: Cambridge University Press, 1953). K. R. Popper, *The Logic of Scientific Discovery* (New York: Basic Books, 1959).

4. See, for example, E. Reichard et al., *Groundwater Contamination Risk Assessment* (Oxfordshire, England: International Association of Hydrological Sciences, 1990), 101ff.; hereafter cited as: Reichard, GCRA.

5. Reichard, GCRA, 177–179. Much of this discussion of value judgments in quantitative risk assessment is based on K. S. Shrader-Frechette, *Risk and Rationality* (Berkeley, Los Angeles, London: University of California Press, 1991), 53–74; hereafter cited as: *Risk*. For a discussion of risk assessment and its components, see Shrader-Frechette, *Risk*, 5ff. For an analysis of needed improvements in risk assessment, see Shrader-Frechette, *Risk*, 169–219.

6. R. Rudner, "The Scientist *Qua* Scientist Makes Value Judgments," in *Introductory Readings in the Philosophy of Science*, ed. E. D. Klemke, R. Hollinger, and A. Kline (Buffalo: Prometheus Books, 1980), 236; B. Allen and K. Crump, "Aspects of Quantitative Risk Assessment as Applied to Cancer," in *Quantitative Risk Assessment*, ed. J. Humber and R. Almeder (Clifton, N.J.: Humana Press, 1987), 129–146.

7. C. Whipple, "Nonpessimistic Risk Assessment," in *The Risk Assessment of Environmental and Human Health Hazards*, ed. D. Paustenbach (New York: John Wiley, 1989), 1105–1120; U.S. NRC, *Reactor Safety Study*, Report no. (NUREG-75/014) WASH-1400 (Washington, D.C.: U.S. Government Printing Office, 1975), 37; C. Starr and C. Whipple, "Risks of Risk Decisions," *Science* 208, no. 4448 (June 1980): 1116; B. Cohen and I. Lee, "A Catalog of Risks," *Health Physics* 36, no. 6 (1979): 707; W. Hafele, "Energy," in *Science, Technology, and the Human Prospect*, ed. C. Starr and P. Ritterbush (New York: Pergamon, 1979), 139; M. Maxey, "Managing Low-Level Radioactive Wastes," in *Low-Level Radioactive Waste Management*, ed. J. Watson (Williamsburg, Va.: Health Physics Society, 1979), 410, 417; B. Cohen, "Risk Analyses of Buried Wastes," in Paustenbach, *Risk Assessment*, 575; R. Andrews, "Environmental Impact Assessment and Risk Assessment," in *Environmental Impact Assessment*, ed. P. Wathern (London: Unwin Hyman, 1988), 85–97; S. Dreyfus, "Formal Models vs. Human Situational Understanding ...," *Technology and People* 1 (1982): 61;

D. MacLean, "Understanding the Nuclear Power Controversy," in *Scientific Controversies*, ed. A. Caplan and H. Engelhardt (Cambridge: Cambridge University Press, 1987), part V; L. Clarke, *Acceptable Risk?* (Berkeley, Los Angeles, London: University of California Press, 1989).

8. P. Ricci and A. Henderson, "Fear, Fiat, and Fiasco," in *Phenotypic Variation in Populations*, ed. A. Woodhead et al. (New York: Plenum, 1988), 285–293; R. Setlow, "Relevance of Phenotypic Variation in Risk," in Woodhead et al., 1–5.

9. M. Schneiderman, "Risk Assessment: Where Do We Want It To Go? What Do We Do To Make It Go There?" in Humber and Almeder, *Quantitative Risk Assessment*, 107–128; E. Foulkes, "Factors Determining Target Doses," in *Hazard Assessment of Chemicals*, ed. J. Saxena (New York: Taylor and Francis, 1989), 31–47.

10. K. Busch, "Statistical Approach to Quantitative Risk Assessment," in Humber and Almeder, *Quantitative Risk Assessment*, 9–55; see also Setlow, "Relevance of Phenotypic Variation in Risk."

11. E. Reichard et al., *Groundwater Contamination Risk Assessment* (Oxfordshire, England: International Association of Hydrological Sciences, 1990), 177.

12. For discussion of the difficulties with "real risk" and with the distinction between "real risk" and "perceived risk," see, for example, W. Freudenburg, "Perceived Risk, Real Risk," *Science* 242 (October 7, 1988): 44–49; P. Slovic, "Perception of Risk," *Science* 236 (1987): 280–285; P. Slovic, B. Fischoff, and S. Liechtenstein, "Characterizing Perceived Risk," in *Perilous Progress*, ed. R. Kates, C. Hohemser, and H. Kasperson (Boulder: Westview, 1985); P. Slovic, B. Fischoff, and S. Liechtenstein, "Perception and Acceptability of Risk from Energy Systems," in *Public Reactions to Nuclear Power*, ed. W. Freudenburg and E. Rosa (Boulder: American Association for the Advancement of Science/Westview, 1984), 115–135; and K. Shrader-Frechette, *Risk*, 77–88.

13. For discussion of some of these other risk factors, see W. Freudenburg and T. Jones, "Attitudes and Stress in the Presence of Technological Risk," *Social Forces* 69, no. 4 (June 1991): 999–1024; J. Short, "Social Dimensions of Risk," *The American Sociologist* (Summer 1987): 167–172; J. Short, "The Social Fabric at Risk," *American Sociological Review* 49 (December 1984): 711–725; S. Rayner and R. Canton, "How Fair Is Safe Enough?" *Risk Analysis* 7, no. 1 (March 1987): 3–9; K. Shrader-Frechette, *Risk*, 89–168; K. Shrader-Frechette, *Risk Analysis and Scientific Method* (Boston: Kluwer/Reidel, 1985), 55–125; R. Dunlap, M. Kraft, and E. Rosa (eds.), *The Public and Nuclear Waste: Citizens' Views of Repository Siting* (Durham: Duke University Press, 1993).

14. H. Longino, "Comments on 'What's Wrong with Quantitative Risk Assessment?,'" remarks delivered at the Philosophy of Science Association Meeting, Pittsburgh, 24 October 1986, pp. 3–11; J. Fabrikant et al., Committee on the Biological Effects of Ionizing Radiation, *Health Risks of Radon and Other Internally Deposited Alpha-Emitters: BEIR IV* (Washington, D.C.: National Academy Press, 1988); K. S. Shrader-Frechette, *Nuclear Power and*

Public Policy (Boston: Reidel, 1983), 25–27; D. Paustenbach (ed.), *The Risk Assessment of Environmental and Human Health Hazards* (New York: John Wiley, 1989); J. Saxena (ed.), *Hazard Assessment of Chemicals* (New York: Taylor and Francis, 1989); A. Woodhead et al. (eds.), *Phenotypic Variation in Populations* (New York: Plenum, 1988).

15. Longino, "Comments," 3; J. Purdham, "Whose Life Is It Anyway?" *At The Centre: The Canadian Centre for Occupational Health and Safety* 10, no. 1 (March 1987): 9; Foulkes, "Factors," 43ff.; Fabrikant, BEIR IV, 442ff.; Woodhead et al., *Phenotypic Variation.*

16. F. von Hippel and T. Cochran, "Chernobyl, The Emerging Story: Estimating Long-Term Health Effects," *Bulletin of the Atomic Scientists* 42, no. 7 (August/September 1986): 18–24 (note: this volume was originally misnumbered as vol. 43, no. 1 due to a misprint); E. Marshall, "Reactor Explodes Amid Soviet Silence," *Science* 232, no. 4752 (16 May 1986): 814–815.

17. D. Nebert, "Genes Encoding Drug-Metabolizing Enzymes," in Woodhead et al., *Phenotypic Variation,* 59.

18. L. Cox and P. Ricci, "Legal and Philosophical Aspects of Risk Analysis," in Paustenbach, *Risk Assessment,* 1038ff.; S. Samuels, "The Arrogance of Intellectual Power," in Woodhead et al., *Phenotypic Variation,* 113–120; K. S. Shrader-Frechette, *Science Policy, Ethics, and Economic Methodology* (Boston: Reidel, 1985), esp. chaps. 2, 5, 6, and 7.

19. V. Bond, "Causality of a Given Cancer After Known Radiation Exposure," in *Hazards,* ed. R. Kates et al. (Washington, D.C.: National Academy Press, 1986), 24–43.

20. L. J. Carter, *Nuclear Imperatives and Public Trust* (Washington, D.C.: Resources for the Future, 1987), 417.

Notes to Chapter Four

1. C. Bernard, *Bulletin of the New York Academy of Medicine* 4 (1928): 997.

2. U.S. Department of Energy, *Nuclear Waste Policy Act, Environmental Assessment, Yucca Mountain Site, Nevada Research and Development Area, Nevada,* DOE/RW-0073, 3 vols. (Washington, D.C.: U.S. DOE, 1986), vol. 3, pp. C.5–C.55; hereafter cited as: DOE, NWPA-Yucca.

3. DOE, NWPA-Yucca, pp. C.5–56. The same admission is made in U.S. DOE, *Nuclear Waste Policy Act, Environmental Assessment, Reference Repository Location, Hanford Site, Washington,* DOE/RW-0070, 3 vols. (Washington, D.C.: U.S. DOE, 1986), vol. 2: 6–294; hereafter cited as: DOE, NWPA-Hanford.

4. See note 17, chap. 1, of this volume.

5. See, for example, R. Bryan, *State of Nevada Comments on the U.S. Department of Energy Draft Environmental Assessment for the Proposed High-Level Nuclear Waste Site at Yucca Mountain,* 2 vols. (Carson City: Nuclear Waste Project Office, Office of the Governor, 1985), vol. 1: I-42, I-43;

R. Peters, *The Effect of Percolation Rate on Water Travel Time in Deep, Partially Saturated Zones,* SAND85-0854 (Albuquerque: Sandia National Labs., 1986), 32; see G. Sawyer, "Statement," *Nuclear Waste Program,* Hearings before the Committee on Energy and Natural Resources, U.S. Senate, 100th Congress, First Session on the Current Status of the Department of Energy's Civilian Nuclear Waste Activities, 29 January, 4 and 5 February 1987, part 1 (Washington, D.C.: U.S. Government Printing Office, 1987), 709–712; hereafter cited as: U.S. Congress, *Nuclear.*

6. R. Barnard and H. Dockery, *Technical Summary of the Performance Assessment Calculational Exercises for 1990 (PACE-90), Vol. 1: "Nominal Configuration" Hydrogeologic Parameters and Calculation Results,* SAND90-2726 (Albuquerque: Nuclear Waste Repository Technology Department, Sandia National Labs., 1991).

7. Barnard and Dockery, *Technical Summary,* 5–6.

8. Thompson Engineering Company, *Review and Comment on the U.S. Department of Energy Site Characterization Plan Conceptual Design Report,* NWPO-TR-009-88 (Carson City: State of Nevada, Agency for Projects/ Nuclear Waste Project Office, October 1988) (Item 329 in US DOE, DE90006793).

9. See R. A. Watson, "Explanation and Prediction in Geology," *Journal of Geology* 77 (1969): 488–494.

10. R. A. Watson, "Absence as Evidence in Geology," *Journal of Geological Education* 30 (1982): 300–301.

11. See, for example, J. Beavers and N. Thompson, *Environmental Effects on Corrosion in the Tuff Repository* (Washington, D.C.: U.S. NRC, 1990) (Item 118 in US DOE, DE91000566); W. Halsey, "Selection Criteria for Container Materials at the Proposed Yucca Mountain High Level Nuclear Waste Repository," in *NACE Corrosion '90* (Las Vegas: U.S. DOE, 1990) (Item 60 in US DOE, DE91000566); J. Perry, "A Lineament Analysis of Yucca Mountain, Nevada: The Proposed High-Level Nuclear Waste Repository," in *6th Thematic Conference on Remote Sensing for Exploration Geology: Applications, Technology, Economics* (Ann Arbor: Environmental Research Institute of Michigan, 1988) (Item 135 in US DOE, DE91000566); D. Dobson et al., "Plans for Characterization of the Potential Geologic Repository Site at Yucca Mountain, Nevada," in *International Conference for High-Level Radioactive Waste Management* (Las Vegas: U.S. DOE, 1990) (Item 8 in US DOE, DE91000566).

12. See G. Sawyer, *Report of the State of Nevada Commission on Nuclear Projects* (Carson City: Nevada Commission on Nuclear Projects, December 1990), 73.

13. K. V. Hodges, "Comment," in J. L. Younker, S. L. Albrecht, W. J. Arabasz, J. H. Bell, F. W. Cambray, S. W. Carothers, J. I. Drever, J. T. Einaudi, D. E. French, K. V. Hodges, R. H. Jones, D. K. Kreamer, W. G. Pariseau, T. A. Vogel, T. Webb, W. B. Andrews, G. A. Fasano, S. R. Mattson, R. C. Murray, L. B. Ballou, M. A. Revelli, A. R. Ducharme, L. E. Shephard, W. W. Dudley, D. T. Hoxie, R. J. Herbst, E. A. Patera, B. R. Judd, J. A. Docka, L. R. Rickertsen, J. M. Boak, and J. R. Stockey, *Report of the Peer Review Panel on the Early Site Suitability Evaluation of the Potential Repository*

Site at Yucca Mountain, Nevada, SAIC-91/8001 (Washington, D.C.: U.S. DOE, 1992), 362; hereafter cited as: Younker, Albrecht, et al.

14. N. Oreskes, "Comments on Uncertainty, Expert Error, and Radioactive Waste," unpublished remarks, 23 March 1992, 6.

15. K. V. Hodges, "Comment," in Younker, Albrecht, et al., 362–363.

16. K. V. Hodges, "Comment," in Younker, Albrecht, et al., 363.

17. K. V. Hodges, "Comment," in Younker, Albrecht, et al., 384.

18. "Consensus Position," in Younker, Albrecht, et al., p. B-2.

19. D. Hawkins, Assistant Administrator for Air and Waste Management, U.S. EPA, *Considerations of Environmental Protection Criteria for Radioactive Waste* (Washington, D.C.: U.S. EPA, February 1978); hereafter cited as: U.S. EPA, *Considerations.*

20. U.S. EPA, *Considerations,* 10, 26.

21. C. B. Raleigh and the Panel on Coupled Processes at Yucca Mountain, *Ground Water at Yucca Mountain: How High Can It Rise?* (Washington, D.C.: National Academy Press, 1992); hereafter cited as: Raleigh.

22. Nevada NWPO, *State of Nevada Comments on the U.S. Department of Energy Consultation Draft Site Characterization Plan, Yucca Mountain Site, Nevada: Vol. 1* (Carson City: U.S. DOE, 1989) (Item 335 in US DOE, DE90006793).

23. R. Stein and P. Collyer, "Pilot Research Projects for Underground Disposal of Radioactive Wastes in the United States of America," in *Radioactive Waste Management. Vol. 3. Proceedings of an International Conference Held by the IAEA in Seattle, 16–20 May 1983* (Washington, D.C.: U.S. DOE, 1984) (Item 157 in US DOE, DE89005394).

24. K. G. Knauss et al., *Hydrothermal Interaction of Solid Wafers of Topopah Spring Tuff with J-13 Water at 90 and 150/Degree/C Using . . . Long-Term Experiments* (Livermore, Calif.: Lawrence Livermore National Lab., 1987) (Item 18 in US DOE, DE89005394); D. Hoffman et al., "Review of a Field Study of Radionuclide Migration from an Underground Nuclear Explosion at the Nevada Test Site," in *International Conference on Radioactive Waste Management* (Los Alamos: Los Alamos National Lab., 1983) (Item 140 in US DOE, DE89005394).

25. See, respectively, R. Jacobson et al., *A Reconnaissance Investigation of Hydrogeochemistry and Hydrology of Rainier Mesa* (Reno: Desert Research Institute, 1986) (Item 183 in US DOE, DE89005394); Knauss et al., *Hypothermal Interaction;* J. Bates and T. Gerding, "Performance of Actinide-Containing SRL 165 Type Glass in Unsaturated Conditions," in *Scientific Basis for Nuclear Waste Management 11: Volume 112: Proceedings,* ed. M. Apted and R. Westerman (Boston: Materials Research Society, 1987) (Item 14 in US DOE, DE89005394).

26. H. D. Smith, *Electrochemical Corrosion-Scoping Experiments: An Evaluation of the Results* (Richland, Wash.: Westinghouse Hanford Co., 1988) (Item 151 in US DOE, DE90006793); H. D. Smith, *Initial Report on Stress-Corrosion-Cracking Experiments Using Zircaloy-4 Spent Fuel Cladding C-Rings* (Richland, Wash.: Westinghouse Hanford Co., 1988) (Item 153 in US DOE, DE90006793).

27. J. Bates et al., "Identification of Secondary Phases Formed During Unsaturated Reaction of UO₂ with EJ-13 Water," in *Materials Research Society Fall Meeting* (Argonne, Ill.: Argonne National Lab., 1989) (Item 102 in US DOE, DE90006793); J. Bates et al., "Parametric Effects of Glass Reaction Under Unsaturated Conditions," in *Materials Research Society Fall Meeting* (Argonne, Ill.: Argonne National Lab., 1989) (Item 103 in US DOE, DE90006793); McCright et al., *Progress Report in the Results of Testing Advanced Conceptual Design Metal Barrier Materials Under Relevant Environmental Conditions for a Tuff Repository* (Livermore, Calif.: Lawrence Livermore National Lab., 1987) (Item 114 in US DOE, DE90006793); see R. Westerman et al., *Corrosion Testing of Type 304L Stainless Steel in Tuff Groundwater Environments* (Richland, Wash.: Pacific Northwest Lab., 1987) (Item 135 in US DOE, DE90006793); H. Weiss et al., *Metallurgical Analysis of a 304L Stainless Steel Canister from the Spent Fuel Test-Climax* (Livermore, Calif.: Lawrence Livermore National Lab., 1985) (Item 119 in US DOE, DE88004834).

28. C. Hadlock, *Technical Support of Standards for High-Level Radioactive Waste Management*, vol. D: *Release Mechanisms*, EPA 520/4-79-007D (Washington, D.C.: U.S. EPA, 1980), 49.

29. J. Blacic et al., *Effects of Long-Term Exposure of Tuffs to High-Level Nuclear Waste Repository Conditions, Final Report* (Los Alamos: Los Alamos National Lab., 1986) (Item 67 in US DOE, DE88004834).

30. S. Pitman et al., "Corrosion and Slow-Strain-Rate Testing of Type 304L Stainless in Tuff Groundwater Environments," in *Corrosion '87* (San Francisco: Pacific Northwest Lab, 1986) (Item 172 in US DOE, DE88004834).

31. DOE, NWPA-Hanford, vol. 2: 6–24, 6–25.

32. P. O'Brien, *Technical Support for High-Level Radioactive Waste Management, Task C Report: Assessment of Migration Pathways*, EPA 520/4-79-007C (Washington, D.C.: U.S. EPA, 1977), 134.

33. See C. Smith et al., *Population Risks from Disposal of High-Level Radioactive Wastes in Geologic Repositories*, EPA-520/3-80-006 (Washington, D.C.: U.S. EPA, 1982), 10, 51.

34. U.S. DOE, Office of Scientific and Technical Information, "Project History," in *Yucca Mountain Project Bibliography, 1988–1989*, DOE/OSTI-3406 (Suppl.2) (DE90006793) (Oak Ridge: U.S. DOE, November 1990), vii–xvii.

35. DOE, NWPA-Yucca, vol. 2: 6–242.

36. U.S. Geological Survey, *Vegetation and Climates of the Last 45,000 Years in the Vicinity of the Nevada Test Site, South-Central Nevada* (Reston, Va.: U.S. Geological Survey, 1985) (Item 394 in US DOE, DE88004834).

37. R. French, *Daily, Seasonal, and Annual Precipitation at the Nevada Test Site, Nevada* (Las Vegas: University of Nevada Water Resources Center, 1986) (Item 186 in US DOE, DE89005394).

38. See J. Braithwaite and F. Nimick, *Effect of Host-Rock Dissolution and Precipitation on Permeability in a Nuclear Waste Repository in Tuff,* SAND84-0192 (Albuquerque: Sandia National Labs., 1984) (Item D161 in

US DOE, NVO-96-24 [REV. 5]). R. French, *Effects of the Length of Record on Estimates of Annual and Seasonal Precipitation at the Nevada Test Site, Nevada* (Las Vegas: Nevada University Desert Research Institute, 1987) (Item 220 in US DOE, DE89005394).

39. DOE, NWPA-Yucca, vol. 2: 6–298, 6–299.

40. The three quotes are taken, respectively, from DOE, NWPA-Yucca, vol. 2: 6–32, 6–32, and 6–257.

41. L. Benson, "Effect of Paleoclimatic Fluctuations on the Transport of Radionuclides from Potential Waste Disposal Sites in the Great Basin of the Western United States," *Earth Sciences* 3, no. 1 (March): 7–9 (Item 90 in US DOE, DE89005394).

42. S. Mara, *Assessment of Effectiveness of Geologic Isolation Systems. Geologic Factors in the Isolation of Nuclear Waste: Evaluation of Long-Term Geomorphic Processes and Catastrophic Events* (Seattle: Battelle Pacific Northwest Lab., 1980) (Item 92 in US DOE, DE89005394).

43. L. Metcalf, *Preliminary Review and Summary of the Potential for Tectonic, Seismic, and Volcanic Activity at the Nevada Test Site Defense Waste Disposal Site* (Reno: Desert Research Institute, 1983) (Item 142 in US DOE, DE89005394). See also B. Crowe, *Volcanic Hazard Assessment for Disposal of High-Level Radioactive Waste* (Los Alamos: Los Alamos National Laboratory, 1986).

44. J. Czarnecki, "Characterization of the Subregional Groundwater Flow System of a Potential Site for a High-Level Nuclear Waste Repository," Ph.D. diss., University of Minnesota, 1988. (Item 278 in US DOE, DE90006793).

45. T. Dunne and L. Leopold, *Water in Environmental Planning* (San Francisco: W. H. Freeman, 1978), 52, 54, 70.

46. J. Davis, *Geological Reconnaissance and Chronologic Studies, Technical Report no. 33* (Las Vegas: Desert Research Institute, 1983) (Item 143 in US DOE, DE89005394).

47. U.S. DOE, "NNWSI History," in *Bibliography of the Published Reports, Papers, and Articles on the Nevada Nuclear Waste Storage Investigations, January 1985*, NVO-96-24 (Rev. 5) (Las Vegas: U.S. DOE, Nevada Operations Office, 1985), 1–30.

48. H. MacDougall et al., *Site Characterization Plan: Conceptual Design Report, Vol. 3: Appendices A–E: Nevada Nuclear Waste Storage Investigations Project* (Albuquerque: Sandia National Labs., 1987) (Item 177 in US DOE, DE90006793).

49. J. Robinson, *Water Levels in Periodically Measured Wells in the Yucca Mountain Area, Nevada, 1981–1987* (Denver: U.S. Geological Survey, 1988) (Item 271 in US DOE, DE90006793). See also Raleigh.

50. Raleigh, 144.

51. Raleigh, 7, 122, 135.

52. Stein and Collyer, "Pilot Research Projects."

53. I. Roxburgh, *Geology of High-Level Nuclear Waste Disposal* (London: Chapman and Hall, 1987), 183; hereafter cited as: *Geology*.

54. I. Walker, *Geologic and Hydrogeologic Evaluation of a Proposed Site . . .* (Frankfort, Ky.: State Department of Health, 1962), 3.

55. S. Papadopulos and I. Winograd, *Storage of Low-Level Radioactive*

Wastes in the Ground: Hydrogeologic and Hydrochemical Factors, EPA-520/3-74-009 (Washington, D.C.: U.S. EPA, Office of Radiation Programs, 1974), 29–30.

56. N. Bixler and R. Eaton, "Modeling of Multiphase Flow in Permeable Media: (1) Mathematical Model; (2) Analysis of Imbibation and Drying Experiments," in *Gordan Research Conference on Modeling of Flow in Permeable Media* (Albuquerque: Sandia National Labs., 1986) (Item 187 in US DOE, DE90006793).

57. R. Watson, "A Critique of Chronostratigraphy," *American Journal of Science* 283 (February 1983): 173–177; see also R. Watson and H. Wright, "The End of the Pleistocene: A General Critique of Chronostratigraphic Classification," *Boreas* 9 (1980): 153–163.

58. L. Ramspott, "Assessment of Engineered Barrier System and Design of Waste Packages," in *American Nuclear Society Annual Meeting* (Livermore, Calif.: Lawrence Livermore National Lab., 1988) (Item 147 in US DOE, DE90006793).

59. C. Cooper, *Numerical Simulation of Gas Flow through Unsaturated Fractured Rock at Yucca Mountain, Nevada*, NWPO-TR-014-90 (Las Vegas and Reno: Water Resources Center, Desert Research Institute, University of Nevada System, January 1990).

60. C. Sastre et al., *Waste Package Reliability*, NUREG/CR-4509 (Washington, D.C.: U.S. NRC, 1986), 22–24.

61. U.S. NRC, *Reactor Safety Study*, Report no. (NUREG-75/014) WASH-1400 (Washington, D.C.: U.S. Government Printing Office, 1975).

62. See chap. 6 and R. Cooke, *Subjective Probability and Expert Opinion* (New York: Oxford University Press, 1991), chap. 9.

63. Nevada NWPO, *State of Nevada Comments on the U.S. Department of Energy Consultation Draft Site Characterization Plan, Yucca Mountain Site, Nevada: Vol. 1* (Carson City: U.S. DOE, 1989) (Item 335 in US DOE, DE90006793). Nevada NWPO, *State of Nevada Comments on the U.S. Department of Energy Consultation Draft Site Characterization Plan, Yucca Mountain Site, Nevada: Vol. 2* (Carson City: U.S. DOE, 1989) (Item 336 in US DOE, DE90006793).

64. See, for example, G. Bertozzi, M. Hill, J. Lewi, and R. Storck, "Long-Term Risk Assessment of Geological Disposal," ed. R. Simon, *Radioactive Waste Management and Disposal* (Cambridge: Cambridge University Press, 1986), 639, 647.

65. M. Board, *Examination of the Use of Continuum Versus Discontinuum Models for Design and Performance Assessment for the Yucca Mountain Site*, NUREG/CR-5426 (Washington, D.C.: U.S. NRC, Division of Waste Management, Office of Nuclear Material Safety and Safeguards, August 1989); T. Brikowski, *Yucca Mountain Program Summary of Research, Site Monitoring and Technical Review Activities (January 1987–June 1988)* (Carson City: State of Nevada, Agency for Projects/Nuclear Waste Project Office, December 1988); C. Cooper, *Numerical Simulation of Gas Flow*; see GeoTrans Inc., *Review of Modeling Efforts Associated with Yucca Mountain, Nevada*, NWPO-TR-004-87 (Carson City: State of Nevada, Agency for Nuclear Projects/Nuclear Waste Project Office, September 1986), 9.

66. M. Board, *Examination*, 66.

67. See J. Lemons and D. Brown, "The Role of Science in the Decision to Site a High-Level Nuclear Waste Repository at Yucca Mountain, Nevada, USA," *The Environmentalist* 10, no. 1 (1990): 7.

68. T. Brikowski, *Yucca Mountain Program Summary*, 75.

69. GeoTrans Inc., *Review of Modeling Efforts*, 1.

70. See, for example, S. Sinnock and T. Lin, *Preliminary Bounds on the Expected Postclosure Performance of the Yucca Mountain Repository Site, Southern Nevada*, SAND84-1492 (Albuquerque: Sandia National Labs., 1984), 8; Sinnock et al., *Preliminary Estimates of Groundwater Travel Time and Radionuclide Transport at the Yucca Mountain Repository Site*, SAND85-2701 (Albuquerque: Sandia National Labs., 1986), 8; E. Jacobson, *Investigation of Sensitivity and Uncertainty in Some Hydrologic Models of Yucca Mountain and Vicinity*, SAND84-7212 (Albuquerque: Sandia National Labs., 1984), 5; F. Thompson et al., *Preliminary Upper-Bound Consequence Analysis for a Waste Repository at Yucca Mountain, Nevada*, SAND83-7475 (Albuquerque: Sandia National Labs., 1984), iii; N. Hayden, *Benchmarking NNMSI Flow and Transport Codes: Cove 1 Results*, SAND84-0996 (Albuquerque: Sandia National Labs., 1985), 3–1; A. Dudley et al., *Total System Performance Assessment Code (TOSPACO): Vol. 1, Physical and Mathematical Bases: Yucca Mountain Project*, SAND85-0002 UC-70 (Albuquerque: Sandia National Labs., 1988) (Item 182 in US DOE, DE90006793), 36–44; C. Smith et al., *Population Risks*, 39; Y. Lin, *Sparton—A Simple Performance Assessment Code for the Nevada Nuclear Waste Storage Investigations Project*, SAND85-0602 (Albuquerque: Sandia National Labs., 1985), i; see GeoTrans Inc., *Review of Modeling Efforts*, 13, 17.

71. See K. Shrader-Frechette, "Values and Hydrogeological Method: How Not to Site the World's Largest Nuclear Dump," in *Planning for Changing Energy Conditions, Energy Policy Studies*, vol. 4, ed. J. Byrne and D. Rich (New Brunswick, N.J.: Transaction Books, 1988); K. Shrader-Frechette, "Idealized Laws, Antirealism, and Applied Science: A Case in Hydrogeology," *Synthese* 81 (1989): 329–352.

72. See R. Loux, *State of Nevada Comments on the U.S. Department of Energy Site Characterization Plan, Yucca Mountain Site, Nevada* (Carson City: Nevada Agency for Nuclear Projects, 1989), vol. 3: 6.

73. See N. Cartwright, *How the Laws of Physics Lie* (Oxford: Clarendon Press, 1983), 111; Shrader-Frechette, "Values and Hydrogeological Method"; Shrader-Frechette, "Idealized Laws, Antirealism, and Applied Science."

74. See M. Friedman, "The Methodology of Positive Economics," in *The Philosophy of Economics*, ed. D. Hausman (Cambridge: Cambridge University Press, 1984).

75. See A. Berusch and E. Gause, "DOE Progress in Assessing the Long Term Performance of Waste Materials," in *Scientific Basis for Nuclear Waste Management X*, ed. J. Bates and W. Seefeldt (Boston: Materials Research Society, 1987) (Item 190 in US DOE, DE89005394).

76. See, for example, D. Zyvoloski, "Simulation of Heat Transfer in the Unsaturated Zone," in *International Conference for High-Level Radioactive*

Waste Management (Las Vegas: U.S. DOE, 1990) (Item 23 in US DOE, DE91000566); K. Karasaki et al., "Building of a Conceptual Model at UE25-c Hole Complex," in *International Conference for High-Level Radioactive Waste Management* (Las Vegas: U.S. DOE, 1990) (Item 35 in US DOE, DE91000566); T. Wolery et al., "The EQ3/6 Software Package for Geochemical Modeling," in *American Chemical Society National Meeting* (Los Angeles: ACS, 1988) (Item 45 in US DOE, DE91000566); A. Richardson, *Yucca Mountain Project: Preliminary Shaft Liner Design Criteria and Methodology Guide* (Las Vegas: U.S. DOE, 1990) (Item 69 in US DOE, DE91000566); J. Kotcras, *Studies of Computational Models for Jointed Media with Orthogonal Sets of Joints* (Las Vegas: U.S. DOE, 1990) (Item 70 in US DOE, DE91000566); L. Costin, "Application of Models for Jointed Rock to the Analysis of Prototype Testing for the Yucca Mountain Project," in *U.S. Symposium on Rock Mechanics* (Golden, Colo.: U.S. DOE, 1990) (Item 81 in US DOE, DE91000566); R. Glass, "Laboratory Research Program to Aid in Developing and Testing the Validity of Conceptual Models for Flow and Transport through Unsaturated Porous Media," in *GEOVAL '90* (Stockholm: U.S. DOE, 1990) (Item 83 in US DOE, DE91000566).

77. For one such admission, see DOE, NWPA-Hanford, vol. 2: 6–52, 6–69.

78. See, for example, U.S. DOE, *Nuclear Waste Policy Act, Environmental Assessment, Davis Canyon Site, Utah,* 3 vols., DOE/RW-0071 (Washington, D.C.: U.S. DOE, 1986), vol. 2: 6–120; hereafter cited as: DOE, NWPA-Davis.

79. See K. Shrader-Frechette, "Three Arguments Against Simplicity," in *Aesthetic Factors in Natural Science,* ed. N. Rescher (New York: University Press of America, 1990).

80. See, for example, Dudley et al., *Total System Performance.*

81. F. Gelbard et al., "One-Dimensional Radionuclide Transport Under Time-Varying Conditions," in *International Conference for High-Level Radioactive Waste Management* (Las Vegas: U.S. DOE, 1989) (Item 123 in US DOE, DE91000566); see also, for example, B. Sagar and A. Runchal, *A Mathematical Model for Fluid Flow, Heat, and Mass Transport in Variably Saturated Geological Media* (Las Vegas: U.S. DOE, 1990) (Item 131 in US DOE, DE91000566).

82. C. Cooper, *Numerical Simulation of Gas Flow;* Dudley et al., *Total System Performance,* 1; Jacobson, *Investigation of Sensitivity and Uncertainty,* 12; B. Travis et al., *Preliminary Estimates of Water Flow and Radionuclide Transport in Yucca Mountain* (Los Alamos: Los Alamos National Lab, 1984), 3; R. Peters, *The Effect of Percolation Rate on Water Travel Time in Deep, Partially Saturated Zones,* SAND85-0854 (Albuquerque: Sandia National Labs., 1986), i; Sastre et al., *Waste Package Reliability,* 24; Lin, *Sparton—A Simple Performance Assessment Code,* 1; Sinnock et al., *Preliminary Estimates of Groundwater Travel Time,* 66.

83. Sinnock et al., *Preliminary Estimates of Groundwater Travel Time,* 5, 13.

84. L. Mondy et al., *Comparison of Waste Emplacement Configurations for*

a Nuclear Waste Repository in Tuff: IV: Thermo-Hydrological Analysis (Albuquerque: Sandia National Labs., 1983), 6.

85. Sinnock et al., *Preliminary Estimates of Groundwater Travel Time*, 80.

86. GeoTrans, *Review of Modeling Efforts*, esp. 11, 13; Thompson Engineering Company, *Review and Comment on the U.S. Department of Energy Site Characterization Plan Conceptual Design Report*, NWPO-TR-009-88 (Carson City: State of Nevada, Agency for Projects/Nuclear Waste Project Office, October 1988) (Item 329 in US DOE, DE90006793), esp. 1–15.

87. T. Nelson et al., *Yucca Mountain Project Waste Package Design for MRS [Monitored Retrievable Storage] System Studies* (Livermore, Calif.: Lawrence Livermore National Lab., 1989) (Item 132 in US DOE, DE90006793).

88. Smith et al., *Population Risks*, 183.

89. E. Reichard et al., *Groundwater Contamination Risk Assessment* (Oxfordshire, England: International Association of Hydrological Sciences, 1990), 180.

90. Sinnock et al., *Preliminary Estimates of Groundwater Travel Time*, 79.

91. Thompson Engineering Company, *Review and Comment*.

92. N. Goodman, "Safety, Strength, Simplicity," *Philosophy of Science* 28 (1961): 150–151; K. Friedman, "Empirical Simplicity as Testability," *British Journal for the Philosophy of Science* 23 (1972): 25–33; Shrader-Frechette, "Three Arguments Against Simplicity."

93. K. Wilson and B. Lyons, *Ground-Water Levels and Tritium Concentrations at the Maxey-Flats Low-Level Radioactive Waste Disposal Site Near Morehead, Kentucky, June 1984 to April 1989*, Report 90-4189 (Louisville: U.S. Geological Survey, 1991), 20.

94. EMCON Associates and J. McCollough, *Geotechnical Investigation and Waste Management Studies, Nuclear Waste Disposal Site, Fleming County, Kentucky, Project 108–5.2* (Unpublished report, 1975). Available from EMCON, 326 Commercial Street, San Jose, California.

95. D. Polluck and H. Zehner, "A Conceptual Analysis of the Ground-Water Flow System at the Maxey Flats Radioactive Waste Burial Site, Fleming County, Kentucky," U.S. Geological Survey Open-File Report, in *Modeling and Low-Level Waste Management*, ORO-821, ed. C. Little and L. Stratton (Springfield, Va.: National Technical Information Service, U.S. Department of Commerce, 1981); E. Werner, *Joint Intensity Survey in the Morehead Kentucky Area*, unpublished study, Louisville: U.S. Geological Survey, Water Resources Division, 1980.

96. G. Meyer, "Maxey Flats Radioactive Waste Burial Site: Status Report," unpublished report, Advanced Science and Technology Branch, U.S. Environmental Protection Agency, 1975, 9.

97. W. Naedele, "Nuclear Grave Is Haunting Kentucky," *Philadelphia Bulletin*, 17 May 1979, in U.S. Geological Survey, Maxey Flats—Publicity, Vertical File, Louisville, Kentucky Water Resources Division, U.S. Division of the Interior, 1–3; F. Browning, "The Nuclear Wasteland," *New Times* 7 (1976): 43.

98. D. K. Kreamer in Younker, Albrecht, et al., 423.

99. DOE, NWPA-Yucca, vol. 2: 6–162.

100. For tuff sampling, see, for example, C. Voss and L. Shotwell, "An Investigation of the Mechanical and Hydrologic Behavior of Tuff Fractures Under Saturated Conditions," in *International Conference for High-Level Radioactive Waste Management* (Las Vegas: U.S. DOE, 1990) (Item 40 in US DOE, DE91000566); see also R. Peters et al., *Fracture and Matrix Hydrologic Characteristics of Tuffaceous Materials from Yucca Mountain, Nye County, Nevada*, SAND84-1471 (Albuquerque: Sandia National Labs., 1984) (Item D170 in US DOE, NVO-96-24 [REV. 5]). For sampling of properties of glass see, for example, T. Abrajano et al., *The Reaction of Glass During Gamma Irradiation in a Saturated Tuff Environment: Part 3, Long-Term Experiments at 1 × 10⁴ rad/hour* (Argonne, Ill.: Argonne National Lab., 1988) (Item 23 in US DOE, DE89005394).

101. R. Einziger and H. Buchanan, *Long-Term, Low-Temperature Oxidation of PWR Spent Fuel: Interim Transition Report* (Richland, Wash.: Westinghouse Hanford Co., 1988) (Item 26 in US DOE, DE89005394).

102. S. Tyler, "Deep Installations of Monitoring in Unsaturated Welded Tuff," in *International Congress on Hydrology of Rocks of Low Permeability* (Las Vegas: University of Nevada System, 1985) (Item 173 in US DOE, DE89005394); see L. Candy and N. Mao, "Nuclear Waste Repository Characterization: A Spatial Estimation/Identification Approach," in *Eighth Triennial World Congress-International Federation of Automatic Control* (Kyoto, Japan: Lawrence Livermore National Lab., 1981) (Item 105 in US DOE, DE89005394).

103. See, respectively, Y. Chuang et al., *Laboratory Analysis of Fluid Flow and Solute Transport Through a Variably Saturated Fracture Embedded in Porous Tuff* (Washington, D.C.: U.S. NRC, 1990) (Item 120 in US DOE, DE91000566); W. Lin and W. Daily, "Laboratory Study of Fracture Healing in Topopah Spring Tuff," in *Nuclear Waste Isolation in the Unsaturated Zone* (Las Vegas: U.S. DOE, 1989) (Item 47 in US DOE, DE91000566); J. Connolly and F. Nimick, *Mineralogic and Chemical Data Supporting Heat Capacity Determination for Tuffaceous Rocks* (Las Vegas: U.S. DOE, 1990) (Item 66 in US DOE, DE91000566).

104. L. Carter, NIPT, 37.

105. D. Broxton, "Clinoptilolite Compositions in Diagenetically Altered Tuffs at a Potential Nuclear Waste Repository, Yucca Mountain, Nevada," in *Interface Science and Engineering*, ed. P. Hofmann (Columbus: Battelle Memorial Institute, 1987) (Item 90 in US DOE, DE90006793); see W. Linderfelt, *Characterization of Infiltration into Fractured, Welded Tuff Using Small Borehole Data Collection Technique*, NWPO-TR-005-87 (Carson City: State of Nevada, Agency for Nuclear Projects/Nuclear Waste Project Office, October 1986).

106. D. Bish and S. Chipera, *Revised Mineralogic Summary of Yucca Mountain, Nevada* (Los Alamos: Los Alamos National Lab., 1988) (Item 64 in US DOE, DE90006793).

107. S. Knight and K. Thomas, "Sorption of Radionuclides in Tuff Using Groundwaters of Various Compositions," in *194th National Meeting of the*

American Chemical Society (New Orleans: ACS, 1987) (Item 4 in US DOE, DE89005394); K. Thomas, *Summary of Sorption Measurements Performed with Yucca Mountain, Nevada, Tuff Samples and Water from Well J-13* (Los Alamos: Los Alamos National Lab., 1987) (Item 6 in US DOE, DE89005394); R. Beckman et al., *Preliminary Report on the Statistical Evaluation of Sorption Data* (Los Alamos: Los Alamos National Lab., 1988) (Item 7 in US DOE, DE89005394).

108. U.S. NRC, *In the Matter of Proposed Rulemaking on the Storage and Disposal of Nuclear Waste (Waste Confidence Rulemaking)*, PR-50, 51 (44FR61372) (Washington, D.C.: U.S. NRC, 1980), p. B-60.

109. H. Fuentes et al., *Preliminary Report on Sorption Modeling* (Los Alamos: Los Alamos National Lab., 1987) (Item 50 in US DOE, DE890006793).

110. M. Morgenstein, *Physics and Chemistry of the Transition of Glass to Authigenic Minerals: State of Nevada, Agency of Nuclear Projects/Nuclear Waste Project Office* (Carson City: Nevada Nuclear Waste Project Office, 1984) (Item 291 in US DOE, DE90006793); Bechman et al., *Preliminary Report*; D. Bish and S. Chipera, *Revised Mineralogic Summary of Yucca Mountain, Nevada* (Los Alamos: Los Alamos National Lab., 1989) (Item 64 in US DOE, DE90006793); see also D. Finnegan and E. Bryant, *Methods for Obtaining Sorption Data from Uranium-Series Disequilibria* (Los Alamos: Los Alamos National Lab., 1987) (Item 55 in US DOE, DE890006793); K. Campbell, *Statistical Guidelines for Planning a Limited Drilling Program* (Los Alamos: Los Alamos National Lab., 1988) (Item 60 in US DOE, DE90006793).

111. See K. Shrader-Frechette, "Scientific Progress and Models of Justification: A Case in Hydrogeology," in *Science, Technology, and Social Progress*, Research in Technology Studies, vol. 2, ed. S. Goldman (London and Toronto: Associated University Press, 1989).

112. See, for example, A. Meijer et al., "Sorption of Radionuclides on Yucca Mountain Tuffs," in *Nuclear Waste Isolation in the Unsaturated Zone: FOCUS '89* (Los Alamos: Los Alamos National Lab., 1989) (Item 82 in US DOE, DE90006793); J. Thompson, *Laboratory and Field Studies Related to the Radionuclide Migration Project: Progress Report, October 1, 1986–September 30, 1987* (Los Alamos: Los Alamos National Lab., 1988) (Item 358 in US DOE, DE90006793); J. Thompson, "Actinide Behavior on Crushed Rock Columns," *Journal of Radioanalytical and Nuclear Chemistry* 130, no. 2 (April 1989): 353–364 (Item 90 in US DOE, DE90006793); W. Daniels, *Laboratory and Field Studies Related to the Radionuclide Migration Project. Progress Report, October 1, 1980–September 30, 1981* (Los Alamos: Los Alamos National Lab., 1982) (Item 125 in US DOE, DE89005394); C. Duffy and S. Al-Hassan, "Time and Frequency Domain Analysis of Tracer Migration in Crushed Tuff," in *Workshop on Modeling of Solute Transport in the Unsaturated Zone* (Los Alamos: Utah State University, 1987) (Item 211 in US DOE, DE89005394); R. Rundberg et al., "Observation of Time Dependent Dispersion in Laboratory Scale Experiments with Intact Tuff," in *Second International Conference on Chemistry and Migration Behavior of Actinides*

and Fission Products in the Geosphere (Monterey: U.S. DOE, 1989) (Item 19 in US DOE, DE91000566).

113. See U.S. Congress, *Nuclear,* 204.

114. A. Kelmers et al., "Evaluation of DOE Radionuclide Solubility Data and Selected Retardation Parameters: Description of Calculational and Confirmatory Experimental Activities," in *NRC Research Annual Review Meeting of Nuclear Waste Management Research on Geochemistry of HLW Disposal* (Tallahassee: Oak Ridge National Lab., 1983) (Item 139 in US DOE, DE89005394).

115. U.S. DOE, "Project History," in *Yucca Mountain Project Bibliography, 1988–1989.*

116. A. Norris et al., "Infiltration at Yucca Mountain, Nevada, Traced by ^{36}Cl," *Nuclear Instruments and Methods in Physics Research, Section B: Beam Interactions with Materials and Atoms (Netherlands)* 29, no. 1/2 (November 1987): 376–379 (Item 92 in US DOE, DE90006793).

117. GeoTrans, *Review of Modeling Efforts,* 1.

118. H. Zehner, *Hydrologic Investigation of the Maxey Flats Radioactive Waste Burial Site, Fleming County, Kentucky,* Open-File Report (Louisville: U.S. Geological Survey, 1981), 110.

119. Carter, NIPT, 38.

120. H. Fuentes et al., "Solute Leaching from Resin/Tuff Media in Unsaturated Flow," *Radioactive Waste Management* 10, no. 4 (June 1988): 285–320 (Item 10 in US DOE, DE89005394); see Rundberg et al., "Observation of Time Dependent Dispersion"; V. Oversby and R. McCright, "Laboratory Experiments Designed to Provide Limits on the Radionuclide Source Term for the NNWSI Project," in *Workshop on the Source Term for Radionuclide Migration from HLW or Spent Nuclear Fuel* (Albuquerque: Lawrence Livermore National Lab., 1985) (Item 122 in US DOE, DE88004834).

121. See, for example, E. Weeks and W. Wilson, *Preliminary Evaluation of Hydrologic Properties of Cores of Unsaturated Tuff, Test Well USW H-1, Yucca Mountain, Nevada,* Report 84-4193 (Denver: U.S. Geological Survey, 1984) (Item E111 in US DOE, NVO-96-24 [REV. 5]).

122. See R. Loux, *State of Nevada Comments on the U.S. Department of Energy Consultation Draft Site Characterization Plan, Yucca Mountain Site, Nevada Research and Development Area, Nevada,* 2 vols. (Carson City: State of Nevada, Agency for Nuclear Projects/Nuclear Waste Project Office, 1988), vol. 1: I-9, I-10, II-2, II-3.

123. U.S. DOE, "Project History," in *Yucca Mountain Project Bibliography, 1988–1989.*

124. See, for example, F. Heuze, "Geomechanics in Hard Rock Mining-Lessons from Two Case Histories," *Preprint, Society of Mining Engineers of AIME* 82-364 (September 1982): 14 (Item 134 in US DOE, DE89005394).

125. Roxburgh, *Geology,* 181.

126. Roxburgh, *Geology,* 181.

127. R. Peters et al., *Fracture and Matrix Hydrologic Characteristics of Tuffaceous Materials from Yucca Mountain, Nye County, Nevada,* SAND84-

1471 (Albuquerque: Sandia National Labs., 1984) (Item D170 in US DOE, NVO-96-24 [REV. 5]), i.

128. D. Evans et al., "Fracture System Characterization for Unsaturated Rock," in *Waste Management '87: Waste Isolation in the U.S., Technical Programs, and Public Education,* ed. R. Post (Tucson: University of Arizona Nuclear Engineering Dept., 1987) (Item 196 in US DOE, DE89005394).

129. W. Daily and A. Ramirez, "Geophysical Tomography for Imaging Water Movement in Welded Tuff," in *Second International Congress on Nuclear Waste Management* (Livermore, Calif.: Lawrence Livermore National Lab., 1986) (Item 142 in US DOE, DE90006793); K. Pruess and T. Narasimhan, "Numerical Modeling of Multiphase and Nonisothermal Flow in Fractured Media," in *International Conference on Fluid Flow in Fractured Rocks* (Atlanta: Lawrence Berkeley Lab., 1988) (Item 43 in US DOE, DE89005394); see E. Majer et al., "VSP [Vertical Seismic Profiling] and Cross Hole Tomographic Imaging for Fracture Characterization," in *Nuclear Waste Isolation in the Unsaturated Zone: FOCUS '89* (Livermore, Calif.: Lawrence Berkeley Lab., 1989) (Item 108 in US DOE, DE90006793).

130. E. Klavetter et al., *Experimental Plan for Investigating Water Movement Through Fractures: Yucca Mountain Project* (Albuquerque: Sandia National Labs., 1989) (Item 172 in US DOE, DE90006793).

131. Nevada NWPO, *State of Nevada Comments on the U.S. Department of Energy Consultation Draft Site Characterization Plan, Yucca Mountain Site, Nevada: Vol. 1* (Carson City: U.S. DOE, 1989) (Item 335 in US DOE, DE90006793); C. Malone, "The Yucca Mountain Project," *Environ. Sci. Technol.* 23, no. 12 (1989): 1453; Loux, *State of Nevada Comments,* vol. 3: 6.

132. See Karasaki et al. "Building of a Conceptual Model"; J. Yow, "Block Analysis for Preliminary Design of Underground Excavations," in *U.S. Symposium on Rock Mechanics* (Golden, Colo.: U.S. DOE, 1990) (Item 55 in US DOE, DE91000566); Costin, "Application of Models for Jointed Rock"; J. Tillerson et al., "Uncertainties in Sealing a Nuclear Waste Repository in Partially Saturated Tuff," in *Proceedings of an NEA/CEC Workshop* (Paris: OECD, 1989) (Item 88 in US DOE, DE91000566); R. Zimmerman and G. Bodvarsson, "Combined Analytical/Numerical Approaches to Solving Fluid Flow Problems in the Unsaturated Zone at Yucca Mountain," in *International Conference for High-Level Radioactive Waste Management* (Las Vegas: U.S. DOE, 1990) (Item 90 in US DOE, DE91000566); K. Lee et al., "Application of Geophysical Methods for Fracture Characterization," in *International Conference for High-Level Radioactive Waste Management* (Las Vegas: U.S. DOE, 1990) (Item 114 in US DOE, DE91000566); L. Pyrak-Nolte and N. Cook, "A Stratified Percolation Model for Saturated and Unsaturated Flow through Natural Fractures," in *International Conference for High-Level Radioactive Waste Management* (Las Vegas: U.S. DOE, 1990) (Item 115 in US DOE, DE91000566).

133. L. Greenwade and G. Cederberg, "Preliminary Geochemical/Geophysical Model of Yucca Mountain," in *Symposium on the Scientific Basis for Nuclear Waste Management* (Los Alamos: Los Alamos National Lab., 1987) (Item 74 in US DOE, DE90006793).

134. See, for example, T. Buscheck and J. Nitao, *Preliminary Scoping Calculations of Hydrothermal Flow in Variably Saturated Sign Test at the Yucca Mountain Exploratory Shaft Test Site* (Livermore, Calif.: Lawrence Livermore National Lab., 1988) (Item 130 in US DOE, DE90006793); K. Erickson et al., "Approximate Methods to Calculate Radionuclide Discharges for Performance Assessment of HLW Repositories in Fractured Rock," in *Waste Management '86. Volume 2: High-Level Waste*, ed. R. Post (Albuquerque: Sandia National Labs., 1986) (Item 175 in US DOE, DE89005394); see J. Cuderman, *Design and Modeling of Small Scale Multiple Fracturing Experiments* (Albuquerque: Sandia National Labs., 1981) (Item 121 in US DOE, DE89005394); for use of single flow equations see, for example, R. Peters and E. Klavetter, "Continuum Model for Water Movement in an Unsaturated Fractured Rock Mass," *Water Resources Research* 24, no. 3 (March 1988): 416–430 (Item 38 in US DOE, DE89005394).

135. See, for example, A. Ramirez and W. Daily, "Electromagnetic Experiment to Map In Situ Water in Heated Welded Tuff: Preliminary Results," in *Rock Mechanics: Proceedings of the 28th U.S. Symposium on Rock Mechanics* (Tucson: A. A. Balkema Publishers, 1987) (Item 154 in US DOE, DE90006793).

136. U.S. DOE, "Project History," in *Yucca Mountain Project Bibliography, 1988–1989*, xiii; see Norris et al., "Infiltration at Yucca Mountain."

137. Sinnock and Lin, *Preliminary Bounds*, 14–15.

138. Linderfelt, *Characterization of Infiltration*.

139. Sinnock and Lin, *Preliminary Bounds*, 17.

140. Sinnock and Lin, *Preliminary Bounds*, 24.

141. Sinnock and Lin, *Preliminary Bounds*, 16, 41.

142. Peters, *The Effect of Percolation Rate*, i; Travis et al., *Preliminary Estimates of Water Flow*, 4.

143. K. Pruess et al., *Effective Continuum Approximation for Modeling Fluid and Heat Flow in Fractured Porous Tuff: Nevada Nuclear Waste Storage Investigations Project* (Livermore, Calif.: Lawrence Berkeley Lab., 1988) (Item 42 in US DOE, DE89005394).

144. Evans et al., "Fracture System Characterization for Unsaturated Rock"; J. Rulon et al., *Preliminary Numerical Simulations of Groundwater Flow in the Unsaturated Zone, Yucca Mountain, Nevada* (Berkeley, Calif.: Lawrence Berkeley Lab., 1986) (Item 181 in US DOE, DE89005394); see T. Rasmussen and D. Evans, *Unsaturated Flow and Transport Through Fractured Rock Related to High-Level Waste Repositories: Final Report, Phase 2* (Tucson: Arizona University Department of Hydrology and Water Resources, 1987) (Item 216 in US DOE, DE89005394); Thompson, *Laboratory and Field Studies Related to the Radionuclide Migration Project: Project Report, October 1, 1985–September 30, 1986*.

145. Thompson Engineering Company, *Review and Comment*, 13.

146. See J. L. Younker, W. B. Andrews, G. A. Fasano, C. C. Herrington, S. R. Mattson, R. C. Murray, L. B. Ballou, M. A. Revelli, A. R. Ducharme, L. E. Shepard, W. W. Dudley, D. T. Hoxie, R. J. Herbst, E. A. Patera, B. R. Judd, J. A. Docka, and L. R. Rickertsen, *Report of the Early Site Suitabil-*

ity Evaluation of the Potential Repository Site at Yucca Mountain, Nevada, SAIC-91/8000 (Washington D.C.: U.S. DOE, 1992), 214, 2–13; hereafter cited as: Younker, Andrews, et al.

147. Younker, Albrecht, et al., 181, 240, 427–430, 472, 506.

148. Pruess and Narasimhan, "Numerical Modeling."

149. R. Blanchard et al., *Supplementary Radiological Measurements at the Maxey Flats Radioactive Waste Burial Site—1976–1977,* EPA-520/5-78-011 (Montgomery: U.S. EPA, 1978), 1, 29; see K. Shrader-Frechette, "Models, Scientific Method, and Environmental Ethics," in *Upstream/Downstream,* ed. D. Scherer (Philadelphia: Temple University Press, 1990).

150. Sinnock and Lin, *Preliminary Bounds,* 16, 41.

151. C. Malone, "Geologic and Hydrologic Issues Related to Siting a Repository for High-Level Nuclear Waste at Yucca Mountain, Nevada, USA," *Journal of Environmental Management* 30 (1990): 381–396. J. Raloff, "Fall-out Over Nevada's Nuclear Destiny," *Science News* 137, no. 1 (16 January 1990): 11–12.

152. J. Neel, "Statement," in *Low-Level Radioactive Waste Disposal,* Hearings before a Subcommittee of the Committee on Government Operations, House of Representatives, 94th Congress, Second Session, 23 February, 12 March, and 6 April 1976 (Washington, D.C.: U.S. Government Printing Office, 1976), 258; see also A. Weiss and P. Columbo, *Evaluation of Isotope Migration—Land Burial,* NUREG/CR-1289 BNL-NUREG-51143 (Washington D.C.: U.S. NRC, 1980), 5; Meyer, "Maxey Flats Radioactive Waste Burial Site: Status Report," 9.

153. Neel, "Statement," 258; EMCON, *Geotechnical Investigation and Waste Management Studies.*

154. Zehner, *Hydrologic Investigation,* 35, 40; Werner, *Joint Intensity Survey,* 45; see Wilson and Lyons, *Ground-Water Levels and Tritium Concentrations;* Shrader-Frechette "Values and Hydrogeological Method"; Shrader-Frechette, "Idealized Laws, Antirealism, and Applied Science"; Shrader-Frechette, "Models, Scientific Method, and Environmental Ethics."

155. Zehner, *Hydrologic Investigation,* 3.

156. Zehner, *Hydrologic Investigation,* 132.

157. Zehner, *Hydrologic Investigation,* 134.

158. Loux, *State of Nevada Comments,* vol. 2: 2.

159. See R. Williams, *A Technique for the Geothermic Modeling of Underground Surfaces: Nevada Nuclear Waste Storage Investigations Project* (Albuquerque: Sandia National Labs., 1988) (Item 171 in US DOE, DE90006793); K. Campbell, *Kriging for Interpolation of Sparse and Irregularly Distributed Geologic Data* (Los Alamos: Los Alamos National Lab., 1986) (Item 73 in US DOE, DE90006793).

160. Norris et al., "Infiltration at Yucca Mountain."

161. W. Glassley, "Evaluation of the Postimplacement Environment of High Level Radioactive Waste Packages at Yucca Mountain, Nevada," in *Waste Management '89* (Livermore, Calif.: Lawrence Livermore National Lab., 1989) (Item 150 in US DOE, DE90006793); see R. Aines, "Estimates

of Radionuclide Release from Glass Waste Forms in a Tuff Repository and the Effects on Regulatory Compliance," in *Nuclear Waste Management II*, ed. W. Passchier and B. Bosnjakovik (Westerville, Okla.: American Ceramic Society Inc., 1986) (Item 155 in US DOE, DE90006793).

162. Nevada NWPO, *State of Nevada Comments*, vol. 1.

163. U.S. DOE, *Yucca Mountain Project Bibliography, 1988–1989*, 3–18.

164. DOE, NWPA-Yucca, vol. 1: 1–5.

165. U.S. DOE, *Yucca Mountain Project Bibliography, 1988–1989*.

166. Younkers, Andrews, et al., 3–46.

167. Thompson et al., *Preliminary Upper-Bound Consequence Analysis*, i.

168. Thompson et al., *Preliminary Upper-Bound Consequence Analysis*, i.

169. Thompson et al., *Preliminary Upper-Bound Consequence Analysis*, vi–vii.

170. Smith et al., *Population Risks*, 222.

171. U.S. Congress, *Nuclear Waste Program*, 195.

172. See note 2, chap. 1.

173. U.S. EPA, *Draft Environmental Impact Statement, 40 CFR, Part 191, Environmental Standards for Management and Disposal of Spent Nuclear Fuel, High Level, and Transuranic Radioactive Wastes* (Washington, D.C.: U.S. EPA, 1982), 54,57; hereafter cited as: EPA, EIS.

174. EPA, EIS, 109.

175. R. Goble et al., *Potential Retrieval of Radioactive Wastes at the Proposed Yucca Mountain Repository: A Preliminary Review of Risk Issues*, NWPO-SE-010-88 (Carson City: State of Nevada, Agency for Nuclear Projects/Nuclear Waste Project Office, June 1988), 40.

176. J. Emel et al., *Yucca Mountain Socioeconomic Project*, #RA001–RA005 (Las Vegas: Coopers and Lybrand, 1987), 44; D. Golding and A. White, *Guidelines on the Scope, Content, and Use of Comprehensive Risk Assessment in the Management of High-Level Nuclear Waste Transportation*, NWPO-TN-007-90 (Carson City: State of Nevada, Agency for Projects/Nuclear Waste Project Office, December 1990), 5.

177. Golding and White, *Guidelines*, 5–8; see also S. Tuler et al., *The Effects of Human Reliability in the Transportation of Spent Nuclear Fuel*, NWPO-SE-007-88 (Carson City: State of Nevada, Agency for Nuclear Projects/Nuclear Waste Project Office, June 1988) (Item 305 in US DOE, DE90006793), 91.

178. Emel et al., *Yucca Mountain Socioeconomic Project*, 108, 110; J. Emel et al., *Risk Management and Organizational Systems for High-Level Radioactive Waste Disposal: Issues and Priorities*, NWPO-SE-008-88 (Carson City: State of Nevada, Agency for Projects/Nuclear Waste Project Office, September 1988), 9; Golding and White, *Guidelines*, 2, 28; W. Burns et al., *Social Amplification of Risk: An Empirical Study*, NWPO-SE-027-90 (Carson City: State of Nevada, Agency for Projects/Nuclear Waste Project Office, September 1990), ii; Tuler et al., *The Effects of Human Reliability*; see also J. Petterson, *Goiania Incident Case Study*, NWPO-SE-015-88 (Carson City: State of Nevada, Agency for Nuclear Projects/Nuclear Waste Project Office,

June 1988); H. Peters and L. Hennen, *The Accident at Gorleben: A Case Study of Risk Communication and Risk Amplification in the Federal Republic of Germany*, NWPO-SE-012-88 (Carson City: State of Nevada, Agency for Nuclear Projects/Nuclear Waste Project Office, July 1988). For discussion of the social amplification of risk see, for example, J. F. Short, "On Defining, and Explaining Elephants (and Reactions to Them): Hazards, Disasters, and Risk Analysis," *International Journal of Mass Emergencies and Disasters* 7, no. 3 (November 1989): 397–418; J. F. Short, "Hazards, Risks, and Enterprise," *Law and Society Review* 24, no. 1 (1990): 179–198; W. Freudenburg, "Nothing Recedes Like Success? Risk Analysis and the Organizational Amplification of Risks," *Risk: Issues in Health and Safety* 3 (1992): 1–35.

179. M. Lyverse, *Records of Wells for the Period June 13, 1984 to December 4, 1986 at the Maxey Flats Radioactive Waste Disposal Site*, Report 87-214 (Louisville: U.S. Geological Survey, 1987), 15–16.

180. See note 170 above and R. Lipschutz, *Radioactive Waste* (Cambridge: Ballinger, 1980), 157ff.

181. U.S. Congress, *Safety of DOE Nuclear Facilities*, Hearing before the Subcommittee on Energy and Power of the Committee on Energy and Commerce, House of Representatives, 101st Congress, First Session, 22 February 1989, Serial no. 101-1 (Washington D.C.: U.S. Government Printing Office, 1989); U.S. Congress, *DOE: Pollution at Fernald, Ohio*, Hearing before the Subcommittee on Transportation, Tourism, and Hazardous Materials of the Committee on Energy and Commerce, House of Representatives, 100th Congress, Second Session on H.R. 3783, H.R. 3784, and H.R. 3785, 14 October 1988, Serial no. 100-236 (Washington, D.C.: U.S. Government Printing Office, 1989).

182. U.S. Congress, *DOE Nuclear Facility at Fernald, OH*, Hearing before the Subcommittee on Energy Conservation and Power of the Committee on Energy and Commerce, House of Representatives, 99th Congress, Second Session, 13 August 1986, Serial no. 99-163 (Washington, D.C.: U.S. Government Printing Office, 1987), 2ff., 9ff. See note 12, chap. 1, for further information on DOE violations. See also DOE, NWPA-Yucca, vol. 3: C.2–6 through C.3–23 and DOE, NWPA-Hanford, C.2–9 through C.8–21.

183. H. Reid, U.S. Senator from Nevada, "Statement," in *Nuclear Waste Policy Act*, Hearing before the Subcommittee on Energy and the Environment of the Committee on Interior and Insular Affairs, House of Representatives, 100th Congress, 18 September 1987 (Washington, D.C.: U.S. Government Printing Office, 1988), 46; hereafter. cited as: NWPA-88. See the discussion and notes in chapter 1 for additional information and references.

184. U.S. Congress, *Safety of DOE Nuclear Facilities*, 36.

185. Rep. P. Sharp, "Statement," NWPA-88, 3; A. Bringloe, "Statement," in U.S. Congress, *High-Level Nuclear Waste Issues*, Hearings before the Subcommittee on Nuclear Regulation of the Committee on Environment and Public Works, U.S. Senate, 100th Congress, 23 April, 2, 3, 18 June 1987 (Washington, D.C.: U.S. Government Printing Office, 1987), 237; hereafter cited as: HLNWI.

186. C. Fultz, "Statement," in U.S. Congress, *Safety of DOE Nuclear*

Facilities, 36, 41–45; U.S. Congress, *DOE: Pollution at Fernald, Ohio*; Emel et al., *Risk Management and Organizational Systems,* 68–74.

187. U.S. Congress, *DOE Nuclear Facility at Fernald, OH,* 143–146.

188. U.S. Congress, *DOE: Pollution at Fernald, Ohio,* 27–28, 52. See also U.S. Congress, NWPA–88, 211ff., 393ff.

189. U.S. Congress, *DOE Nuclear Facility at Fernald, Ohio,* 54.

190. U.S. Congress, *DOE: Pollution at Fernald, Ohio,* 67.

191. U.S. Congress, *DOE: Pollution at Fernald, Ohio,* 134.

192. Shrader-Frechette, "Values and Hydrogeological Method," 127.

193. W. Carey et al., *Hillslope Erosion at the Maxey Flats, Radioactive Waste Disposal Site,* Report 89–4199 (Louisville: U.S. Geological Survey, 1990), 1.

194. GeoTrans, *Review of Modeling Efforts,* 1.

195. See, for example, C. Malone, "Environmental Performance Assessment: A Case Study of an Emerging Methodology," *J. Environmental Systems* 19, no. 2 (1990): 171.

196. J. Lemons et al., "America's High-Level Nuclear Waste Repository: A Case Study of Environmental Science and Public Policy," *Intern. J. Environmental Studies* 34 (1989): 31; M. Winsor and C. Malone, "State of Nevada Perspective on Environmental Program Planning for the Yucca Mountain Project," *The Environmental Professional* 12 (1990): 197, 205; Golding and White, *Guidelines.*

197. U.S. Congress, *Nuclear Waste Program,* 271.

198. U.S. Congress, *Mission Plan for the Civilian Radioactive Waste Management Program,* Hearing before the Subcommittee on Energy Research and Development of the Committee on Energy and Natural Resources, U.S. Senate, 99th Congress, First Session on the Department on Energy's Mission Plan for the Civilian Radioactive Waste Management Program, 12 September 1985 (Washington, D.C.: U.S. Government Printing Office, 1986), 325; U.S. Congress, *Nuclear Waste Program,* 245.

199. U.S. Congress, *Mission Plan,* 625.

200. U.S. Congress, *Mission Plan,* 736. See notes 174, 177 in this chapter.

201. U.S. Congress, *Nuclear Waste Program,* 70ff., 216.

202. U.S. Congress, *Nuclear Waste Program,* 726.

203. U.S. Congress, *Nuclear Waste Program,* 923.

Notes to Chapter Five

1. For discussion of the Ford-Mitre and UCS studies see K. Shrader-Frechette, *Risk and Rationality* (Berkeley, Los Angeles, London: University of California Press, 1991), 100–101; hereafter cited as: Risk.

2. J. King, "Approach to Developing a Ground-Motion Design Basis for Facilities Important to Safety at Yucca Mountain," in *International Confer-*

ence for High-Level Radioactive Waste Management (Las Vegas: U.S. DOE, 1990) (Item 4 in US DOE, DE91000566).

3. U.S. DOE, "NNWSI History," in *Bibliography of the Published Reports, Papers, and Articles on the Nevada Nuclear Waste Storage Investigations, January 1985,* NVO-96-24 (Rev. 5) (Las Vegas: U.S. DOE, Nevada Operations Office, 1985), 1–30.

4. J. King et al., "Assessment of Seismic Hazards at Yucca Mountain," in *American Nuclear Society Annual Meeting* (Las Vegas: Science Applications International Corp., 1988) (Item 1 in US DOE, DE90006793).

5. B. Crowe, *Volcanic Hazard Assessment for Disposal of High-Level Radioactive Waste* (Los Alamos: Los Alamos National Lab., 1986) (Item 61 in US DOE, DE88004834).

6. L. Metcalf, *Preliminary Review and Summary of the Potential for Tectonic, Seismic, and Volcanic Activity at the Nevada Test Site Defense Waste Disposal Site* (Reno: Desert Research Institute, 1983) (Item 142 in US DOE, DE89005394).

7. J. Emel et al., *Postclosure Risks at the Proposed Yucca Mountain Repository: A Review of Methodological and Technical Issues,* NWPO-SE-011-88 (Carson City: State of Nevada, Agency for Nuclear Projects/Nuclear Waste Project Office, June 1988), 10.

8. E. Smith et al., *Regional Importance of Post-6 M. Y. Old Volcanism in the Southern Great Basin: Implications for Risk Assessment of Volcanism at the Proposed Nuclear Waste Repository at Yucca Mountain, Nevada,* Report no. 10, Annual Report for the Period 7/1/87 to 6/30/88. Submitted to the Nuclear Waste Project Office (Las Vegas: Center for Volcanic and Tectonic Studies, Department of Geoscience, University of Nevada, September 1988), 1–37.

9. L. Jardine et al., "Preliminary Preclosure Safety Analysis for a Prospective Yucca Mountain Repository," in *Waste Management '87: Waste Isolation in the U.S., Technical Programs, and Public Education,* ed. R. Post, (Tucson: University of Arizona Nuclear Engineering Dept., 1987) (Item 249 in US DOE, DE90006793).

10. Emel et al., *Postclosure Risks,* 40–41; J. Emel et al., *Nuclear Waste Management: A Comparative Analysis of Six Countries,* NWPO-SE-034-90 (Carson City: State of Nevada, Agency for Projects/Nuclear Waste Project Office, November 1990), 4–5.

11. Emel et al., *Nuclear Waste Management,* 5–10.

12. W. Williams, *Population Risks from Uranium Ore Bodies,* EPA 520/3-80-009 (Washington, D.C.: U.S. EPA, 1980), 1–23.

13. W. Carey et al., *Hillslope Erosion at the Maxey Flats, Radioactive Waste Disposal Site,* Report 89-4199 (Louisville: U.S. Geological Survey, 1990), 34.

14. L. Cox and P. Ricci, "Risk, Uncertainty, and Causation," in *The Risk Assessment of Environmental and Human Health Hazards,* ed. D. Paustenbach (New York: John Wiley, 1989), 1026.

15. U.S. ERDA (Energy Research and Development Administration), *Final Environmental Statement: Waste Management Operations, Hanford Reservation, Richland, Washington,* 2 vols. (ERDA-1538) (Springfield, Va.:

National Technical Information Service, October 1975), vol. 1, p. X-74; see K. Shrader-Frechette, *Nuclear Power and Public Policy* (Boston: Reidel, 1983), chap. 2.

16. U.S. AEC (Atomic Energy Commission), *Comparative Risk-Cost-Benefit Study of Alternative Sources of Electrical Energy* (WASH-1224) (Washington, D.C.: U.S. Government Printing Office, December 1974), 3–83.

17. See J. Tillerson et al., "Uncertainties in Sealing a Nuclear Waste Repository in Partially Saturated Tuff," in *Proceedings of an NEA/CEC Workshop* (Paris: OECD, 1989) (Item 88 in US DOE, DE91000566).

18. See J. Lemons and D. Brown, "The Role of Science in the Decision to Site a High-Level Nuclear Waste Repository at Yucca Mountain, Nevada, USA," *The Environmentalist* 10, no. 1 (1990): 7.

19. U.S. DOE, Office of Civilian Radioactive Waste Management, *Yucca Mountain Project Bibliography, 1988–1989*, DOE/OSTI-3406 (Suppl.2) (DE90006793) (Oak Ridge: U.S. DOE, November 1990), 3–13.

20. U.S. DOE, Office of Civilian Radioactive Waste Management, *Yucca Mountain Project*, 3–8 and 3–9.

21. R. Peters et al., *Fracture and Matrix Hydrologic Characteristics of Tuffaceous Materials from Yucca Mountain, Nye County, Nevada*, SAND84-1471 (Albuquerque: Sandia National Laboratories, 1984) (Item D170 in US DOE, NVO-96-24 [REV. 5]), i.

22. M. Cloninger et al., "Waste Package for Yucca Mountain Repository: Strategy for Regulatory Compliance," in *Waste Management '89* (Livermore, Calif.: Lawrence Livermore National Lab., 1989) (Item 149 in US DOE, DE90006793).

23. J. King et al., *Assessment of Faulting and Seismic Hazards at Yucca Mountain* (Las Vegas: Science Applications International Corp., 1989) (Item 15 in US DOE, DE90006793).

24. See note 14, this chapter.

25. U.S. DOE, *Nuclear Waste Policy Act, Environmental Assessment, Yucca Mountain Site, Nevada Research and Development Area, Nevada*, DOE/RW-0073, 3 vols. (Washington, D.C.: U.S. DOE, (1986), vol. 3, pp. C-54 and C-55; hereafter cited as: DOE, NWPA-Yucca.

26. See C. Smith et al., *Population Risks from Disposal of High-Level Radioactive Wastes in Geologic Repositories*, EPA-520/3-80-006 (Washington, D.C.: U.S. EPA, 1982); A. Dudley et al., *Total System Performance Assessment Code (TOSPAC): Vol. 1, Physical and Mathematical Bases: Yucca Mountain Project*, SAND85-0002 UC-70 (Albuquerque: Sandia National Labs., 1988) (Item 182 in US DOE, DE90006793), 118.

27. J. Jackson et al., "Safety Assessment of Accident Radiological Releases: A Study Performed for the Conceptual Design of a Geologic Repository at Yucca Mountain, Nevada," *Nuclear Safety* 26, no. 4 (July–August 1985): 477–487 (Item 237 in US DOE, DE88004834). Regarding fracture flow, see for example, M. Wilson and A. Dudley, "Radionuclide Transport in an Unsaturated, Fractured Medium," in *American Geophysical Union Fall Meeting* (San Francisco: Spectra Research Institute, 1986) (Item 253 in US DOE, DE88004834); S. Sinnock and T. Lin, *Preliminary Bounds on the Expected*

Postclosure Performance of the Yucca Mountain Repository Site, Southern Nevada, SAND84-1492 (Albuquerque: Sandia National Labs., 1984), 16. See R. Loux, *State of Nevada Comments on the U.S. Department of Energy Consultation Draft Site Characterization Plan, Yucca Mountain Site, Nevada Research and Development Area, Nevada*. 2 vols. (Carson City: State of Nevada, Agency for Nuclear Projects/Nuclear Waste Project Office, 1988), vol. 1: I-10, II-2, and II-3.

28. NRC Staff Comments, in U.S. Congress, *Nuclear Waste Program*, Hearings before the Committee on Energy and Natural Resources, U.S. Senate, 100th Congress, First Session on the Current Status of the Department of Energy's Civilian Nuclear Waste Activities, 29 January, 4 and 5 February 1987, part 1 (Washington, D.C.: U.S. Government Printing Office, 1987), 199; see also 712; hereafter cited as: U.S. Congress, *Nuclear Waste Program*.

29. Regarding the weapons-testing case, see DOE, NWPA-Yucca, vol. 2: 6–47. Regarding DOE avoidance of worst-case analysis at Hanford, see U.S. DOE, *Nuclear Waste Policy Act*, Environmental Assessment, Reference Repository Location, Hanford Site, Washington, 3 vols., DOE/RW-0070 (Washington, D.C.: U.S. DOE, 1986), vol. 3, pp. C.4–15 and vol. 3, pp. C.8–21; hereafter cited as: DOE, NWPA-Hanford. R. Goble et al., *Potential Retrieval of Radioactive Wastes at the Proposed Yucca Mountain Repository: A Preliminary Review of Risk Issues*, NWPO-SE-010-88 (Carson City: State of Nevada, Agency for Nuclear Projects/Nuclear Waste Project Office, June, 1988), 31.

30. See Loux, *State of Nevada Comments*, I-7, II-1.

31. Goble et al., *Potential Retrieval of Radioactive Wastes*, 40.

32. K. Wilson and B. Lyons, *Ground-Water Levels and Tritium Concentrations at the Maxey-Flats Low-Level Radioactive Waste Disposal Site Near Morehead, Kentucky, June 1984 to April 1989*, Report 90–4189 (Louisville: U.S. Geological Survey, 1991), 47.

33. See P. O'Brien, *Technical Support for High-Level Radioactive Waste Management, Task C Report: Assessment of Migration Pathways*, EPA 520/4-79-007C (Washington, D.C.: U.S. EPA, 1977).

34. Shrader-Frechette, *Risk*, chap. 8.

35. O'Brien, *Technical Support*, 106–169.

36. G. Sawyer et al., *Report of the Nevada Commission on Nuclear Projects* (Carson City: Nevada Commission on Nuclear Projects, 1990), 47. See also D. G. Schweitzer and C. Sastre, *Assumptions, Uncertainties, and Limitations in the Predictive Capabilities of Models for Sensitization in 304 Stainless Steels* (Upton, N.Y.: Brookhaven National Lab., 1987).

37. S. Pitman et al., "Corrosion and Slow-Strain-Rate Testing of Type 304L Stainless in Tuff Groundwater Environments," in *Corrosion '87* (San Francisco: Pacific Northwest Lab., 1986) (Item 172 in US DOE, DE88004834).

38. B. Rusche, "Statement," in U.S. Congress, *Nuclear Waste Program*, 906–907.

39. See Shrader-Frechette, *Risk*, chap. 9.

40. Shrader-Frechette, *Risk*, chap. 9.

41. E. Reichard et al., *Groundwater Contamination Risk Assessment* (Oxfordshire, England: International Association of Hydrological Sciences, 1990), 144, 160.

42. E. Jacobson, *Investigation of Sensitivity and Uncertainty in Some Hydrologic Models of Yucca Mountain and Vicinity*, SAND84-7212 (Albuquerque: Sandia National Labs., 1985), 90. For evidence of DOE acceptance of such *average* values, see DOE, NWPA-Yucca, vol. 2: 6–162ff.

43. S. Sinnock et al., *Preliminary Estimates of Groundwater Travel Time and Radionuclide Transport at the Yucca Mountain Repository Site*, SAND85-2701 (Albuquerque: Sandia National Labs., 1986), i.

44. Sinnock et al., *Preliminary Estimates*, i.

45. R. Bryan, *State of Nevada Comments on the U.S. Department of Energy Draft Environmental Assessment for the Proposed High-Level Nuclear Waste Site at Yucca Mountain.* 2 vols. (Carson City: Nuclear Waste Project Office, Office of the Governor, 1985), vol. 1: I-43; R. Peters, *The Effect of Percolation Rate on Water Travel Time in Deep, Partially Saturated Zones*, SAND85-0854 (Albuquerque: Sandia National Labs., 1986), 32; see G. Sawyer, "Statement," in U.S. Congress, *Nuclear Waste Program*, 709–712.

46. See Shrader-Frechette, *Nuclear Power and Public Policy*, 148ff.; K. Shrader-Frechette, *Risk Analysis*, 144, 174. For problems with using averages in QRA, see R. Cooke, *The European Communities' Expert Judgment Study* (Delft, The Netherlands: University of Technology, 1991), 8ff.; hereafter cited as: Cooke, *European*.

47. R. Peters et al., *Fracture and Matrix Hydrologic Characteristics of Tuffaceous Materials from Yucca Mountain, Nye County, Nevada*, SAND84-1471 (Albuquerque: Sandia National Labs., 1984) (Item D170 in US DOE, NVO-96-24 [REV. 5]), i.

48. Sinnock and Lin, *Preliminary Bounds*, 8–11.

49. Smith et al., *Population Risks*, 49.

50. Dudley et al., *Total System Performance Assessment Code*, 72.

51. Sinnock and Lin, *Preliminary Bounds*, 41.

52. Carey et al., *Hillslope Erosion*, 1, 34.

53. B. Carpenter, "A Nuclear Graveyard," *U.S. News and World Report* 110, no. 10 (March 1991): 74.

54. See note 17, chap. 1.

55. For discussion of expert judgment and the Kahneman and Tversky results, see Shrader-Frechette, *Risk and Rationality*, 128ff.; R. Cooke, *Experts in Uncertainty* (New York: Oxford University Press, 1991). For discussion of the 90-percent confidence bands and associated problems, see Cooke, *European*, 9ff.

56. L. Hamilton et al., *Toward a Risk Assessment of the Spent Fuel and High-Level Nuclear Waste Disposal System*, Contract DE-AC02-76CH00016 (Washington, D.C.: U.S. DOE, 1986), 10–25.

57. See Williams, *Population Risks from Uranium*, 23.

58. G. Sawyer, *Report of the State of Nevada Commission on Nuclear Projects* (Carson City: Nevada Commission on Nuclear Projects, November 1986), 9.

59. Emel et al., *Nuclear Waste Management*, 5. See A. Milnes, *Geology*

and Radwaste (New York: Academic, 1985), 286ff.; U.S. Congress, *Nuclear Waste Program*, 29ff. See also C. Nyquist, "Nuclear Waste Disposal in Sweden," *Public Utilities Fortnightly* (14 May 1987): 34–35.

60. Emel et al., *Nuclear Waste Management*, 206.

61. See, for example, M. Board, *Examination of the Use of Continuum Versus Discontinuum Models for Design and Performance Assessment for the Yucca Mountain Site*, NUREG/CR-5426 (Washington, D.C.: U.S. NRC, Division of Waste Management, Office of Nuclear Material Safety and Safeguards, August 1989), 66; K. Stephens et al., *Methodologies for Assessing Long-Term Performance of High-Level Radioactive Waste Packages*, NUREG/CR-4477 ATR-85(5810-01)1ND (Washington, D.C.: U.S. NRC, Division of Waste Management, Office of Nuclear Material Safety and Safeguards, January 1986), xv.

62. See J. Rawls, *A Theory of Justice* (Cambridge: Harvard University Press, 1971); R. Kasperson and S. Abdollahzadeh, *Distributional Equity Problems at the Proposed Yucca Mountain Facility*, NWPO-SE-009-88 (Carson City: State of Nevada, Agency for Projects/Nuclear Waste Project Office, July 1988); Shrader-Frechette, *Nuclear Power and Public Policy*, 25ff., 136ff.; Shrader-Frechette, *Risk Analysis and Scientific Method*, 32ff., 210ff.; Shrader-Frechette, *Science Policy, Ethics, and Economic Methodology* (Boston: Reidel, 1985), 55ff.; Shrader-Frechette, *Risk*; K. Shrader-Frechette, *Environmental Ethics* (Pacific Grove, Calif.: Boxwood Press, 1991).

63. J. Passmore, *Man's Responsibility for Nature* (New York: Scribner's, 1974); see Kasperson and Abdollahzadeh, *Distributional Equity Problems*.

64. Rawls, *A Theory of Justice*.

65. A. Sen, *Collective Choice and Social Welfare* (San Francisco: Holden-Day); see Kasperson and Abdollahzadeh, *Distributional Equity Problems*. For a libertarian ethics, see R. Nozick, *Anarchy, State, and Utopia* (New York: Basic Books, 1974). For discussion of problems with the Pareto-based ethics, see Shrader-Frechette, *Science Policy, Ethics, and Economic Methodology*, 231ff.

66. See R. Kasperson et al., "Confronting Equity Radioactive Waste Management: Modest Proposals for a Socially Just and Acceptable Program," in *Equity Issues in Radioactive Waste Management*, ed. R. Kasperson (Cambridge, Mass.: Oegleschlager, Gunn, and Hain, 1983); R. Kasperson et al., *Assessing the State/Nation Distributional Equity Issues Associated with the Proposed Yucca Mountain Repository: A Conceptual Approach*, NWPO-SE-018-89 (Carson City: State of Nevada, Agency for Nuclear Waste Projects/Nuclear Waste Project Office, June 1988); Kasperson and Abdollahzadeh, *Distributional Equity Problems*; P. Kleindorfer et al., *Valuation and Assessment of Equity in the Siting of a Nuclear Waste Repository*, Report 88-67 (Philadelphia: Risk and Decision Process Center, the Wharton School, University of Pennsylvania, 1988); A. Kneese et al., "Economic Issues in the Legacy Problem," in *Equity Issues in Radioactive Waste Management*, ed. R. Kasperson; D. MacLean (ed.), *Values at Risk* (Totowa, N.J.: Rowman and Allanheld, 1986); Rawls, *A Theory of Justice*; S. Rayner and R. Cantor, "How Free Is Safe Enough? The Cultural Approach to Societal Technology Choice," *Risk Analysis* 7 (March 1987): 3–13; W. Schultze and A. Kneese, "Risk and

Benefit-Cost Analysis," *Risk Analysis* 1 (1981): 81–88; Shrader-Frechette, *Nuclear Power and Public Policy*, 25ff., 136ff.; Shrader-Frechette, *Risk Analysis and Scientific Method*, 210ff.; Shrader-Frechette, *Risk*; Shrader-Frechette, *Environmental Ethics*; Shrader-Frechette, "Ethical Dilemmas and Radioactive Waste: A Survey of the Issues," *Environmental Ethics* 13 (Winter 1991): 327–343.

67. For discussion of substantive and procedural equality, see Shrader-Frechette, *Science Policy, Ethics, and Economic Methodology*, 219ff.

68. Reichard et al., *Groundwater Contamination Risk Assessment*, 167.

69. Kneese et al., "Economic Issues in the Legacy Problem"; Shrader-Frechette, *Science Policy, Ethics, and Economic Methodology*, 261ff.

70. For discussion of equity and the NIMBY syndrome, see W. Freudenburg and S. Pastor, "NIMBY's and LULU's: Stalking the Syndromes," *Journal of Social Issues*, forthcoming.

71. See Shrader-Frechette, *Risk Analysis and Scientific Method*, 84ff., 142ff.; Shrader-Frechette, *Risk*, chap. 8.

72. See Reichard et al., *Groundwater Contamination Risk Assessment*, 162–163, 181.

73. See Reichard et al., *Groundwater Contamination Risk Assessment*, 164–168.

74. See Reichard et al., *Groundwater Contamination Risk Assessment*, 164.

75. See Shrader-Frechette, *Risk*, chap. 8.

76. U.S. Congress, *DOE: Pollution at Fernald, Ohio*, Hearing before the Subcommittee on Transportation, Tourism, and Hazardous Materials of the Committee on Energy and Commerce, House of Representatives, 100th Congress, Second Session on H.R. 3783, H.R. 3784, and H.R. 3785, 14 October 1988, Serial no. 100-236 (Washington, D.C.: U.S. Government Printing Office, 1989), esp. 27–28.

77. S. Mattson et al., "Geology and Hydrogeology of the Proposed Nuclear Waste Repository at Yucca Mountain, Nevada and the Surrounding Area," in *Geological Society of America Annual Meeting* (Las Vegas: Science Applications International Corp., 1989) (Item 3 in US DOE, DE90006793). For further discussion of this point, see text and references, chapter 2.

78. J. Lemons et al., "America's High-Level Nuclear Waste Repository: A Case Study of Environmental Science and Public Policy," *Intern. J. Environmental Studies* 34 (1989): 38.

79. U.S. DOE, "Foreword," in *Bibliography of the Published Reports, Papers, and Articles on the Nevada Nuclear Waste Storage Investigations, January 1985*, NVO-96-24 (Rev. 5) (Las Vegas: U.S. DOE, Nevada Operations Office, 1985), 111. G. Jacob, "Conflict, Location, and Politics: Siting a Nuclear Waste Repository" (Ph.D. diss., University of Michigan. Available from University Microfilms, Ann Arbor, Michigan) (Item 136 in US DOE, DE91000566); J. Davis, "Wasting of Nevada," *Sierra* 73, no. 4 (July 1988): 31–35 (Item 251 in US DOE, DE89005394); J. Karkut, "Nevada v. Herrington: An Effective Check on the DOE," *Journal of Energy and Policy (USA)* 8, no. 2 (1988): 301–318 (Item 425 in US DOE, DE90006793);

R. Bryan, "Politics and Promises of Nuclear Waste Disposal," *Environment* 29, no. 8 (October 1987): 32–38 (Item 229 in US DOE, DE89005394); See L. Carter, "Nuclear Wastes: Popular Antipathy Narrows Search for Disposal Sites," *Science* 197, no. 4310 (September): 1265–1266 (Item 68 in US DOE, DE89005394); U.S. Congress, *Civilian Nuclear Waste Program*, Hearing Before the Committee on Energy and Natural Resources, U.S. Senate, 101st Congress, Second Session, 2 March 1990 (Washington, D.C.: U.S. Government Printing Office, 1990), 213–214; U.S. Congress, *Nuclear Waste Program*, 210; U.S. Congress, *Mission Plan for the Civilian Radioactive Waste Management Program*, Hearing before the Subcommittee on Energy Research and Development of the Committee on Energy and Natural Resources, U.S. Senate, 99th Congress, First Session on the Department of Energy's Mission Plan for the Civilian Radioactive Waste Management Program, 12 September 1985 (Washington, D.C.: U.S. Government Printing Office, 1986), 45; H. Kunreuther et al., "Public Attitude Toward Siting a High-Level Nuclear Waste Repository in Nevada," *Risk Analysis* 10, no. 4 (December 1990): 470; M. Winsor and C. Malone, "State of Nevada Perspective on Environmental Program Planning for the Yucca Mountain Project," *The Environmental Professional* 12 (1990): 197.

80. See Emel et al., *Postclosure Risks*, 20.

81. U.S. Congress, *Mission Plan*, 235.

82. G. Sawyer, *Report of the State of Nevada Commission on Nuclear Projects* (Carson City: Nevada Commission on Nuclear Projects, 1990), 2.

83. Emel et al., *Nuclear Waste Management*, 5.

84. Loux, *State of Nevada Comments*, 33–34.

85. Nevada NWPO (Nuclear Waste Project Office), *State of Nevada Comments on the U.S. Department of Energy Draft Environmental Assessment for the Proposed High-Level Nuclear Waste Site at Yucca Mountain: Vol. 2* (Carson City: U.S. DOE, 1985) (Item 339 in US DOE, DE90006793).

86. See R. Keeney, "Analysis of the Portfolio of Sites to Characterize for Selecting a Nuclear Repository," *Risk Analysis* 7, no. 2 (June 1987): 195–218 (Item 218 in US DOE, DE89005394).

87. For further discussion of begging the question in a different context, see the next chapter.

88. See E. Marshall, "Nevada Wins the Nuclear Waste Lottery," *Science* (Washington, D.C.) 239 (January 1988): 15 (Item 241 in US DOE, DE89005394).

89. For discussion of the single-site choice, see E. Russell et al., "Fabrication and Closure Development of Nuclear Waste Containers for Storage at the Yucca Mountain, Nevada Repository," in *Joint International Waste Management Conference* (Kyoto: U.S. DOE, 1989) (Item 46 in US DOE, DE91000566); U.S. GAO, *Nuclear Waste* (Gaithersburg, Md.: U.S. GAO, 1988) (Item 111 in US DOE, DE91000566); U.S. GAO, *Nuclear Waste* (Gaithersburg, Md.: U.S. GAO, 1989) (Item 112 in US DOE, DE91000566).

90. See D. Zettwock, "Interview with K. S. Shrader-Frechette," 2 August 1985. Available from Dr. Shrader-Frechette of the University of South

Florida, Tampa, Florida; K. Shrader-Frechette, "Values and Hydrogeological Method: How Not to Site the World's Largest Nuclear Dump," in *Planning for Changing Energy Conditions, Energy Policy Studies*, vol. 4, ed. J. Byrne and D. Rich (New Brunswick: Transaction Books, 1988), 126ff.

91. Rusche, "Statement," in U.S. Congress, *Mission Plan*, 484, 655.

92. Rusche, "Statement," in U.S. Congress, *Mission Plan*, 484–485.

93. M. Koryakin, "State of the Soviet Nuclear Industry," *WISE (World Information Service on Energy) News Communique* 332 (18 May 1990): 2 (P.O. Box 5627, NL-1007 AP Amsterdam, The Netherlands).

94. Shrader-Frechette, *Risk*; Shrader-Frechette, *Nuclear Power and Public Policy*.

95. *Price-Anderson Amendments Act of 1988*, P.L. 100–408, Stat. 102, pp. 1066–1085.

96. Koryakin, "State of the Soviet Nuclear Industry"; Shrader-Frechette, *Risk*; Shrader-Frechette, *Nuclear Power and Public Policy*.

97. Koryakin, "State of the Soviet Nuclear Industry"; see M. Resnikoff, *Probabilistic Risk Assessment and Nuclear Waste Transportation: A Case Study of the Use of RADTRAN in the 1986 Environmental Assessment for Yucca Mountain*, NWPO-TN-066-90 (New York: Radioactive Waste Management Associates, December 1990).

98. F. Parker, "Testimony," in U.S. Congress, NWP, 88.

99. Resnikoff, *Probabilistic Risk Assessment*, 44; see Shrader-Frechette, *Nuclear Power and Public Policy*, 73ff.

100. L. Hamilton et al., *Toward a Risk Assessment of the Spent Fuel and High-Level Nuclear Waste Disposal System*, Contract DE-AC02-76CH00016 (Washington, D.C.: U.S. DOE, 1986), 10–25.

101. See, for example, U.S. Congress, *Safety of DOE Nuclear Facilities*, Hearing before the Subcommittee on Energy and Power of the Committee on Energy and Commerce, House of Representatives, 101st Congress, First Session, 22 February 1989, Serial no. 101–1 (Washington D.C.: U.S. Government Printing Office, 1989). See also U.S. Congress, NWP, 82ff.; U.S. DOE, NWPA-Hanford, vol. 3, pp. c. 2–9, c. 2–28, c. 2–29.

102. U.S. Congress, *Safety of DOE Nuclear Facilities*, 2. For citizens' requests for liability coverage, see U.S. DOE, NWPA-Yucca, vol. 3, p. c. 2–8.

103. Rusche, "Statement," in U.S. Congress, *Nuclear Waste Program*, 376. See Williams, *Population Risks from Uranium*, 1ff.

104. W. Freudenburg and T. Jones, "Attitudes and Stress in the Presence of Technological Risk," *Social Forces* 69, no. 4 (June 1991): 1143–1168; W. Freudenburg and J. Gervers, *Empirical Studies of Hazard Management*, Draft Report (Carson City: Nevada Nuclear Waste Projects Office, 1991).

105. G. E. Moore, *Principia Ethica* (Cambridge: Cambridge University Press, 1951), viii–ix; 23–40, 60–63, 108, 146.

106. Shrader-Frechette, *Nuclear Power and Public Policy*, chap. 6, esp. 142–152.

107. See Moore, *Principia Ethica*, 36–40; Shrader-Frechette, *Nuclear Power and Public Policy*, chap. 9.

108. U.S. DOE, NWPA-Yucca, vol. 2: 6–121.

109. See Williams, *Population Risks from Uranium*, 23.

110. O'Brien, *Technical Support for High-Level Radioactive Waste Management*, 125ff.; Smith et al., *Population Risks*, 183.

Notes to Chapter Six

1. U.S. Geological Survey, "Memo, 1 July 1962" vertical file, "Maxey Flats: Correspondence and Phone Conversations," (Louisville: U.S. Department of the Interior, USGS, Water Resources Division, 1962); J. Neel, "Statement," in U.S. Congress, *Low-Level Radioactive Waste Disposal*, Hearings before a Subcommittee of the Committee on Government Operations, House of Representatives, 94th Congress, Second Session, 23 February, 12 March, and 6 April 1976 (Washington, D.C.: U.S. Government Printing Office, 1976), 258; hereafter cited as: U.S. Congress, *LLRWD*. See also A. Weiss and P. Columbo, *Evaluation of Isotope Migration—Land Burial*, NUREG/CR-1289 BNL-NUREG-51143 (Washington, D.C.: U.S. NRC, 1980), 5.

2. D. Montgomery and R. Blanchard, "Radioactivity Measurement in the Environment at the Maxey Flats Waste Burial Site," in *Management of Low-Level Radioactive Waste*, vol. 2, ed. M. Carter et al. (New York: Pergamon, 1979), 784; U.S. Congress, *LLRWD*, 28; G. Meyer, *Preliminary Data on the Occurrence of Transuranium Nuclides in the Environment at the Radioactive Waste Burial Site, Maxey Flats, Kentucky* (Washington, D.C.: U.S. EPA, Office of Radiation Programs, February 1976), x.

3. P. Zurer, "U.S. Charts Plans for Nuclear Waste Disposal," *Chemical and Engineering News* 61, no. 27 (July 1983): 20–38.

4. R. Kasperson and S. Abdollahzadeh, *Distributional Equity Problems at the Proposed Yucca Mountain Facility*, NWPO-SE-009-88 (Carson City: State of Nevada, Agency for Projects/Nuclear Waste Project Office, July 1988), 13.

5. USGS, "Memo, 1 July 1962"; G. Meyer, "Maxey Flats Radioactive Waste Burial Site: Status Report," unpublished report (Advanced Science and Technology Branch, U.S. Environmental Protection Agency, 1975), 9; Pacific Northwest Laboratory et al., *Research Program at Maxey Flats and Consideration of Other Shallow Land Burial Sites*, NUREG/CR-1832 (Washington, D.C.: U.S. NRC, 1980), esp. v, I-1, I-2, I-14, IV-6, IV-9, V-7ff.

6. L. Cox and P. Ricci, "Legal and Philosophical Aspects of Risk Analysis," in *The Risk Assessment of Environmental and Human Health Hazards*, ed. D. Paustenbach (New York: John Wiley, 1989), 1026.

7. H. Kunreuther et al., "A Decision-Process Perspective on Risk and Policy Analysis," in *Resolving Locational Conflict*, ed. L. Lake (New Brunswick, N.J.: Center for Urban Policy Research, Rutgers University, 1987), 261.

8. T. Rasmussen, "Methods of Hazard Analysis and Nuclear Safety Engineering," in *The Three Mile Island Nuclear Accident*, ed. T. Moss and D. Sills (New York: New York Academy of Sciences, 1981).

9. U.S. DOE, *Nuclear Waste Policy Act, Environmental Assessment, Yucca*

Mountain Site, Nevada Research and Development Area, Nevada, DOE/RW-0073, 3 vols. (Washington, D.C.: U.S. DOE, 1986), vol. 2: 6–280; hereafter cited as: U.S. DOE, NWPA-Yucca.

10. U.S. DOE, NWPA-Yucca, vol. 2: 6–292.

11. U.S. DOE, NWPA-Yucca, vol. 2: 6–12 and 6–25.

12. J. L. Younker, W. B. Andrews, G. A. Fasano, C. C. Herrington, S. R. Mattson, R. C. Murray, L. B. Ballou, M. A. Revelli, A. R. Ducharme, L. E. Shephard, W. W. Dudley, D. T. Hoxie, R. J. Herbst, E. A. Patera, B. R. Judd, J. A. Docka, and L. R. Rickertsen, *Report of Early Site Suitability Evaluation of the Potential Repository Site at Yucca Mountain, Nevada,* SAIC-91/8000 (Washington, D.C.: U.S. Department of Energy, 1992), E-11; hereafter cited as: Younker, Andrews, et al.

13. Younker, Andrews, et al., E-11.

14. J. L. Younker, S. L. Albrecht, W. J. Arabasz, J. H. Bell, F. W. Cambray, S. W. Carothers, J. I. Drever, J. T. Einaudi, D. E. French, K. V. Hodges, R. H. Jones, D. K. Kreamer, W. G. Pariseau, T. A. Vogel, T. Webb, W. B. Andrews, G. A. Fasano, S. R. Mattson, R. C. Murray, L. B. Ballou, M. A. Revelli, A. R. Ducharme, L. E. Shephard, W. W. Dudley, D. T. Hoxie, R. J. Herbst, E. A. Patera, B. R. Judd, J. A. Docka, L. R. Rickertsen, J. M. Boak, and J. R. Stockey, *Report of the Peer Review Panel on the Early Site Suitability Evaluation of the Potential Repository Site at Yucca Mountain, Nevada,* SAIC-91/8001 (Washington, D.C.: U.S. Department of Energy, 1992), B-2; hereafter cited as: Younker, Albrecht, et al.

15. Younker, Andrews, et al., E-5.

16. Younker, Andrews, et al., E-11.

17. K. Shrader-Frechette, *Risk and Rationality* (Berkeley, Los Angeles, London: University of California Press, 1991), 133–145; hereafter cited as: *Risk.*

18. L. Libby et al., "Evaluation of Great Deserts of the World for Perpetual Radwaste Storage," *The Environmental Professional* 4, no. 2 (1982): 111–128 (Item 122 in US DOE, DE89005394).

19. U.S. NRC, *In the Matter of Proposed Rulemaking on the Storage and Disposal of Nuclear Waste (Waste Confidence Rulemaking),* PR-50, 51 (44FR61372) (Washington, D.C.: U.S. NRC, 1980), I-25.

20. U.S. NRC, *In the Matter of Proposed Rulemaking,* IV-1.

21. See K. Shrader-Frechette, *Nuclear Power and Public Policy,* 49ff.

22. F. Thompson et al., *Preliminary Upper-Bound Consequence Analysis for a Waste Repository at Yucca Mountain, Nevada,* SAND83-7475 (Albuquerque: Sandia National Labs., 1984), i, v–vi, 7, 47.

23. Y. Lin, *Sparton—A Simple Performance Assessment Code for the Nevada Nuclear Waste Storage Investigations Project,* SAND85-0602 (Albuquerque: Sandia National Labs., 1985), i, 1.

24. C. St. John, *Thermal Analysis of Spent Fuel Disposal in Vertical Emplacement Boreholes in a Welded Tuff Repository,* SAND84-7207 (Albuquerque: Sandia National Labs., 1985), 2.

25. U.S. DOE, *Nuclear Waste Policy Act, Environmental Assessment, Reference Repository Location, Hanford Site, Washington,* 3 vols., DOE/RW-

0070 (Washington, D.C.: U.S. DOE, 1986), vol. 2: 6–75; hereafter cited as: DOE, NWPA-Hanford.

26. I. Borg et al., *Information Pertinent to the Migration of Radionuclides in Ground Water at the Nevada Test Site. Part 1. Review and Analysis of Existing Information* (Livermore, Calif.: Lawrence Livermore Lab., 1976) (Item 53 in US DOE, DE89005394).

27. J. Wang and T. Narasimhan, *Hydrologic Mechanisms Governing Fluid Flow in Partially Saturated, Fractured, Porous Tuff at Yucca Mountain* (Berkeley, Calif.: Lawrence Berkeley Lab., 1984) (Item 105 in US DOE, DE88004834); J. Wang and T. Narasimhan, *Hydrologic Mechanisms Governing Partially Saturated Fluid Flow in Fractured Welded Units and Porous Non-Welded Units at Yucca Mountain* (Berkeley, Calif.: Lawrence Berkeley Lab., 1986) (Item 282 in US DOE, DE88004834).

28. K. Pruess et al., *Effective Continuum Approximation for Modeling Fluid and Heat Flow in Fractured Porous Tuff: Nevada Nuclear Waste Storage Investigations Project* (Berkeley, Calif.: Lawrence Berkeley Lab., 1988) (Item 42 in US DOE, DE89005394).

29. Nevada NWPO, *State of Nevada Comments on the U.S. Department of Energy Consultation Draft Site Characterization Plan, Yucca Mountain Site, Nevada Research and Development Area, Nevada: Vol. 2* (Carson City: Nevada Nuclear Waste Project Office, 1988) (Item 334 in US DOE, DE90006793).

30. Nevada NWPO, *State of Nevada Comments on the U.S. Department of Energy Consultation Draft Site Characterization Plan, Yucca Mountain Site, Nevada: vol. 1* (Carson City: Nevada Nuclear Waste Project Office, 1988) (Item 335 in US DOE, DE90006793).

31. C. Jantzen et al., *Scientific Basis for Nuclear Waste Management VIII. Volume 44* (Pittsburgh: Materials Research Society, 1989) (Item 403 in US DOE, DE90006793).

32. Younker, Andrews, et al., 2–150.

33. Younker, Andrews, et al., 2–150.

34. Younker, Andrews, et al., 2–157.

35. Younker, Andrews, et al., 2–155.

36. Younker, Andrews, et al., 2–155.

37. Meyer, "Maxey Flats Radioactive Waste Burial Site," 9; Pacific Northwest Laboratory et al., *Research Program at Maxey Flats*, esp. v, I-1, I-2, I-14, IV-6, IV-9, V-7ff.

38. S. Sinnock and T. Lin, *Preliminary Bounds on the Expected Postclosure Performance of the Yucca Mountain Repository Site, Southern Nevada*, SAND84-1492 (Albuquerque: Sandia National Labs., 1984), 7, 37.

39. Sinnock and Lin, *Preliminary Bounds*, 47.

40. S. Pitman et al., "Corrosion and Slow-Strain-Rate Testing of Type 304L Stainless in Tuff Groundwater Environments," in *Corrosion '87* (San Francisco: Pacific Northwest Lab., 1986) (Item 172 in US DOE, DE88004834).

41. C. Sastre et al., *Waste Package Reliability*, NUREG/CR-4509 (Washington, D.C.: U.S. NRC, 1986), 22.

42. Sastre et al., *Waste Package Reliability*, 65.

43. Sastre et al., *Waste Package Reliability*, 66.

44. S. Sinnock et al., *Preliminary Estimates of Groundwater Travel Time and Radionuclide Transport at the Yucca Mountain Repository Site*, SAND85-2701 (Albuquerque: Sandia National Labs., 1986), 58.

45. Sinnock et al., *Preliminary Estimates*, 77.

46. Sinnock et al., *Preliminary Estimates*, 1–2.

47. P. Zhang, *Evaluation of the Geologic Relations and Seismotectonic Stability of the Yucca Mountain Area, Nevada Waste Site Investigation*, 2 vols. (NNWSI) (Reno: Center for Neotectonic Studies, Mackay School of Mines, University of Nevada, 1989), vol. 2.

48. Sinnock and Lin, *Preliminary Bounds*, 53.

49. Sinnock and Lin, *Preliminary Bounds*, 53.

50. R. Einziger and H. Buchanan, *Long-Term, Low-Temperature Oxidation of PWR Spent Fuel: Interim Transition Report* (Richland, Wash.: Westinghouse Hanford Co., 1988) (Item 26 in US DOE, DE89005394).

51. H. D. Smith, *Electrochemical Corrosion-Scoping Experiments: An Evaluation of the Results* (Richland, Wash.: Westinghouse Hanford Co., 1988) (Item 151 in US DOE, DE90006793); H. D. Smith, *Initial Report on Stress Corrosion-Cracking Experiments Using Zircaloy-4 Spent Fuel Cladding C-Rings* (Richland, Wash.: Westinghouse Hanford Co., 1988) (Item 153 in US DOE, DE90006793).

52. Younker, Andrews, et al., E-5, E-11.

53. Younker, Albrecht, et al., 57.

54. C. Baylis, "Are Some Propositions Neither True Nor False?" *Philosophy of Science* 3 (1936): 156–166; C. Ducasse, "Truth, Verifiability, and Propositions about the Future," *Philosophy of Science* 8 (1941): 329–337; O. Helmer and P. Oppenheim, "A Syntactical Definition of Probability and Degree of Confirmation," *The Journal of Symbolic Logic* 10 (1945): 25–60; C. Hempel, "Eine rein topologische Form nichtaristotelischer Logik," *Erkenntnis* 6 (1936–1937): 436–442; N. Rescher, *Many-Valued Logic* (New York: McGraw-Hill, 1969).

55. See, for example, K. R. Popper, *The Logic of Scientific Discovery* (New York: Basic Books, 1959); K. R. Popper, *Conjectures and Refutations* (London: Routledge and Kegan Paul, 1963); C. Hempel, *Philosophy of Natural Science* (Englewood Cliffs, N.J.: Prentice-Hall, 1966).

56. See Popper, *The Logic of Scientific Discovery*; Popper, *Conjectures and Refutations*; Hempel, *Philosophy of Natural Science*.

57. Younker, Albrecht, et al., B-2.

58. Younker, Albrecht, et al., B-2.

59. See, for example, Popper, *The Logic of Scientific Discovery*; Popper, *Conjectures and Refutations*; Hempel, *Philosophy of Natural Science*; J. Fetzer, "The Frame Problem: Artificial Intelligence Meets David Hume," *International Journal of Expert Systems* 3, no. 3 (1991): 219–232.

60. M. Resnick, *Choices* (Minneapolis: University of Minnesota, 1986); R. D. Luce and H. Raiffa, *Games and Decisions* (New York: Wiley, 1957), 275–326.

61. Shrader-Frechette, *Risk*, 100–130.

62. See Rescher, *Many-Valued Logic*.

63. Fetzer, "The Frame Problem," 223, 227.

64. Younker, Andrews, et al., 1–31.

65. J. Bates, J. Bradley, A. Teetsov, C. Bradley, M. Buchholtz, and M. B. ten Brink, "Colloid Formation During Waste Form Reaction: Implications for Nuclear Waste Disposal," *Science* 256 (1 May 1992): 649–651.

66. J. Raloff, "Radwastes May Escape Glass via New Route," *Science News* 141, no. 18 (1992): 141.

67. C. Ducasse, "Truth, Verifiability, and Propositions about the Future," *Philosophy of Science* 8 (1941): 329–337; Rescher, *Many-Valued Logic*.

68. Younker, Albrecht, et al., B-2.

69. Younker, Albrecht, et al., 40–51, 257, 460.

70. See Rescher, *Many-Valued Logic*, 328ff.; Helmer and Oppenheim, "A Syntactical Definition of Probability."

71. Younker, Andrews, et al., 1–18.

72. Younker, Andrews, et al., 1–13.

73. H. Otway and M. Peltu, *Regulating Industrial Risks* (London: Buttersworths, 1985), 4.

74. See, for example, Younker, Albrecht, et al., 13.

75. Younker, Albrecht, et al., 460.

76. Younker, Andrews, et al., 2–123, 2–124.

77. Younker, Andrews, et al., 2–123, 2–124.

78. Younker, Andrews, et al., E-5.

79. Younker, Andrews, et al., 2–123, 2–124.

80. J. Thompson, *Laboratory and Field Studies Related to the Radionuclide Migration Project: Progress Report, October 1, 1986–September 30, 1987* (Los Alamos: Los Alamos National Lab., 1988) (Item 358 in US DOE, DE90006793).

81. B. Kiernan et al., *Report of the Special Advisory Committee on Nuclear Waste Disposal*, no. 142 (Frankfort, Ky.: Legislative Research Commission, 1977), ix–17; U.S. Energy Research and Development Administration (U.S. ERDA), "ERDA-1538," *Final Environmental Statement: Waste Management Operations, Hanford Reservation, Richland, Washington*, (Springfield, Va.: National Technical Information Service, 1975), vol. 2, 11.1-H-1 through 11.1-H-4.

82. G. Hart, "Address to the Forum," U.S. Environmental Protection Agency, *Proceedings of a Public Forum on Environmental Protection Criteria for Radioactive Wastes*, (ORP/CSD-78-2) (Washington, D.C.: U.S. Government Printing Office, 1978), 6.

83. U.S. ERDA, "ERDA-1538," vol. 1, X-74; see Shrader-Frechette, *Nuclear Power and Public Policy*, chaps. 2–3.

84. U.S. ERDA, "ERDA-1538," vol. 1, p. II.1–57.

85. U.S. ERDA, "ERDA-1538," vol. 1, p. III.2–2.

86. U.S. ERDA, "ERDA-1537," *Waste Management Operations: Savannah River Plant, Aiken, South Carolina*, (UC-2-11-70) (Springfield, Va.: National Technical Information Service, September 1977), II-20 and IV-2; see also U.S. ERDA, "ERDA-1536," *Waste Management Operations, Idaho National Engineering Laboratory, Idaho* (Springfield, Va.: National Technical Information Service, September 1977), E-41. For data on the 1061 figure, see U.S. Congress, *Nuclear Waste Policy Act*, Hearings before the Subcommittee on Energy and Environment of the Committee on Interior and Insu-

lar Affairs, House of Representatives, 100th Congress, 18 September 1987 (Washington, D.C.: U.S. Government Printing Office, 1988), 46; hereafter cited as: U.S. Congress, NWPA.

87. U.S. EPA, *Considerations of Environmental Protection Criteria for Radioactive Waste* (Washington, D.C.: U.S. EPA, 1978), 26.

88. Lin, *Sparton—A Simple Performance Assessment Code*, i, 1.

89. U.S. DOE, NWPA-Hanford, vol. 2: 6–7.

90. D. Alexander et al., "High Level Radioactive Waste Management," vol. 2, in *Proceedings of the International Topical Meeting* (La Grange Park, Ill.: American Nuclear Society, April 1990), 1283.

91. GeoTrans, *Review of Modeling Efforts Associated with Yucca Mountain, Nevada,* NWPO-TR-004-87 (Carson City: State of Nevada, Agency for Nuclear Projects/Nuclear Waste Project Office, September 1986), 1.

92. Sinnock et al., *Preliminary Estimates,* 1–2. See also R. Loux, *Nevada State and Local Government Comments on the U.S. Department of Energy's Report to Congress Pursuant to Section 175 of the Nuclear Waste Policy Act, as Amended,* NWPO SE 020 89 (Carson City: The Nevada Agency for Nuclear Projects and Affected Local Government, March 1989), 3; G. Sawyer, *Report of the State of Nevada Commission on Nuclear Projects* (Carson City: Nevada Commission on Nuclear Projects, December 1990), 37.

93. R. Beers and R. Morey, *Subsurface Radar Profiling Field Tests at Low-Level Nuclear Waste Burial Sites: Maxey Flats, Kentucky and Beatty, Nevada,* NUREG/CR-1272 GC-TR-79-1023 WL (Washington, D.C.: U.S. NRC, Division of Health, Siting and Waste Management Office of Regulatory Research, June 1981), 43.

94. R. McGuire et al., *Demonstration of a Risk-Based Approach to High-Level Waste Repository Evaluation,* NP-7057 Research Project 3055–2 (Palo Alto, Calif.: EEI/UWASTE and Electric Power Research Institute, October 1990), iii, 12–2.

95. M. Board, *Examination of the Use of Continuum Versus Discontinuum Models for Design and Performance Assessment for the Yucca Mountain Site,* NUREG/CR-5426 (Washington, D.C.: U.S. NRC, Division of Waste Management, Office of Nuclear Material Safety and Safeguards, August 1989), iii, 66.

96. J. Lemons and D. Brown, "The Role of Science in the Decision to Site a High-Level Nuclear Waste Repository at Yucca Mountain, Nevada, USA," *The Environmentalist* 10, no. 1 (1990): 6.

97. U.S. Congress, NWPA, 211ff. See also U.S. Congress, *Nuclear Waste Program,* Hearing before the Committee on Energy and Natural Resources, U.S. Senate, 100th Congress, 29 June 1987 (Washington, D.C.: U.S. Government Printing Office, 1987); hereafter sited as: U.S. Congress, NWP–June. R. Loux, *State of Nevada Comments on the U.S. Department of Energy Site Characterization Plan, Yucca Mountain Site, Nevada* (Carson City: Nevada Agency for Nuclear Projects, 1989), vol. 2: 2.

98. Loux, *State of Nevada Comments on the U.S. Department of Energy Consultation Draft Site,* vol. 1: I-1 through I-4.

99. Loux, *State of Nevada Comments on the U.S. Department of Energy Site Characterization Plan,* vol. 1: 3.

100. Younker, Albrecht, et al., 128.

101. Younker, Albrecht, et al., 128.

102. See, for example, K. Shrader-Frechette, *Expert Judgment in Assessing Radwaste Risks* (Carson City: Nevada Agency for Nuclear Projects, Yucca Mountain Socioeconomic Project, 1992).

103. Younker, Albrecht, et al., 120.

104. Younker, Albrecht, et al., 120–121.

105. Younker, Albrecht, et al., 122.

106. See, for example, I. C. Yang, *Climatic Changes Inferred from Analyses of Lake Sediment Cores, Walker Lake*, USGS-WRI-84-4006 (Las Vegas: Water-Resources Investigations Report, U.S. Geological Survey, 1989); S. S. Levy, "Mineralogic Alteration History and Paleohydrology at Yucca Mountain, Nevada," in *High Level Radioactive Waste Management, Proceedings of the Second Annual International Conference*, 28 April–3 May, 1991, Las Vegas (La Grange Park, Ill.: American Nuclear Society, Inc., 1991), 477–485.

107. Levy, "Mineralogic Alteration History."

108. See Yang, *Climatic Changes*.

109. C. B. Raleigh and the panel on Coupled Hydrologic/Techtonic/Hydrothermal Systems at Yucca Mountain, *Groundwater at Yucca Mountain: How High Can It Rise?* (Washington, D.C.: National Academy Press, 1992).

110. Raleigh, *Groundwater at Yucca Mountain*, 140, C-9 through C-23.

111. Younker, Andrews, et al., 2–69.

112. Younker, Andrews, et al., 2–67.

113. Younker, Albrecht, et al., 520.

114. Younker, Albrecht, et al., 2–70.

115. U.S. DOE, NWPA-Hanford, vol. 3, p. c. 2–28, and R. Bryan, *State of Nevada Comments on the U.S. Department of Energy Draft Environmental Assessment for the Proposed High-Level Nuclear Waste Site at Yucca Mountain*, 2 vols. (Carson City: Nuclear Waste Project Office, Office of the Governor, 1985), vol. 1: I-48 through I-49.

116. M. Winsor and C. Malone, "State of Nevada Perspective on Environmental Program Planning for the Yucca Mountain Project," *The Environmental Professional* 12 (1990): 196, 205–206; see C. Malone, "Geologic and Hydrologic Issues Related to Siting a Repository for High-Level Nuclear Waste at Yucca Mountain, Nevada, USA," *Journal of Environmental Management* 30 (1990): 381–396.

117. U.S. DOE, NWPA-Yucca, vol. 2: 6–298, 6–299.

118. R. Loux, *Comments on U.S. Department of Energy, Office of Civilian Radioactive Waste Management, Draft 1988 Mission Plan Amendment (DOE/RW-0187, June 1988)* (Carson City: State of Nevada, Agency for Nuclear Projects/Nuclear Waste Project Office, September 1988), 39.

119. R. Hunter and C. Mann, *Techniques for Determining Probabilities of Events and Processes Affecting the Performance of Geologic Repositories*, NUREG/CR-3964 SAND86-0196, vol. 1 (Washington, D.C.: U.S. NRC, Division of High-Level Waste Management, Office of Nuclear Material Safety and Safeguards, June 1989), 3.

120. Hunter and Mann, *Techniques for Determining Probabilities*, 7.

121. Hunter and Mann, *Techniques for Determining Probabilities*, 10.

122. N. Matuska, *Ground-Water Sampling of the NNWSI Water Table Test Wells Surrounding Yucca Mountain, Nevada*, NWPO-TR-010-89 (Las Vegas and Reno: Water Resources Center Desert Research Institute, December 1988), 11–12.

123. See C. Whipple, "Nonpessimistic Risk Assessment," in *The Risk Assessment of Environmental and Human Health Hazards*, ed. D. Paustenbach, 1112–1113; B. Cohen, "Risk Analyses of Buried Wastes," in *The Risk Assessment of Environmental and Human Health Hazards*, ed. D. Paustenbach, 575.

124. See Whipple, "Nonpessimistic Risk Assessment," 1113; E. Liebow, "Letter to Kristin Shrader-Frechette" (Seattle: Batelle Human Affairs Research Center, 17 July 1987); E. Liebow and J. Fawcett, "Socioeconomic Aspects of Repository-Related Risk Perceptions: A Preliminary Literature Review" (Seattle: Batelle, 16 July 1987); E. Liebow and D. Herborn, "Assessing the Economic and Social Effects of Perceiving the Repository as 'Risky': A Preliminary Approach" (Seattle: Batelle, 28 May 1987); S. Nealy and E. Liebow (eds.), *Assessing Social and Economic Effects of Perceived Risk*, PNL-6515, BHARC-800/88/005 UC-70 (Richland, Wash.: Pacific Northwest Laboratory, March 1988).

125. See, for example, U.S. DOE, NWPA-Hanford, vol. 2: 6–294, and U.S. DOE, NWPA-Yucca, vol. 3, p. c.5–56.

126. See W. Freudenburg, "Perceived Risk, Real Risk: Social Science and the Art of Probabilistic Risk Assessment," *Science* 242 (7 October 1988): 44–49; W. Freudenburg and T. Jones, "Attitudes and Stress in the Presence of Technological Risk," *Social Forces* 69, no. 4 (June 1991): 1143–1168; L. Gould et al., *Perceptions of Technological Risks and Benefits* (New York: Sage, 1988); C. Heimer, "Social Structure, Psychology and the Estimation of Risk," *Annual Review of Sociology* 14: 491–519; B. Johnson and V. Covello (eds.), *The Social and Cultural Construction of Risk*, (Dordrecht: Reidel, 1987); J. Petterson, "The Reality of Perception," *Practicing Anthropology* 10 (1988): 8–9, 12; J. Petterson, *Goiania Incident Case Study*, NWPO-SE-015-88 (Carson City. State of Nevada, Agency for Nuclear Projects/Nuclear Waste Project Office, June 1988); P. Slovic, "Perception of Risk," *Science* 236 (1987): 280–285; P. Slovic et al., "Rating the Risks: the Structure of Expert and Lay Perceptions," *Environment* 21 (April 1979); and A. Tversky and D. Kahneman, "Judgment Under Uncertainty: Heuristics and Biases," *Science* 185 (1974): 1124–1131.

127. D. MacLean (ed.), *Values at Risk* (Totowa, N.J.: Rowman and Allanheld, 1986); K. Shrader-Frechette, *Risk Analysis and Scientific Method* (Boston: Reidel, 1985), 55–124; K. Shrader-Frechette, *Science Policy, Ethics, and Economic Methodology* (Boston: Reidel, 1985), 67ff., 121ff., 210ff., 261ff., 286ff.; K. Shrader-Frechette, *Risk*, chap. 2; R. Andrews, "Environmental Impact Assessment and Risk Assessment," in *Environmental Impact Assessment*, ed. P. Wathern (London: Unwin Hyman, 1988), 85–97; L. Cox and P. Ricci, "Legal and Philosophical Aspects of Risk Analysis," in *The Risk Assessment of Environmental and Human Health Hazards*, ed. D. Paustenbach, 1017–1046.

128. See Shrader-Frechette, *Risk*, chap. 8.

129. P. Ricci and A. Henderson, "Fear, Fiat, and Fiasco," in *Phenotypic Variation in Populations*, ed. A. Woodhead et al. (New York: Plenum, 1988), 288–293; D. Paustenbach, "A Survey of Health Risk Assessment," in *The Risk Assessment of Environmental and Human Health Hazards*, ed. Paustenbach, 38–39; R. Gammage and C. Travis, "Formaldehyde Exposure and Risk," in *The Risk Assessment of Environmental and Human Health Hazards*, ed. D. Paustenbach, 601–611.

130. A. Tversky and D. Kahneman, "Belief in the Law of Small Numbers," in *Judgment Under Uncertainty: Heuristics and Biases*, ed. D. Kahneman et al. (Cambridge: Cambridge University Press, 1982), 23–31; D. Kahneman and A. Tversky, "Subjective Probability," in *Judgment Under Uncertainty*, ed. D. Kahneman et al., 46–47.

131. See S. Oskamp, "Overconfidence in Case-Study Judgments," in *Judgment Under Uncertainty*, ed. Kahneman et al., 287–293.

132. Whipple, "Nonpessimistic Risk Assessment"; Cohen, "Risk Analyses of Buried Wastes."

133. L. Cox, "Comparative Risk Measures," in *Phenotypic Variation in Populations*, ed. Woodhead et al., 233–243; see B. Ames et al., "Ranking Possible Carcinogens," in *The Risk Assessment of Environmental and Human Health Hazards*, ed. D. Paustenbach, 1083ff.; M. Layard and A. Silvers, "Epidemiology in Environmental Risk Assessment," in *The Risk Assessment of Environmental and Human Health Hazards*, ed. D. Paustenbach, 159; N. Harley, "Environmental Lung Cancer Risk from Radon Daughter Exposure," in *The Risk Assessment of Environmental and Human Health Hazards*, ed. D. Paustenbach, 620; and Cohen, "Risk Analyses of Buried Wastes," 574.

134. See Shrader-Frechette, *Risk*, chap. 6.

135. For discussions of risk perception see, for example, Freudenburg, "Perceived Risk, Real Risk"; Freudenburg and Jones, "Attitudes and Stress"; Gould et al., *Perceptions of Technological Risks and Benefits*; Heimer, "Social Structure, Psychology and the Estimation of Risk"; Johnson and Covello, *The Social and Cultural Construction of Risk*; J. Petterson, "The Reality of Perception"; J. Petterson, *Goiania Incident Case Study*; Slovic, "Perception of Risk"; Slovic et al., "Rating the Risks"; and Tversky and Kahneman, "Judgment Under Uncertainty."

136. J. Yasinsky, "Nuclear Waste Management—Choosing Among the Options," *Proceedings of the American Power Conference* 45 (1983): 851–854 (Item 137 in US DOE, DE89005394). For further examples of this problem, see U.S. DOE, NWPA-Hanford, vol. 2: 6–294, and U.S. DOE, NWPA-Yucca, vol. 3, p. c. 5–56.

137. See U.S. Congress, *Nuclear Waste Program*, Hearings before the Committee on Energy and Natural Resources, U.S. Senate, 29 April and 7 May 1987 (Washington, D.C.: U.S. Government Printing Office, 1987), 41, for the 80-percent figure. See also J. Davis, "Wasting of Nevada," *Sierra* 73, no. 4 (July 1988): 31–35 (Item 251 in US DOE, DE89005394). For another confirmation of the 80-percent figure, see P. Slovic, J. Flynn, and M. Layman, "Perceived Risk, Trust, and the Politics of Nuclear Waste," *Science* 254 (13 December 1991): 1604.

138. See Shrader-Frechette, *Risk*, chap. 4.

139. P. Slovic et al., *Perceived Risk, Stigma, and Potential Economic Impacts of a High-Level Nuclear Waste Repository in Nevada*, NWPO-SE-023-89 (Carson City: State of Nevada, Agency for Nuclear Projects/Nuclear Waste Projects Office, July 1989). W. Burns et al., *Social Amplification of Risk: An Empirical Study*, NWPO-SE-027-90 (Carson City: State of Nevada, Agency for Projects/Nuclear Waste Project Office, September 1990). For other discussions of social amplifications of risk, see chapter three, notes 12–13 and chapter four, note 170.

140. Burns et al., *Social Amplification of Risk*, 660. See J. Petterson, "The Reality of Perception"; J. Petterson, *Goiania Incident Case Study*; H. Peters and L. Hennen, *The Accident at Gorleben: A Case Study of Risk Communication and Risk Amplification in the Federal Republic of Germany*, NWPO-SE-012-88 (Carson City: State of Nevada, Agency for Nuclear Projects/Nuclear Waste Project Office, July 1988).

141. P. Slovic et al., *What Comes to Mind When You Hear the Words "Nuclear Waste Repository"?: A Study of 10,000 Images*, NWPO-SE-028-90 (Carson City: State of Nevada, Agency for Projects/Nuclear Waste Project Office, 1990), i.

142. Slovic et al., *What Comes to Mind When You Hear the Words "Nuclear Waste Repository"?*.

143. Cohen, "Risk Analyses of Buried Wastes," 575; Whipple, "Non-pessimistic Risk Assessment," 1112–1113; K. Shrader-Frechette, "Economics, Risk-Cost Benefit Analysis, and the Linearity Assumption," in *PSA 1982*, ed P. Asquith and T. Nickles (East Lansing, Mich.: Philosophy of Science Association, 1982).

144. Cox and Ricci, "Legal and Philosophical Aspects of Risk Analysis," 1017–1046; W. Rowe, *An Anatomy of Risk* (New York: John Wiley and Sons, 1977), 926.

145. B. Fischhoff et al., "Facts and Fears," in *Societal Risk Assessment*, ed. R. Schwing and W. Albers (New York: Plenum, 1980), 207; R. Kates et al., *Hazards: Technology and Fairness* (Washington, D.C.: National Academy Press, 1986)

146. S. Samuels, "The Arrogance of Intellectual Power," in *Phenotypic Variation in Populations*, ed. Woodhead et al., 113–120; see also P. Pahner, "The Psychological Displacement of Anxiety: An Application to Nuclear Energy," in *Risk-Benefit Methodology and Application*, ed. D. Okrent (Los Angeles: University of California School of Engineering and Applied Science, 1975), 575.

147. P. Gleick and J. Holdren, "Assessing the Environmental Risks of Energy," *American Journal of Public Health* 71, no. 9 (September 1981): 1046; A. Van Horn and R. Wilson, "The Status of Risk-Benefit Analysis," discussion paper (Cambridge, Mass.: Harvard University Energy and Environmental Policy Center, 1976), 19.

148. U.S. DOE, NWPA-Yucca, vol. 2: 6–121.

149. See, for example, U.S. DOE, NWPA-Hanford, vol. 2: 6–24 and 6–25.

150. U. Park and C. Pflum, "Requirements for Controlling a Repository's Releases of Carbon–14 Dioxide: The High Costs and Negligible Benefits," in *International Conference for High-Level Radioactive Waste Management* (Las Vegas: U.S. DOE, 1990) (Item 2 in US DOE, DE91000566).

151. See Shrader-Frechette, *Risk*, 70ff.

152. C. Comar, "Risk: A Pragmatic *De Minimis* Approach," *Science* 203, no. 4378 (1979): 319; Cox and Ricci, "Legal and Philosophical Aspects of Risk Analysis," 1028–1041.

153. C. Starr, *Current Issues in Energy*, (New York: Pergamon, 1979), 14ff.; L. Cox and P. Ricci, "Risk, Uncertainty, and Causation," in *The Risk Assessment of Environmental and Human Health Hazards*, ed. D. Paustenbach, 134–135.

154. See Shrader-Frechette, *Risk*, 71ff.

155. Office of Civilian Radioactive Waste Management, *Performance Assessment Strategy Plan for the Geologic Repository Program* (Washington, D.C.: U.S. DOE, 1990).

156. For the DOE claim, see B. Rusche, "Statement," in *Mission Plan for the Civilian Radioactive Waste Management Program*, Hearing before the Subcommittee on Energy Research and Development of the Committee on Energy and Natural Resources, U.S. Senate, 99th Congress, First Session on the Department on Energy's Mission Plan for the Civilian Radioactive Waste Management Program, 12 September 1985 (Washington, D.C.: U.S. Government Printing Office, 1986), 484–485. For regulations concerning other nuclear facilities, see Shrader-Frechette, *Risk*, chap. 5.

157. See Shrader-Frechette, *Risk*, chaps. 5, 7.

158. K. Neuhauser et al., "Projected Environmental Impacts of Radioactive Material Transportation to the First U.S. Repository Site," in *International Symposium on the Packaging and Transport of Radioactive Materials (PATRAM '86)* (Albuquerque: Sandia National Labs., 1986) (Item 180 in US DOE, DE89005394). See also U.S. DOE, NWPA-Yucca, vol. 2: 6–121.

159. C. Brown, "Equalizing Differences in the Labor Market," *Quarterly Journal of Economics* 94, no. 1 (February 1980): 113–134; A. Dillingham, "The Injury Risk Structure of Occupations and Wages," Ph.D. diss., Cornell University, 1979; R. McLean et al., "Compensating Wage Differentials for Hazardous Work: An Empirical Analysis," *Quarterly Review of Economics and Business* 18, no. 3 (1978): 97–107; C. Olson, "Trade Unions, Wages, Occupational Injuries, and Public Policy," Ph.D. diss., University of Wisconsin, 1979; R. Smith, "Compensating Wage Differentials and Hazardous Work," Technical Analysis Paper no. 5 (Washington, D.C.: Office of Evaluation, Office of the Assistant Secretary for Policy Evaluation and Research, U.S. Department of Labor, 1973); R. Thaler and S. Rosen, "The Value of Saving a Life," in *Household Production and Consumption*, ed. N. Terleckyi (New York: National Bureau of Economic Research, 1976), 265–298; W. Viscusi, *Employment Hazards*, (Cambridge, Mass.: Harvard University Press, 1979); J. Graham and D. Shakow, "Risk and Reward," *Environment* 23, no. 8 (October 1981): 14–20, 44–45; J. Graham et al., "Risk Compensation," *Environment* 25, no. 1 (January/February 1983): 14–27.

160. E. Eckholm, "Unhealthy Jobs," *Environment* 19, no. 6 (August/September 1977): 31–33; D. Berman, *Death on the Job* (London: Monthly Review Press, 1978); see also D. Paustenbach, "A Survey of Health Risk Assessment," 34–35, and Samuels, "The Arrogance of Intellectual Power," 113–120.

161. See Shrader-Frechette, *Risk*, 72ff.

162. U.S. Congress, *Nuclear Waste Program*, Hearings before the Committee on Energy and Natural Resources, U.S. Senate, 100th Congress, First Session on the Current Status of the Department of Energy's Civilian Nuclear Waste Activities, 29 January, 4 and 5 February 1987, Part 1 (Washington, D.C.: U.S. Government Printing Office, 1987), 212; hereafter cited as: *Nuclear Waste Program–January*.

163. U.S. Congress, *Nuclear Waste Program–January*, 213. For a discussion of the importance of supplying risk information to the public, see M. Baram, "Rights and Duties Concerning the Availability of Environmental Risk Information to the Public," in *Communicating Risks to the Public*, ed. R. E. Kasperson and P. M. Stallen (Boston: Kluwer, 1991), 67–78.

164. U.S. Congress, *Nuclear Waste Program–January*, 216, 726.

165. U.S. Congress, *Nuclear Waste Program–January*, 699–746.

166. U.S. Congress, *Nuclear Waste Program–January*, 216–245, 466–509.

167. U.S. Congress, *Nuclear Waste Program–January*, 923.

168. U.S. Congress, *Nuclear Waste Program–January*, 747.

169. O. Morgenstern, *On the Accuracy of Economic Observations* (Princeton, N.J.: Princeton University Press, 1963), 62.

170. See, for instance, W. Roberds et al., *In-Situ Test Programs Related to Design and Construction of High-Level Nuclear Waste (HLW) Deep Geologic Repositories. Final Report (Task 2), June 1981–November 1982* (Bellevue, Wash.: Golder Associates, Inc., 1983) (Item 145 in US DOE, DE89005394).

171. See, for example, K. Erickson et al., "Approximate Methods to Calculate Radionuclide Discharges for Performance Assessment of HLW Repositories in Fractured Rock," in *Waste Management '86. Vol. 2: High-Level Waste*, ed. R. Post (Albuquerque: Sandia National Labs., 1986) (Item 175 in US DOE, DE89005394).

172. See, for example, S. Sinnock and T. Lin, "Preliminary Estimates of Groundwater Travel Time at Yucca Mountain," in *American Nuclear Society Meeting* (Albuquerque: Sandia National Labs., 1988) (Item 214 in US DOE, DE90006793); P. Huyakorn et al., "Finite Element Simulation of Moisture Movement and Solute Transport in a Large Caisson," in *Workshop on Modeling of Solute Transport in the Unsaturated Zone* (Herndon, Va.: GeoTrans, Inc., 1987) (Item 212 in US DOE, DE89005394); A. Gutjahr et al., "Panel Summary Report," in *Workshop on Modeling of Solute Transport in the Unsaturated Zone* (Socorro, N.M.: New Mexico Institute of Mining and Technology, 1987) (Item 213 in US DOE, DE89005394).

173. J. Rulon et al., *Preliminary Numerical Simulations of Groundwater Flow in the Unsaturated Zone, Yucca Mountain, Nevada* (Berkeley, Calif.: Lawrence Berkeley Lab., 1986) (Item 181 in US DOE, DE89005394).

174. See U.S. DOE, "Project History," in *Yucca Mountain Project Bibliography, 1988–1989*, DOE/OSTI-3406 (Suppl.2) (DE90006793) (Oak Ridge: U.S. DOE, November 1990), viii.

175. S. Mara, *Assessment of Effectiveness of Geologic Isolation Systems. Geologic Factors in the Isolation of Nuclear Waste: Evaluation of Long-Term Geomorphic Processes and Catastrophic Events* (Seattle: Battelle Pacific Northwest Lab., 1980) (Item 92 in US DOE, DE89005394).

176. Office of Civilian Radioactive Waste Management, *Performance Assessment Implementation Plan.*

177. U.S. Congress, *DOE Nuclear Facility at Fernald, OH*, Hearing before the Subcommittee on Energy Conservation and Power of the Committee on Energy and Commerce, House of Representatives, 99th Congress, Second Session, 13 August 1986, Serial No. 99-163 (Washington, D.C.: U.S. Government Printing Office, 1987), 5, 6.

178. U.S. Congress, *DOE Nuclear Facility at Fernald, OH*, 7–9; see C. Malone, "Environmental Review and Regulation for Siting a Nuclear Repository at Yucca Mountain, Nevada," *Environ. Impact Assess. Rev.* 9: 92; Loux, *Comments on U.S. Department of Energy*, 20–23; Alexander et al., "High Level Radioactive Waste Management."

179. U.S. Congress, *Mission Plan for the Civilian Radioactive Waste Management Program*, 107; U.S. Congress, *DOE Nuclear Facility at Fernald, OH*, 144. See also U.S. Congress, NWPA, 244, and U.S. Congress, *Nuclear Waste Program–April/May*, 185. For DOE's admissions regarding its "schedule pushing," see DOE, NWPA-Yucca, vol. 3, p. c. 3–23.

180. U.S. Congress, *DOE Nuclear Facility at Fernald, OH*, 108; U.S. Congress, *DOE: Pollution at Fernald, Ohio*. Hearing before the Subcommittee on Transportation, Tourism, and Hazardous Materials of the Committee on Energy and Commerce, House of Representatives, 100th Congress, Second Session on H.R. 3783, H.R. 3784, and H.R. 3785, 14 October 1988, Serial No. 100-236 (Washington, D.C.: U.S. Government Printing Office, 1989), 1–3, 54ff.

181. For Luken's comment, see U.S. Congress, *DOE: Pollution at Fernald, Ohio*, 25. U.S. Congress, *Mission Plan*, 133ff., 235ff., 269ff., 506ff., 625, 667ff. U.S. Congress, *Nuclear Waste Program–January*; U.S. Congress, *DOE Nuclear Facility at Fernald, OH.*; U.S. Congress, *Safety of DOE Nuclear Facilities*, Hearing before the Subcommittee on Energy and Power of the Committee on Energy and Commerce, House of Representatives, 101st Congress, First Session, 22 February 1989, Serial No. 101-1 (Washington, D.C.: U.S. Government Printing Office, 1989); U.S. Congress, *DOE: Pollution at Fernald, Ohio*.

182. U.S. Congress, *DOE Nuclear Facility at Fernald, OH*, 2.

183. U.S. Congress, *DOE: Pollution at Fernald, Ohio*, 36–45.

184. Loux, *State of Nevada Comments on the US Department of Energy Site Characterization Plan*, vol. 1: 3.

185. A. J. Keesler, "Testimony," in U.S. Congress, *The Federal Program for the Disposal of Spent Nuclear Fuel and High-Level Radioactive Waste*, Hearing before the Subcommittee on Nuclear Regulation of the Committee

on Environment and Public Works, U.S. Senate, 101st Congress, 2 October 1990 (Washington, D.C.: U.S. Government Printing Office, 1990), 145.

186. Sinnock et al., *Preliminary Estimates of Groundwater Travel Time*, 75; see Loux, *Comments on U.S. Department of Energy*, 20–23.

187. See, for example, Board, *Examination of the Use of Continuum Versus Discontinuum Models*, 66.

188. U.S. Congress, *Nuclear Waste Program–January*, 212–213.

189. U.S. Congress, *Nuclear Waste Program–January*, 245–271.

190. See, for example, Loux, *State of Nevada Comments on the U.S. Department of Energy Site Characterization Plan*, vol. 1: 3; vol. 2: 2.

191. Sinnock et al., *Preliminary Estimates of Groundwater Travel Time*.

192. L. Costin and S. Bauer, *Thermal and Mechanical Codes First Benchmark Exercise, Part I: Thermal Analysis*, SAND88-1221 UC-814 (Albuquerque: Sandia National Labs., 1990), i; see N. Hayden, *Benchmarking: NNMSI Flow and Transport Codes: Cove 1 Results*, SAND84-0996 (Albuquerque: Sandia National Labs., 1985), 1–1, 1–2. For those who speak of "verifying" their models, see, for example, R. Barnard and H. Dockery, *Technical Summary of the Performance Assessment Calculational Exercises for 1990 (PACE-90). Vol. 1: "Nominal Configuration" Hydrogeologic Parameters and Calculation Results*, SAND90-2727 (Albuquerque: Nuclear Waste Repository Technology Department, Sandia National Labs., 1991), 1–3: Hunter and Mann, *Techniques for Determining Probabilities of Events and Processes*, 5. For those who claim to "validate" their models, see, for example, T. Brikowski et al., *Yucca Mountain Program Summary of Research, Site Monitoring and Technical Review Activities (January 1987–June 1988)*, (Carson City: State of Nevada, Agency for Projects/Nuclear Waste Project Office, December 1988), 51; Hunter and Mann, *Techniques for Determining Probabilities of Events and Processes*, 4; K. Stephens et al., *Methodologies for Assessing Long-Term Performance of High-Level Radioactive Waste Packages*, NUREG/CR-4477 ATR-85 (5810–01)1ND (Washington, D.C.: U.S. NRC, Division of Waste Management, Office of Nuclear Material Safety and Safeguards, January 1986), xvi; Barnard and Dockery, *Technical Summary of the Performance Assessment Calculational Exercises for 1990 (PACE-90). Vol. 1*: 1–3.

193. For these who believe in program "verification" see, for example, E. Dijstra, *A Discipline of Programming* (Englewood Cliffs, N.J.: Prentice-Hall, 1976); C. Hoare, "An Axiomatic Basis for Computer Programming," *Communications of the ACM* 12 (1969): 576–580, 583; C. Hoare, "Mathematics of Programming," *BYTE* (August 1986): 115–149.

194. J. H. Fetzer, "Program Verification: The Very Idea," *Communications of the ACM* 31, no. 9 (September 1988): 1048–1063. See also J. H. Fetzer, "Philosophical Aspects of Program Verification," *Minds and Machines* 1 (1991): 197–216; and J. H. Fetzer, "Mathematical Proofs of Computer System Correctness," *Notices of the American Mathematical Society* 36, no. 10 (December 1989): 1352–1353. For discussions regarding program verification, I am indebted to J. H. Fetzer.

195. Office of Civilian Radioactive Waste Management, *Performance Assessment Implementation Plan*.

196. Office of Civilian Radioactive Waste Management, *Performance Assessment Implementation Plan.*

197. J. H. Fetzer, "Another Point of View," *Communications of the ACM* 32, no. 8 (August 1989): 921.

198. S. Savitzky, "Letters," *Communications of the ACM* 32, no. 3 (March 1989): 377.

199. D. Nelson, "Letters," *Communications of the ACM,* 32, no. 7 (July 1989): 792.

200. J. Dobson and B. Randell, "Program Verification," *Communications of the ACM* 32, no. 4 (April 1989): 422.

201. See, for example, P. Hopkins, *Cone 2A Benchmarking Calculations Using LLUVIA,* SAND88-2511-UC-814 (Albuquerque: Sandia National Labs., 1990), 1.

202. J. Emel et al., *Postclosure Risks at the Proposed Yucca Mountain Repository: A Review of Methodological and Technical Issues,* NWPO-SE-011-88 (Carson City: State of Nevada, Agency for Nuclear Projects/Nuclear Waste Project Office, June 1988), 41.

203. Thompson et al., *Preliminary Upper-Bound Consequence Analysis,* i, v–vi.

204. Thompson et al., *Preliminary Upper-Bound Consequence Analysis,* 1984, 7, 47.

205. Lin, *Sparton—A Simple Performance Assessment Code,* i, 1.

206. U.S. DOE, NWPA-Yucca, vol. 3, C. 5–54 and C. 5–55.

207. U.S. DOE, NWPA-Yucca, vol. 3, C. 5–56 and U.S. DOE, NWPA-Hanford, vol. 2, p. 6–294.

208. See, for example, Yonker, Andrews, et al., 1–18, 2–6.

209. Younker, Albrecht, et al., 13, 47, 107, 149.

210. Younker, Albrecht, et al., 13, 47, 107, 149.

211. Younker, Albrecht, et al., 7.

212. Younker, Albrecht, et al., 112.

213. Younker, Albrecht, et al., 47.

214. Younker, Albrecht, et al., 511.

215. Younker, Albrecht, et al., 247, 411, 467.

216. U.S. NRC, *In the Matter of Proposed Rulemaking,* I-3.

217. U.S. Congress, *DOE Nuclear Facility at Fernald, OH;* U.S. Congress, *Safety of DOE Nuclear Facilities;* U.S. Congress, *DOE: Pollution at Fernald, Ohio.* See also note 12, chapter 1, for other evidence of DOE failures.

218. U.S. NRC, *In the Matter of Proposed Rulemaking,* I-4.

219. K. Wilson and B. Lyons, *Ground-Water Levels and Tritium Concentrations at the Maxey-Flats Low-Level Radioactive Waste Disposal Site Near Morehead, Kentucky, June 1984 to April 1989,* Report 90-4189 (Louisville: U.S. Geological Survey, 1991), 36.

220. U.S. Congress, *DOE: Pollution at Fernald, Ohio,* 67.

221. U.S. Congress, *DOE: Pollution at Fernald, Ohio,* 132.

222. U.S. NRC, *Reactor Safety Study,* Report no. (NUREG-75/014) WASH-1400 (Washington, D.C.: U.S. Government Printing Office, 1975).

223. See Shrader-Frechette, *Risk and Rationality.*

224. U.S. Congress, *Nuclear Waste Program–January*, 446.

225. For example, U.S. Congress, *Nuclear Waste Program–January*; U.S. Congress, *DOE Nuclear Facility at Fernald, OH*; U.S. Congress, *Safety of DOE Nuclear Facilities*; U.S. Congress, *DOE: Pollution at Fernald, Ohio*.

226. For example, H. Kunreuther et al., "Public Attitude Toward Siting a High-Level Nuclear Waste Repository in Nevada," *Risk Analysis* 10, no. 4 (December 1990): 483.

227. Loux, *Nevada State and Local Government Comments*, 2; Winsor and Malone, "State of Nevada Perspective on Environmental Program Planning, 197, 205; G. Sawyer, *Report of the State of Nevada Commission on Nuclear Projects* (Carson City: Nevada Commission on Nuclear Projects, November 1988), 8–9, 13.

228. U.S. Congress, *Mission Plan*, 133, 219, 321, 328; D. Golding and A. White, *Guidelines on the Scope, Content, and Use of Comprehensive Risk Assessment in the Management of High-Level Nuclear Waste Transportation*, NWPO-TN-007-90 (Carson City: State of Nevada, Agency for Projects/ Nuclear Waste Project Office, December 1990), 28ff.; J. Lemons et al., "America's High-Level Nuclear Waste Repository: A Case Study of Environmental Science and Public Policy," *Intern. J. Environmental Studies* 34 (1989): 25; J. Emel et al., *Postclosure Risks at the Proposed Yucca Mountain Repository: A Review of Methodological and Technical Issues*, NWPO-SE-011-88 (Carson City: State of Nevada, Agency for Nuclear Projects/Nuclear Waste Project Office, June 1988), 42.

229. U.S. Congress, *Nuclear Waste Program–January*, 446.

230. U.S. Congress, *Nuclear Waste Program–January*, 726.

231. See U.S. Congress, *Nuclear Waste Program*, 747; see G. Sawyer, *Report of the State of Nevada Commission on Nuclear Projects* (Carson City: Nevada Commission on Nuclear Projects, November 1986), 92ff.; C. Malone, "Environmental Performance Assessment: A Case Study of an Emerging Methodology," *J. Environmental Systems* 19, no. 2 (1990): 171–184.

232. Burns et al., *Social Amplification of Risk*, 1ff. For further information on social amplification of risk, see notes 12–13, chapter 3, and note 170, chapter 4.

233. Petterson, "The Reality of Perception"; Petterson, *Goiania Incident Case Study*.

234. Peters and Hennen, *The Accident at Gorleben*.

235. More than a billion dollars has already been spent in site-characterization activities at Yucca Mountain, and the site characterization work has just begun. R. Loux, "Will the Nation's Nuclear Waste Policy Succeed at Yucca Mountain?" *Public Utilities Fortnightly* (22 November 1990): 26–28 and U.S. Congress, *Nuclear Waste Program–January*, 268.

236. For a fuller discussion of problems of scientific method in Yucca Mountain QRAs and recommendations about improving these methods, see Shrader-Frechette, *Expert Judgment in Assessing Radwaste Risks*. See also K. S. Shrader-Frechette, *Expert Judgment and the Frame Problem: Analysis of the "Early Site Suitability Evaluation," Yucca Mountain* (Carson City: Nevada Agency for Nuclear Projects, June 1992).

237. Younker, Albrecht, et al., p. B-2.

Notes to Chapter Seven

1. R. K. Waddell, J. H. Robison, and R. K. Blankennagel, *Hydrology of Yucca Mountain and Vicinity, Nevada–California—Investigative Results through Mid-1983* (Denver: U.S. Geological Survey, Water Resources Investigations Report 84–4267, 1984).

2. S. Sinnock et al., *Preliminary Estimates of Groundwater Travel Time and Radionuclide Transport at the Yucca Mountain Repository Site*, SAND85-2701 (Albuquerque: Sandia National Labs., 1986), i.

3. U.S. DOE, *Nuclear Waste Policy Act, Environmental Assessment, Yucca Mountain Site, Nevada Research and Development Area, Nevada*, DOE/RW-0073, 3 vols. (Washington, D.C.: U.S. DOE, 1986), vol. 2: 6–165; hereafter cited as: U.S. DOE, NWPA-Yucca.

4. U.S. DOE, NWPA-Yucca, vol. 2: 6–167.

5. See L. Hamilton et al., *Toward a Risk Assessment of the Spent Fuel and High-Level Nuclear Waste Disposal System*, Contract DE-AC02-76CH00016 (Washington, D.C.: U.S. DOE, 1986), 9–12.

6. Lovins is quoted in A. K. Bates, "The Karma of Kerma: Nuclear Wastes and Natural Rights," *Environmental Law and Litigation* 3 (1988): 19.

7. R. Peters et al., "Effect of Percolation Rate on Water-Travel Time in Deep, Partially Saturated Zones," in *Symposium on Groundwater flow and Transport Modeling for Performance Assessment of Deep Geologic Disposal of Radioactive Waste* (Albuquerque: Sandia National Labs., 1985) (Item 227 in US DOE, DE88004834).

8. Board on Radioactive Waste Management, U.S. NAS, *Rethinking High-Level Radioactive Waste Disposal* (Washington, D.C.: National Academy Press, 1990), v; see also 27; hereafter cited as: Board, NAS.

9. B. Travis et al., *Preliminary Estimates of Water Flow and Radionuclide Transport in Yucca Mountain* (Los Alamos: Los Alamos National Lab., 1984), 3–4.

10. A. Dudley et al., *Total System Performance Assessment Code (TOSPAC): Vol. 1, Physical and Mathematical Bases: Yucca Mountain Project*, SAND85-0002 UC-70 (Albuquerque: Sandia National Labs., 1988) (Item 182 in US DOE, DE90006793), 92.

11. Travis et al., *Preliminary Estimates of Water Flow*, 16.

12. Travis et al., *Preliminary Estimates of Water Flow*, 25; Sinnock et al., *Preliminary Estimates of Groundwater Travel Time*, i.

13. U.S. DOE, *Tectonic Stability and Expected Ground Motion at Yucca Mountain. Final Report. Revision 1. August 7–8, 1984–January 25–26, 1985* (La Jolla: Science Applications International Corp., 1985) (Item 18 in US DOE, DE88004834); J. Emel et al., *Risk Management and Organizational Systems for High-Level Radioactive Waste Disposal: Issues and Priorities*, NWPO-SE-008-88 (Carson City: State of Nevada, Agency for Projects/Nuclear Waste Project Office, September 1988); J. Emel et al., *Postclosure Risks at the Proposed Yucca Mountain Repository: A Review of Methodological and Technical Issues*, NWPO-SE-011-88 (Carson City: State of Nevada, Agency for Nuclear Projects/Nuclear Waste Project Office, June 1988).

14. P. O'Brien, *Technical Support for High-Level Radioactive Waste Management, Task C Report: Assessment of Migration Pathways*, EPA 520/4-79-007C (Washington, D.C.: U.S. EPA, 1977), 68.

15. NRC, "Staff Comments," in U.S. Congress, *Nuclear Waste Program*, Hearings before the Committee on Energy and Natural Resources, U.S. Senate, 100th Congress, First Session on the Current Status of the Department of Energy's Civilian Nuclear Waste Activities, 29 January, 4 and 5 February 1987, part 1 (Washington, D.C.: U.S. Government Printing Office, 1987), 204; hereafter cited as: *Nuclear Waste Program–January*. For the NAS claim, see Board, NAS, 4.

16. B. Rusche, "Statement," in U.S. Congress, *Nuclear Waste Program–January*, 917.

17. U.S. DOE, NWPA-Yucca, vol. 2: 6–78.

18. U.S. DOE, NWPA-Yucca, vol. 2: 6–334 and 6–335.

19. Sinnock et al., *Preliminary Estimates of Groundwater Travel Time*, 58.

20. S. Raker and R. Jacobson, *Chemistry of Groundwater in Tuffaceous Rocks, Central Nevada*, NWPO-TR-006-87 (Carson City: State of Nevada, Agency for Projects/Nuclear Waste Project Office, January 1987), 72.

21. K. Stephens et al., *Methodologies for Assessing Long-Term Performance of High-Level Radioactive Waste Packages*, NUREG/CR-4477 ATR-85 (5810–01)1ND (Washington, D.C.: U.S. NRC, Division of Waste Management, Office of Nuclear Material Safety and Safeguards, January 1986), xvi, 8–2.

22. C. Malone, "Geologic and Hydrologic Issues Related to Siting a Repository for High-Level Nuclear Waste at Yucca Mountain, Nevada, USA," *Journal of Environmental Management* 30: 381; D. Brown and J. Lemons, "Scientific Certainty and the Laws That Govern Location of a Potential High-Level Nuclear Waste Repository," *Environmental Management* 15, no. 3 (1990): 319. See note 84 regarding the impossibility of quantifying uncertainties at present.

23. J. Lemons and D. Brown, "The Role of Science in the Decision to Site a High-Level Nuclear Waste Repository at Yucca Mountain, Nevada, USA," *The Environmentalist* 10, no. 1 (1990): 10.

24. J. Emel et al., *Nuclear Waste Management: A Comparative Analysis of Six Countries*, NWPO-SE-034-90 (Carson City: State of Nevada, Agency for Projects/Nuclear Waste Project Office, November 1990), 5.

25. R. Hunter and C. Mann, *Techniques for Determining Probabilities of Events and Processes Affecting the Performance of Geologic Repositories*, NUREG/CR-3964 SAND86-0196, vol. 1, June (Washington, D.C.: U.S. NRC, Division of High-Level Waste Management, Office of Nuclear Material Safety and Safeguards, 1989), 1.

26. Hunter and Mann, *Techniques for Determining Probabilities of Events*, 2.

27. Thompson Engineering Company, *Review and Comment on the U.S. Department of Energy Site Characterization Plan Conceptual Design Report*, NWPO-TR-009-88 (Carson City: State of Nevada, Agency for Projects/Nuclear Waste Project Office, October 1988) (Item 329 in US DOE, DE90006793), 13.

28. C. Malone, "The Yucca Mountain Project," *Environ. Sci. Technol.* 23, no. 12 (1989): 1453. For the utility-industry claim, See M. Yates, "Council Report Finds High-Level Nuclear Waste Repository Rules 'Unrealistic'," *Public Utilities Fortnightly* (16 August 1990): 40–41. For the NAS worries, see Board, NAS.

29. J. L. Younker, S. L. Albrecht, W. J. Arabasz, J. H. Bell, F. W. Cambray, S. W. Carothers, J. I. Drever, J. T. Einaudi, D. E. French, K. V. Hodges, R. H. Jones, D. K. Kreamer, W. G. Pariseau, T. A. Vogel, T. Webb, W. B. Andrews, G. A. Fasano, S. R. Mattson, R. C. Murray, L. B. Ballou, M. A. Revelli, A. R. Ducharme, L. E. Shephard, W. W. Dudley, D. T. Hoxie, R. J. Herbst, E. A. Patera, B. R. Judd, J. A. Docka, L. R. Rickertsen, J. M. Boak, and J. R. Stockey, *Report of the Peer Review Panel on the Early Site Suitability Evaluation of the Potential Repository Site at Yucca Mountain, Nevada,* SAIC-91/8001 (Washington, D.C.: U.S. Department of Energy, 1992), B-2; hereafter cited as: Younker, Albrecht, et al.

30. Thompson Engineering Company, *Review and Comment,* 5.

31. Sinnock et al., *Preliminary Estimates of Groundwater Travel Time,* 57.

32. Sinnock et al., *Preliminary Estimates of Groundwater Travel Time,* i.

33. R. Peters, *The Effect of Percolation Rate on Water Travel Time in Deep, Partially Saturated Zones,* SAND85-0854 (Albuquerque: Sandia National Labs., 1986), i.

34. E. Reichard et al., *Groundwater Contamination Risk Assessment,* (Oxfordshire, England: International Association of Hydrological Sciences, 1990), 101.

35. R. Bryan, *State of Nevada Comments on the U.S. Department of Energy Draft Environmental Assessment for the Proposed High-Level Nuclear Waste Site at Yucca Mountain,* 2 vols. (Carson City: Nuclear Waste Project Office, Office of the Governor, 1985), vol. 1: I-42 and I-43; Peters, *The Effect of Percolation Rate,* 32; see G. Sawyer, "Statement," in U.S. Congress, *Nuclear Waste Program–January,* 709, 712.

36. Sinnock et al., *Preliminary Estimates of Groundwater Travel Time,* 58, 75.

37. Sinnock et al., *Preliminary Estimates of Groundwater Travel Time,* i–ii.

38. S. Sinnock and T. Lin, *Preliminary Bounds on the Expected Postclosure Performance of the Yucca Mountain Repository Site, Southern Nevada,* SAND84-1492 (Albuquerque: Sandia National Labs., 1984), 41.

39. Sinnock and Lin, *Preliminary Bounds on the Expected Postclosure Performance,* 37.

40. Sinnock and Lin, *Preliminary Bounds on the Expected Postclosure Performance,* 53.

41. Sinnock and Lin, *Preliminary Bounds on the Expected Postclosure Performance,* 41.

42. Sinnock and Lin, *Preliminary Bounds on the Expected Postclosure Performance,* 53.

43. E. Jacobson, *Investigation of Sensitivity and Uncertainty in Some Hydrologic Models of Yucca Mountain and Vicinity,* SAND84-7212 (Albuquerque: Sandia National Labs., 1985), 90.

44. Sinnock and Lin, *Preliminary Bounds on the Expected Postclosure Performance,* 29.

45. Sinnock and Lin, *Preliminary Bounds on the Expected Postclosure Performance*, 24; C. Smith et al., *Population Risks from Disposal of High-Level Radioactive Wastes in Geologic Repositories*, EPA-520/3-80-006 (Washington, D.C.: U.S. EPA), 91.

46. Sinnock and Lin, *Preliminary Bounds on the Expected Postclosure Performance*, 16.

47. Sinnock and Lin, *Preliminary Bounds on the Expected Postclosure Performance*, 37.

48. Sinnock et al., *Preliminary Estimates of Groundwater Travel Time*, 58.

49. Sinnock et al., *Preliminary Estimates of Groundwater Travel Time*, 75.

50. Sinnock et al., *Preliminary Estimates of Groundwater Travel Time*, 77.

51. Sinnock et al., *Preliminary Estimates of Groundwater Travel Time*, 80.

52. Smith et al., *Population Risks*, 49.

53. Smith et al., *Population Risks*, 183.

54. Sinnock et al., *Preliminary Estimates of Groundwater Travel Time*, 77.

55. F. Thompson et al., *Preliminary Upper-Bound Consequence Analysis for a Waste Repository at Yucca Mountain, Nevada*, SAND83-7475 (Albuquerque: Sandia National Labs., 1984), v–vi.

56. Dudley et al., *Total System Performance Assessment Code*, 56.

57. See, for example, J. L. Younker, W. B. Andrews, G. A. Fasano, C. C. Herrington, S. R. Mattson, R. C. Murray, L. B. Ballou, M. A. Revelli, A. R. Ducharme, L. E. Shephard, W. W. Dudley, D. T. Hoxie, R. J. Herbst, E. A. Patera, B. R. Judd, J. A. Docka, and L. R. Rickertsen, *Report of Early Site Suitability Evaluation of the Potential Repository Site at Yucca Mountain, Nevada*, SAIC-91/8000 (Washington, D.C.: U.S. Department of Energy, 1992), pp. 2–94, 2–163; hereafter cited as: Younker, Andrews, et al.

58. Younker, Albrecht, et al., 25.

59. Younker, Albrecht, et al., 259.

60. Younker, Albrecht, et al., 214.

61. Younker, Albrecht, et al., 214.

62. Younker, Andrews, et al., 2–121, 1–3.

63. Younker, Andrews, et al., 1–9.

64. Younker, Andrews, et al., 2–117.

65. U.S. EPA, *Report to Congress on Hazardous Waste Disposal* (Washington, D.C.: U.S. Government Printing Office, June 1973), 133.

66. S. Papadopulos and I. Winograd, *Storage of Low-Level Radioactive Wastes in the Ground: Hydrogeologic and Hydrochemical Factors*, EPA-520/3-74-009 (Washington, D.C.: U.S. EPA, Office of Radiation Programs, 1974), 29, 33.

67. H. Zehner, *Preliminary Hydrogeologic Investigation of the Maxey Flats Radioactive Waste Burial Site*, USGS 79-1329 (Louisville: U.S. Department of the Interior, USGS, 1979), 48–52.

68. See Board, NAS, 4. See also A. Radin, Chair, Monitored Retrievable Storage Review Commission, *Nuclear Waste: Is There a Need for Federal Interim Storage?* (Washington, D.C.: U.S. Government Printing Office, 1989), 103, 10, xvii.

69. Bates, "The Karma of Kerma: Nuclear Wastes and Natural Rights," 13.

70. U.S. DOE, *Nuclear Waste Policy Act, Environmental Assessment*,

Reference Repository Location, Hanford Site, Washington, 3 vols., DOE/ RW-0070 (Washington, D.C.: U.S. DOE, 1986), vol. 2: 6–148; hereafter cited as: U.S. DOE, NWPA-Hanford.

71. B. Barry, *Liberty and Justice* (Oxford: Clarendon Press, 1991), 271– 273.

72. M. E. Rosen, "Nevada v. Watkins: Who Gets the Shaft?" *Virginia Environmental Law Journal* 10 (1991): 239–309.

73. M. Yates, "DOE Reassesses Civilian Radioactive Waste Management Program," *Public Utilities Fortnightly* (15 February 1990): 36–38.

74. F. L. Parker et al., Board on Radioactive Waste Management, U.S. National Research Council, *Rethinking High-Level Radioactive Waste Disposal* (Washington, D.C.: National Academy Press, 1990), 1, 4, 6.

75. Radin, *Nuclear Waste,* D3, D18.

76. Radin, *Nuclear Waste,* D5, see also D4, D18. For problems with fracturing caused by the heat of the waste, see chapter 4.

77. Radin, *Nuclear Waste,* D6, D7, D18.

78. Radin, *Nuclear Waste,* D8, D9, D18.

79. Radin, *Nuclear Waste,* D10, D18.

80. Radin, *Nuclear Waste,* D11, D12, D18. See A. Milnes, *Geology and Radwaste* (New York: Academic Press, 1985), 286ff.; hereafter cited as: G. R. See also U.S. NAS, *A Review of the Swedish KBS-II Plan for Disposal of Spent Nuclear Fuel* (Washington, D.C.: U.S. NAS, 1980); and C. E. Nyquist, "Nuclear Waste Disposal in Sweden," *Public Utilities Fortnightly* (14 May 1987): 34–35.

81. Radin, *Nuclear Waste,* D13–D15, D18.

82. Radin, *Nuclear Waste,* D15–D18.

83. Radin, *Nuclear Waste,* D17.

84. Younker, Albrecht, et al., B-2.

85. C. Fairhurst, Board on Radioactive Waste Management, National Research Council, in *The Federal Program for the Disposal of Spent Nuclear Fuel and High-Level Radioactive Waste,* Hearing before the Subcommittee on Nuclear Regulation of the Committee on Environment and Public Works, U.S. Senate, 101 Congress (Washington, D.C.: U.S. Government Printing Office, 1990), 35; hereafter cited as: *The Federal Program for the Disposal of Spent Nuclear Fuel.*

86. See, for example, K. Shrader-Frechette, *Risk,* chap. 9.

87. See Sinnock et al., *Preliminary Estimates of Groundwater Travel Time,* 80.

88. Shrader-Frechette, *Risk,* 132–134.

89. H. Shue, "Exporting Hazards," in *Boundaries: National Autonomy and Its Limits,* ed. P. Brown and H. Shue (Totowa, N.J.: Rowman and Littlefield, 1981), 107–145; J. Lichtenberg, "National Boundaries and Moral Boundaries," in Brown and Shue, *Boundaries,* 79–100.

90. See, for example, L. Becker, "Rights," in *Property,* ed. L. Becker and K. Kipnis (Englewood Cliffs, N.J.: Prentice-Hall, 1984), 76. For a discussion of the flaws in this view of rights, see A. Baier, "Poisoning the Wells," in *Values at Risk,* ed. D. MacLean (Totowa, N.J.: Rowman and Allenheld, 1986), 49–74.

91. Shrader-Frechette, *Risk*, 136–137.

92. Shrader-Frechette, *Risk*, 137–138.

93. Shrader-Frechette, *Risk*, 138–139.

94. For a discussion of this argument, see W. K. Frankena, "Concept of Social Justice," in *Social Justice*, ed. R. Brandt, (Englewood Cliffs, N.J.: Prentice-Hall, 1962), 15; Shrader-Frechette, *Risk*, chap. 8.

95. R. Miller, "Letter," in *The Federal Program for the Disposal of Spent Nuclear Fuel*, 126.

Notes to Chapter Eight

1. A. M. Weinberg, "Social Institutions and Nuclear Energy," *Science* 177 (7 July 1972): 27–34.

2. F. L. Parker, *Rethinking High-Level Radioactive Waste Disposal: A Position Statement of the Board on Radioactive Waste Management* (Washington, D.C.: National Academy Press, 1990), 2; hereafter cited as: NAS, HLRW.

3. For an excellent analysis of equity issues in radioactive waste management/disposal, see R. E. Kasperson (ed.), *Equity Issues in Radioactive Waste Management* (Cambridge, Mass.: Oelgeschlager, Gunn, and Hain, 1983).

4. K. Shrader-Frechette, *Risk and Rationality* (Berkeley, Los Angeles, London: University of California Press, 1991), 117ff.; hereafter cited as: Risk.

5. See, for example, R. Williams, *A Technique for the Geothermic Modeling of Underground Surfaces: Nevada Nuclear Waste Storage Investigations Project* (Albuquerque: Sandia National Labs., 1980) (Item 171 in US DOE, DE90006793), 1–23; S. Sinnock and T. Lin, *Preliminary Bounds on the Expected Postclosure Performance of the Yucca Mountain Repository Site, Southern Nevada*, SAND84-1492 (Albuquerque: Sandia National Labs., 1984).

6. By virtue of 10 CFR 60.113, U.S. repositories are required to provide "substantially complete containment" within the waste packages for three hundred to one thousand years and a controlled release rate from the engineered barrier system for ten thousand years of 1 part in 10^5 per year for radionuclides present in defined quantities one hundred years after permanent closure. See A. Berusch and E. Gause, "DOE Progress in Assessing the Long Term Performance of Waste Materials," in *Scientific Basis for Nuclear Waste Management X*, ed. J. Bates and W. Seefeldt (Boston: Materials Research Society, 1987) (Item 190 in US DOE, DE89005394).

7. See note 86 in the preceding chapter.

8. W. T. Blackstone, "On the Meaning and Justification of the Equality Principle," in *The Concept of Equality*, ed. W. T. Blackstone (Minneapolis: Burgess, 1969), 121.

9. J. Rawls, "Justice as Fairness," in *Philosophy of Law*, ed. J. Feinberg and H. Gross (Encino, Calif.: Dickenson, 1975), 284. For a discussion of rights theories in the context of risk assessments, see A. Baier, "Poisoning the Wells," in *Values at Risk*, ed. MacLean (Totowa, N.J.: Rowman and Allenheld, 1986), 49–74.

10. For arguments to this effect, see M. C. Beardsley, "Equality and Obedience to Law," in *Law and Philosophy*, ed. S. Hook (New York: New York University Press, 1964), 35–36. See also I. Berlin, "Equality," in *Law and Philosophy*, ed. Hook, 33; W. K. Frankena, "Some Beliefs about Justice," in *Philosophy of Law*, ed. Feinberg and Gross, 250–251; M. Marcovic, "The Relationship between Equality and Local Autonomy," in *Equality and Social Policy*, ed. W. Feinberg (Urbana: University of Illinois Press, 1978), 93; Rawls, "Justice as Fairness," 277, 280, 282; G. Vlastos, "Justice and Equality," in *Social Justice*, ed. R. B. Brandt (Englewood Cliffs, N.J.: Prentice-Hall, 1962), 50, 56.

11. J. R. Pennock, "Introduction," in *The Limits of the Law*, Nomos 15, Yearbook of the American Society for Political and Legal Philosophy, ed. J. R. Pennock and J. W. Chapman (New York: Lieber-Atherton, 1974), 2, 6.

12. See J. Rawls, "Justice as Fairness," *Journal of Philosophy* 54, no. 22 (October 1957): 653–662; J. Rawls, "Justice as Fairness," *Philosophical Review* 67 (April 1958): 164–194. See also Rawls, *A Theory of Justice* (Cambridge, Mass.: Harvard University Press, 1971), 3–53. For discussion of compensation regarding risks, see *Hazards: Technology and Fairness*, ed. R. W. Kates et al. (Washington, D.C.: National Academy Press, 1986), part 2.

13. K. S. Shrader-Frechette, *Science Policy, Ethics, and Economic Methodology* (Boston: Reidel, 1985), 221–222; hereafter cited as: *Science Policy*.

14. Morally relevant grounds for discrimination are grounds for saying that there are differences between cases, even when we apply the principle that similar cases ought to be treated similarly. We have come to believe that skin color, for example, is not a morally relevant basis, but that ability to do a certain job might be. For analysis of this question, see W. K. Frankena, "The Concept of Social Justice," in *Social Justice*, ed. Brandt, 10, 14. See Taylor, "Justice and the Common Good," in *Concept of Equality*, ed. Blackstone, 94–97; Rawls, *A Theory of Justice*, 586; and A. Sen, "Welfare Inequalities and Rawlsian Axiomatics," in *Foundational Problems in the Special Sciences*, ed. R. E. Butts and J. Hintikka (Boston: Reidel, 1977), vol. 2: 288.

15. See Shrader-Frechette, *Science Policy*, 220–221. See also L. Cox and P. Ricci, "Legal and Philosophical Aspects of Risk Analysis," in *The Risk Assessment of Environmental and Human Health Hazards*, ed. D. Paustenbach (New York: John Wiley, 1989), 1026–1027. See also K. Shrader-Frechette, *Science Policy*, 222ff.; Frankena, "Beliefs about Justice," 252–257. The position described here as "prima facie political egalitarianism" appears to be close to what Frankena defends as "procedural egalitarianism." For Frankena, procedural egalitarians are to be distinguished from substantive egalitarians, who believe that there is some factual respect in which all human beings are equal. Procedural egalitarians deny that there is some such factual respect.

16. NAS, HLRW, 16.

17. L. Lave and B. Leonard (in "Regulating Coke Oven Emissions," in *The Risk Assessment of Environmental and Human Health Hazards*, ed. D. Paustenbach, 1068–1069) make such an argument. See H. Bethe, "The Necessity of Fission Power," *Scientific American* 234, no. 1 (January 1976): 26ff., who also makes such an argument. For a brief defense of the thesis that

we can define rationality in terms of efficiency, see A. C. Michalos, *Foundations of Decisionmaking* (Ottowa: Canadian Library of Philosophy, 1987), 135–142. K. Shrader-Frechette, *Nuclear Power and Public Policy* (Boston: Reidel, 1983), 29; J. Maddox, *The Doomsday Syndrome* (London: Macmillan, 1972), 213; P. Drucker, "Saving the Crusade," in *Environmental Ethics*, K. Shrader-Frechette (Pacific Grove, Calif.: Boxwood Press, 1991), 102, 103, 200; hereafter cited as: *Environmental Ethics*. M. M. Maxey, "Radwastes and Public Ethics," *Health Physics* 34, no. 2 (February 1978): 129–135, esp. 132. See also Cox and Ricci, "Legal and Philosophical aspects," 1038.

18. A. V. Kneese et al., "Economic Issues in the Legacy Problem," in *Equity Issues in Radioactive Waste Management*, ed. R. Kasperson (Cambridge, Mass.: Oelgeschlager, Gunn and Hain, 1983), 203–226, esp. 219. For other discussions of discounting, see D. Parfit, "Energy Policy and the Further Future: The Social Discount Rate," in *Energy and the Future*, ed. D. MacLean and P. Brown (Totowa, N.J.: Rowman and Littlefield, 1983), 31–37.

19. K. Shrader-Frechette, *Nuclear Power and Public Policy*.

20. Frankena (in "Concept of Social Justice," in *Social Justice*, ed. Brandt, 15) uses this argument. He offers it as a sound (and apparently the only) basis for justifying inequalities and differences in treatment among persons.

21. See Markovic, "Equality and Local Autonomy," 85, 87–88; Patterson, "Inequality, Freedom, and the Equal Opportunity Doctrine," in *Equality and Social Policy*, ed. Feinberg, 33–34; H. Laski, "Liberty and Equality," in *The Concept of Equality*, ed. Blackstone, 170, 173; J. Rees, *Equality* (New York: Praeger, 1971), 61–79; and H. J. Gans, "The Costs of Inequality," in *Small Comforts for Hard Times*, ed. M. Mooney and F. Stuber (New York: Columbia University Press, 1977), 50–51.

22. For a discussion of distributive risk assessment, see D. MacLean, "Social Values and the Distribution of Risk," in *Values at Risk*, ed. MacLean. These Census Bureau statistics are cited by A. Larkin, "The Ethical Problem of Economic Growth vs. Environmental Degradation," in *Environmental Ethics*, Shrader-Frechette, 212. See also D. C. North and R. L. Miller, *The Economics of Public Issues* (New York: Harper and Row, 1971), 151, who substantiate this same point. Similar statistics for England are cited by Rees, *Equality*, 30–32. See Patterson, "Inequality," 36.

23. See Shrader-Frechette, *Science Policy*, chap. 7, sec. 3.2; note 22 above; Patterson, "Inequality," 21–30; B. Williams, "The Idea of Equality," in *Concept of Equality*, ed. Blackstone, 49–53; and J. H. Scharr, "Equality of Opportunity and Beyond," in *Equality*, Nomos 9, Yearbook of the American Society for Political and Legal Philosophy, ed. J. R. Pennock and J. W. Chapman (New York: Lieber-Atherton, 1968), 231–240. See also J. R. Pennock, *Democratic Political Theory* (Princeton, N.J.: Princeton University Press, 1979), 36–37; and J. P. Plamenatz, "Equality of Opportunity," in *Concept of Equality*, ed. Blackstone.

24. See A. Gibbard, "Risk and Value," in *Values at Risk*, ed. D. MacLean (Totowa, N.J.: Rowman and Allenheld, 1986), 97–99. See also E. J. Mishan, *21 Popular Economic Fallacies* (New York: Praeger, 1969), 236; Shrader-Frechette, *Nuclear Power and Public Policy*, 123ff.

25. See Mishan, *Economic Fallacies*, 232–233, 245ff.; Rees, *Equality*, 36. See also Plamenatz, "Equality of Opportunity," and Larkin, "The Ethical Problem of Economic Growth."

26. R. B. Stewart, "Pyramids of Sacrifice? Problems of Federalism in Mandating State Implementation of Natural Environmental Policy," in *Land Use and Environmental Law Review, 1978*, ed. F. A. Strom (New York: Clark Boardman, 1978), 172. Numerous detailed economic analyses support this point. See, for example, A. M. Freeman, "Distribution of Environmental Quality," in *Environmental Quality Analyses*, ed. A. V. Kneese and B. T. Bower (Baltimore: Johns Hopkins University Press, 1972), 271–275. See also A. V. Kneese and C. L. Schultze, *Pollution, Prices, and Public Policy* (Washington, D.C.: Brookings Institution, 1975), 28.

27. See V. Brodine, "A Special Burden," *Environment* 13, no. 2 (March 1971): 24. See D. N. Dane, "Bad Air for Children," *Environment* 18, no. 9 (November 1976): 26–34. See also A. M. Freeman, "Income Distribution and Environmental Quality," in *Pollution, Resources, and the Environment*, ed. A. C. Enthoven and A. M. Freeman (New York: Norton, 1973), 101. Enthoven and Freeman make the same point, regarding air pollution, that Kneese and Haveman make (A. V. Kneese, "Economics and the Quality of the Environment," in Enthoven and Freeman, *Pollution*, 74–79; A. M. Freeman, R. H. Haveman, and A. V. Kneese, *The Economics of Environmental Policy* [New York: Wiley, 1973], 143). See also Asch and J. J. Seneca, "Some Evidence on the Distribution of Air Quality," *Land Economics* 54, no. 3 (August 1978): 278–297; and D. D. Ramsey, "A Note on Air Pollution, Property Values, and Fiscal Variables," *Land Economics* 52, no. 2 (May 1976): 230–234. See Gibbard, "Risk and Value," 96. See also S. Samuels, "Arrogance of Intellectual Power" in *Phenotypic Variation in Populations*, ed. A. Woodhead et al. (New York: Plenum, 1988); and, for example, J. Stein, "Water for the Wealthy," *Environment* 19, no. 4 (May 1977): 6–14. The point is documented well by Freeman (in "Distribution of Environmental Quality," 275), who argues that pollution is not "the great leveler," since the wealthy have "the means to protect themselves" from environmental insults. Even the issue of who benefits most from pollution controls is complex (see Freeman, "Distribution of Environmental Quality," 271–273; "Income Distribution," 101–104; *Economics of Environmental Policy*, 144–145; and Kneese, "Economics and Quality of Environment," 78–80). Freeman, Haveman, Kneese, and other economists conclude: "on balance, . . . the improvement would be pro poor" (Freeman, *Economics of Environmental Policy*, 143–144). In any case, there are several means whereby the costs of pollution control can be shifted from the poor and middle class to members of higher-income groups (see Freeman, "Income Distribution," 104–105, and *Economics of Environmental Policy*, 145–148).

28. Public Law No. 100–203, 101 stat. 1330–227. See also M. E. Rosen, "Nevada v. Watkins: Who Gets the Shaft?" *Virginia Environmental Law Journal* 10 (1991): 241–242, 250.

29. D. Parfit, "Energy Policy and the Further Future: The Identity Problem," in *Energy and the Future*, ed. D. MacLean and P. Brown (Totowa, N.J.: Rowman and Littlefield, 1983), 166–179.

30. For discussion of some of the arguments against our duty to members

of future generations, see B. Barry, *Liberty and Justice* (Oxford: Clarendon Press, 1991), 242ff. See also E. Partridge, "Introduction," in *Responsibilities to Future Generations*, ed. E. Partridge (Buffalo: Prometheus Books, 1981), 7.

31. See Partridge, "Introduction," 8ff. for discussion of some of these arguments.

32. D. MacLean, "A Moral Requirement of Energy Policies," in *Energy and the Future*, ed. MacLean and Brown, 180–197.

33. See, for example, J. Feinberg, "The Rights of Animals and Unborn Generations," in *Social Ethics*, ed. T. A. Mappes and J. S. Zembaty (New York, McGraw-Hill, 1977), 358–359.

34. J. Rawls, *A Theory of Justice*, secs. 44–45, pp. 284–298.

35. See, for example, Barry, *Liberty and Justice*, 269. See also D. Mac-Lean, "A Problem of Morality Between Generations," in *Equity Issues in Radioactive Waste Management*, ed. Kasperson, 175–188.

36. See Daniel Callahan, "What Obligations Do We Have to Future Generations?" *The American Ecclesiastical Review* 164, no. 4 (April 1971): 265–280.

37. Feinberg, "The Rights of Animals and Unborn Generations," 358.

38. For other arguments for our duties to members of future generations, see E. B. Weiss, *In Fairness to Future Generations* (Tokyo, Japan: United Nations University, 1989), and K. S. Shrader-Frechette, *Environmental Ethics*.

39. D. MacLean, "Introduction," in *Energy and the Future*, ed. MacLean and Brown, 9.

40. See, for example, notes 27–36.

41. Barry, *Liberty and Justice*, 259ff.

42. See the previous note; see also T. Page, "Intergenerational Justice as Opportunity," in *Energy for the Future*, ed. MacLean and Brown, 38ff. and T. Cochran, "Conflicting Views on a Neutrality Criterion for Radioactive Waste Management," in *Energy for the Future*, ed. MacLean and Brown, 110.

43. W. Williams, *Population Risks from Uranium Ore Bodies*, EPA 520/3-80-009 (Washington, D.C.: U.S. EPA, 1980), 1–23.

44. Regarding the importance of the consent of the governed, see, for example, J. Locke, *Second Treatise of Government*, ed. C. B. Macpherson (Indianapolis: Hackett, 1980), esp. chap. VIII, chap. XIII, and A. Gewirth, *Human Rights* (Chicago: University of Chicago Press, 1982), 282.

45. Quoted in A. K. Bates, "The Karma of Kerma: Nuclear Wastes and Natural Rights," *Environmental Law and Litigation* 3 (1988): 27.

46. See the preceding note.

47. Quoted in Bates, "The Karma of Kerma," 28.

48. Quoted in Bates, "The Karma of Kerma," 33.

49. The term, "second-party consent," is from T. L. Beauchamp and J. F. Childress, *Principles of Biomedical Ethics* (New York: Oxford University Press, 1989), 75, who define it as "consent on behalf of a person given by another." Second-party consent is accomplished by proxy decisionmakers who typically make decisions for another person on the basis of beneficence and nonmaleficence toward the person on whose behalf they speak. For discussion of the ethical criteria for proxy decisionmaking, see Beauchamp and Childress, *Principles of Biomedical Ethics*, 177ff.

50. For one person who uses this argument, see D. Bodde, "Radioactive

Wastes: Pragmatic Strategies and Ethical Perspectives," in *Energy and the Future*, ed. MacLean and Brown, esp. 121.

51. Rawls, *A Theory of Justice*, 355.

52. Rawls, *A Theory of Justice*, 356ff.

53. See T. Cochran, "A Criterion for Radioactive Waste Management," in *Energy and the Future*, ed. MacLean and Brown, 114, 116.

54. See Cochran, "A Criterion," 116.

55. C. Montange, "Federal Nuclear Waste Disposal Policy," *Natural Resources Journal* 27 (Spring 1987): 408.

56. According to B. Carpenter, "A Nuclear Graveyard," *U.S. News and World Report* 110, no. 10 (18 March 1991): 74, a full 80 percent of Nevadans oppose the Yucca Mountain facility. See notes 1 and 2 in chapter 2. For further confirmation of the 80-percent figure, see R. H. Bryan, Governor of Nevada, "Statement," in *Nuclear Waste Program*, Hearings before the Committee on Energy and Natural Resources, U.S. Senate, 100th Congress, 29 April and 7 May 1987 (Washington, D.C.: U.S. Government Printing Office, 1987), 41. For another confirmation of the 80-percent figure, see P. Slovic, J. Flynn, and M. Layman, "Perceived Risk, Trust, and the Politics of Nuclear Waste," *Science* 254 (13 December 1991): 1604.

57. Rawls, *A Theory of Justice*, 355.

58. One of the best accounts of technological risk and consent is given by D. MacLean, "Risk and Consent," in *Values at Risk*, ed. D. MacLean, 17–30. See also R. L. Goldsteen and J. K. Schorr, *Demanding Democracy After Three Mile Island* (Gainesville: University of Florida Press, 1991), 218ff.

59. One of the best accounts of consent in medical ethics, and the account followed here, is that of Beauchamp and Childress, *Principles of Biomedical Ethics*, 74ff. See also M. Curry and L. May, *Professional Responsibility for Harmful Actions* (Dubuque: Kendall/Hunt, 1984), and R. Faden and T. Beauchamp, *A History and Theory of Informed Consent* (New York: Oxford University Press, 1986).

60. See Beauchamp and Childress, *Principles of Biomedical Ethics*, 74ff.

61. Beauchamp and Childress, *Principles of Biomedical Ethics*, 85–99. See also, for example, C. Keown, P. Slovic, and S. Lichtenstein, "Attitudes of Physicians, Pharmacists, and Laypersons Toward Seriousness and Need for Disclosure of Prescription Drug Side Effects," *Health Psychology* 3 (1984): 1–11.

62. Beauchamp and Childress, *Principles of Biomedical Ethics*, 99–106, esp. 101.

63. Beauchamp and Childress, *Principles of Biomedical Ethics*, 111; see 106–111. See also Bernard Gert, "Coercion and Freedom," in *Coercion: Nomos XIV*, ed. J. R. Pennock and J. W. Chapman (New York: Aldine, 1972), 36–37, and H. Beecher, *Research and the Individual* (Boston: Little, Brown, 1970).

64. See Beauchamp and Childress, *Principles of Biomedical Ethics*, 78ff., 79–85.

65. Montange, "Federal Nuclear Waste Disposal Policy," 398–399.

66. F. L. Parker et al., Board on Radioactive Waste Management, *Rethinking High-Level Radioactive Waste Disposal* (Washington, D.C.: National Academy Press, 1990), 17.

67. See A. Blowers, D. Lowry, and B. Solomon, *The International Politics of Nuclear Waste* (New York: St. Martin's Press, 1991), 216.

68. D. Olinger, *St. Petersburg Times*, 1 December 1991, p. D1. See also A. Keesler, "Testimony," in C. Fairhurst, Board on Radioactive Waste Management, National Research Council, *The Federal Program for the Disposal of Spent Nuclear Fuel and High-Level Radioactive Waste*, Hearing before the Subcommittee on Nuclear Regulation of the Committee on Environment and Public Works, U.S. Senate, 101 Congress (Washington, D.C.: U.S. Government printing Office, 1990), 1–2, and K. Schneider, "Nuclear Industry Plans Ads to Counter Critics," *New York Times* (13 November 1991).

69. Olinger, *St. Petersburg Times*, 1 December 1991, p. D1.

70. According to B. Carpenter, "A Nuclear Graveyard," *U.S. News and World Report* 110, no. 10 (18 March 1991): 74, a full 80 percent of Nevadans oppose the Yucca Mountain facility. See note 56 for other sources of the 80-percent figure.

71. 42 USC, section 10173a (1987); see M. E. Rosen, "Nevada v. Watkins: Who Gets the Shaft?" *Virginia Environmental Law Journal* 10 (Spring 1991): 239–309, esp. 250.

72. For discussion of the compensating wage differential and problems with it, see chapter 6 of this volume and Shrader-Frechette, *Risk*, 72ff., 153ff.

73. B. Carpenter, "A Nuclear Graveyard," 74. See note 56 for the sources of the 80-percent figure.

74. C. H. Montange, "Federal Nuclear Waste Disposal Policy," *Natural Resources Journal* 27 (Spring 1987): 309–408, esp. 408.

75. B. Rusche, "Statement," in U.S. Congress, *Mission Plan for the Civilian Radioactive Waste Management Program*. Hearing before the Subcommittee on Energy Research and Development of the Committee on Energy and Natural Resources, U.S. Senate, 99th Congress, First Session on the Department on Energy's Mission Plan for the Civilian Radioactive Waste Management Program, 12 September 1985 (Washington, D.C.: U.S. Government Printing Office, 1986), 484–485, 655.

76. M. Koryakin, "State of the Soviet Nuclear Industry," *WISE (World Information Service on Energy) News Communique* 332 (18 May 1990): 2 (P.O. Box 5627, NL-1007 AP Amsterdam, The Netherlands).

77. Beauchamp and Childress, *Principles of Biomedical Ethics*, 87ff.

78. Beauchamp and Childress, *Principles of Biomedical Ethics*, 88.

79. Carpenter, "A Nuclear Graveyard," 74.

80. See Beauchamp and Childress, *Principles of Biomedical Ethics*, 95.

81. Beauchamp and Childress, *Principles of Biomedical Ethics*, 95; see also J. F. Childress, *Who Should Decide? Paternalism in Health Care* (New York: Oxford University Press, 1982), chapter 4, for discussion of several kinds of consent.

82. Beauchamp and Childress, *Principles of Biomedical Ethics*, 98.

83. Beauchamp and Childress, *Principles of Biomedical Ethics*, 97.

84. See chapters 4 through 7 in this volume; see also Kneese et al., "Economic Issues in the Legacy Problem," in *Equity Issues in Radioactive Waste Management*, ed. Kasperson, 201–206.

85. Weiss, *In Fairness to Future Generations*, 28–34.

86. 42 USC 4331(b).

87. National Environmental Policy Act, cited in EPA, "Criteria for Radioactive Wastes," *Federal Register* 43 (November 1978), 53262–67.

88. T. Cochran, "A Criterion for Radioactive Waste Management," in *Energy and the Future*, ed. MacLean and Brown, 115–116 and EPA, "Criteria for Radioactive Wastes," 53262.

89. Montange, "Federal Nuclear Waste Disposal Policy," 381–382.

90. 50 Fed. Reg. 38,086–38,087, promulgating 40 C.F.R., section 191.15–191.16. See C. Montange, "Federal Nuclear Waste Disposal Policy," 382.

91. 42 U.S.C., section 300ff.

92. See Montange, "Federal Nuclear Waste Disposal Policy," 383ff.

93. 40 C.F.R. section 144.12; Montange, "Federal Nuclear Waste Disposal Policy," 358, 387.

94. Montange, "Federal Nuclear Waste Disposal Policy," 383–389.

95. H. Green, "Legal Aspects of Intergenerational Equity," in *Equity Issues in Radioactive Waste Management*, ed. Kasperson, 193.

96. Green, "Legal Aspects of Intergenerational Equity," 194.

97. Green, "Legal Aspects of Intergenerational Equity," 195–196.

98. J. Sax, "The Public Trust Doctrine in Natural Resource Law: Effective Judicial Intervention," *Michigan Law Review* 68 (1970): 473–566, and *Michigan Law Review, Note*, "Proprietary Duties of the Federal Government under the Public Land Trust," *Michigan Law Review* 75 (1977): 586–626. See also Green, "Legal Aspects of Intergenerational Equity," 199ff.

99. 10 C.F.R., sections 60.113(a)(1) and 60.113(a)(2). See also Montange, "Federal Nuclear Waste Disposal Policy," 381.

100. Carpenter, "A Nuclear Graveyard," 74.

101. R. Monastersky, "First Nuclear Waste Dump Finally Ready," *Science News* 140 (12 October 1991): 228.

102. J. Lemons, D. Brown, and G. Varner, "Congress, Consistency, and Environmental Law: Nuclear Waste at Yucca Mountain, Nevada," *Environmental Ethics* 12 (Winter 1990): 311–327.

103. Kneese et al., "Economic Issues in the Legacy Problem," 217.

Notes to Chapter Nine

1. N. Lenssen, *Nuclear Waste* (Washington, D.C.: Worldwatch, 1991), 35.

2. A. Weinberg, "Statement," in U.S. Congress, *Nuclear Waste Program*, Hearings before the Committee on Energy and Natural Resources, U.S. Senate, First Session, Part 2, (Washington, D.C.: U.S. Government Printing Office, 1987), 2–3; hereafter cited as: Weinberg, "Statement" and NWP-2.

3. See chapter 2, especially text and notes 1–9. See also C. Flavin, *Nuclear Power: The Market Test* (Washington, D.C.: Worldwatch Institute, December 1983).

4. Although the feasibility of a variety of "soft" technologies needs to be substituted on a case by case basis, it is possible to outline some of the argu-

ments for feasibility. See, for example, C. Flavin and S. Postel, "Developing Renewable Energy," in *State of the World 1984*, ed. L. R. Brown et al. (New York: Norton, 1984), 137ff.; C. Flavin, "Reforming the Electric Power Industry," in *State of the World 1986*, ed. L. R. Brown et al. (New York: Norton, 1986), 105–116; C. Flavin and C. Polluck, "Harnessing Renewable Energy," in *State of the World 1985*, ed. L. R. Brown et al. (New York: Norton, 1985), 180ff.; L. R. Brown, "The Coming Solar Age," in *Environment*, ed. J. Allen (Guilford, Conn.: Dushkin, 1985), 61ff.; W. U. Chandler, "Increasing Energy Efficiency," in Brown, *State of the World 1985*, 151–164. See *Energy Future*, ed. R. Stobaugh and D. Yergin (New York: Random House, 1979); and C. Flavin, "Reassessing the Economics of Nuclear Power," in *State of the World 1984*, ed. Brown, esp. 118–132. See also C. Flavin, "Building a Bridge to Sustainable Energy," in *State of the World 1992*, ed. L. R. Brown et al. (New York: Norton, 1992), 27–45.

5. According to L. S. Johns and associates of the OTA Solar Energy Staff (in *Application of Solar Technology to Today's Energy Needs*, 2 vols. [Washington, D.C.: U.S. Office of Technology Assessment, 1978], vol. 1: 3), "Onsite solar devices could be made competitive in markets representing over 40 percent of U.S. energy demand by the mid-1980's." The OTA staff goes on to say that low-temperature solar uses, which comprise 40 percent of total U.S. energy needs, are currently competitive economically with existing alternatives (pp. 13–14), even in cities such as Boston, Alburquerque, and Omaha, where heating needs are often significant (pp. 31ff.). See also the previous note.

6. H. Kendall, "Calling Nuclear Power to Account," *Calypso Log* 18, no. 5 (October 1991): 8.

7. A. Bates, "The Karma of Kerma: Nuclear Wastes and Natural Rights," *Environmental Law and Litigation* 3 (1988): 39–40. Senator J. Sasser, "Testimony," in U.S. Congress, *Nuclear Waste Policy Act*, Hearing before the Subcommittee on Energy and the Environment of the Committee on Interior and Insular Affairs, House of Representatives, 100th Congress, First Session (Washington, D.C.: U.S. Government Printing Office, 1988), 395 (hereafter cited as: U.S. Congress, NWPA) says that there will be between 86,200 and 130,300 MTUs needing to be stored by the year 2020. He also says that the U.S. DOE estimate of 130,300 is more than 50 percent higher than those of other experts.

8. Weinberg, "Statement," 2–5; see also N. Lenssen, *Nuclear Waste*, 27–28.

9. Weinberg, "Statement," 5. D. Vieth, "Statement," in U.S. Congress, *Nuclear Waste Program*, Hearing before the Committee on Energy and Natural Resources, U.S. Senate, 100th Congress, First Session, 29 June 1987, Part 4 (Washington, D.C.: U.S. Government Printing Office, 1987), 130. See also A. Weinberg, "Statement," *Civilian Radioactive Waste Disposal*, Hearing before the Committee on Energy and Natural Resources, U.S. Senate, 100th Congress, First Session, 16–17 July 1987 (Washington, D.C.: U.S. Government Printing Office, 1987), 202ff.; see also 276ff., 335ff., 387ff.; hereafter cited as: U.S. Congress, CRWD.

10. As we mentioned in chapter 6, scientists have learned that, contrary to

previous scientific opinion, radioactive wastes may escape from glass via a new route. They discovered a previously unknown mechanism for directly generating colloids, particles too tiny to settle out of water. By releasing only one drop of water per week over an inch-long, half-inch diameter, glassy cylinder—containing neptunium, americium, and plutonium—scientists showed that exposure to slow dripping of water can change the largely nonreactive borosilicate glass into a form that facilitates the flaking of mineralized shards containing radionuclides. Hence, any claims about the suitability or unsuitability of vitrification for controlling radwastes depend on whether we have gained closure on the problems associated with vitrification. See J. Bates, J. Bradley, A. Teetsov, C. Bradley, M. Buchholtz ten Brink, "Colloid Formation During Waste Form Reaction: Implications for Nuclear Waste Disposal," *Science* 256 (1 May 1992): 649–651.

11. I. S. Roxburgh, *Geology of High-Level Nuclear Waste Disposal* (London: Chapman and Hall, 1987), 183.

12. Bates, "The Karma of Kerma," 38.

13. For some persons who favor this option, see, for example, L. Carter, *Nuclear Imperatives and Public Trust* (Washington, D.C.: Resources for the Future, 1987), 397, who argues for this option as a compromise solution between disposal and recycling. See also Weinberg, "Statement," 1–11, who argues for temporary storage for one hundred years, prior to permanent disposal. For more information on monitored retrievable storage, see Boeing Engineering and Construction Company, *Monitored Retrievable Storage Conceptual System Study: Cask-in-Trench*, BEC-MRS-3303 (1 November 1983); GA Technologies, Inc., *Monitored Retrievable Storage Conceptual System Study: Closed-Cycle Vault*, GA-A-17322 (1 February 1984); Boeing Engineering and Construction Company, *Monitored Retrievable Storage Conceptual System Study: Concrete Storage Casks*, BEC/MRS-3302 (1 November 1983); Raymond Kaiser Engineers, Inc., *Monitored Retrievable Storage Conceptual System Study: Dry Receiving and Handling Facility*, KEH/R-83-96 (1 January 1984); Westinghouse Electric Corporation, *Monitored Retrievable Storage Conceptual System Study: Metal Storage Leaks*, WYSD-TME010 (1 August 1983); Boeing Engineering and Construction Company, *Monitored Retrievable Storage Conceptual System Study: Open Cycle Vault*, BEC/MRS-3304 (1 November 1983); Westinghouse Electric Corporation, *Monitored Retrievable Storage Conceptual System Study: Transportable Storage Casks*, WTSD-TME-013 (1 August 1983); Westinghouse Electric Corporation, *Monitored Retrievable Storage Conceptual System Study: Tunnel Drywells*, WTDS-TME-012 (1 August 1983); GA Technologies, Inc., *Monitored Retrievable Storage Conceptual System Study: Tunnel-Rack*, GA-A-17323 (1 February 1984); Office of the Secretary, U.S. DOE, *Monitored Retrievable Storage Proposal Research and Development Report*, DOE/S-0021 (1 June 1983). See also U.S. DOE, *Monitored Retrievable Storage Submission to Congress*, 3 vols. (Washington, D.C.: U.S. DOE, 1987).

14. Many of these suggestions are closely related to some of those suggested by R. Kasperson, P. Derr, and R. Kates, "Confronting Equity in Radioactive Waste Management: Modest Proposals for a Socially Just and Acceptable Program," in *Equity Issues in Radioactive Waste Management*, ed.

R. Kasperson (Cambridge, Mass.: Oelgeschlager, Gunn, and Hain, 1983), 168–331.

15. For discussion of the laws and policy relevant to NMRS facilities for radwaste, see C. H. Montange, "Federal Nuclear Waste Disposal Policy," *Natural Resources Journal* 27 (Spring 1987): 401ff.

16. Weinberg, "Statement," 24.

17. See K. B. Krauskopf, *Radioactive Waste Disposal and Geology* (London: Chapman and Hall, 1988), 23ff., 52ff., for this argument.

18. A. Radin, D. Klein, and F. Parker, Monitored Retrievable Storage Review Commission, *Nuclear Waste: Is There a Need for Federal Interim Storage?* (Washington, D.C.: U.S. Government Printing Office, 1989), 4.

19. For discussion of the Tennessee proposals and the events surrounding them, see Montange, "Federal Nuclear Waste Disposal Policy," 403ff.

20. Radin et al., *Nuclear Waste: Is There a Need for Federal Interim Storage?*, 4.

21. Kasperson et al., "Confronting Equity in Radioactive Waste," 346.

22. H. Kendall, "Calling Nuclear Power to Account," *Calypso Log* 18, no. 5 (October 1991): 9; see also, for example, J. Tomain, "Nuclear Catacomb," *Jurimeterics Journal* 29, no. 1 (Fall 1988): 103.

23. J. B. Johnston, U.S. Senator, "Statement," in U.S. Congress, NWP-2.

24. C. R. Malone, "High-Level Nuclear Waste Disposal," *Growth and Change* 22, no. 2 (Spring 1991): 72. See also, for example, D. J. Fiorino, "Environmental Risk and Democratic Process," *Columbia Journal of Environmental Law* 14, no. 2 (1989): 501–547; D. J. Fiorino, "Citizen Participation and Environmental Risk," *Science, Technology, and Human Values* 15, no. 2 (1990): 226–243; B. D. Solomon and D. M. Cameron, "Nuclear Waste Repository Siting," *Energy Policy* 13 (1985): 564–580; A. Kirby and G. Jacob, "The Politics of Transportation and Disposal," *U.S. Policy and Politics* 14, no. 1 (1986): 27–42; D. Bella, C. Mosher, and S. Calvo, "Technocracy and Trust," *Journal of Professional Issues in Engineering* 114, no. 1 (1988): 27–39; M. Kraft, "Evaluating Technology Through Public Participation," in *Technology and Politics*, ed. M. Kraft and N. Vig (Durham, N.C.: Duke University Press, 1988), 252–277.

25. See K. Shrader-Frechette, *Risk*, chaps. 11–12; K. Shrader-Frechette, *Science Policy, Ethics, and Economic Methodology* (Boston: Reidel, 1985), chaps. 8–9; hereafter cited as: Science Policy. M. Heiman, "From 'Not in My Backyard' to 'Not in Anybody's Backyard'," *Journal of the American Planning Association* 56 (1990): 359–362; P. Rennick and R. Greyell, "Opting for Cooperation," *Waste Management* 90 (1990): 307–314; Malone, "High-Level Nuclear Waste Disposal," 72.

26. F. L. Parker et al., Board on Radioactive Waste Management, *Rethinking High-Level Radioactive Waste Disposal* (Washington, D.C.: National Academy Press, 1990), 99; hereafter cited as: U.S. NAS, HLRW.

27. H. Inhaber, "Hands Up for Toxic Waste," *Nature* 347 (1990): 611–612. H. Inhaber, "Can an Economic Approach Solve the High-Level Nuclear Waste Problem?" *Risk: Issues in Health and Safety* 2, no. 4 (Fall 1991): 341–356.

28. See K. Shrader-Frechette, *Risk*, esp. chap. 10.

29. Malone, "High-Level Nuclear Waste Disposal," 72.

30. Regarding adversary assessment and negotiation, see Shrader-Frechette, *Risk and Rationality*, chaps. 11–12; Shrader-Frechette, *Science Policy*, chaps. 8–9.

31. Parker et al., U.S. NAS, HLRW, 29.

32. Parker et al., U.S. NAS, HLRW, 11.

33. See, for example, U.S. Congress, *Waste Isolation Pilot Plant Land Withdrawal*, Hearings before the Committee on Energy and Natural Resources, U.S. Senate, 101st Congress, Second Session (Washington, D.C.: U.S. Government Printing Office, 1990), especially M. Mercola, Concerned Citizens for Nuclear Safety, "Testimony," 289–296. See also Kasperson et al., "Confronting Equity in Radioactive Waste," 351; see also A. Blowers, D. Lowry, and B. Solomon, *The International Politics of Nuclear Waste* (New York: St. Martin's Press, 1991), 219–224. See also R. Monastersky, "Nuclear Waste Plans Blocked," *Science News* 141, no. 7 (15 February 1992): 101.

34. Kasperson et al., "Confronting Equity in Radioactive Waste," 349.

35. Kasperson et al., *Social and Economic Aspects of Radioactive Waste Disposal* (Washington, D.C.: National Academy Press, 1984), 62.

36. See Radin et al., *Nuclear Waste: Is There a Need for Federal Interim Storage?*, 81, I–1. For more information on the amount of waste needing to be stored, see note 7.

37. See, for example, Krauskopf, *Radioactive Waste Disposal and Geology*, 128.

38. R. Loux, "Statement," in U.S. Congress, *High-Level Nuclear Waste Issues*, 100th Congress, First Session (Washington, D.C.: U.S. Government Printing Office, 1987), 319; hereafter cited as: U.S. Congress, HLNWI. See also Carter, *Nuclear Imperatives and Public Trust*, 175–176.

39. H. R. Bryan, Governor of Nevada, "Statement," in U.S. Congress, *Nuclear Waste Program*, Hearings before the Committee on Energy and Natural Resources, U.S. Senate, 100th Congress, First Session, part 3 (Washington, D.C.: U.S. Government Printing Office, 1987), 88ff.; hereafter cited as: U.S. Congress, NWP-3.

40. T. A. Duncan et al., Morgan County MRS Study Group, "Feasibility and Desirability of Monitored Retrievable Storage System Locating in Morgan County, Tennessee," in U.S. Congress, NWP-3, 540–558. Information on the Yakima Indian Nation proposal was obtained from Dr. G. Rosa, Washington State University, Pullman, Wash., personal communication, 15 April 1992.

41. Duncan et al., "Feasibility and Desirability," 547–550.

42. See note 28.

43. See, for example, Krauskopf, *Radioactive Waste Disposal and Geology*, 132.

44. This suggestion comes from Kasperson et al., "Confronting Equity in Radioactive Waste," 366.

45. Kasperson et al., "Confronting Equity in Radioactive Waste," 363, 368.

46. See for example, U.S. DOE, *Nuclear Waste Policy Act, Environmental*

Assessment, Yucca Mountain Site, Nevada Research and Development Area, Nevada, DOE/RW-0073, vol. 3 (Washington, D.C.: U.S. DOE, 1986), C.2–8.

47. For discussion of needed improvements in this area, see C. Cranor, *Regulating Toxics.* . . . (New York: Oxford University Press, 1992), and Shrader-Frechette, *Risk,* chaps. 11–12.

48. Cited in Kasperson et al., "Confronting Equity in Radioactive Waste," 348.

49. W. Freudenburg and T. Jones, "Attitudes and Stress in the Presence of Technological Risk: A Test of the Supreme Court Hypothesis," *Social Forces* 69, no. 4 (June 1991): 1143–1168.

50. See Radin et al., *Nuclear Waste: Is There a Need for Federal Interim Storage?,* 77.

51. See for example, J. W. Chapman (ed.), *Compensatory Justice: NOMOS XXXIII* (New York: New York University Press, 1991).

52. See Radin et al., *Nuclear Waste: Is There a Need for Federal Interim Storage?,* 77ff.

53. See, for example, Shrader-Frechette, *Risk,* chaps. 11–12. For discussion of compensation and incentive schemes regarding high-level radwaste, see U.S. Congress, NWP-2.

54. See Kasperson et al., "Confronting Equity in Radioactive Waste," 352–354.

55. Kasperson et al., "Confronting Equity in Radioactive Waste," 349.

56. Kasperson et al., "Confronting Equity in Radioactive Waste," 349.

57. For discussion of these issues, see the two previous chapters and also U.S. NAS, HLRW, 16ff.

58. Kasperson et al., "Confronting Equity in Radioactive Waste," 362, make a similar suggestion.

59. See Radin et al., *Nuclear Waste: Is There a Need for Federal Interim Storage?,* xv, 11.

60. See Radin et al., *Nuclear Waste: Is There a Need for Federal Interim Storage?,* 79–81.

61. Radin et al., *Nuclear Waste: Is There a Need for Federal Interim Storage?,* xvi.

62. See Radin et al., *Nuclear Waste: Is There a Need for Federal Interim Storage?,* I–2. See also K. Shrader-Frechette, *Nuclear Power and Public Policy* (Boston: Reidel, 1983).

63. Radin et al., *Nuclear Waste: Is There a Need for Federal Interim Storage?,* 37.

64. Radin et al., *Nuclear Waste: Is There a Need for Federal Interim Storage?,* xvi, 11.

65. Parker et al., U.S. NAS, HLRW, v.

66. For discussion of subseabed disposal, see R. Kaplan, "Into the Abyss," *University of Pennsylvania Law Review* 139, no. 3 (January 1991): 769–800; A. G. Milnes, *Geology and Radwaste* (New York: Academic, 1985), 284ff.; U.S. Congress, CRWD, 259ff., 309ff.; J. Kelly, Seabed Corp., "Statement," in U.S. Congress, *Nuclear Waste Policy Act,* Hearing before the Subcom-

mittee on Energy and the Environment, of the Committee on Interior and Insular Affairs, House of Representatives, 100th Congress, First Session (Washington, D.C.: U.S. Government Printing Office, 1988), 118ff., 383ff.; hereafter cited as: U.S. Congress, NWPA.

67. See Lenssen, *Nuclear Waste*, 7, 21, 43ff.; Radin et al., *Nuclear Waste: Is There a Need for Federal Interim Storage?*, 10; M. Yates, "DOE Reassesses Civilian Radioactive Waste Management Program," *Public Utilities Fortnightly* (15 February 1990): 36–38. M. Yates, "Council Report Finds High-Level Nuclear Waste Repository Rules 'Unrealistic,'" *Public Utilities Fortnightly* (16 August 1990): 40–41. R. R. Loux, "Will the Nation's Nuclear Waste Policy Succeed at Yucca Mountain?" *Public Utilities Fortnightly* (22 November 1990): 27–28. See also R. E. Dunlap, M. E. Kraft, and E. A. Rosa (eds.), *The Public and Nuclear Waste: Citizen's Views of Repository Siting* (Durham, N.C.: Duke University Press, 1993); hereafter cited as: Dunlap, Kraft, and Rosa, PNW.

68. Parker et al., U.S. NAS, HLRW, 31.

69. Radin et al. *Nuclear Waste: Is There a Need for Federal Interim Storage?*, xvii, 1.

70. See Radin et al., *Nuclear Waste: Is There a Need for Federal Interim Storage?*, 13.

71. Radin et al., *Nuclear Waste: Is There a Need for Federal Interim Storage?*, xvii.

72. Parker et al., *Rethinking*, 29.

73. D. Gibson, "Can Alchemy Solve the Nuclear Waste problem?" *The Bulletin of the Atomic Scientists* 47 (July/August 1991): 12–17; G. Lawrence, "High-Power Proton Linac for Transmuting the Long-Lived Fission Products in Nuclear Waste," LA-UR-91-1335 (Los Alamos: Los Alamos National Laboratory, 1991); T. Pigford, "Waste Transmutation and Public Acceptance," unpublished paper, University of California, Berkeley, Department of Nuclear Energy, 1991.

74. R. Kasperson et al., *Social and Economic Aspects of Radioactive Waste Disposal* (Washington, D.C.: National Academy Press, 1984), 2.

75. Radin et al., *Nuclear Waste: Is There a Need for Federal Interim Storage?*, xvii.

76. Parker et al., U.S. NAS, HLRW, 4.

77. A similar argument is made by Blowers et al., *The International Politics of Nuclear Waste*, 318.

78. Radin et al., *Nuclear Waste: Is There a Need for Federal Interim Storage?*, xvii, 11.

79. See Radin et al., *Nuclear Waste: Is There a Need for Federal Interim Storage?*, 13.

80. Parker et al., U.S. NAS, HLRW, 4, 27.

81. See Radin et al., *Nuclear Waste: Is There a Need for Federal Interim Storage?*, 11–12.

82. See B. B. Yeager, Sierra Club, "Regarding the Department of Energy's Proposal for Monitored Retrievable Storage (MRS) and the Role of MRS in the Federal High-Level Nuclear Waste Program," in U.S. Congress,

NWP-2, 302–312. For variants of this argument, see Carter, *Nuclear Imperatives and Public Trust*, chap. 3; Krauskopf, *Radioactive Waste Disposal and Geology*, 21ff.; Kasperson et al., "Confronting Equity in Radioactive Waste," 361, argue that permanent disposal, after long (110 years) temporary storage is safer than indefinite short-term storage at the surface.

83. See Radin et al., *Nuclear Waste: Is There a Need for Federal Interim Storage?*, 11–12.

84. D. Deere, "Statement," U.S. Congress, *The Federal Program for the Disposal of Spent Nuclear Fuel and High-Level Radioactive Waste*, Hearing before the Subcommittee on Nuclear Regulation of the Committee on Environment and Public Works, U.S. Senate, 101st Congress, Second Session (Washington, D.C.: U.S. Government Printing office, 1990), 19.

85. Kasperson et al., "Confronting Equity in Radioactive Waste," 362.

86. Radin et al., *Nuclear Waste: Is There a Need for Federal Interim Storage?*, 37.

87. Quoted in Montange, "Federal Nuclear Waste Disposal Policy," 401–402.

88. Radin et al., *Nuclear Waste: Is There a Need for Federal Interim Storage?*, xv, xvii, 10, D-5.

89. T. A. Duncan and F. E. Freytag, Morgan County (Tenn.) MRS Study Group, "Statement," in U.S. Congress, NWP-2, 543ff.

90. See Radin et al., *Nuclear Waste: Is There a Need for Federal Interim Storage?*, 30–31.

91. See Radin et al., *Nuclear Waste: Is There a Need for Federal Interim Storage?*, 37.

92. See Radin et al., *Nuclear Waste: Is There a Need for Federal Interim Storage?*, 52.

93. See, for example, Krauskopf, *Radioactive Waste Disposal and Geology*, 78–79.

94. C. Fairhurst, National Research Council, "Statement," in U.S. Congress, *The Federal Program for the Disposal of Spent Nuclear Fuel and High-Level Radioactive Waste*, Hearing before the Subcommittee on Nuclear Regulation of the Committee on Environment and Public Works, U.S. Senate, 101st Congress, Second Session (Washington, D.C.: U.S. Government Printing office, 1990), 35.

95. For variants of this argument, for example, see Carter, *Nuclear Imperatives and Public Trust*, chap. 3.

96. See Roxburgh, *Geology of High-Level Nuclear Waste Disposal*.

97. For the higher figure, see B. Rusche, DOE, "Statement," in U.S. Congress, NWP-3, 167. For the lower figure, see Radin et al., *Nuclear Waste: Is There a Need for Federal Interim Storage?*, I-1.

98. Johnston, "Statement," 147.

99. For the $51,077 billion figure, see C. Anderson, "Why Evaluate the IWM Process?" in U.S. Congress, NWP-3, 577. See Radin et al., *Nuclear Waste: Is There a Need for Federal Interim Storage?*, 63, who estimate the total lifecycle costs for a permanent repository at $40 billion.

100. Rusche, "Statement," 192.

101. R. G. Rabben, DOE, "Answer," in U.S. Congress, NWP-3, 373.

102. See Radin et al., *Nuclear Waste: Is There a Need for Federal Interim Storage?*, xv, 11. It is important to point out that this conclusion is based on a single NMRS facility, rather than on multiple, regional NMRS sites.

103. Edison Electric Institute, American Nuclear Energy Council, Utility Nuclear Waste Management Group, Electric Utility Companies' Nuclear Transportation Group, Atomic Industrial Forum, "Statement," in U.S. Congress, NWP-3, 629.

104. See D. Parfit, "The Further Future: The Social Discount Rate," in *Energy and the Future*, ed. D. MacLean and P. Brown (Totowa, N.J.: Rowman and Littlefield, 1983), 31–37.

105. See K. S. Shrader-Frechette, *Environmental Ethics* (Pacific Grove, Calif.: Boxwood, 1991), esp. chap. 3.

106. A similar argument is made by Blowers et al., *The International Politics of Nuclear Waste*, 318.

107. A similar argument is made by Blowers et al., *The International Politics of Nuclear Waste*, 319.

108. See Yeager (Sierra Club spokesperson), "Regarding the Department of Energy's Proposal," 302–312. Others who make this same argument include, for example, Krauskopf, *Radioactive Waste Disposal and Geology*, 23ff.

109. See Radin et al., *Nuclear Waste: Is There a Need for Federal Interim Storage?*, 4, 93, 95. See also R. F. Pruett, Mayor, Oak Ridge, Tenn., "Statement," in U.S. Congress, NWP-2, 224–225; and B. B. Yeager, "Statement," in U.S. Congress, HLNWI, 773.

110. See Radin et al., *Nuclear Waste: Is There a Need for Federal Interim Storage?*, 11, 92.

111. See Lenssen, *Nuclear Waste*, 7, 43–44; and R. Watson, "Waste, Waste, Nuclear Waste" (St. Louis: Washington University, February 1990), 13, unpublished manuscript. See also Dunlap, Kraft, and Rosa, PNW; Radin et al., *Nuclear Waste: Is There a Need for Federal Interim Storage?*, D-7.

112. Carter, *Nuclear Imperatives and Public Trust*, 414–433.

113. This argument is similar to one advanced by R. Watson, "Goals for Nuclear Waste Management," NUREG-0412 (Washington, D.C.: U.S. Nuclear Regulatory Commission, 1978); see also J. Lemons, D. Brown, and G. Varner, "Congress, Consistency, and Environmental Law: Nuclear Waste at Yucca Mountain, Nevada," *Environmental Ethics* 12 (Winter 1990): 324.

114. Duncan and Freytag, "Statement," in U.S. Congress, NWP-2, 541. See also note 7, this chapter, for information regarding the volume of waste needing to be stored.

115. Lenssen, *Nuclear Power*, 8, 47.

116. A. Lowry and M. Irwin, "Independent Ukraine to Shut Down Chernobyl Reactors," *World Information Service on Energy (WISE) News Communique* 359 (29 September 1991): 8.

117. See notes 6 and 18, chapter 2, for the casualties and costs associated with Chernobyl.

118. A. Lowry and M. Irwin, "UK Trade Unions Vote Nuclear Phase-Out," *World Information Service on Energy (WISE) News Communique* 359 (29 September 1991): 8.

119. A. Lowry, M. Irwin, and C. Mercy, "Yankee Rowe Shutdown Encourages U.S. Activists," *World Information Service on Energy (WISE) News Communique* 361 (8 November 1991): 5–6; and A. Lowry, M. Irwin, and C. Mercy, "Aging U.S. Reactors," *World Information Service on Energy (WISE) News Communique* 361 (8 November 1991): 6.

120. H. Kendall, "Calling Nuclear Power to Account," *Calypso Log* 18, no. 5 (October 1991): 8.

121. Dunlap, Kraft, and Rosa, PNW. See B. B. Yeager, "Statement," in U.S. Congress, NWPA, 273ff.; see also 307ff. Finally, see R. H. Bryan, Governor of Nevada, "Statement," in U.S. Congress, NWP-3, 44ff.

122. H. Reid, "Statement," in U.S. Congress, NWP-3, 31. See also U.S. Congress, HLNWI, 237ff.

123. F. Millar, "Statement," in U.S. Congress, NWP-3, 117.

124. B. Gardner, Governor of Washington, "Statement," in U.S. Congress, NWP-3, 185.

125. Radin et al., *Nuclear Waste: Is There a Need for Federal Interim Storage?*, 100

126. See, for example, J. Rhodes, "Nuclear Power: Waste Disposal," Address to the 102nd Annual Convention of the National Association of Regulatory Utility Commissioners (Orlando, 1991), 27–28, 41; and M. Steinberg, " Transmutation of High-Level Nuclear Waste," *Science* (16 November 1990): 887–888. Finally see Dunlap, Kraft, and Rosa, PNW.

127. Radin et al., *Nuclear Waste: Is There a Need for Federal Interim Storage?*, D-17. For other accounts of the actions of nuclear nations regarding radioactive waste, see Lenssen, *Nuclear Waste*, 37–49.

128. Bates, "The Karma of Kerma," 38.

129. R. Rosa and W. Freudenburg, "The Historical Development of Public Reactions to Nuclear Power: Implications for Nuclear Waste Policy," in Dunlap, Kraft, and Rosa, PNW. See also R. L. Goldsteen and J. K. Schorr, *Demanding Democracy After Three Mile Island* (Gainesville: University of Florida Press, 1991), 117ff.

Index of Names

Index of Subjects